365 Great
Cakes and Pies

Carol Prager

A JOHN BOSWELL ASSOCIATES BOOK

■ HarperCollins*Publishers*

HarperCollins books may be purchased for educational, business, or sales promotional use. For information, please write: Special Markets Department, HarperCollins Publishers, Inc., 10 East 53rd Street, New York, NY 10022.

FIRST EDITION

Series Editor: Susan Wyler
Design: Nigel Rollings
Index: Maro Riofrancos

Library of Congress Cataloging-in-Publication Data

Prager, Carol.
    365 great cakes & pies / Carol Prager.—1st ed.
        p. cm.
    Includes index.
    ISBN 0-06-016959-1
    1. Cakes. 2. Pies. I. Title. II. Title: Three hundred sixty-five great cakes & pies. III. Title: 365 great cakes and pies.
TX771.P69   1995
841.8′652—dc20   94-23826

95 96 97 98 99 HC 10 9 8 7 6 5 4 3 2 1

Contents

Welcome to the comfort zone. Worth their weight in gold, these irresistible buttery pound cakes, upside-down cakes, pudding cakes, coffee, tea, and snacking cakes may only need a dusting of confectioners' sugar or a simple fruit glaze. Choose from a warm and cozy Granny's Gingerbread Cake, Upside-Down Plum Poppyseed Cake, or Buttermilk Berry Coffee Cake with Lemon Spice Topping.

A bake sale's best collection of frosted cakes and other layered delights that could only be made in the U.S.A. You'll love these updated classics like Classic Boston Cream Pie with a vanilla bean filling and mocha glaze, or a caramelized Burnt Sugar Cake, plus America's "pop" favorites: a triple-layer Southwest Chocolate Chili Cake with Fluffy Fudge Frosting, Fudgy Marbled Mayo Cake, or Mystery Spice Cake with tomato soup as its surprise ingredient.

Consider these cakes the best finishing touch for your next celebration! Fast and festive, a delicate bridal or baby shower Raspberry Princess Cake with white chocolate won't leave you in a time crunch. Or try a summertime Firecracker Spud 'n' Spice Cake adorned with cinnamon red-hots. Plus a complete roundup of best birthday cakes, including a richly dark Macaroon Midnight Cake for the sophisticate or a Classic Checkerboard Cake for the kid in all of us.

Kids of all ages will certainly find Tin Roof Cupcakes with Fluffy Peanut Butter Icing, Batter-Up Butterscotch Cupcakes, or Iced Cappuccino Cupcakes with Espresso Glaze as much fun to make as they are to eat.

Totally indulgent, irresistibly rich, and smooth as velvet, these are our favorite cakes to die for! There's no holding back when it comes to a caramel- and pecan-filled Chocolate Turtle Cheesecake, Malted Marble Cheesecake with a cookies 'n' cream crust, or Fresh Strawberry-Glazed Marzipan Cheesecake.

Introduction: Perfect Cakes and Pies

For all of us with a passion for baking and savoring desserts, homemade cakes and pies are in a league of their own. Ask anyone and you'll hear a personal favorite—a towering chocolate birthday cake, an elegant fresh berry tart, or a silky custard pie that signifies a special occasion or evokes a fond memory. Whether they're plain or fancy, frosted and layered, upside down, air-raised, flourless, fruit-filled, or frozen, and nestled in a bowl, pie plate, or tart pan, cakes and pies are truly the glories of baking and the final flourish to any meal.

From start to finish, step by step, there's nothing that can beat the sweet satisfaction of preparing a cake or pie from scratch. It's a process that makes any baker feel good. I know I'll always remember mastering my first angel food cake and marveling at how the miracle of whipped egg whites and sugar could allow a simple batter to rise to such beautiful heights. Or my discovery of fresh rhubarb, bubbly with strawberries, in my first homemade flaky pie crust with a fancy lattice top. Quickly I realized that rather than being difficult, complicated, or intimidating, successful baking simply requires a careful attention to basic techniques and principles. Practice and experience definitely make perfect, and as a serious baker I'm always learning, but the wonder of cakes and pies is that there is so much variety, with plenty of room for everyone to experience the sweet success of creating a fabulous dessert.

Even the simplest cakes and pies aren't just created from a pinch of this or that in any haphazard order; they're a precise combination of ingredients and techniques. Here are some essential guidelines for foolproof baking you won't be able to do without:

A Baker's Best Secret: Get Organized: Always read the recipe in its entirety, from start to finish. Then gather and assemble all your equipment and ingredients before getting started.

The Perfect Measure: Flour, sugar, and other dry ingredients should always be measured with graduated-sized metal cups and measuring spoons, all liquid ingredients in clear measuring cups with spouts. For accuracy in measuring flour, first stir it in its package or canister to aerate, then gently spoon it into the appropriate measuring cup, taking care not to pack the flour into the cup. Level off any excess with a metal spatula or the flat side of a knife. For best results when measuring liquids, fill the clear glass measuring cup so it is correct at eye level.

The Temperature of Your Oven: Given the fact that oven temperatures can vary greatly, it's a good idea to check your oven temperature whenever you plan to bake. An oven thermometer placed on the center rack is a worthwhile investment. Always remember to begin by preheating your oven, which takes about 15 minutes. If the oven temperature varies more than 25 degrees from your setting, adjust the gauge accordingly. For recipes tested, all cakes and pies were baked on a rack set in the center of the oven except for layer cakes, which were baked on two racks arranged on the center and upper levels of the oven.

Testing for Doneness: There's nothing like the aroma of a homemade cake or pie when it's ready to come out of the oven, but unfortunately this wonderful scent is an imprecise way of telling if your dessert is ready. Given the variables of oven temperature, I've supplied a range of baking times for all recipes tested. For split-second accuracy, I've found a digital timer an invaluable tool. Always inspect your cake or pie after the minimum baking time given. For cakes, the top should be golden brown and for those prepared in greased pans, the cake should begin to pull away from the sides of the pan. Quickly insert a toothpick into the center of the cake; it should come out clean. If particles of cake batter cling, bake a few minutes longer as directed. The cheesecakes should just be set and gently jiggle in the center when removed from the oven.

Visual clues are more reliable with pies. For double-crust and deep-dish pies, the top crust should be a rich golden brown and the filling bubbly in the center. Single-crust pie with baked fillings should have a golden pastry and be set in the center.

STORING: Many cakes and pies have the built-in benefit of permitting advance preparation. Whatever method you follow, it's important always to allow baked cakes and pies to cool completely before storing. Here are some guidelines:

• *Cakes:* As a general rule, frosted layer cakes and cakes containing custard, whipped cream, or fresh fruit fillings can be refrigerated, loosely covered, up to 24 hours. Cheesecakes can be refrigerated up to several days, and they should be served chilled. Well-wrapped pound cakes, plain butter cakes, and unfrosted cake layers can be stored at room temperature for several days without a sacrifice of fresh flavor. Chiffon and angel food cakes can be kept in the pan, covered loosely, and stored at room temperature as well for several days. If a cake is refrigerated, allow it to stand at room temperature 1 hour before serving for maximum flavor.

Rich cakes, such as pound cakes, coffee cakes, and creamed butter cakes, can be frozen up to several months. Quite often I freeze unfrosted butter cake layers in advance, then thaw and frost the cake the day I plan to serve it. Always double-wrap cakes if freezing for airtight storage. Frozen cakes can be allowed to thaw at room temperature. For a just-baked taste, briefly heat the thawed cake in a preheated 300°F oven for 10 minutes, or until just fragrant; then cool completely before assembling or serving.

Cheesecakes, well-wrapped, can be frozen for up to 1 month. Thaw in the refrigerator overnight.

• *Pies:* Double-crust and streusel-topped fruit pies can be stored at room temperature, loosely covered, overnight. If the crust begins to become soft, briefly heat in a preheated 425°F oven for 10 minutes to recrisp. Pies with egg-based or dairy fillings, such as chiffon, cream, and custard pies, should be refrigerated if not served within a few hours of baking. For maximum taste if chilled overnight, allow these pies to stand at room temperature for about 30 minutes before serving. Dairy and egg-based pies do not benefit from freezing.

I believe that freezing unbaked fruit pies is a great way to preserve their fresh flavor. Prepare the fruit filling as usual, but for juicier fruits, such as peaches or any type of berry filling, add an extra tablespoon of thickener per pie (whether flour, tapioca, or cornstarch). Finish the pie as directed, but for a double-crust pie, do not cut vents in the top crust and do not glaze if directed. Wrap the pie airtight in freezer wrap and freeze up to 3 months. To bake a frozen pie, preheat the oven. Unwrap the unthawed pie, place on a cookie sheet, cut vents, and glaze if desired. Bake frozen as directed in the recipe, but add 15 to 20 minutes to the baking time, until the center of the filling is bubbly and the top crust is golden.

Pies without cream or custard fillings, such as nut pies and tarts, can be frozen once baked. Cooled completely and wrapped airtight, they can be stored up to 3 months. Thaw at room temperature 1 hour. Unwrap and bake in a preheated 350°F oven for 30 minutes.

Disks of unbaked pie dough well wrapped in plastic wrap can be refrigerated up to 2 days. Unbaked frozen pie shells and crumb crusts can be wrapped and stored several months. Pie shells can be baked directly from their frozen state. Crumb crusts should be allowed to thaw to room temperature about 30 minutes before baking. Baked pie crusts can be frozen, covered, up to 1 week before filling. Let thaw completely at room temperature, then crisp in the oven at 350°F for 10 minutes.

THE RIGHT STUFF: Beautiful cakes and pies are definitely the sum of their parts, and choosing the right ingredients and knowing how to handle them makes all the difference. It's always important to keep in mind that there's not much room for substitution of ingredients or changing proportions, for that may significantly alter the baked results. Here are a few of the basic ingredients:

• *Flour:* The majority of recipes tested in this book call for all-purpose flour. Although both bleached and unbleached varieties can be used, I prefer bleached all-purpose flour for cakes and pies. Bleached flour, with a lower protein content, absorbs less liquid and produces on average a tenderer and more delicate baked result. Unless specified otherwise, all flour is measured unsifted.

For some light and delicate cakes I use cake flour, an enriched bleached variety made from a high-quality soft wheat. Be sure to purchase plain cake flour and not the variety labeled "self-rising," which contains leavening and salt. I measure cake flour by pouring it directly from the box into the appropriate dry measure and leveling off the excess with a spatula.

Once it is measured, I find the best way to combine flour with other dry ingredients and remove lumps is to sift them together through a wire mesh strainer.

• *Butter and shortening:* In my opinion, for the best taste you can get when creating cakes and pies from scratch, nothing rivals the rich flavor and performance of real butter. I tested with both U.S. Grade AA salted and unsalted varieties and found that in the majority of cases they can be used interchangeably. Be sure to use only butter that comes in sticks and not any whipped, reduced-fat, or tub products. Here there's an enormous difference in the fat and moisture content that can radically affect your baked results. When a recipe calls for "softened" butter, it should be at room temperature between 68° and 70°F. To soften butter, simply remove it from the refrigerator 20 to 30 minutes ahead of time and leave it on your counter. If you forget or you are in a hurry, microwave on High 8 to 10 seconds per stick.

For flaky pie crusts, solid vegetable shortening should be stored and used at room temperature. Some brands of vegetable shortening are available in sticks, but the majority are sold in 1- and 3-pound containers and should be measured with graduated dry-measuring cups and spoons.

• *Sugar:* For the majority of cake and pie recipes, I used granulated white sugar, which is measured as you would flour and other dry ingredients. Granulated sugar is refined from sugarcane or sugar beets and when you purchase it, be sure it is 99.94 percent pure.

For recipes specifying brown sugar, a combination of refined white sugar and molasses, both light and dark brown varieties can be used, depending on what you have on hand and the quantity of rich molasses flavor you seek. All the recipes in this book call for firmly packed brown sugar. To measure, place your dry measuring cup on a sheet of wax paper and pour a generous amount of brown sugar into the cup so that it exceeds the level of the rim. With the flat side of a knife or metal spatula, firmly pack the sugar into the cup and level off any excess.

Powdered sugar, or confectioners' sugar, a combination of finely granulated white sugar and cornstarch, can be quite lumpy. As with brown sugar, place a dry measuring cup on a sheet of wax paper. Add the approximate quantity of powdered sugar to a wire mesh strainer and place it over the cup, sifting the sugar into the cup so that it exceeds the level of the rim. Then pack the sugar into the cup with the flat side of a knife or spatula and sweep off the excess.

• *Eggs:* All recipes in this book were tested with eggs graded large. When selecting eggs, choose grade A or AA that have been stored under refrigeration, with clean uncracked shells. For the safest storage, always keep eggs refrigerated in their carton until you are ready to use them. While the majority of recipes do not require bringing eggs to room temperature before using them, in the case of some cakes in particular I prefer using eggs that are not chilled. Overall, it is not a good idea to leave eggs out at room temperature for longer than 1 hour. For cakes that call for separated eggs or egg whites, where egg whites reach their fullest volume when beaten at room temperature, I separate the egg when chilled, then allow the whites to stand at room temperature about 30 minutes before beating. When a recipe calls for room-temperature whole eggs, as in cheesecake fillings, for instance, where cold eggs could curdle the batter, remove the eggs from the refrigerator about 30 minutes before using or let stand in a bowl of very warm water to cover for 10 minutes.

• *Leavenings*: Leavening is the agent in cakes that makes them rise. With the exception of a few pound cakes and air-raised cakes, for the majority of recipes in this book, I used baking powder and baking soda. These leaveners, when combined with liquid or heat, produce a carbon dioxide gas that releases bubbles in the batter, causing it to expand and rise.

• *Double-acting baking powder:* This is the most common form of baking powder. It is a mixture of acid, baking soda, and starch, which releases the carbon dioxide gas in 2 stages: first, when the powder comes in contact with liquid; then again when it is heated during baking. Baking powder is perishable and should be stored airtight and used within 1 year of purchase.

• *Baking soda:* Also known as bicarbonate of soda, this leavener is used as a neutralizing agent in combination with acidic ingredients, such as molasses, fruit, buttermilk, sour cream, yogurt, and chocolate. Kept in a cool, dry place, baking soda has an indefinite shelf life.

• *Cream of tartar:* An acid found in baking powder, cream of tartar is primarily added to beaten egg whites to act as a stabilizer and to increase volume.

• *Chocolate:* No gathering of cakes and pies would be complete without the inclusion of chocolate, and in this collection you'll find it in several forms. Varieties of chocolate are determined by the amount of chocolate liquor, or the essence of cocoa beans, they contain. These give chocolate its flavor and color.

Unsweetened chocolate (baking, bitter, or cooking chocolate): This is pure chocolate liquor that contains no sugar; it has been cooled and molded into blocks and is most commonly available in packages containing 8 (1-ounce) squares.

Semisweet chocolate (or dark chocolate): This is a combination of chocolate liquor, sugar, cocoa butter, and vanilla. It's been my experience that semisweet chocolate in bar form has a superior quality in baking, and I use it in the majority of recipes. While semisweet varieties are available in chips or morsels and can be melted, they are specially formulated to hold their shape when baked and contain a reduced amount of cocoa butter, which can affect the quality of your finished dessert.

Bittersweet chocolate: Often imported in bar form and slightly sweetened with extra cocoa butter for easier melting, bittersweet chocolate can be substituted for semisweet chocolate in fancier cakes and pies.

Sweet cooking chocolate: Available in 4-ounce bars, this has a higher sugar content than semisweet chocolate and is good both for baking and for melting in frostings.

Milk chocolate: Contains at least 10 percent chocolate liquor and is best used for melting. It is not recommended as a substitute when baking.

White chocolate: Made from cocoa butter, sugar, milk solids, and flavorings, this technically is not chocolate because it contains no chocolate liquor. As with semisweet chocolate, I prefer using white chocolate in bar form for baking. Use white chocolate only in recipes where it is specified; it should not be used as a substitute for other varieties.

Unsweetened cocoa powder: This is the powdered chocolate that remains after the cocoa butter has been removed. Naturally low in fat and sodium, it has no additives or preservatives. Regular and Dutch-process cocoa can be used interchangeably in all recipes.

The way to melt chocolate: Whether you choose the microwave, a regular oven, or a double boiler, melting chocolate is a simple procedure, but it requires some care. If chocolate combines with water or steam or is overheated, it may scorch, seize into a solid mass, or turn grainy. Keep in mind that white and milk chocolate, with a higher quantity of milk solids, need to be stirred sooner and more frequently than unsweetened or semisweet varieties. To microwave, place coarsely chopped chocolate in a microwaveproof bowl. Microwave on Medium (50 percent power) 1½ to 3 minutes or longer, depending on the time stated in the recipe, stirring every minute, until the chocolate begins to melt. Remove the bowl from the microwave and continue to stir until chocolate is completely melted and shiny. If using a double boiler, place coarsely chopped chocolate in the top of a double boiler, then insert the pan into the bottom over hot, not simmering, water. Melt the chocolate, stirring occasionally, until smooth. Remove the top part of the double boiler from the bottom, making sure that the chocolate never comes in contact with steam or simmering water, which could cause it to "seize up" —that is, tighten and turn granular.

   • *Vanilla:* Perhaps no other flavor is more commonly used or beloved than vanilla in baking and desserts. For testing recipes in this book, I always baked with pure vanilla extract, which acts as a natural enhancement to other flavors, such as chocolate and coffee. For a more intense flavor infusion for custard and cream fillings, I used the whole vanilla bean. Whole vanilla beans are the dried pods of tropical orchids. To use, the pod is split, heated until softened, then discarded, and the tiny seeds inside are scraped out and incorporated in the batter or frosting. The flavor of a whole vanilla bean is equivalent to approximately 2 teaspoons of vanilla extract.

   • *Nuts:* A wide assortment of nuts is an essential ingredient in many cakes and pies. Walnuts and pecans can be used interchangeably in most recipes, as can hazelnuts and almonds. Nuts are highly perishable due to the high percentage of natural oils they contain and can quickly go rancid if not properly stored. A good rule of thumb is to purchase nuts in sealed packages or vacuum-packed cans. I keep nuts well wrapped in the freezer, where they remain fresh up to 1 year. Before using, lightly toast frozen nuts in a preheated 350°F oven about 8 minutes to enhance their flavor, then let cool completely.

TOOLS OF THE TRADE: Carefully selected, a few pieces of basic equipment are all it takes to start baking cakes and pies from scratch. While nothing fancy is required, the correct equipment will make all the difference. For example, while the type of rolling pin is unimportant, and you can use whatever feels the most comfortable, it's critical always to pay close attention to the proper size and capacity of your cake and pie pans. Here are some basic guidelines to follow:

• *Electric mixer:* If I had to choose my most important piece of kitchen equipment for both cake and pie baking, it would be my electric mixer. I would recommend a standing mixer over a portable hand-held model for most recipes. With its extra horsepower, a standing mixer performs an enormous variety of tasks in minutes, creaming butter, whipping egg whites, and blending pie pastry dough, just to name a few. For lighter batters, a hand-held mixer is an acceptable substitute, but your mixing time will increase.

• *Cake and pie pans:* When selecting a cake pan, first note the size and stick to those produced by better known manufacturers. Pans made from aluminum or heavy tin-plated steel are excellent choices. With the proper greasing of your pans, nonstick coated styles are not essential. I don't recommend black and dark metal pans. These pans are high conductors of heat, are better suited for bread baking, and will give your cakes a dark, overbaked crust. Tube and bundt pans are often produced by different manufacturers, and there's room for substitutions, so it's always a good idea to check the volume in cups (use water) needed to fill the pan to capacity.

All pies were tested in 9-, 9-inch deep-dish, or 10-inch pie plates either constructed of ovenproof glass or heavy-duty aluminum. While both types worked well, my personal preference is ovenproof glass. The glass generates a high but even amount of heat, and its transparent surface allows you to see how the bottom crust is browning.

Aluminum foil pans can be substituted for your regular cake or pie pans, provided that the capacity is about the same. These pans are a bit thinner and more flimsy, so for baking I like to place them on a cookie sheet in the oven. For pies, I recommend using the deep-dish capacity aluminum pans.

• *Wire racks:* For cooling cakes and pies, metal wire cake racks are indispensable. Available in a variety of sizes, these racks elevate the hot dessert from the countertop, allowing air to flow underneath for even cooling. This is particularly helpful to prevent pies from developing a soggy bottom crust after baking.

In brief, here's a general listing of useful equipment to have on hand. By no means definitive, it's a reference when getting started.

Dry measuring cups: 1/4, 1/3, 1/2, and 1 cup standard metal preferred
Liquid measure: 8- and 16-ounce heatproof glass
Measuring spoons: stainless or plastic 1/8, 1/4, 1/2 teaspoon, 1 teaspoon, and 1 tablespoon
Wire mesh strainer: for sifting

Other helpful equipment and gadgets include:

Cake testers or toothpicks
Candy thermometer
Citrus juicer
Double boiler
Dough scraper, metal or
    plastic
Electric stand mixer
Food processor
Four-sided hand-held grater
Hand-held mixer
Heatproof rubber spatulas
Kitchen scale (in ounces)
Kitchen timer (digital is
    great)
Long chef's knife

Long offset metal spatula
Long straight metal spatula
Microwave oven
Oven thermometer
Pastry blender
Pastry brush
Small, medium, and large
    mixing bowls
Small, sharp paring knife
Swivel-bladed vegetable
    peeler
Wire cooling racks
Wire whisks
Wooden spoons

With this knowledge at your fingertips, now comes the fun part: baking your next cake or pie. Although some recipes may require a few more steps than others, all were created with simplicity in mind. In each recipe, suggestions are given to match pie crusts and fillings or cakes with frostings, but no hard and fast rules apply. Feel free to be creative and come up with your own combinations of flavors, decorations, and garnishes. Now with 365 cakes and pies to choose from, you'll never have trouble finding something perfect to whip up for dessert!

Chapter 1

Butter Cakes Plain and Simple

Here are the cakes that take only one slice to sat-
isfy. Fine-crumbed, a bit rich and indulgent, this homestyle
assortment of old-fashioned pound cakes, comforting coffee
cakes, tea loaves, and spicy fruit-and-nut-topped cakes don't
need much embellishment beyond a dusting of powdered
sugar. These are the cakes created with butter in mind, simply
creamed with sugar and eggs and blended with flour in your
mixing bowl. Less fuss to make, without sacrificing an ounce
of flavor, these wonderful buttery cakes are totable, picnic-
perfect, and ideal for gift-giving. Any butter cake is easy as
1-2-3 to prepare. Here's how:

Creaming butter: Whenever a cake calls for butter,
the secret of success is in learning how to beat your butter and
sugar together properly. This technique will ensure your cake
has a smooth texture and will rise properly. Before you even
start, the butter must be softened. Then it's ready to incorporate air into your cake batter by being beaten until smooth and
creamy at medium-high speed. Gradually add the sugar,
scraping the sides of the mixing bowl with a rubber spatula,
until the creamed mixture is completely smooth. Continue to
beat a few minutes longer until very light and fluffy.

Adding the eggs: Eggs give moisture and volume to
your butter cake. When they are at room temperature, they
blend more easily with the creamed butter and sugar. In most
cases I add eggs 1 at a time, on medium or medium-low
speed, beating about 1 minute after each addition until thoroughly blended.

Adding the dry ingredients: To avoid overmixing,
which toughens a cake, I add the dry ingredients at low speed
just until blended. If adding dry ingredients with a liquid,
always begin and end with the dry ingredients to avoid a
curdled-looking batter.

The flavor of many pound, tea, and coffee cakes
benefits if the cake is baked a day in advance. Simply wrap it
tightly in plastic wrap and store at room temperature. These
cakes also freeze beautifully. They are generally served in thin
slices, about ½ inch thick. Pound cakes are also delicious
toasted, or served with ice cream or with whipped cream and
fresh fruit. Some favorite cakes by the pound in this collection
include Golden Almond Pound Cake with cornmeal and
almond paste, spicy Black Pepper Pound Cake, Coconut Marble Butter Cake with a rich fudge swirl, and a fragrant Orange

Flower Yogurt Cake. Choose your teatime treats among a Triple Ginger Tea Loaf or citrusy Apricot Poppyseed Tea Loaf. Coffee cake is simple or indulgent with a speedy Buttermilk Berry Coffee Cake with Lemon Spice Topping, or try a big and beautiful Hazelnut Coffee Cake with Espresso Glaze.

Butter cakes are great for snacking, too, whipped up in minutes, the perfect after-school treat when cut into generous squares right out of the pan. Kids will love the streusel-topped Chocolate Chip Banana Snackin' Cake packed with cinnamon, or Old-Fashioned Oatmeal Cake with plenty of spice and crunch. Fruit lovers can choose from a gorgeous Upside-Down Plum Poppyseed Cake, Chunky Apple-Cranberry Spice Cake, or a delicate Peach Kiss-Me Crumble Cake with moist summery sliced fruit and crushed gingersnap cookies.

1 BEST BUTTER CAKE
Prep: 20 minutes   Bake: 50 to 55 minutes   Serves: 12

This is a serious butter cake, supermoist thanks to a vanilla-scented melted butter glaze.

1½ sticks (6 ounces) unsalted butter, softened	½ teaspoon freshly grated nutmeg
2 cups sugar	2½ cups flour
4 large eggs, at room temperature	1 teaspoon baking powder
1 tablespoon vanilla extract	½ teaspoon baking soda
2 teaspoons grated lemon zest	½ teaspoon salt
	1 cup buttermilk

1. Preheat oven to 350°F. Grease an 8-cup bundt pan. Dust with flour; tap out excess.

2. In a large bowl, beat together 1 stick of butter and 1½ cups sugar with an electric mixer on medium-high speed until light and fluffy, 1 to 2 minutes. Add eggs, 1 at a time, beating well after each addition. Beat in 2 teaspoons of vanilla, lemon zest, and nutmeg.

3. Sift together flour, baking powder, baking soda, and salt. With mixer on low speed, alternately add flour mixture and buttermilk to butter mixture, beginning and ending with flour, and beat only until blended. Turn batter into prepared pan.

4. Bake 50 to 55 minutes, or until a cake tester inserted in center comes out clean. Let cake cool in pan 10 minutes, then unmold onto a wire rack placed over a large sheet of wax paper or foil.

5. In a small saucepan, combine remaining ½ cup sugar, ½ stick butter, and ¼ cup water. Cook over medium heat, stirring occasionally, until sugar is dissolved and butter is melted, about 3 minutes. Remove from heat and stir in remaining 1 teaspoon vanilla. Gradually brush buttery glaze all over hot cake until absorbed. Let cool completely before serving.

2   CHUNKY APPLE-CRANBERRY SPICE CAKE
Prep: 25 minutes   Bake: 65 to 70 minutes   Serves: 10

Served warm and packed with a homemade chunky applesauce and tart fresh cranberries, this cake is the perfect late afternoon treat to take away a winter's chill.

2½ cups peeled, diced (½-inch) Golden Delicious apples	1 teaspoon cinnamon
1½ sticks (6 ounces) butter, softened	½ teaspoon baking soda
⅔ cup packed brown sugar	½ teaspoon ground ginger
½ cup plus 2 tablespoons granulated sugar	¼ teaspoon ground allspice
3 large eggs	¼ teaspoon salt
2 cups flour	½ cup buttermilk
1½ teaspoons baking powder	1 cup fresh cranberries
	½ cup chopped walnuts
	Classic Custard Sauce (page 84)

1. Preheat oven to 350°F. In a 9-inch glass pie plate, arrange apples in a single layer. Cover loosely with wax paper and microwave on High 5 to 6 minutes, stirring once after 3 minutes, or until apples are tender when tested with small sharp knife. Coarsely mash apples with back of a spoon and let cool. (You should have 1 cup apples.)

2. In a large bowl, beat together butter, brown sugar, and ½ cup granulated sugar with an electric mixer on medium-high speed until light and fluffy. Add eggs, 1 at a time, beating well after each addition.

3. Sift together flour, baking powder, cinnamon, baking soda, ginger, allspice, and salt. With mixer on low speed, alternately add flour mixture and buttermilk to butter mixture, beginning and ending with flour, and beat just until blended.

4. With a rubber spatula, fold apple mixture into batter. Coarsely chop ½ cup of cranberries and stir into batter with walnuts. Turn into a well-greased 9-inch springform pan; smooth top. Sprinkle top with remaining whole cranberries and 2 tablespoons granulated sugar.

5. Bake 65 to 70 minutes, or until a cake tester inserted in center comes out clean. Let cake cool in pan on a wire rack 10 minutes. Remove springform side of pan. Serve warm or at room temperature with Classic Custard Sauce.

3   KAHLÚA CHOCOLATE CAKE

Prep: 30 minutes   Bake: 55 to 60 minutes   Serves: 12

This is fudge heaven! A chocolate and coffee indulgence in every bite.

5 (1-ounce) squares
   unsweetened chocolate
   cut up
2 sticks (8 ounces) butter, cut
   up
¾ cup brewed coffee
¼ cup Kahlúa or other coffee
   liqueur
2 large eggs

2 cups sugar
1 teaspoon vanilla extract
2 cups flour
½ teaspoon baking powder
½ teaspoon baking soda
½ teaspoon salt
½ cup sour cream
   Kahlúa Fudge Glaze (recipe
   follows)

1. Preheat oven to 350°F. Grease an 8-cup bundt pan. Dust with flour; tap out excess.

2. In a small double boiler over simmering water, place chocolate, butter, and coffee. Cook just until chocolate begins to melt, about 5 minutes. Remove from heat and stir until completely smooth. Stir in Kahlúa and let cool.

3. In a large bowl, beat together eggs, sugar, and vanilla with an electric mixer on medium-high speed until light and fluffy, 1 to 2 minutes. Beat in chocolate mixture until smooth.

4. Sift together flour, baking powder, baking soda, and salt. With mixer on low speed, alternately add flour mixture and sour cream to butter mixture, beginning and ending with flour, and beat only until blended. Turn batter into prepared pan.

5. Bake 55 to 60 minutes, or until a cake tester inserted in center comes out clean. Let cake cool in pan 10 minutes, then unmold onto a wire rack and let cool completely. Drizzle Kahlúa Fudge Glaze over top and let stand 30 minutes, or until glaze is set.

4   KAHLÚA FUDGE GLAZE

Prep: 5 minutes   Cook: 1 to 2 minutes   Makes: ½ cup

4 ounces semisweet
   chocolate, cut into small
   pieces
¼ cup heavy cream

2 tablespoons butter
2 tablespoons Kahlúa or other
   coffee liqueur

Place chocolate in a small heatproof bowl. In a small saucepan, combine cream, butter, and Kahlúa. Bring to a boil. Pour over chocolate in bowl and whisk until chocolate is melted and glaze is completely smooth. Let cool until slightly thickened.

5 CHOCOLATE CHIP BANANA SNACKIN' CAKE

Prep: 25 minutes   Bake: 35 to 40 minutes   Serves: 12

These thick and fruity squares are topped off with a melt-in-your-mouth cinnamon-chocolate chip streusel.

1 stick (4 ounces) butter, softened	¼ cup sour cream
1 cup sugar	1¾ cups flour
2 large eggs	½ teaspoon baking powder
1 teaspoon vanilla extract	½ teaspoon baking soda
3 large ripe bananas, peeled and cut into 1-inch chunks	½ teaspoon salt
	Cinnamon-Chocolate Chip Streusel (recipe follows)

1. Preheat oven to 350°F. In a large bowl, beat together butter and sugar with an electric mixer on medium-high speed until light and fluffy, 1 to 2 minutes. Add eggs, 1 at a time, beating well after each addition. Beat in vanilla.

2. In a food processor, puree bananas and sour cream until smooth. Sift together flour, baking powder, baking soda, and salt. With mixer on low speed, alternately add flour mixture and banana mixture to butter mixture, beginning and ending with flour, and beat only until blended.

3. Spread half of batter evenly in a well-greased 13 x 9-inch baking pan. Top with half of Cinnamon-Chocolate Chip Streusel. Carefully spread half of remaining batter over filling. Top with remaining streusel.

4. Bake 35 to 40 minutes, or until a cake tester inserted in center comes out clean. Let cool completely on a wire rack. Cut into squares to serve.

6 CINNAMON-CHOCOLATE CHIP STREUSEL

Prep: 5 minutes   Cook: none   Makes: 2 cups

1 (6-ounce) package semisweet chocolate chips	1 cup chopped walnuts or pecans
	½ cup packed brown sugar
	2½ teaspoons cinnamon

In a medium bowl, combine all ingredients. Stir to mix.

7 ORANGE FLOWER YOGURT CAKE
Prep: 25 minutes   Bake: 50 to 55 minutes   Serves: 12

This supermoist cake is perfect served with fresh fruit.

1½ sticks (6 ounces) unsalted butter, softened	2¾ cups cake flour
2 cups sugar	1½ teaspoons baking powder
3 large eggs, at room temperature	½ teaspoon baking soda
2 teaspoons grated orange zest	½ teaspoon salt
1 teaspoon vanilla extract	1 cup plain yogurt
	Orange Flower Glaze (recipe follows)

1. Preheat oven to 350°F. Grease an 8-cup bundt pan. Dust with flour; tap out excess.

2. In a large bowl, beat together butter and sugar with an electric mixer on medium-high speed until light and fluffy, 1 to 2 minutes. Add eggs, 1 at a time, beating well after each addition. Beat in orange zest and vanilla.

3. Sift together cake flour, baking powder, baking soda, and salt. With mixer on low speed, alternately add flour mixture and yogurt to butter mixture, beginning and ending with flour, and beat only until blended. Turn batter into prepared pan.

4. Bake 50 to 55 minutes, or until a cake tester inserted in center comes out clean. Let cake cool in pan 10 minutes, then unmold onto a wire rack placed over a large sheet of wax paper or foil. Gradually brush Orange Flower Glaze all over hot cake until absorbed. Let cool completely before serving.

8 ORANGE FLOWER GLAZE
Prep: 2 minutes   Cook: 2 to 4 minutes   Makes: ½ cup

Orange flower water is what gives this buttery glaze an unusual citrus flavor, and is worth seeking out here. It can be found in specialty food shops.

½ cup sugar	1 tablespoon orange flower water
4 tablespoons unsalted butter, cut up	

In a small saucepan, combine sugar, butter, and ¼ cup water. Cook over medium heat, stirring occasionally, until sugar is dissolved and butter is melted, 2 to 4 minutes. Remove from heat and stir in orange flower water.

9 COCONUT MARBLE BUTTER CAKE
Prep: 25 minutes   Bake: 65 to 70 minutes   Serves: 10 to 12

¼ cup unsweetened cocoa
   powder
1 cup plus 3 tablespoons
   sugar
2 tablespoons light corn syrup
⅛ teaspoon baking soda
2 sticks (8 ounces) unsalted
   butter, softened
3 large eggs, at room
   temperature

1 teaspoon vanilla extract
2 cups flour
½ teaspoon baking powder
½ teaspoon salt
⅓ cup milk
½ teaspoon coconut extract
¾ cup flaked coconut

1. Preheat oven to 350°F. Grease a 9 x 5 x 3-inch loaf pan. Dust with flour; tap out excess. In a small saucepan, combine cocoa, 3 tablespoons sugar, corn syrup, and ¼ cup water. Bring to boil over medium heat, stirring constantly until smooth. Remove from heat and let cool completely. Stir in baking soda.

2. In a large bowl, beat butter with an electric mixer on medium-high speed until smooth and creamy, about 2 minutes. Gradually add remaining 1 cup sugar and continue beating until light and fluffy, about 5 minutes. Add eggs, 1 at a time, beating well after each addition. Beat in vanilla.

3. Sift together flour, baking powder, and salt. With mixer on low speed, alternately add flour mixture and milk to butter mixture, beginning and ending with flour, and beat only until blended.

4. In a medium bowl, combine ¼ (about 1 cup) of yellow batter with cocoa mixture. Fold gently until blended. Stir coconut extract and flaked coconut into remaining yellow batter. Spoon ¾ of coconut batter into prepared pan. Spoon chocolate batter on top, then spoon on remaining coconut batter. With a long thin knife, gently swirl through batters to marbleize.

5. Bake 65 to 70 minutes, or until a cake tester inserted in center comes out clean. Let cake cool in pan 10 minutes, then turn out onto a wire rack to cool completely.

10   BLACK PEPPER POUND CAKE

Prep: 20 minutes   Bake: 75 to 80 minutes   Serves: 8 to 10

Freshly ground black pepper from the peppermill is essential for this subtly spicy pound cake; make sure the pepper is finely ground.

2 sticks (8 ounces) unsalted butter, softened	1½ teaspoons vanilla extract
1 cup sugar	2 cups flour
4 large eggs, at room temperature	1 teaspoon freshly ground black pepper
1 tablespoon fresh lemon juice	1 teaspoon baking powder
	½ teaspoon salt
	½ teaspoon ground allspice

1. Preheat oven to 325°F. Grease a 9 x 5 x 3-inch loaf pan. Dust with flour; tap out excess.

2. In a large bowl, beat butter with an electric mixer on medium-high speed until smooth and creamy. Gradually add sugar and continue beating until light and fluffy, about 5 minutes. Add eggs, 1 at a time, beating well after each addition. Beat in lemon juice and vanilla.

3. Sift together flour, pepper, baking powder, salt, and allspice. On low speed, gradually add flour mixture, beating just until blended. Turn batter into prepared pan.

4. Bake 75 to 80 minutes, or until a cake tester inserted in center comes out clean. Let cake cool in pan 10 minutes, then unmold onto a wire rack to cool completely.

11   GOLDEN ALMOND POUND CAKE

Prep: 20 minutes   Bake: 60 to 65 minutes   Serves: 8 to 10

Stone-ground yellow cornmeal and almond paste give this buttery cake a lovely golden crumb and a subtle nutty flavor.

2 sticks (8 ounces) unsalted butter, softened	½ teaspoon vanilla extract
⅓ cup almond paste	½ teaspoon almond extract
1 cup sugar	1½ cups flour
4 large eggs, at room temperature	1 teaspoon baking powder
2 teaspoons grated lemon zest	½ teaspoon salt
	½ cup yellow cornmeal
	¼ cup milk

1. Preheat oven to 325°F. Grease an 8-cup bundt pan. Dust with flour; tap out excess.

2. In a large bowl, beat together butter and almond paste with an electric mixer on medium-high speed until smooth and creamy. Gradually add sugar and continue beating until light and fluffy, about 5 minutes longer. Add eggs, 1 at a time, beating well after each addition. Beat in lemon zest, vanilla, and almond extract.

3. Sift together flour, baking powder, and salt; stir in cornmeal. With mixer on low speed, alternately add flour mixture and milk to butter mixture, beginning and ending with flour, and beat only until blended. Turn batter into prepared pan.

4. Bake 60 to 65 minutes, or until a cake tester inserted in center comes out clean. Let cake cool in pan 10 minutes, then unmold onto a wire rack and cool completely.

12 BUTTERMILK BERRY COFFEE CAKE WITH LEMON SPICE TOPPING

Prep: 20 minutes   Bake: 65 to 70 minutes   Serves: 8

This easy streusel coffee cake is also wonderful with fresh raspberries.

1 stick (4 ounces) butter, softened	¼ teaspoon salt
1 cup sugar	½ cup buttermilk
2 large eggs	1½ cups fresh or frozen blueberries
1 teaspoon vanilla extract	2 teaspoons fresh lemon juice
1⅔ cups flour	Lemon Spice Topping
½ teaspoon baking powder	(recipe follows)
½ teaspoon baking soda	

1. Preheat oven to 350°F. In a large bowl, beat together butter and sugar with an electric mixer on medium-high speed until light and fluffy, 2 minutes. Add eggs, 1 at a time, beating well after each addition. Beat in vanilla.

2. Sift together flour, baking powder, baking soda, and salt. With mixer on low speed, alternately add flour mixture and buttermilk to butter mixture, beginning and ending with flour, and beat only until blended.

3. Turn half of batter into a greased 9-inch springform pan. In a medium bowl, toss berries with lemon juice; sprinkle berries on top of batter. Cover berries with remaining batter. Sprinkle Lemon Spice Topping over all.

4. Bake 65 to 70 minutes, or until a cake tester inserted in center comes out clean. Transfer to a wire rack and let cool 15 minutes. Remove springform side of pan. Serve cake warm or at room temperature.

13 LEMON SPICE TOPPING

Prep: 5 minutes   Cook: none   Makes: ¾ cup

½ cup packed brown sugar	½ teaspoon grated lemon zest
⅓ cup flour	3 tablespoons butter, softened
¾ teaspoon cinnamon	

In a medium bowl, combine brown sugar, flour, cinnamon, and lemon zest. With pastry blender or 2 knives, cut in butter until mixture resembles coarse crumbs.

14 OLD-FASHIONED OATMEAL CAKE

Prep: 30 minutes   Bake: 35 to 40 minutes   Serves: 12

This comfort classic features a slightly unusual crunchy broiled-on oat topping. Watch the topping carefully to make sure it doesn't burn.

1¼ cups boiling water
1 cup old-fashioned oats
1 stick (4 ounces) butter,
    softened
¾ cup packed brown sugar
½ cup granulated sugar
2 large eggs
1 teaspoon vanilla extract

¾ cup all-purpose flour
¾ cup whole wheat flour
1 teaspoon baking soda
1 teaspoon cinnamon
½ teaspoon salt
   Oat Crunch Topping (recipe
   follows)

1. In a heatproof bowl, pour boiling water over oats. Let cool to lukewarm, stirring occasionally, about 30 minutes.

2. Meanwhile, preheat oven to 350°F. In a large bowl, beat butter with an electric mixer on medium-high speed until smooth and creamy. Gradually add brown sugar and granulated sugar and continue beating until light and fluffy, about 3 minutes. Add eggs, 1 at a time, beating well after each addition. Beat in vanilla, then stir in softened oats.

3. Sift together all-purpose flour, whole wheat flour, baking soda, cinnamon, and salt. With mixer on low speed, add flour mixture to butter mixture, beating just until blended. Turn batter into a greased 13 x 9-inch baking pan. Bake 35 to 40 minutes, or until a cake tester inserted in center comes out clean.

4. Preheat boiler. Spread Oat Crunch Topping over top of hot cake. Broil topping 5 inches from heat until brown and bubbly, 2 to 3 minutes. Let cake cool completely on a wire rack.

15 OAT CRUNCH TOPPING

Prep: 5 minutes   Cook: none   Makes: about 1⅔ cups

½ cup packed brown sugar
⅓ cup heavy cream
⅓ cup butter, melted
   Pinch of ground nutmeg
⅓ cup old-fashioned oats

⅓ cup chopped walnuts or
   pecans
⅓ cup flaked coconut
¼ cup wheat germ

In a medium bowl, whisk together brown sugar, cream, melted butter, and nutmeg until smooth. Stir in oats, nuts, coconut, and wheat germ.

16 UPSIDE-DOWN PLUM POPPYSEED CAKE
Prep: 40 minutes   Cook: 6 to 8 minutes   Bake: 50 to 55 minutes
Serves: 8

Prepare the ruby red plum topping first to allow time for it to cool before adding the buttery poppyseed cake batter. This is a perfect late-summer dessert with whipped cream or vanilla ice cream.

6 medium purple plums, pitted
1 stick (4 ounces) plus 2 tablespoons butter, softened
1¼ cups plus 2 tablespoons sugar
2 large eggs, separated, at room temperature

1 teaspoon vanilla extract
1½ cups flour
1 teaspoon baking powder
½ teaspoon salt
1 tablespoon poppyseeds
¼ cup milk

1. Grease a 9 x 2-inch round cake pan. Dust with flour; tap out excess. Cut each plum into 6 wedges; discard pits. In a large skillet, heat 2 tablespoons butter over medium-high heat. Add plums and ½ cup sugar. Cook, stirring occasionally, until plums are just tender and sugar is completely melted, about 5 minutes. With a slotted spoon, transfer fruit to a plate; reserve syrup in skillet. Let cool slightly.

2. Arrange plums, cut sides down, along bottom of prepared pan in concentric circles. Bring reserved fruit syrup in skillet to a boil. Boil until slightly thickened, stirring constantly, about 1 minute. Pour syrup over plums and let fruit cool completely.

3. Preheat oven to 350°F. In a large bowl, beat together remaining 1 stick butter and ¾ cup of remaining sugar with an electric mixer on medium-high speed until light and fluffy, about 2 minutes. Add egg yolks, 1 at a time, beating well after each addition. Beat in vanilla.

4. Sift together flour, baking powder, and salt; stir in poppyseeds. With mixer on low speed, alternately add flour mixture and milk to butter mixture, beginning and ending with flour, and beat only until blended.

5. In a medium bowl, beat egg whites in clean bowl with an electric mixer with clean beaters on medium speed until soft peaks form. Gradually beat in remaining 2 tablespoons sugar and continue to beat to stiff peaks. With a rubber spatula, gently fold ⅓ of whites into cake batter, then fold in remaining whites just until blended. Spread batter evenly over plums in prepared pan.

6. Bake 50 to 55 minutes, or until a cake tester inserted in center comes out clean. Let cake cool completely in pan. Run a small knife around edge of pan, then invert cake onto serving plate.

17 CHOCOLATE-CHERRY SOUR CREAM COFFEE CAKE

Prep: 35 minutes   Bake: 55 to 60 minutes   Serves: 12 to 14

This ultrarich sour cream cake is studded with dried cherries and a bitter-sweet chocolate streusel.

1½ **sticks (6 ounces) unsalted butter, softened**
1¼ **cups granulated sugar**
3 **large eggs**
1½ **teaspoons vanilla extract**
3 **cups flour**
1½ **teaspoons baking powder**
1½ **teaspoons baking soda**
½ **teaspoon salt**
2 **cups sour cream**
1 **cup walnuts**

1 **(3-ounce) bar bittersweet chocolate, cut up, or** ½ **cup semisweet chocolate chips**
⅔ **cup packed brown sugar**
⅓ **cup dried cherries or raisins, chopped**
1 **tablespoon unsweetened cocoa powder**
2 **teaspoons cinnamon**
 Powdered sugar

1. Preheat oven to 350°F. Grease a 12-cup bundt pan or a 10-inch tube pan. Dust with flour; tap out excess.

2. In a large bowl, beat butter with an electric mixer on medium speed until smooth and creamy. Gradually beat in granulated sugar until light and fluffy, about 3 minutes. Add eggs, 1 at a time, beating well after each addition. Beat in vanilla.

3. Sift together flour, baking powder, baking soda, and salt. On low speed, alternately add flour mixture and sour cream to butter mixture, beginning and ending with flour, and beat just until blended.

4. In a food processor, combine walnuts, chocolate, brown sugar, dried cherries, cocoa powder, and cinnamon. Turn machine quickly on and off until mixture is coarsely ground.

5. Spread ⅓ (about 2 cups) of cake batter into prepared pan. Sprinkle with half of chocolate filling (1½ cups), then cover with half of remaining batter. Repeat process with remaining chocolate filling and batter.

6. Bake 55 to 60 minutes, or until a cake tester inserted in center comes out clean. Let cake cool in pan 15 minutes, then unmold onto a wire rack and cool completely. Dust top with powdered sugar before serving.

18 HOLIDAY HONEY PEAR CAKE
Prep: 20 minutes   Bake: 65 to 72 minutes   Serves: 12

This honey- and spice-scented cake is a favorite during the Jewish holiday of Rosh Hashanah. Dark, dense, and moist, my version is distinguished by the addition of dried pears, though golden raisins can be substituted. For maximum flavor, bake this cake a day ahead.

½ cup walnuts
2 cups flour
1 teaspoon cinnamon
¾ teaspoon baking powder
¾ teaspoon baking soda
½ teaspoon salt
¼ teaspoon ground allspice
¼ teaspoon grated nutmeg
¾ cup diced dried pears or
   golden raisins
3 large eggs

¾ cup packed brown sugar
¾ cup honey
3 tablespoons melted butter
   or vegetable oil
½ teaspoon grated orange zest
½ teaspoon grated lemon zest
½ cup cold strongly brewed
   coffee
¼ cup fresh orange juice
1 tablespoon whiskey or
   brandy

1. Preheat oven to 350°F. Spread out walnuts on a small baking sheet. Bake 5 to 7 minutes, or until nuts are lightly browned and fragrant. Let cool, then coarsely chop. Grease a 9 x 5 x 3-inch loaf pan. Dust with flour; tap out excess.

2. Sift together flour, cinnamon, baking powder, baking soda, salt, allspice, and nutmeg. In small bowl, toss toasted chopped walnuts and pears or raisins with 1 tablespoon flour mixture.

3. In a large bowl, beat together eggs and brown sugar with an electric mixer on medium speed to blend. Beat in honey, melted butter, orange zest, and lemon zest. In a glass measure, combine coffee, orange juice, and whiskey. With mixer on low speed, alternately add flour and coffee mixture to butter mixture, beginning and ending with flour, and beat just until blended. Stir in walnut and pear mixture. Turn batter into prepared pan.

4. Bake 60 to 65 minutes, or until top of cake springs back when lightly touched in center. Let cake cool in pan 10 minutes, then turn out onto a wire rack and cool completely.

19 HAZELNUT COFFEE CAKE WITH ESPRESSO GLAZE

Prep: 30 minutes   Bake: 70 to 80 minutes   Serves: 16

Complete with a double dose of espresso-hazelnut swirl and a translucent espresso glaze, this flavor-packed coffee cake is elegant enough for your most discriminating guests.

1 cup hazelnuts	1 teaspoon baking soda
2 sticks (8 ounces) unsalted	½ teaspoon salt
butter, softened	1½ cups sour cream
2 cups sugar	2 tablespoons instant espresso
3 large eggs	powder
2 teaspoons vanilla extract	Espresso Glaze (page 25)
3 cups flour	
1½ teaspoons baking powder	

1. Preheat oven to 350°F. Arrange hazelnuts on a small cookie sheet. Bake 10 to 15 minutes, or until nuts are lightly browned and dark skins are cracked. Rub warm nuts in a terrycloth towel to remove as much of skins as possible. Let cool, then finely chop. Grease a 12-cup bundt pan. Dust with flour; tap out excess.

2. In a large bowl, beat butter with an electric mixer on medium-high speed until smooth and creamy. Gradually add sugar and continue beating until light and fluffy, about 3 minutes. Add eggs, 1 at a time, beating well after each addition. Beat in vanilla.

3. Sift together flour, baking powder, baking soda, and salt. With mixer on low speed, alternately add flour mixture and sour cream to butter mixture, beginning and ending with flour, and beat only until blended.

4. In a cup, dissolve instant espresso in 2 tablespoons hot water. In a medium bowl, fold dissolved espresso into ⅓ (about 2½ cups) of yellow batter until blended.

5. Fold hazelnuts into remaining batter. Spoon half hazelnut batter into prepared pan. Spoon espresso batter over it, spreading evenly with spatula. Spoon, then spread, remaining hazelnut batter on top.

6. Bake 60 to 65 minutes, or until a cake tester inserted in center comes out clean. Let cake cool in pan 15 minutes, then unmold onto a wire rack and cool completely. Drizzle Espresso Glaze over top of cake. Let stand 30 minutes, or until glaze is set.

20 ESPRESSO GLAZE
Prep: 5 minutes   Cook: none   Makes: ½ cup

2 to 3 tablespoons hot brewed
    coffee or water
1½ teaspoons instant espresso
    powder

½ teaspoon vanilla extract
1⅓ cups sifted powdered sugar

In a medium bowl, stir together 2 tablespoons coffee, espresso powder, and vanilla until espresso is dissolved. Whisk in powdered sugar. Gradually stir in remaining 1 tablespoon coffee if necessary to make a thick glaze.

21 PEACH KISS-ME CRUMBLE CAKE
Prep: 25 minutes   Bake: 40 to 45 minutes   Serves: 8

1 stick (4 ounces) butter,
    softened
½ cup sugar
2 large eggs
1 teaspoon vanilla extract
½ teaspoon grated lemon zest
1 cup flour
1 teaspoon baking powder
¼ teaspoon grated nutmeg

¼ teaspoon salt
1 pound (3 medium) peaches,
    peeled and sliced, or
    1 (16-ounce) can peach
    slices in heavy syrup,
    well drained
Gingersnap Crumble
    Topping (recipe follows)

1. Preheat oven to 350°F. Grease an 8-inch springform pan. In a medium bowl, beat together butter and sugar with an electric mixer on medium-high speed until light and fluffy, 2 minutes. Beat in eggs, 1 at a time, then beat in vanilla and lemon zest.

2. Sift together flour, baking powder, nutmeg, and salt. With mixer on low speed, gradually add flour mixture just until blended. Turn into the prepared pan. Arrange peach slices over top of batter, overlapping slightly in concentric circles. Sprinkle fruit with Gingersnap Crumble Topping.

3. Bake 40 to 45 minutes, or until a cake tester inserted in center comes out clean. Let cake cool in pan 15 minutes. Remove springform side of pan. Serve warm or at room temperature.

22 GINGERSNAP CRUMBLE TOPPING
Prep: 5 minutes   Cook: none   Makes: ⅔ cup

⅓ cup flour
3 tablespoons packed brown
    sugar
3 tablespoons gingersnap
    cookie crumbs

½ teaspoon ground ginger
¼ teaspoon cinnamon
2 tablespoons butter, softened

In a medium bowl, combine flour, brown sugar, cookie crumbs, ginger, and cinnamon. With pastry blender or 2 knives, cut in butter until mixture resembles fine crumbs.

23 STRAWBERRY 'N' CREAM SHORTCAKES
Prep: 20 minutes   Chill: 1 hour   Bake: none   Serves: 8

2 pints fresh whole strawberries, hulled	2 tablespoons powdered sugar
¼ cup granulated sugar	3 tablespoons sour cream
1 tablespoon fresh lemon juice	½ teaspoon vanilla extract
1 cup heavy cream	Cream Shortcakes (recipe follows)

1. In a large bowl, combine 1 pint strawberries and sugar. Crush berries with a potato masher or fork. From remaining pint strawberries, reserve 8 for garnish. Slice remaining strawberries and stir into crushed berry mixture. Mix in lemon juice. Refrigerate 1 hour, stirring occasionally.

2. In a large bowl, beat together heavy cream and powdered sugar with an electric mixer until soft peaks form. Add sour cream and vanilla and continue to beat until stiff.

3. With a serrated knife, split cream shortcakes horizontally; place bottoms on dessert plates. Top with equal amounts of strawberry mixture and 1½ cups whipped cream. Replace tops and spoon a dollop of remaining whipped cream on top of each shortcake. Top each with 1 reserved whole strawberry.

24 CREAM SHORTCAKES
Prep: 10 minutes   Bake: 18 to 20 minutes   Makes: 8 shortcakes

1 cup all-purpose flour	¼ teaspoon salt
1 cup cake flour	1 stick (4 ounces) butter, cut up
3 tablespoons packed brown sugar	1 cup plus 1 tablespoon heavy cream
1 tablespoon baking powder	

1. Preheat oven to 400°F. In a medium bowl, combine all-purpose flour, cake flour, sugar, baking powder, and salt. With a pastry blender or 2 knives, cut in butter until mixture resembles coarse crumbs. Gradually add 1 cup cream, tossing with a fork until dough is evenly moistened.

2. Transfer dough to a work surface and knead gently until it just holds together, about 1 minute. Roll or pat dough ½ inch thick. With a 3-inch cookie or biscuit cutter, cut dough into circles and transfer to a well-greased cookie sheet. Reroll scraps to make a total of 8 circles. Brush tops with remaining 1 tablespoon cream.

3. Bake 18 to 20 minutes, or until tops are golden. Transfer to a wire rack and let cool completely before filling.

25   FROSTED MERINGUE SPICE CAKE

Prep: 25 minutes   Bake: 53 to 55 minutes   Serves: 9

½ cup pecans
1 stick (4 ounces) butter, softened
¾ cup granulated sugar
¾ cup packed light brown sugar
2 large eggs, at room temperature
½ teaspoon vanilla extract

1¼ cups cake flour
½ teaspoon baking powder
½ teaspoon baking soda
½ teaspoon cinnamon
¼ teaspoon grated nutmeg
¼ teaspoon ground cloves
¼ teaspoon salt
Pinch of ground red pepper
½ cup buttermilk

1. Preheat oven to 350°F. Spread out pecans on a small baking sheet. Bake 8 to 10 minutes, or until nuts are lightly browned and fragrant. Let cool, then chop fine. Grease a 9-inch square baking pan. Dust with flour; tap out excess.

2. In a large bowl, beat together butter, ½ cup granulated sugar, and ½ cup brown sugar with an electric mixer on medium-high speed until light and fluffy, about 2 minutes. Separate 1 egg, reserving white for frosting. Add egg yolk, then whole egg, 1 at a time, to butter mixture, beating well after each addition. Beat in vanilla.

3. Sift together cake flour, baking powder, baking soda, cinnamon, nutmeg, cloves, salt, and red pepper. With mixer on low speed, alternately add flour mixture and buttermilk to butter mixture, beginning and ending with flour, and beat just until blended. Turn batter into prepared pan.

4. Bake 35 minutes, or until a cake tester inserted in center comes out clean. Transfer cake to a wire cake rack; leave oven on.

5. Set a sieve over a small bowl; press remaining ¼ cup each granulated and brown sugar through sieve to combine. In a clean medium bowl, beat reserved egg white with an electric mixer with clean beaters on medium speed until soft peaks form. Gradually beat in sugar mixture, 1 tablespoon at a time, until stiff peaks form when beaters are lifted, about 3 minutes. With a rubber spatula, gently fold in chopped pecans.

6. Gently spread meringue over warm cake. Return cake to oven and bake 10 minutes longer, or until top of meringue is golden brown. Let cool completely on a wire rack before serving.

26   GIANT POPPY-BERRY SHORTCAKE RING
Prep: 20 minutes   Chill: 1 hour   Bake: none   Serves: 8

Here's an easy dessert for summer entertaining. The simple shortcake biscuit ring can be prepared ahead, then filled with your favorite assortment of fresh berries.

1 **pint whole fresh** **strawberries, hulled**	1 **cup heavy cream**
¼ **cup granulated sugar**	2 **tablespoons powdered** **sugar**
1 **cup fresh blueberries,**	1 **teaspoon vanilla extract**
blackberries, or	**Buttermilk Poppyseed**
raspberries	**Shortcake Ring (recipe**
2 **tablespoons orange liqueur**	**follows)**

1. In a large bowl, combine strawberries and granulated sugar. Crush berries with potato masher or fork. Refrigerate 1 hour, stirring occasionally.

2. Add blueberries, blackberries, or raspberries to strawberry mixture. Stir in orange liqueur.

3. In a large bowl, beat together cream and powdered sugar with an electric mixer until soft peaks form. Add vanilla and continue to beat until stiff.

4. With a serrated knife, cut top quarter off the Poppyseed Shortcake Ring and place bottom on a large dessert plate. Spoon berry mixture over cake, then add dollops of whipped cream. Cover cream with top of shortcake.

27   BUTTERMILK POPPYSEED SHORTCAKE RING
Prep: 10 minutes   Bake: 18 to 20 minutes   Makes: 8 shortcakes

Circles of tender biscuits are baked close together to form this whimsical shortcake.

2 **cups flour**	¼ **teaspoon salt**
⅓ **cup plus 1 tablespoon sugar**	1 **stick (4 ounces) butter, cut**
1 **tablespoon poppyseeds**	**up**
2 **teaspoons baking powder**	¾ **cup plus 2 tablespoons**
1 **teaspoon baking soda**	**buttermilk**

1. Preheat oven to 425°F. In a medium bowl, combine flour, ⅓ cup sugar, poppyseeds, baking powder, baking soda, and salt. With a pastry blender or 2 knives, cut in butter until mixture resembles coarse crumbs. Gradually add buttermilk, tossing with a fork until dough is evenly moistened.

2. Transfer dough to a work surface and knead gently until it just holds together, about 1 minute. Roll out or pat dough to ½-inch thickness. With a round 3-inch cookie or biscuit cutter, cut dough into circles. Reroll scraps to make a total of 8 circles. Arrange biscuits on a well-greased cookie sheet, with edges touching, to form an 8-inch circle. Sprinkle top with remaining 1 tablespoon sugar.

3. Bake 18 to 20 minutes, or until golden. With a large metal spatula, carefully transfer shortcake ring to a wire rack and let cool completely.

28 APRICOT POPPYSEED TEA LOAF
Prep: 10 minutes   Stand: 1 hour   Bake: 65 to 70 minutes
Serves: 12

Diced dried apricots add just the right amount of tartness to this classic poppyseed pound cake.

¾ **cup finely diced dried**	1 **teaspoon grated lemon zest**
apricots	1 **teaspoon vanilla extract**
1 **tablespoon apricot brandy**	5 **large eggs, at room**
or brandy	**temperature**
2 **sticks (8 ounces) unsalted**	2 **cups cake flour**
butter, softened	¼ **teaspoon salt**
1 **cup sugar**	2 **tablespoons poppyseeds**
1 **teaspoon grated orange zest**	**Citrus Glaze (recipe follows)**

1. In a small bowl, combine apricots and brandy. Let stand at least 1 hour, or overnight.

2. Preheat oven to 350°F. Grease a 9 x 5 x 3-inch loaf pan. Dust with flour; tap out excess.

3. In a large bowl, beat butter with an electric mixer at medium-high speed until smooth and creamy. Gradually add sugar, 1 tablespoon at a time, and continue to beat until very light and fluffy, about 4 minutes. Beat in orange zest, lemon zest, and vanilla. Add eggs 1 at a time, beating 2 minutes after each addition, until batter has increased in volume and is very light.

4. Sift together cake flour and salt. Stir in poppyseeds. With a rubber spatula, gradually fold flour into butter mixture ⅓ at a time. Gently fold in soaked apricots with any brandy remaining in bowl, just until blended. Turn batter into prepared pan.

5. Bake 65 to 70 minutes, or until a cake tester inserted in center comes out clean. Let cake cool in pan 10 minutes, then turn out onto a wire rack placed over a large sheet of wax paper or foil. Gradually brush top of hot cake with Citrus Glaze until absorbed. Let cool completely before serving.

29 CITRUS GLAZE
Prep: 5 minutes   Cook: none   Makes: about ¼ cup

2 **tablespoons fresh orange**	2 **teaspoons fresh lemon juice**
juice	3 **tablespoons sugar**

In a small bowl, combine all ingredients. Stir until sugar is dissolved.

30   GRANNY'S GINGERBREAD CAKE
Prep: 20 minutes   Bake: 35 to 40 minutes   Serves: 9

Best eaten warm, this old-fashioned dark molasses cake is pure nostalgia.

1 stick (4 ounces) butter,
   softened
¾ cup packed brown sugar
¾ cup unsulphured molasses
2 large eggs
2¼ cups flour
1½ teaspoons baking soda
2 teaspoons ground ginger

1 teaspoon cinnamon
½ teaspoon dry mustard
½ teaspoon mace or grated
   nutmeg
½ teaspoon salt
¼ teaspoon ground allspice
1 cup buttermilk
   Vanilla ice cream

1. Preheat oven to 350°F. Grease a 9-inch square baking pan. Dust with flour; tap out excess.

2. In a large bowl, beat together butter and brown sugar with an electric mixer on medium-high speed until light and fluffy, 2 minutes. Gradually beat in molasses, then eggs, 1 at a time, beating well after each addition.

3. Sift together flour, baking soda, ginger, cinnamon, mustard, mace, salt, and allspice. With mixer on low speed, alternately add flour mixture and buttermilk to butter mixture, beginning and ending with flour, and beat just until blended. Turn batter into prepared pan.

4. Bake 35 to 40 minutes, or until a cake tester inserted in center comes out clean. Let cake cool in pan 15 minutes, then cut into 3-inch squares and serve warm with vanilla ice cream.

31   TRIPLE GINGER TEA LOAF
Prep: 20 minutes   Bake: 60 to 65 minutes   Serves: 8 to 10

This fragrant spice cake tastes even better when baked a day ahead.

1 stick (4 ounces) butter,
   softened
1 cup sugar
2 large eggs, at room
   temperature
2 teaspoons grated fresh
   ginger
1 teaspoon grated orange zest
1⅔ cups flour

1 teaspoon ground ginger
1 teaspoon cinnamon
½ teaspoon baking soda
½ teaspoon salt
⅛ teaspoon ground cloves
½ cup buttermilk
¼ cup chopped crystallized
   ginger

1. Preheat oven to 350°F. Grease an 8½ x 4½ x 2½-inch loaf pan. Dust with flour; tap out excess.

2. In a large bowl, beat butter with an electric mixer on medium-high speed until smooth and creamy. Gradually add sugar and continue beating until light and fluffy, about 3 minutes. Add eggs, 1 at a time, beating well after each addition. Beat in grated ginger and orange zest.

3. Sift together flour, ground ginger, cinnamon, baking soda, salt, and cloves. With mixer on low speed, alternately add flour mixture and buttermilk to butter mixture, beginning and ending with flour, and beat only until blended. Stir in crystallized ginger. Turn batter into prepared pan.

4. Bake 60 to 65 minutes, or until a cake tester inserted in center comes out clean. Let cake cool in pan 10 minutes, then turn out onto a wire rack and cool completely.

32   FRESH PERSIMMON CAKE

Prep: 30 minutes   Bake: 62 to 70 minutes   Serves: 8 to 10

A favorite fruit for holiday baking, sweet and fragrant persimmons are available from October through February. Be sure to use a light or pure olive oil here; extra-virgin oil will be overpowering.

1 cup pecans	1½ teaspoons baking soda
3 large eggs	2¼ cups flour
1¼ cups granulated sugar	1 teaspoon cinnamon
½ cup olive oil	½ teaspoon ground ginger
2 tablespoons brandy	½ teaspoon salt
1 teaspoon vanilla extract	½ cup golden raisins
1 pound very ripe	Powdered sugar and
persimmons	whipped cream

1. Preheat oven to 325°F. Spread out pecans on a small baking sheet. Bake 7 to 10 minutes, or until nuts are lightly browned and fragrant. Let cool, then coarsely chop. Grease a 9-inch springform pan. Dust with flour; tap out excess.

2. In a large bowl, beat eggs, sugar, olive oil, brandy, and vanilla with an electric mixer at medium speed until smooth.

3. Remove tops of persimmons and cut in half. With a spoon, carefully scoop out flesh and transfer to a food processor; process until smooth. Measure out 1 cup puree; stir in baking soda. Beat persimmon puree into egg mixture until well combined.

4. Sift together flour, cinnamon, ginger, and salt. With mixer on low speed, gradually beat flour mixture into persimmon batter until just combined. With a rubber spatula, fold in toasted pecans and raisins. Turn batter into prepared pan.

5. Bake 55 to 60 minutes, or until a cake tester inserted in center comes out clean. Let cake cool in pan 15 minutes. Remove springform side of pan; sift powdered sugar over top. Serve warm with whipped cream.

33   FRESH PINEAPPLE PECAN UPSIDE-DOWN CAKE

Prep: 40 minutes   Bake: 45 to 50 minutes   Serves: 8

Golden cornmeal buttermilk cake with the addition of fresh pineapple makes this comfort classic extra-special.

6 slices of fresh peeled pineapple, cut ¾ inch thick	1 teaspoon vanilla extract
1¼ cups granulated sugar	1 cup flour
1 stick (4 ounces) plus 2 tablespoons butter, softened	1½ teaspoons baking powder
	½ teaspoon baking soda
2 large eggs, separated, at room temperature	½ teaspoon salt
	½ cup yellow cornmeal
	½ cup buttermilk
	¾ cup packed brown sugar
	½ cup chopped pecans

1. Remove cores from pineapple slices with a small sharp knife or round cookie cutter. In a 10-inch glass pie plate, combine ¼ cup granulated sugar and ½ cup water. Microwave on High 3½ to 4 minutes, or until liquid comes to a boil and sugar dissolves. Add 3 pineapple slices and microwave on High 4 to 5 minutes, turning once halfway through, or until pineapple is just tender. Drain slices on paper towels. Repeat process with remaining pineapple slices and let cool.

2. Preheat oven to 350°F. In a large bowl, beat together 1 stick butter and remaining 1 cup granulated sugar with an electric mixer on medium-high speed until light and fluffy. Add egg yolks, 1 at a time, beating well after each addition. Beat in vanilla.

3. Sift together flour, baking powder, baking soda, and salt; stir in cornmeal. With mixer on low speed, alternately add flour mixture and buttermilk to butter mixture, beginning and ending with flour, and beat just until blended. In a small clean bowl, beat egg whites with an electric mixer and clean beaters until stiff but not dry. With a rubber spatula, gently fold whites into cake batter.

4. In a 10-inch cast-iron skillet, melt remaining 2 tablespoons butter, brushing sides of pan with butter to coat. Sprinkle an even layer of brown sugar over bottom of pan, then sprinkle on pecans. Arrange fresh or canned pineapple slices on top in a single layer; pour cake batter over all.

5. Bake 45 to 50 minutes, or until a cake tester inserted in center comes out clean. With a small sharp knife, loosen cake from edge of pan and immediately invert onto a serving plate. Let cool completely before serving.

34 SWEET CREAM POUND CAKE

Prep: 20 minutes   Bake: 60 to 65 minutes   Serves: 12

This cardamom-scented pound cake, extra-rich and moist thanks to the addition of heavy cream, needs only a dusting of powdered sugar and a bowl of fresh berries as accompaniments.

2 sticks (8 ounces) unsalted butter, softened	1 teaspoon vanilla extract
1 (16-ounce) box powdered sugar	2½ cups cake flour
	1½ teaspoons baking powder
4 large eggs, at room temperature	1 teaspoon ground cardamom
	½ teaspoon salt
	½ cup heavy cream

1. Preheat oven to 350°F. Grease a 12-cup bundt pan. Dust with flour; tap out excess.

2. In a large bowl, beat butter with an electric mixer on medium-high speed until smooth and creamy. Gradually add powdered sugar and continue beating until light and fluffy, about 5 minutes. Add eggs, 1 at a time, beating well after each addition. Beat in vanilla.

3. Sift together cake flour, baking powder, cardamom, and salt. With mixer on low speed, alternately add flour mixture and cream to butter mixture, beginning and ending with flour, and beat only until blended. Turn batter into prepared pan.

4. Bake 60 to 65 minutes, or until a cake tester inserted in center comes out clean. Let cake cool in pan 15 minutes, then unmold onto a wire rack and cool completely.

35 EDNA PAYNE'S GIANT SOUR CREAM CAKE

Prep: 20 minutes   Bake: 1 hour plus 40 to 45 minutes   Serves: 20

2 sticks (8 ounces) unsalted
   butter, softened
3 cups sugar
6 large eggs, separated, at
   room temperature

1 teaspoon vanilla extract
3 cups flour
¼ teaspoon baking soda
¼ teaspoon salt
1 cup sour cream

1. Preheat oven to 300°F. Grease a 12-cup bundt pan. Dust with flour; tap out excess.

2. In a large bowl, beat butter with an electric mixer on medium-high speed until smooth and creamy. Gradually add sugar, 1 tablespoon at a time, then continue beating until batter has increased in volume and is very light and fluffy, about 8 minutes. Add egg yolks, 1 at a time, beating well after each addition. Beat in vanilla.

3. Sift together flour, baking soda, and salt 3 times. With mixer on low speed, alternately add flour mixture and sour cream to butter mixture, beginning and ending with flour, and beating just until blended.

4. In another clean bowl, beat egg whites with an electric mixer with clean beaters at medium speed until peaks are stiff but not dry, about 4 minutes. With a rubber spatula, gently fold ⅓ of egg whites into sour cream mixture, then fold in remaining whites just until blended. Turn batter into prepared pan.

5. Bake 1 hour plus 40 to 45 minutes, or until a cake tester inserted in center comes out clean. Let cake cool in pan 15 minutes, then unmold onto a wire rack and cool completely.

Chapter 2

Red, White, and Blue Ribbon Cakes

Towering layer cakes and foot-long sheet cakes are totally American, a wonderful part of our taste for country baking. These frosted cakes include bake-sale favorites from the farm that celebrate nature's bounty of fruits and vegetables. Many people love classic Fresh Ginger Carrot Cake, but the same tradition includes more unusual combinations, such as a spicy Sweet Potato Cocoa Cake, Apple Butter Stack Cake, or Spiced Blackberry Jam Cake with a fluffy buttermilk icing. This chapter is also full of whimsy and regional tradition: Southern Buttermilk Lane Cake with its filling of dried fruit, pecans, and bourbon; a down-home and fudgy Dark Chocolate Cola Cake; Fudgy Marbled Mayo Cake; and Mystery Spice Cake with tomato soup are just a few.

I tested these layer cake recipes in standard 8- and 9-inch round cake pans. I like to line my pans with wax paper. This only takes a few minutes, and it guarantees that the layers will turn out easily, even if the cake has cooled in the pan too long. Using the bottom of a cake pan as a guide, depending on the number of layers in your cake, trace a circle on 2 or 3 sheets of wax paper, then cut out the circles with scissors. Lightly grease the bottom and sides of the pans, then line the bottoms with the paper circles. Grease the paper, then flour the pans, tapping out any excess flour. After baking, let the cakes cool in the pans for 10 minutes, then unmold onto wire racks and immediately peel off the wax paper. Invert the cakes again so they are right side up and let them cool completely.

Whether your cake is a single layer or stacked very high, filling and frosting it correctly will make the confection look professional. For layer cakes, place the bottom layer right side up on a cake plate; sweep off excess crumbs with a pastry brush. Tuck 4 strips of wax paper under the cake to catch any drips. With a long metal spatula, cover the bottom layer with frosting or filling, leaving a ¼-inch edge exposed. Repeat the process with the remaining layers, leaving the top of the cake unfrosted. After you fill the cake, next apply a thin layer of frosting to the sides to seal any gaps between the cake layers and to even the sides. Then frost the top of the cake and apply any remaining frosting to the sides. I love to decorate my cakes with circular swirls or peaks of frosting applied with a small spatula or the back of a spoon. This can be done to both the top and the sides of the cake or just to the top or sides alone, leaving the remainder of the cake smooth. After frosting and decorating, slowly pull out the strips of wax paper from the bottom of the cake before serving.

Baked cake layers freeze beautifully for do-ahead ease. Simply thaw them at room temperature for about an hour, then fill and frost as directed. This is particularly convenient for cakes with more perishable custard and whipped cream fillings. All butter cakes and frostings can be fully assembled a day ahead, then kept loosely wrapped or under a bowl or cake cover in the refrigerator. Let stand for about an hour at room temperature before serving for maximum flavor. Take note that boiled icings, like the Classic Seven-Minute Icing and Fluffy Penuche Frosting, are best prepared the day they are served; neither benefit from refrigeration or freezing.

So here you have it, cakes that could only be made in the U.S.A., each a blue ribbon winner. Choose from Burnt Sugar Cake made with caramel syrup, Blue Ribbon Banana Pecan Cake with Creamy Coconut Filling and a Shiny Cocoa Glaze, triple-layer Southwest Chocolate Chili Cake with Fluffy Fudge Frosting, or Plantation Peanut Butter Cake.

36   FRESH COCONUT LAYER CAKE
Prep: 35 minutes   Bake: 50 to 55 minutes   Serves: 12

Truly the queen of layer cakes, this version gets its superior flavor from freshly grated coconut.

1 medium fresh coconut or 3 cups flaked coconut	Up to 1 cup milk
1 stick (4 ounces) butter, softened	2¼ cups cake flour
1½ cups sugar	2 teaspoons baking powder
2 large eggs, separated, at room temperature	½ teaspoon baking soda
1 teaspoon vanilla extract	½ teaspoon salt
	Classic Seven-Minute Icing (recipe follows)

1. If using fresh coconut, preheat oven to 350°F. With a hammer, carefully drive a nail or large metal skewer through each of the coconut's three "eyes." Invert coconut over a bowl and let stand 5 minutes to drain liquid. Strain liquid through a fine sieve and reserve. Bake coconut on a baking sheet 20 minutes. Wrap in a kitchen towel and with a hammer, crack into large pieces. Remove shell and peel off brown skin with a small sharp knife. Finely grate coconut meat; reserve 3 cups.

2. Grease two 9-inch round cake pans. Line bottoms with wax paper; grease paper. Dust pans with flour; tap out excess. In a large bowl, beat together butter and sugar with an electric mixer on medium speed until light and fluffy, about 2 minutes. Add egg yolks, 1 at a time, beating well after each addition. Beat in vanilla.

3. Add enough milk to reserved coconut liquid to equal 1 cup. (If using flaked coconut, measure out 1 cup milk.) Sift together cake flour, baking powder, baking soda, and salt. With mixer on low speed, alternately add flour and coconut-milk mixture or plain milk to butter mixture, beginning and ending with flour. Beat just until blended. Stir in ¾ cup grated coconut.

4. In a clean small bowl, beat egg whites with an electric mixer with clean beaters on medium speed until soft peaks form when beaters are lifted. With a rubber spatula, gently fold beaten egg whites into coconut batter mixture. Turn batter into prepared pans.

5. Bake 30 to 35 minutes, or until a cake tester inserted in center comes out clean. Let cakes cool in pans 10 minutes, then unmold onto wire racks and remove wax paper. Invert cakes again and let cool completely.

6. Arrange 1 cake layer on a serving plate and frost top with about ⅓ (2 cups) of Classic Seven-Minute Icing. Sprinkle top with ¾ cup grated coconut and cover with remaining cake layer. Cover sides of cake with remaining icing. Gently press remaining 1½ cups coconut onto top and sides of cake.

37 CLASSIC SEVEN-MINUTE ICING
Prep: 5 minutes   Cook: 7 minutes   Makes: 6 cups

  3 **large egg whites**
1½ **cups sugar**
  1 **tablespoon light corn syrup**

½ **teaspoon cream of tartar**
1 **teaspoon vanilla extract**

1. In top of a large double boiler over simmering water, combine egg whites, sugar, ⅓ cup water, corn syrup, and cream of tartar. Beat with a hand-held electric mixer on high speed 7 minutes, or until soft but firm peaks form when beaters are lifted.

2. Remove from heat and transfer to a large bowl. With an electric mixer, beat in vanilla. Continue to beat until icing is very stiff and cooled, about 5 minutes.

38   BURNT SUGAR CAKE
Prep: 25 minutes   Cook: 9 to 11 minutes   Bake: 35 to 40 minutes
Serves: 12

Don't let the name throw you—the rich caramel syrup in this cake batter and frosting gives this American classic wonderful butterscotch flavor and golden color. The caramel syrup can be prepared a day ahead and stored at room temperature.

2¼ cups sugar
½ cup boiling water
1½ sticks (6 ounces) butter, softened
3 large eggs, at room temperature
1 teaspoon vanilla extract

3 cups sifted cake flour
2 teaspoons baking powder
½ teaspoon baking soda
½ teaspoon salt
1 cup sour cream
Burnt Sugar Frosting (page 39)

1. In a heavy medium saucepan, cook 1 cup sugar over medium heat, swirling pan occasionally, until sugar is melted and a deep amber color, 8 to 10 minutes. (Do not stir.) Remove from heat and with a long-handled spoon, gradually stir in boiling water. (Mixture will bubble vigorously.) Return pan to heat and simmer until caramel is completely dissolved, about 1 minute longer. Transfer caramel syrup to a glass measure and let cool completely. (There should be about ¾ cup.)

2. Preheat oven to 350°F. Grease two 9-inch round cake pans. Line bottoms with wax paper; grease paper. Dust pans with flour; tap out excess. In a large bowl, beat butter with an electric mixer on medium speed until smooth and creamy. Gradually beat in remaining 1¼ cups sugar until light and fluffy, about 2 minutes. Add eggs, 1 at a time, beating well after each addition. Beat in vanilla.

3. Sift together cake flour, baking powder, baking soda, and salt. In another bowl, whisk together sour cream and ½ cup cooled caramel syrup until smooth. (Reserve remaining ¼ cup caramel syrup for frosting that follows.)

4. With mixer on low speed, alternately add flour and caramel mixture to butter mixture, beginning and ending with flour, and beat just until blended. Turn batter into prepared pans.

5. Bake 35 to 40 minutes, or until a cake tester inserted in center comes out clean. Let cakes cool in pans 10 minutes, then unmold onto wire racks and remove wax paper. Invert cakes again and let cool completely. Fill and frost cake with Burnt Sugar Frosting.

39   BURNT SUGAR FROSTING
Prep: 5 minutes   Cook: none   Makes: 3 cups

1 stick (4 ounces) butter, softened	2 tablespoons sour cream
4 cups sifted powdered sugar	1 teaspoon vanilla extract
¼ cup reserved caramel syrup (from step 1 of Burnt Sugar Cake, page 38)	Pinch of salt

In a large bowl, beat butter with an electric mixer on medium speed until smooth and creamy. Gradually beat in powdered sugar. Add caramel syrup, sour cream, and vanilla and beat on high speed until frosting is smooth and fluffy, about 1 minute longer.

40   SWEET POTATO COCOA CAKE
Prep: 35 minutes   Bake: 40 to 45 minutes   Serves: 12

Mashed fresh sweet potatoes give this mildly spiced cocoa cake a rich buttery flavor and lots of moistness. It is a perfect sheet cake for your next potluck or picnic.

2 sticks (8 ounces) butter, softened	1½ teaspoons baking powder
1¾ cups sugar	1 teaspoon cinnamon
2 teaspoons grated orange zest	½ teaspoon baking soda
4 large eggs	½ teaspoon salt
1 cup mashed cooked sweet potatoes, cooled	½ teaspoon ground allspice
1¾ cups flour	¾ cup buttermilk
½ cup unsweetened cocoa powder	Classic Cream Cheese Frosting (page 92)

1. Preheat oven to 350°F. Grease a 13 x 9-inch baking pan; line bottom with wax paper and grease paper. Dust with flour; tap out excess.

2. In a large bowl, beat together butter and sugar with an electric mixer on medium speed until light and fluffy, about 2 minutes. Beat in orange zest. Add eggs, 1 at a time, beating well after each addition. Beat in sweet potatoes until smooth.

3. Sift together flour, cocoa, baking powder, cinnamon, baking soda, salt, and allspice. With mixer on low speed, alternately add flour mixture and buttermilk to butter mixture, beginning and ending with flour, and beat just until blended. Turn batter into prepared pan.

4. Bake 40 to 45 minutes, or until a cake tester inserted in center comes out clean. Let cake cool in pan 10 minutes, then turn out onto a wire rack and remove wax paper. Invert cake again and let cool completely. Frost top and sides of cake with Classic Cream Cheese Frosting.

41   FRESH GINGER CARROT CAKE
Prep: 25 minutes   Bake: 48 to 55 minutes   Serves: 12

This is a towering triple-ginger version of one of America's favorite layer cakes. Use the large holes of your grater for the carrots, the small to finely grate the fresh ginger.

¾ cup walnuts
1 stick (4 ounces) butter, softened
1 cup granulated sugar
¾ cup packed brown sugar
4 large eggs
1 tablespoon grated fresh ginger
½ cup vegetable oil
2 cups flour

2 teaspoons baking soda
1½ teaspoons cinnamon
1 teaspoon salt
½ teaspoon ground ginger
½ teaspoon grated nutmeg
Pinch of ground cloves
3 cups grated carrots (about 1 pound)
Gingery Cream Cheese Frosting (recipe follows)

1. Preheat oven to 350°F. Spread out walnuts on a small baking sheet. Bake 8 to 10 minutes, or until nuts are lightly browned and fragrant. Transfer to a plate and let cool, then coarsely chop. Grease two 9-inch round cake pans. Line bottoms with wax paper; grease paper. Dust pans with flour; tap out excess.

2. In a large bowl, beat together butter, granulated sugar, and brown sugar with an electric mixer on medium speed until light and fluffy. Add eggs, 1 at a time, beating well after each addition. Beat 2 minutes until mixture is thick and light. Beat in grated ginger. Gradually beat in oil in a thin steady stream until blended.

3. Sift together flour, baking soda, cinnamon, salt, ground ginger, nutmeg, and cloves. With mixer on low speed, add flour mixture to butter mixture just until blended. Stir in carrots and chopped toasted walnuts. Turn batter into prepared pans.

4. Bake 40 to 45 minutes, or until a cake tester inserted in center comes out clean. Let cakes cool in pans 10 minutes, then unmold onto wire racks and remove wax paper. Invert cakes again and let cool completely. Fill and frost cake with Gingery Cream Cheese Frosting.

42   GINGERY CREAM CHEESE FROSTING
Prep: 5 minutes   Cook: none   Makes: 2¼ cups

1 (8-ounce) package cream cheese, softened
4 tablespoons butter, softened
1 teaspoon vanilla extract

½ teaspoon ground ginger
3½ cups sifted powdered sugar
¼ cup finely chopped crystallized ginger

In a large bowl, beat together cream cheese, butter, vanilla, and ground ginger with an electric mixer on medium speed until light and fluffy. Gradually beat in powdered sugar until frosting is spreading consistency. Beat in crystallized ginger.

43   MYSTERY SPICE CAKE

Prep: 15 minutes   Bake: 30 to 35 minutes   Serves: 8 to 10

This old-fashioned spice cake has always relied on that special fruit—the tomato—for its moist, tender crumb.

1 stick (4 ounces) butter, softened	½ teaspoon grated nutmeg
½ cup granulated sugar	¼ teaspoon salt
½ cup packed brown sugar	¼ teaspoon freshly ground black pepper
2 large eggs	Pinch of ground cloves
1 teaspoon vanilla extract	1 (10¾-ounce) can tomato soup
2 cups flour	Toasted Pecan Cream Cheese Frosting (recipe follows)
1½ teaspoons cinnamon	
1 teaspoon baking powder	
1 teaspoon baking soda	

1. Preheat oven to 350°F. Grease two 8-inch round cake pans. Line bottoms with wax paper; grease paper. Dust pans with flour; tap out excess.

2. In a large bowl, beat together butter, granulated sugar, and brown sugar with an electric mixer on medium speed until light and fluffy. Add eggs, 1 at a time, beating well after each addition. Beat in vanilla.

3. Sift together flour, cinnamon, baking powder, baking soda, nutmeg, salt, pepper, and cloves. With mixer on low speed, alternately add flour mixture and tomato soup to butter mixture, beginning and ending with flour, and beat just until blended. Turn batter into prepared pans.

4. Bake 30 to 35 minutes, or until a cake tester inserted in center comes out clean. Let cakes cool in pans 10 minutes, then unmold onto wire racks and remove wax paper. Invert cakes again and let cool completely. Fill and frost cake with Toasted Pecan Cream Cheese Frosting.

44   TOASTED PECAN CREAM CHEESE FROSTING

Prep: 10 minutes   Bake: 8 to 10 minutes   Makes: 2½ cups

½ cup pecans	4 tablespoons butter, softened
1 (8-ounce) package cream cheese, softened	1 teaspoon vanilla extract
	3 cups sifted powdered sugar

1. Preheat oven to 350°F. Spread out pecans on a small baking sheet. Bake 8 to 10 minutes, or until nuts are lightly browned and fragrant. Transfer to a plate and let cool, then chop fine.

2. In a large bowl, beat together cream cheese, butter, and vanilla with an electric mixer on medium speed until light and fluffy. Gradually beat in powdered sugar until frosting reaches spreading consistency. Stir in chopped toasted pecans.

45 OLD KENTUCKY BROWN SUGAR POUND CAKE WITH CHOCOLATE BOURBON GLAZE

Prep: 30 minutes   Bake: 83 to 95 minutes   Serves: 16

1 cup pecans
3 sticks (12 ounces) unsalted butter, softened
1 (16-ounce) box light brown sugar
5 large eggs, separated, at room temperature
3 cups flour
½ teaspoon baking powder

½ teaspoon baking soda
½ teaspoon salt
¾ cup buttermilk
¼ cup bourbon
2 teaspoons vanilla extract
½ cup granulated sugar
   Chocolate Bourbon Glaze (recipe follows)

1. Preheat oven to 350°F. Spread out pecans on a small baking sheet. Bake 8 to 10 minutes, or until nuts are lightly browned and fragrant. Cool and chop coarsely. Grease a 10-inch tube pan. Dust with flour; tap out excess.

2. In a large bowl, beat together butter and brown sugar with an electric mixer on medium-high speed until light and fluffy, 2 minutes. Add egg yolks, 1 at a time, beating well after each addition.

3. Sift together flour, baking powder, baking soda, and salt. In a small bowl, combine buttermilk, bourbon, and vanilla. With mixer on low speed, alternately add flour mixture and buttermilk to butter mixture, beginning and ending with flour, and beat only until blended. Stir in pecans.

4. In another clean bowl, beat egg whites with an electric mixer with clean beaters on medium speed to soft peaks. Gradually add granulated sugar and continue to beat until stiff peaks form when beaters are lifted, about 3 minutes. With a rubber spatula, gently fold ⅓ of egg whites into pecan batter. Then fold in remaining whites just until blended. Turn batter into prepared pan.

5. Bake 75 to 85 minutes, or until a cake tester inserted in center comes out clean. Let cake cool in pan 15 minutes, then unmold onto a wire rack and cool completely. Drizzle top with Chocolate Bourbon Glaze.

46 CHOCOLATE BOURBON GLAZE

Prep: 5 minutes   Cook: 3 minutes   Makes: ½ cup

4 ounces semisweet chocolate, cut into small pieces
4 tablespoons unsalted butter, cut up

2 tablespoons heavy cream
2 tablespoons bourbon

Place chocolate in a medium heatproof bowl. In a small saucepan, bring butter, cream, and bourbon to a boil and pour over chocolate. Whisk until chocolate is melted and glaze is completely smooth. Let cool completely.

47 FUDGY MARBLED MAYO CAKE

Prep: 30 minutes   Bake: 30 to 35 minutes   Serves: 12

Mayonnaise guarantees the moistest marble cake ever.

2 large eggs	**½ teaspoon salt**
1½ cups sugar	**1 cup milk**
1½ teaspoons vanilla extract	**3 tablespoons unsweetened**
¾ cup mayonnaise	**cocoa powder**
2½ cups flour	**3 tablespoons hot water**
1½ teaspoons baking soda	**Fudgy Fudge Frosting**
½ teaspoon baking powder	**(recipe follows)**

1. Preheat oven to 350°F. Grease two 9-inch round cake pans. Line bottoms with wax paper; grease paper. Dust pans with flour; tap out excess.

2. In a large bowl, beat together eggs, sugar, and vanilla with an electric mixer on high speed until light and fluffy, about 3 minutes. Reduce speed to low and beat in mayonnaise.

3. Sift together flour, baking soda, baking powder, and salt. On low speed, alternately add flour mixture and milk to mayonnaise mixture, beginning and ending with flour, and beat just until blended.

4. In a small bowl, whisk together cocoa and hot water until smooth. With a rubber spatula, fold in 1 cup yellow batter to blend. Turn remaining yellow batter into prepared pans, then pour 3 pools of chocolate batter on top of each pan. With a small spatula or knife, cut through batters to marbleize.

5. Bake 30 to 35 minutes, or until a cake tester inserted in center comes out clean. Let cakes cool in pans 10 minutes, then unmold onto wire racks and remove wax paper. Invert cakes again and let cool completely. Fill and frost cake with Fudgy Fudge Frosting.

48 FUDGY FUDGE FROSTING

Prep: 15 minutes   Cook: 2½ to 3 minutes   Makes: 2 cups

5 (1-ounce) squares	**2 cups sifted powdered sugar**
unsweetened chocolate,	**Pinch of salt**
cut into small pieces	**1 teaspoon vanilla extract**
6 tablespoons butter, cut up	**½ cup heavy cream**

1. In a medium glass bowl, combine chocolate and butter. Microwave on Medium 2½ to 3 minutes, or until butter is melted. Whisk butter and chocolate together until completely smooth. Transfer chocolate mixture to a large bowl. Let cool slightly, about 10 minutes.

2. Beat chocolate mixture, 1 cup powdered sugar, salt, and vanilla with an electric mixer on medium speed until light and fluffy. Beat in cream, then remaining 1 cup powdered sugar until smooth and frosting is a spreadable consistency, about 1 minute longer.

49   CLASSIC BOSTON CREAM PIE

Prep: 15 minutes   Bake: 45 to 50 minutes   Serves: 8 to 10

Always a single layer cake, split in half and filled with a luscious vanilla cream filling, this American classic dessert was created at the Parker House Hotel in Boston in the mid-1850s. For chocolate fanatics, here's an exceptionally generous coating of satiny bittersweet glaze.

1 stick (4 ounces) butter, softened	½ teaspoon salt
	¾ cup milk
1 cup sugar	Vanilla Bean Filling (recipe
2 large eggs	follows)
1 teaspoon vanilla extract	Bittersweet Mocha Glaze
2 cups cake flour	(page 45)
2 teaspoons baking powder	

1. Preheat oven to 350°F. Grease a 9-inch springform pan. Dust pan with flour; tap out excess.

2. In a large bowl, beat together butter and sugar with an electric mixer on medium-high speed until light and fluffy, about 2 minutes. Beat in eggs, 1 at a time, beating well after each addition. Beat in vanilla.

3. Sift together cake flour, baking powder, and salt. With mixer on low speed, alternately add flour mixture and milk to butter mixture, beginning and ending with flour, and beat just until blended. Turn batter into prepared pan.

4. Bake 45 to 50 minutes, or until cake tester inserted in center comes out clean. Let cool completely on a wire rack.

5. Run a sharp knife around edge of pan to loosen cake and remove springform side of pan. With a long serrated knife, split cake in half horizontally. Arrange bottom half of cake, cut side up, on serving plate and spread top with Vanilla Bean Filling. Top with remaining cake, cut side down. Spread Bittersweet Mocha Glaze evenly on top of cake, letting some drip down sides. Let stand 30 minutes, until glaze is firm, or refrigerate until ready to serve.

50   VANILLA BEAN FILLING

Prep: 10 minutes   Cook: 8 minutes   Chill: 1 hour   Makes: 1½ cups

⅓ cup sugar	½ vanilla bean, split
2 tablespoons cornstarch	lengthwise, or 1 teaspoon
Pinch of salt	vanilla extract
¾ cup milk	2 large egg yolks
½ cup heavy cream	

1. In a medium saucepan, combine sugar, cornstarch, and salt. Gradually whisk in milk and heavy cream, then stir in vanilla bean. Bring to boil over medium heat, whisking gently, until thickened. Remove from heat.

2. In a small bowl, beat egg yolks lightly. Gradually whisk in ½ cup hot filling mixture. Return to saucepan, whisking constantly. Return to boil and boil 1 minute longer. Remove from heat and carefully remove vanilla bean and scrape out seeds. Discard vanilla pod and return seeds to filling. Transfer filling to bowl and cover surface directly with wax paper or plastic wrap to prevent skin from forming. (If using vanilla extract, add to filling in bowl.) Refrigerate 1 hour, or until cold. Whisk filling to soften before spreading on cake.

51   BITTERSWEET MOCHA GLAZE
Prep: 10 minutes   Cook: 1 to 1½ minutes   Makes: ¾ cup

6 ounces bittersweet or
  semisweet chocolate, cut
  into small pieces
⅓ cup heavy cream

1 tablespoon light corn syrup
1 teaspoon instant coffee
  powder

Place chocolate in a medium bowl. In a small glass bowl, combine cream, corn syrup, and coffee. Microwave on High 1 to 1½ minutes, or until very hot and small bubbles form around sides of bowl. Stir to dissolve coffee. Immediately pour over chocolate and stir until completely smooth.

52   SHINY COCOA GLAZE
Prep: 5 minutes   Cook: 2 to 2½ minutes   Makes: ½ cup

¼ cup heavy cream
1 teaspoon light corn syrup
¼ cup unsweetened cocoa
  powder

¼ cup sugar
1 teaspoon butter
½ teaspoon vanilla extract

1. In a medium glass bowl, combine cream and corn syrup. Sift together cocoa powder and sugar; whisk into cream until smooth (mixture will be thick). Stir in butter.

2. Microwave on Medium 2 to 2½ minutes, stirring once halfway through, until sugar dissolves and mixture is smooth. Stir in vanilla. Let cool slightly.

53 BLUE RIBBON BANANA PECAN CAKE
Prep: 20 minutes   Bake: 38 to 45 minutes   Serves: 12

For maximum flavor, fully ripe bananas are essential to this cake. Simply peel the fruit, place on a sheet of wax paper, and gently mash with a fork.

1 cup pecans	1½ teaspoons baking powder
1½ sticks (6 ounces) butter,	¾ teaspoon baking soda
softened	½ teaspoon salt
1¼ cups sugar	¼ teaspoon grated nutmeg
2 large eggs	½ cup buttermilk
1 cup ripe mashed bananas	Creamy Coconut Filling
(about 2 medium)	(recipe follows)
1 teaspoon vanilla extract	Shiny Cocoa Glaze
2 cups flour	(page 45)

1. Preheat oven to 350°F. Spread out pecans on a small baking sheet. Bake 8 to 10 minutes, or until nuts are lightly browned and fragrant. Transfer to a plate and let cool, then coarsely chop. Grease two 9-inch round cake pans. Line bottoms with wax paper; grease paper. Dust pans with flour; tap out excess.

2. In a large bowl, beat together butter and sugar with an electric mixer on medium speed until light and fluffy, about 2 minutes. Add eggs, 1 at a time, beating well after each addition. Add bananas and vanilla, then beat 1 minute longer.

3. Sift together flour, baking powder, baking soda, salt, and nutmeg. With mixer on low speed, alternately add flour mixture and buttermilk to banana mixture, beginning and ending with flour, and beat just until blended. Stir in nuts. Turn batter into prepared pans.

4. Bake 30 to 35 minutes, or until a cake tester inserted in center comes out clean. Let cakes cool in pans 10 minutes, then unmold onto wire racks and remove wax paper. Invert cakes again and let cool completely. Place 1 cake layer on serving plate; spread top with Creamy Coconut Filling. Top with remaining cake layer, then spread top of cake with Shiny Cocoa Glaze. Let stand until glaze has set, about 30 minutes.

54 CREAMY COCONUT FILLING
Prep: 10 minutes   Cook: 2 to 3 minutes   Chill: 1 hour
Makes: 1½ cups

¼ cup sugar	2 large egg yolks
2 tablespoons cornstarch	¾ cup flaked coconut
Pinch of salt	¾ teaspoon vanilla extract
1 cup half-and-half	

1. In a small saucepan, combine sugar, cornstarch, and salt. Gradually whisk in half-and-half to blend. Bring to a boil over medium heat, stirring gently, until thickened, 1 to 2 minutes. Remove from heat.

2. In a small bowl, beat egg yolks lightly. Gradually whisk in ¼ cup hot filling mixture. Return to saucepan, whisking constantly. Return to a boil and boil 1 minute longer. Remove from heat. Stir in coconut and vanilla. Transfer filling to a bowl and cover surface directly with wax paper or plastic wrap. Refrigerate 1 hour, or until cold.

---

55   PLANTATION PEANUT BUTTER CAKE
Prep: 15 minutes   Bake: 30 to 35 minutes   Serves: 12

Here's a cake packed with peanut flavor for young and old alike. Included is a choice of two frostings—one for double-nut fans, the other for chocolate lovers.

¾ cup smooth peanut butter
1 stick (4 ounces) butter,
       softened
¾ cup granulated sugar
¾ cup packed brown sugar
2 large eggs
1½ teaspoons vanilla extract
2 cups cake flour

2 teaspoons baking powder
½ teaspoon salt
     Pinch of ground allspice
¾ cup milk
¾ cup chopped peanuts
     Fluffy Peanut Butter Icing or
     Peanut Butter Fudge
     Frosting (page 89 or 90)

1. Preheat oven to 350°F. Grease two 9-inch round cake pans. Line bottoms with wax paper; grease paper. Dust pans with flour; tap out excess.

2. In a large bowl, beat together peanut butter and butter with an electric mixer on medium speed until smooth and creamy. Beat in granulated sugar and brown sugar until mixture is light and fluffy, about 3 minutes. Add eggs, 1 at a time, beating well after each addition. Beat in vanilla.

3. Sift together cake flour, baking powder, salt, and allspice. With mixer on low speed, alternately add flour mixture and milk to peanut butter mixture, beginning and ending with flour, and beat just until blended. Stir in ½ cup chopped peanuts. Turn batter into prepared pans.

4. Bake 30 to 35 minutes, or until a cake tester inserted in center comes out clean. Let cakes cool in pans 10 minutes, then unmold onto wire racks and remove wax paper. Invert cakes again and let cool completely. Fill and frost cake with Fluffy Peanut Butter Icing or Peanut Butter Fudge Frosting. Sprinkle remaining ¼ cup chopped peanuts over top of cake.

56 APPLE BUTTER STACK CAKE
Prep: 15 minutes   Bake: 38 to 45 minutes   Serves: 12

This fruity autumn layer cake is not too sweet, and the lemony butter icing lends just the right amount of citrus tang.

¾ cup walnuts
1 stick (4 ounces) butter, softened
1¼ cups sugar
2 large eggs
1 teaspoon vanilla extract
2¼ cups flour
1½ teaspoons baking soda
1 teaspoon baking powder

½ teaspoon salt
½ teaspoon cinnamon
½ teaspoon grated nutmeg
Pinch of ground cloves
¼ cup currants
1½ cups apple butter
Lemon Butter Frosting
(recipe follows)

1. Preheat oven to 350°F. Spread out walnuts on a small baking sheet. Bake 8 to 10 minutes, or until nuts are lightly browned and fragrant. Transfer to a plate and let cool, then coarsely chop. Grease two 9-inch round cake pans. Line bottoms with wax paper; grease paper. Dust pans with flour; tap out excess.

2. In a large bowl, beat together butter and sugar with an electric mixer on medium speed until light and fluffy, 2 minutes. Add eggs, 1 at a time, beating well after each addition. Beat in vanilla.

3. Sift together flour, baking soda, baking powder, salt, cinnamon, nutmeg, and cloves. In a small bowl, toss chopped toasted walnuts and currants with 2 tablespoons of flour mixture. With mixer on low speed, alternately add remaining flour mixture and apple butter to butter mixture, beginning and ending with flour, and beat just until blended. Stir in walnut-currant mixture. Turn batter into prepared pans.

4. Bake 30 to 35 minutes, or until a cake tester inserted in center comes out clean. Let cakes cool in pans 10 minutes, then unmold onto wire racks and remove wax paper. Invert cakes again and let cool completely. Fill and frost cake with Lemon Butter Frosting.

57 LEMON BUTTER FROSTING
Prep: 5 minutes   Cook: none   Makes: 2 cups

2 sticks (8 ounces) unsalted butter, softened
3½ cups sifted powdered sugar

2 tablespoons fresh lemon juice
1 teaspoon grated lemon zest

In a medium bowl, beat butter with an electric mixer until smooth and creamy. Gradually beat in powdered sugar until light and fluffy. Add lemon juice and lemon zest. Beat 1 minute longer for desired spreading consistency.

58 AMERICA'S GOLD LAYER CAKE

Prep: 15 minutes   Bake: 35 to 40 minutes   Serves: 12

Tall and golden cake layers are crowned with a buttery Brown Sugar Caramel Icing. For the moistest and most tender cake crumb, make sure to have all your ingredients at room temperature.

1½ sticks (6 ounces) butter, softened	2 teaspoons baking powder
1½ cups sugar	½ teaspoon salt
2 large whole eggs, at room temperature	1 cup milk, at room temperature
2 large egg yolks, at room temperature	1½ teaspoons vanilla extract
2½ cups cake flour	1 teaspoon fresh lemon juice
	Brown Sugar Caramel Icing (recipe follows)

1. Preheat oven to 350°F. Grease two 9-inch round cake pans. Line bottoms with wax paper; grease paper. Dust pans with flour; tap out excess.

2. In a large bowl, beat together butter and sugar with an electric mixer on medium speed until light and fluffy. Add whole eggs and egg yolks, 1 at a time, beating well after each addition.

3. Sift together cake flour, baking powder, and salt. In a glass measure, combine milk, vanilla, and lemon juice. With mixer on low speed, alternately add milk mixture and flour to butter mixture, beginning and ending with flour. Beat 2 minutes longer on medium speed. Turn batter into prepared pans.

4. Bake 35 to 40 minutes, or a cake tester inserted in center comes out clean and cake pulls away from sides of pan. Let cakes cool in pans 10 minutes, then unmold onto wire racks and remove wax paper. Invert layers again and let cool completely. Fill and frost cake with Brown Sugar Caramel Icing.

59 BROWN SUGAR CARAMEL ICING

Prep: 5 minutes   Cook: 2 minutes   Cool: 20 minutes
Makes: 2½ cups

2 cups packed brown sugar	1½ teaspoons vanilla extract
⅔ cup heavy cream	3½ cups sifted powdered sugar
1 stick (4 ounces) butter, cut up	

1. In a large saucepan, combine brown sugar, cream, and butter. Bring to boil over medium heat. Boil 2 minutes. Remove from heat and stir in vanilla. Transfer to a large bowl and let cool slightly, stirring occasionally, about 20 minutes.

2. Gradually beat in powdered sugar with an electric mixer on medium speed and continue to beat until icing is light and fluffy, about 2 minutes longer.

60   SOUTHERN BUTTERMILK LANE CAKE
Prep: 20 minutes   Bake: 25 to 30 minutes   Serves: 12 to 14

This southern specialty cake is a favorite for the holidays. The addition of buttermilk gives the triple white layers an exceptionally tender crumb. Decorate the top with candied cherries for a festive look.

2 sticks (8 ounces) butter, softened	1 cup buttermilk
1¾ cups sugar	8 large egg whites, at room temperature
1½ teaspoons vanilla extract	Luscious Lane Filling (page 51)
3 cups cake flour	Classic Seven-Minute Icing (page 37)
2½ teaspoons baking powder	
½ teaspoon baking soda	
¼ teaspoon salt	

1. Preheat oven to 350°F. Grease three 9-inch round cake pans. Line bottoms with wax paper; grease paper. Dust pans with flour; tap out excess.

2. In a large bowl, beat butter with an electric mixer on medium speed until smooth and creamy. Gradually beat in sugar, 1 tablespoon at a time, until mixture is light and fluffy, about 3 minutes. Beat in vanilla.

3. Sift together cake flour, baking powder, baking soda, and salt. With mixer on low speed, alternately add flour mixture and buttermilk to butter mixture, beginning and ending with flour, and beat just until blended.

4. In another large bowl, beat egg whites with an electric mixer with clean beaters on medium speed until stiff but not dry peaks form, about 4 minutes. With a rubber spatula, gently fold egg whites into batter ⅓ at a time. Turn into prepared pans.

5. Bake 25 to 30 minutes, or until tops are golden and a cake tester inserted in center comes out clean. Let cakes cool in pans 10 minutes, then unmold onto wire racks and remove wax paper. Invert cakes again and let cool completely.

6. Place 1 cake layer on a serving plate and spread top with half (about 1½ cups) Luscious Lane Filling. Repeat with another cake layer and remaining filling. Top with third cake layer. Frost top and sides with Classic Seven-Minute Icing.

61 LUSCIOUS LANE FILLING
Prep: 15 minutes   Cook: 6 minutes   Makes: 3 cups

¾ cup sugar
6 large egg yolks
¼ cup bourbon or brandy
6 tablespoons butter, softened
and cut into 6 pieces

¾ cup chopped pecans
¾ cup chopped dried figs
¾ cup flaked coconut

1. In a double boiler over simmering water, combine sugar and egg yolks. Cook, stirring, until sugar dissolves and mixture coats back of a spoon, about 6 minutes. Remove from heat and stir in bourbon. Transfer to a large bowl and let cool about 20 minutes.

2. Beat cooled egg mixture with an electric mixer on medium-high speed until smooth and creamy. Gradually beat in butter, 1 tablespoon at a time, until light and fluffy. With a rubber spatula, fold in pecans, figs, and coconut.

62 SPICED BLACKBERRY JAM CAKE
Prep: 10 minutes   Bake: 30 to 35 minutes   Serves: 12

This is a favorite cake from Kentucky and Tennessee, where blackberries grow in abundance. The jam gives these cake layers a beautiful deep berry color, a perfect contrast to the silky buttermilk icing. Any other seedless berry jam can be substituted: Try raspberry, strawberry, or blueberry.

2 sticks (8 ounces) butter,
softened
1¾ cups sugar
4 large eggs
1 cup seedless blackberry jam
2 tablespoons crème de cassis
(black currant liqueur)
2½ cups flour

1 teaspoon baking soda
1 teaspoon cinnamon
½ teaspoon ground cloves
½ teaspoon grated nutmeg
¼ teaspoon salt
1 cup buttermilk
Buttery Buttermilk Icing
(page 52)

1. Preheat oven to 350°F. Grease three 9-inch round cake pans. Line bottoms with wax paper; grease paper. Dust pans with flour; tap out excess.

2. In a large bowl, beat together butter and sugar with an electric mixer on medium speed until light and fluffy. Add eggs, 1 at a time, beating well after each addition. Beat in jam and cassis.

3. Sift together flour, baking soda, cinnamon, cloves, nutmeg, and salt. With mixer on low speed, alternately add flour mixture and buttermilk to jam mixture, beginning and ending with flour, just until blended. Turn batter into prepared pans.

4. Bake 30 to 35 minutes, or until a cake tester inserted in center comes out clean. Let cakes cool in pans 10 minutes, then unmold onto wire racks and remove wax paper. Invert layers again and let cool completely. Fill and frost cake with Buttery Buttermilk Icing.

63   BUTTERY BUTTERMILK ICING
Prep: 5 minutes   Cook: 8 minutes   Makes: 2 cups

1 stick (4 ounces) butter	Pinch of salt
1 (16-ounce) box powdered	6 tablespoons buttermilk
sugar, sifted	1 teaspoon vanilla extract

1. In a small saucepan, melt butter over medium heat, then cook 5 minutes, or until a dark golden brown. Immediately strain butter through a fine sieve into a large bowl; discard browned bits of butter in sieve.

2. Gradually add 1 cup powdered sugar and salt to strained butter, beating with an electric mixer on medium speed until smooth. Alternately add remaining sugar, buttermilk, and vanilla until icing is light and fluffy, about 2 minutes.

64   SOUTHWEST CHOCOLATE CHILI CAKE
Prep: 20 minutes   Bake: 30 to 35 minutes   Serves: 12

Watch out—the secret to this triple-layer devilish cake is the addition of pure ground red chili—do not use commercial chili or chili con carne powder. Trust me, this sweet-peppery combination of flavors is a natural complement to chocolate.

1 stick (4 ounces) butter, softened	2 teaspoons baking soda
1½ cups packed brown sugar	½ teaspoon salt
1 cup granulated sugar	½ cup buttermilk
2 teaspoons vanilla extract	1 cup boiling water
3 large eggs	2 tablespoons mild red pure chili powder or
3 (1-ounce) squares unsweetened chocolate, melted and cooled	⅛ teaspoon ground red pepper
2⅓ cups cake flour	Fluffy Fudge Frosting (recipe follows)

1. Preheat oven to 350°F. Grease three 8-inch round cake pans. Line bottoms with wax paper; grease paper. Dust pans with flour; tap out excess.

2. In a large bowl, beat together butter, brown sugar, and granulated sugar with an electric mixer on medium speed until light and fluffy, about 2 minutes. Beat in vanilla. Add eggs, 1 at a time, beating well after each addition. Beat in melted chocolate.

3. Sift together cake flour, baking soda, and salt. With mixer on low speed, alternately add flour mixture and buttermilk to butter mixture, beginning and ending with flour, and beat just until blended. In a glass measure, combine boiling water and chili powder. Gradually beat chili liquid into batter in a thin stream. Turn batter into prepared pans.

4. Bake 30 to 35 minutes, or until cake begins to pull away from sides of pan. Let cakes cool in pans 10 minutes, then unmold onto wire racks and remove wax paper. Invert cakes again and let cool completely. Fill and frost cake with Fluffy Fudge Frosting.

65   FLUFFY FUDGE FROSTING
Prep: 10 minutes   Cook: 5 to 6 minutes
Stand: 20 minutes   Makes: 3 cups

Because of its white sauce base, this old-fashioned cooked topping, sometimes called "gravy frosting," fluffs up to beautiful heights when whipped in your electric mixer.

¼ cup flour
1 cup milk
1½ sticks (6 ounces) butter,
     softened
2 (1-ounce) squares
     unsweetened chocolate,
     melted and cooled

1½ cups sifted powdered sugar
     Pinch of salt
1 teaspoon vanilla extract

1. In a small saucepan, whisk flour and ¼ cup milk until smooth. Gradually whisk in remaining milk until blended. Bring to a boil over medium heat, whisking constantly, until thickened, 4 to 5 minutes. Boil, whisking, 1 minute. Remove from heat and let stand, whisking occasionally, until completely cool, about 20 minutes.

2. In a medium bowl, beat together butter and chocolate with an electric mixer on medium speed until smooth and creamy. Gradually add powdered sugar and salt and continue to beat until light and fluffy, about 2 minutes. Beat in vanilla. Gradually beat in thickened milk mixture, 1 tablespoon at a time, until frosting is very light, smooth, and spreadable.

66 DARK CHOCOLATE COLA CAKE
Prep: 15 minutes   Bake: 35 to 40 minutes   Serves: 12

The combination of cola and coffee brings out a deep dark chocolate flavor in this rich cake.

2 sticks (8 ounces) butter, cut up	2 cups flour
½ cup miniature marshmallows	2 cups sugar
	1 teaspoon baking soda
½ teaspoon instant coffee powder	¼ teaspoon salt
	2 large eggs
¼ cup unsweetened cocoa powder	½ cup buttermilk
	1 teaspoon vanilla extract
1 cup cola	Chocolate Cola Frosting (recipe follows)

1. Preheat oven to 350°F. Grease two 9-inch round cake pans. Line bottoms with wax paper; grease paper. Dust pans with flour; tap out excess.

2. In a medium saucepan, melt butter and marshmallows over medium heat, whisking, until smooth. Remove from heat and stir in coffee powder until dissolved. Stir in cocoa powder until smooth, then stir in cola.

3. In a large bowl, sift together flour, sugar, baking soda, and salt. Beat in cola mixture with an electric mixer on low speed until moistened. Add eggs, buttermilk, and vanilla. Increase speed to medium and beat 2 minutes longer, or until batter is completely smooth.

4. Bake 35 to 40 minutes, or until a cake tester inserted in center comes out clean. Let cakes cool in pans 10 minutes, then unmold onto wire racks and remove wax paper. Invert cakes again and let cool completely. Fill and frost cake with Chocolate Cola Frosting.

67 CHOCOLATE COLA FROSTING
Prep: 10 minutes   Cook: 2½ to 3 minutes   Makes: 2 cups

5 (1-ounce) squares unsweetened chocolate, cut into small pieces	2½ cups sifted powdered sugar
	½ teaspoon vanilla extract
	⅓ cup cola
4 tablespoons butter	

1. In a medium glass bowl, combine chocolate and butter. Microwave on Medium 2½ to 3 minutes, or until butter is melted. Whisk butter and chocolate together until completely smooth. Transfer chocolate mixture to a large bowl. Let cool until lukewarm, about 10 minutes.

2. Beat chocolate mixture, 1 cup powdered sugar, and vanilla with an electric mixer on medium speed until light and fluffy. Beat in cola, then remaining 1½ cups powdered sugar until smooth and frosting is a spreadable consistency, about 1 minute longer.

68 CAN'T BE BEET SHEET CAKE
Prep: 10 minutes   Bake: 25 to 30 minutes   Serves: 20

With only one bowl and a whisk, here's a blue ribbon cake for a crowd. Dark, dense, and delicious, pureed beets are a favorite farm addition to chocolate cake.

1 (16-ounce) can whole or sliced beets with liquid	3 large eggs
2⅓ cups sugar	1 tablespoon vanilla extract
1½ cups unsweetened cocoa powder	2⅔ cups flour
⅔ cup vegetable oil	2½ teaspoons baking soda
¼ cup sour cream	½ teaspoon salt
	Fluffy Penuche Frosting (recipe follows)

1. Preheat oven to 350°F. Grease an 18 x 11 x 1-inch sheet pan. In a food processor, puree beets and liquid until smooth. In a very large bowl, sift together sugar and cocoa powder. Whisk in beet puree, oil, sour cream, eggs, and vanilla until blended.

2. Sift together flour, baking soda, and salt. Whisk flour mixture into beet mixture just until smooth. Turn batter into prepared pan.

3. Bake 25 to 30 minutes, or until a cake tester inserted in center comes out clean. Transfer to a wire rack and let cool completely. Leaving cake in pan, spread Fluffy Penuche Frosting over top of cake.

69 FLUFFY PENUCHE FROSTING
Prep: 5 minutes   Cook: 7 minutes   Makes: 6 cups

Molasses gives this classic boiled brown sugar frosting an additional hit of butterscotch flavor. It makes a wonderful frosting for any spice layer cake.

3 large egg whites	½ teaspoon cream of tartar
1½ cups packed dark brown sugar	1½ teaspoons vanilla extract
1 tablespoon unsulphured molasses	

1. In top of a large double boiler over simmering water, combine egg whites, brown sugar, ⅓ cup water, molasses, and cream of tartar. Beat with a hand-held electric mixer on high speed 7 minutes, or until soft but firm peaks form when beaters are lifted.

2. Remove from heat and transfer to a large bowl. Beat in vanilla with electric mixer on high speed. Continue to beat until icing is very stiff and cooled, about 5 minutes.

70 SUNSHINE CITRUS CAKE
Prep: 20 minutes   Bake: 25 to 30 minutes   Serves: 12

Sun-kissed oranges star in this delicate layer cake, which can be completely assembled a day ahead, loosely covered, and refrigerated. Just let stand at room temperature for an hour before serving.

1½ sticks (6 ounces) unsalted butter, softened	1 tablespoon baking powder
1½ cups sugar	½ teaspoon salt
2 teaspoons grated orange zest	1 cup fresh orange juice
3 large eggs, separated, at room temperature	Fresh Orange Filling (recipe follows)
2 cups cake flour	Citrus Meringue
¼ cup cornstarch	Buttercream (page 57)

1. Preheat oven to 350°F. Grease three 9-inch round cake pans. Line bottoms with wax paper; grease paper. Dust pans with flour; tap out excess.

2. In a large bowl, beat butter with an electric mixer on medium speed until smooth and creamy. Gradually beat in sugar until mixture is light and fluffy, about 3 minutes. Beat in orange zest. Add egg yolks, 1 at a time, beating well after each addition; then beat 2 minutes longer, or until very light.

3. Sift together cake flour, cornstarch, baking powder, and salt. With mixer on low speed, alternately add flour mixture and orange juice, beginning and ending with flour and beating just until blended.

4. In a small clean bowl, beat egg whites with an electric mixer with clean beaters on medium speed until stiff but not dry peaks form. With a rubber spatula, gently fold beaten egg whites into orange mixture ⅓ at a time. Turn batter into prepared pans.

5. Bake 25 to 30 minutes, or until a cake tester inserted in center comes out clean. Let cakes cool in pans 10 minutes, then unmold onto wire racks and remove wax paper. Invert cakes again and let cool completely. Place 1 cake layer on a serving plate. Spread half (1 cup) of Fresh Orange Filling over top of cake. Add another cake layer and cover top with remaining filling. Top with third cake layer. Frost top and sides with Citrus Meringue Buttercream.

71 FRESH ORANGE FILLING
Prep: 15 minutes   Cook: 10 minutes   Chill: 1 hour   Makes: 2 cups

1 cup sugar	2 large egg yolks
¼ cup cornstarch	1 tablespoon butter
Pinch of salt	2 teaspoons grated orange zest
1½ cups fresh orange juice	

1. In a medium nonreactive saucepan, combine sugar, cornstarch, and salt. Gradually whisk in orange juice until smooth. Bring to a boil over medium heat, stirring gently; boil 1 minute. Remove from heat.

2. In a small bowl, beat egg yolks. Gradually whisk in ½ cup hot filling mixture. Return yolk mixture to saucepan, whisking constantly. Return to a boil and boil 1 minute. Remove from heat and whisk in butter and orange zest until butter is melted and filling is smooth. Transfer to a bowl, cover surface directly with plastic wrap or wax paper, and refrigerate until cold, about 1 hour.

72 CITRUS MERINGUE BUTTERCREAM
Prep: 15 minutes   Cook: 5 to 6 minutes   Makes: 4 cups

1¼ cups sugar
¼ cup fresh orange juice
5 large egg whites, at room
   temperature

3 sticks (12 ounces) butter, at
   room temperature
1½ teaspoons grated orange zest
1 teaspoon vanilla extract

1. In a small saucepan, bring 1 cup of sugar and orange juice to a boil over medium-high heat, stirring to dissolve sugar. Boil without stirring until syrup reaches 240°F on a candy thermometer or forms a soft ball, 5 to 6 minutes.

2. Meanwhile, in a large bowl, beat egg whites with an electric mixer on medium speed until soft peaks form. Add remaining ¼ cup sugar, 1 tablespoon at a time, and beat until stiff peaks form. Gradually pour in boiling syrup in a thin stream. Increase mixer speed to high and beat until meringue is thick and glossy and completely cooled, about 8 minutes.

3. In another large bowl, beat butter with an electric mixer on medium-high speed until smooth and creamy. Beat in meringue, ¼ cup at a time, blending well after each addition, and beat 2 minutes longer, or until buttercream is thick and spreadable. Beat in orange zest and vanilla.

73   RED VELVET CAKE
Prep: 10 minutes   Bake: 30 to 35 minutes   Serves: 12

Here's a down-home favorite from my friend Barbara Stratton.

1   stick (4 ounces) butter,
   softened
1½ cups sugar
2   large eggs
1   (1-ounce) bottle liquid red
   food coloring
1   teaspoon vanilla extract
2¼ cups cake flour
¼   cup unsweetened cocoa
   powder

1   teaspoon baking powder
½   teaspoon salt
1   cup buttermilk
1   teaspoon baking soda
1   tablespoon distilled white
   vinegar
   White Velvet Icing
   (recipe follows)

1. Preheat oven to 350°F. Grease two 9-inch round cake pans. Line bottoms with wax paper; grease paper. Dust pans with flour; tap out excess.

2. In a large bowl, beat together butter and sugar with an electric mixer on medium speed until light and fluffy, about 2 minutes. Add eggs, 1 at a time, beating well after each addition. Beat in red food coloring and vanilla.

3. Sift together cake flour, cocoa powder, baking powder, and salt. With mixer on low speed, alternately add flour mixture and buttermilk to butter mixture, beginning and ending with flour, just until blended. Dissolve baking soda in vinegar and stir thoroughly into batter. Turn into pans.

4. Bake 30 to 35 minutes, or a cake tester inserted in center comes out clean and cake comes away from sides of pan. Let cakes cool in pans 10 minutes, then unmold onto wire racks and remove wax paper. Invert layers again and let cool completely. Fill and frost cake with White Velvet Icing.

74   WHITE VELVET ICING
Prep: 10 minutes   Cook: 5 to 6 minutes   Cool: 20 minutes
Makes: 2½ cups

¼   cup flour
1   cup milk
1½ sticks (6 ounces) butter,
   softened

1½ cups sifted powdered sugar
   Pinch of salt
1   teaspoon vanilla extract

1. In a small saucepan, whisk flour and ¼ cup milk until smooth. Gradually whisk in remaining milk until blended. Bring to a boil over medium heat, whisking constantly, until thickened, 4 to 5 minutes. Boil, whisking, 1 minute. Remove from heat and let stand, whisking occasionally, until completely cool, about 20 minutes.

2. In a medium bowl, beat butter with an electric mixer on medium speed until smooth and creamy. Gradually add powdered sugar and salt and continue to beat until light and fluffy, about 2 minutes. Beat in vanilla. Gradually beat in thickened milk mixture, 1 tablespoon at a time, until icing is very light, smooth, and spreadable.

Chapter 3

Birthday and Other Party Cakes

What to make for dessert? That's not a question often asked when it's time for someone's birthday party. Of course, it has to be cake, and the kind we all love and remember: layered, frosted, and studded with glowing candles. A cake simple and easy on the inside, but a bit dressier on the outside, complete with an extra flourish of piped frosting, a drizzle of melted chocolate, or a sprinkling of nuts and candy. These same dolled-up cakes are also the perfect finale for a bridal shower, Valentine's Day, or a special holiday or dinner party. Here is a collection of specialty cakes designed to be festive, some with an air of sophistication, some simple and just plain fun. Filled with ice cream, iced with chocolate truffle frosting, slathered with whipped cream, here are the cakes you'll love to make when you feel like showing off—even if there is no birthday in sight.

Any cake can be transformed into a party cake if you know how to decorate it. Decorating is easy, fun, and rewarding even for the novice baker. Always keep in mind that simplicity is best; a single garnish makes the strongest visual impression. For unfrosted cakes, like the Chocolate Avalanche, a generous dusting of powdered sugar gives the top a delightful snowy effect; an added sprinkling of cocoa on top of the sugar can add further interest. You can also hold a doily or stencil over a cake and dust with powdered sugar to create an intricate pattern.

Chocolate is made for decoration. Frosted and glazed chocolate cakes love to be garnished with shaved chocolate. Shavings can be easily achieved with the aid of the wide holes on a standing four-sided grater. Try mixing dark semisweet, lighter milk chocolate, and white chocolate shavings for a fancy effect. If the cake has a chocolate glaze, be sure to apply the shavings on the top and sides before the glaze sets. For nut cakes, such as the Hazelnut Sacher Torte, whole almonds, hazelnuts, pecans, or walnuts can be dipped halfway in melted chocolate and arranged along the outer edge of the cake.

Other tips for a festive touch are to apply chopped nuts, toasted coconut, toasted cake crumbs, cookie crumbs, or chocolate chips around the sides of a frosted cake. A mound of fresh berries garnished with a sprig of fresh mint is a beautiful topping, as is a sprinkling of small candies, candied ginger, or citrus peel. If using fresh flowers, arrange them along the edge of the top of the cake, taking care to choose blooms that are not poisonous and are untreated by toxic chemicals. One of the prettiest decorations I know and a simple way to make a birthday cake look gift-wrapped and elegant is to tie a wide plain ribbon loosely around the sides of the cake. Another easy trick is to purchase candles of different heights or mix them with festive sparklers to create a beautiful glowing crown of birthday light.

Piped rosettes of frosting are a wonderful decoration for party cakes. A set of decorating piping bags and tips can be purchased at modest cost and can easily give the simplest cake a polished, professional look, even with just a little practice. Plain whipped cream and buttercream varieties of frosting are best for piping. I also like to fit a pastry bag with a ridged star tip and pipe circular swirls of frosting along the top and bottom edges of the cake.

Some cakes in this collection were especially created with birthdays in mind. A tender yellow Buttermilk Birthday Cake layered with old-fashioned chocolate frosting is a classic, but other suggestions include pretty pink Cherry Chip Cake and the easiest ever Classic Checkerboard Cake, which requires no special pan to prepare. Special occasion cakes include a Macaroon Midnight Cake for a bachelor party or football gathering, Raspberry Princess Cake with white chocolate for a bridal or baby shower, and Sweetheart Chocolate-Raspberry Cake for Valentine's Day or any other occasion when you want to say "I love you." Cakes for entertaining round out the collection, including a do-ahead Meringue-Nut Ice Cream Torte and a light-as-a-feather Italian Marsala Mascarpone Cake.

75 BUTTERMILK BIRTHDAY CAKE
Prep: 15 minutes   Bake: 35 to 40 minutes   Serves: 12

Kids and grown-ups will agree that all you'll need are birthday candles to crown this traditional golden layer cake with fudgy buttermilk frosting.

2 **sticks (8 ounces) butter, softened**
2 **cups sugar**
4 **large eggs, at room temperature**
2½ **cups cake flour**
1½ **teaspoons baking powder**

½ **teaspoon baking soda**
½ **teaspoon salt**
1 **cup buttermilk, at room temperature**
1½ **teaspoons vanilla extract**
Chocolate Buttermilk Frosting (recipe follows)

1. Preheat oven to 350°F. Grease two 9-inch round cake pans. Line bottoms with wax paper; grease paper. Dust pans with flour; tap out excess.

2. In a large bowl, beat together butter and sugar with an electric mixer on medium speed until light and fluffy. Add eggs, 1 at a time, beating well after each addition.

3. Sift together cake flour, baking powder, baking soda, and salt. In a glass measure, combine buttermilk and vanilla. With mixer on low speed, alternately add flour and buttermilk mixture to butter mixture, beginning and ending with flour. Beat 2 minutes longer at medium speed. Turn batter into prepared pans.

4. Bake 35 to 40 minutes, or until a cake tester inserted in center comes out clean. Let cakes cool in pans 10 minutes, then unmold onto wire racks and remove wax paper. Invert cakes again and let cool completely. Fill and frost cake with Chocolate Buttermilk Frosting.

76 CHOCOLATE BUTTERMILK FROSTING
Prep: 10 minutes   Cook: 2 to 2½ minutes   Makes: 2 cups

4 **(1-ounce) squares unsweetened chocolate, cut up**
4 **tablespoons butter, cut up**

2½ **cups sifted powdered sugar**
1 **teaspoon vanilla extract**
⅓ **cup buttermilk**

1. In a small glass bowl, combine chocolate and butter. Microwave on Medium 2 to 2½ minutes, or until butter is melted. Whisk butter and chocolate together until completely smooth.

2. Transfer chocolate mixture to a large bowl. Beat in 1 cup powdered sugar and vanilla with an electric mixer on medium speed until smooth. Beat in buttermilk, then remaining 1½ cups powdered sugar, until light and fluffy, about 1 minute longer.

77 FRUITED SPICE LAYER CAKE
Prep: 20 minutes   Bake: 38 to 45 minutes   Serves: 12

Sometimes called a hummingbird cake for its golden color, this layered treat owes its moistness to crushed sweet pineapple and chopped ripe bananas.

¾ cup pecans or walnuts
1 stick (4 ounces) butter, softened
1½ cups sugar
½ cup vegetable oil
3 large eggs
1½ teaspoons vanilla extract
3 cups flour
1 teaspoon baking soda
½ teaspoon baking powder

1 teaspoon cinnamon
1 teaspoon salt
¼ teaspoon grated nutmeg
1 (8-ounce) can crushed pineapple in juice
2 cups chopped ripe bananas (2 medium)
Classic Cream Cheese Frosting (page 92)

1. Preheat oven to 350°F. Spread out pecans on a small baking sheet. Bake 8 to 10 minutes, or until nuts are lightly browned and fragrant. Transfer to a plate and let cool, then coarsely chop. Grease three 8- or 9-inch round cake pans. Line bottoms with wax paper; grease paper. Dust pans with flour; tap out excess.

2. In a large bowl, beat together butter and sugar with an electric mixer on medium speed until light and fluffy, about 2 minutes. Gradually beat in oil in a thin steady stream until blended. Add eggs, 1 at a time, beating well after each addition. Add vanilla and beat 2 minutes longer, until mixture is thick and light.

3. Sift together flour, baking soda, baking powder, cinnamon, salt, and nutmeg. In a medium bowl, combine pineapple and bananas. With mixer on low speed, alternately add flour and fruit mixture to butter mixture, beginning and ending with flour, and beat just until blended. Turn batter into prepared pans.

4. Bake 30 to 35 minutes, or until a cake tester inserted in center comes out clean. Let cakes cool in pans 10 minutes, then unmold onto wire racks and remove wax paper. Invert cakes again and let cool completely. Fill and frost cake with Classic Cream Cheese Frosting.

78   CLASSIC CHECKERBOARD CAKE

Prep: 15 minutes   Bake: 25 to 30 minutes   Serves: 12

It's simple—just spoon rings of chocolate and vanilla batters for this party cake, and like magic you've created a whimsical checkerboard pattern.

1½ **sticks (6 ounces) butter, softened**
1¾ **cups sugar**
6 **large egg whites, at room temperature**
2 **teaspoons vanilla extract**
2½ **cups cake flour**
1 **tablespoon baking powder**

½ **teaspoon salt**
1 **cup milk, at room temperature**
3 **tablespoons unsweetened cocoa powder**
Extra-Rich Fudge Frosting (page 64)

1. Preheat oven to 350°F. Grease three 8-inch round cake pans. Line bottoms with wax paper; grease paper. Dust pans with flour; tap out excess.

2. In a large bowl, beat together butter and sugar with an electric mixer on medium speed until smooth and creamy. Add egg whites and vanilla. Increase speed to high and beat until thick and fluffy, about 2 minutes longer.

3. Sift together cake flour, baking powder, and salt. With mixer on low speed, alternately add flour mixture and milk to butter mixture, beginning and ending with flour, and beat just until blended.

4. Turn half of batter (about 2½ cups) into a medium bowl. Sift cocoa powder over top. With a rubber spatula, gently fold in cocoa until blended.

5. Carefully spoon a 2-inch ring of remaining white batter around outer edge of 2 prepared cake pans, then spoon a 2-inch ring of chocolate batter right next to white batter. Finish with a small circle of white batter in center of each pan. In remaining pan, spoon chocolate batter for outer ring, white batter for next ring, then finish with a center circle of chocolate.

6. Bake 25 to 30 minutes, or until a cake tester inserted in center comes out clean. Let cakes cool in pans 10 minutes, then unmold onto wire racks and remove wax paper. Invert cakes again and let cool completely. Fill and frost cake with Extra-Rich Fudge Frosting, using identical layers for top and bottom of cake and different layer for middle.

79   EXTRA-RICH FUDGE FROSTING

Prep: 5 minutes   Cook: 4 to 5 minutes   Makes: 2½ cups

This custard-style frosting is pure indulgence.

5 ounces semisweet chocolate, cut up	½ cup sugar
1 (1-ounce) square unsweetened chocolate	4 large egg yolks
2 tablespoons coffee or water	½ teaspoon vanilla extract
	2 sticks (8 ounces) butter, softened and cut up

1. In a medium glass bowl, combine semisweet and unsweetened chocolate and coffee. Microwave on Medium 1½ to 2 minutes, or until coffee is hot. Whisk coffee and chocolate together until completely smooth.

2. In a double boiler over simmering water, whisk together sugar and egg yolks. Cook, whisking constantly, until mixture is thickened and coats the back of a spoon, about 3 minutes. Transfer to a large bowl. Add vanilla.

3. Add chocolate to egg mixture and beat with an electric mixer on medium-high speed until completely cooled, about 5 minutes. Beat in butter, 1 piece at a time, blending well after each addition, until smooth and spreadable.

80   HAZELNUT SACHER TORTE

Prep: 25 minutes   Bake: 60 to 65 minutes   Stand: 1 hour
Serves: 12

Toasted hazelnuts update this Viennese classic, which features an apricot jam filling and a shiny chocolate glaze.

¾ cup hazelnuts	1 teaspoon vanilla extract
¾ cup plus 2 tablespoons sugar	½ teaspoon lemon zest
1½ sticks (6 ounces) butter, softened	¼ teaspoon salt
5 large eggs, separated, at room temperature	½ cup cake flour
5 ounces bittersweet or semisweet chocolate, melted and cooled	½ cup apricot preserves
	Bittersweet Chocolate Glaze (recipe follows)
	Whipped cream

1. Preheat oven to 350°F. Arrange hazelnuts on a small cookie sheet. Bake 15 minutes, or until nuts are lightly browned and dark skins are cracked. Rub warm nuts in a terrycloth towel to remove as much of skins as possible. Let cool. In a food processor, process nuts and 2 tablespoons sugar until finely ground. Grease a 9-inch springform pan. Line bottom with wax paper; grease paper. Dust pan with flour; tap out excess.

2. In a large bowl, beat butter with an electric mixer on medium speed until smooth and creamy. Gradually add ½ cup sugar and continue to beat until light and fluffy, about 2 minutes. Add egg yolks, 1 at a time, beating well after each addition. Beat in melted chocolate, vanilla, and lemon zest. With a rubber spatula, fold in nut mixture.

3. In another large clean bowl, beat egg whites and salt with an electric mixer with clean beaters on medium-low speed until foamy, about 2 to 4 minutes. Increase speed to medium and gradually add remaining ¼ cup sugar, 1 tablespoon at a time, beating well after each addition. Continue beating on medium speed until mixture holds very firm peaks when beaters are lifted, about 2 minutes longer.

4. Gently fold ⅓ of whites into chocolate mixture; repeat twice more with remaining whites just until blended. Sift cake flour over top and fold into batter until just blended. Turn into prepared pan.

5. Bake 45 to 50 minutes, or until a cake tester inserted in center comes out clean. Let cake cool 10 minutes, then remove springform side of pan. Invert cake onto a wire rack set over a large sheet of wax paper or foil and remove bottom of pan. Peel off wax paper and let cake cool completely.

6. With a long serrated knife, split cake horizontally into 2 even layers. Leave one layer, cut side up, on wire rack. In a small saucepan, heat apricot preserves over low heat until melted. Strain through a fine sieve into a small bowl, then spread over bottom cake layer. Top with second layer, cut side down. Pour warm chocolate glaze onto cake, quickly spreading over top and sides with a long, narrow metal spatula. Let stand 1 hour, or until glaze sets. Run metal spatula along base of cake and carefully transfer to serving plate. Serve with whipped cream.

---

81 BITTERSWEET CHOCOLATE GLAZE
Prep: 5 minutes   Cook: 1 to 2 minutes   Makes: 1½ cups

3 tablespoons light corn syrup
2 tablespoons butter

6 ounces bittersweet or semisweet chocolate, cut into small pieces

In a medium saucepan, bring corn syrup, butter, and 3 tablespoons water to a boil, 1 to 2 minutes. Remove from heat and whisk in chocolate until melted and smooth.

82   MACAROON MIDNIGHT CAKE
Prep: 15 minutes   Bake: 35 to 40 minutes   Serves: 12

Perfect for a groom's party or a chocolate lover's birthday celebration, this tender dark cake is enhanced by fluffy almond-scented buttercream and snowy white coconut.

3 (1-ounce) squares unsweetened chocolate, chopped	2 large eggs
	2 cups flour
	1½ teaspoons baking powder
1 teaspoon instant coffee powder	½ teaspoon baking soda
	¼ teaspoon salt
1½ sticks (6 ounces) butter, softened	¾ cup milk
	Marzipan Buttercream (recipe follows)
1¾ cups sugar	
1 teaspoon vanilla extract	2 cups flaked coconut

1. Preheat oven to 350°F. Grease two 9-inch round cake pans. Line bottoms with wax paper; grease paper. Dust pans with flour; tap out excess.

2. In a medium glass bowl, combine chocolate, ⅓ cup water, and coffee powder. Microwave on Medium 1½ minutes, or until water is very hot and coffee is dissolved. Whisk until mixture is completely smooth. Let cool completely.

3. In a large bowl, beat together butter and sugar with an electric mixer on medium speed until light and fluffy, about 2 minutes. Beat in vanilla. Add eggs, 1 at a time, beating well after each addition. Beat in chocolate mixture.

4. Sift together flour, baking powder, baking soda, and salt. With mixer on low speed, alternately add flour mixture and milk to butter mixture, beginning and ending with flour, and beat just until blended. Turn batter into prepared pans.

5. Bake 35 to 40 minutes, or until cakes spring back when lightly touched in center and come away from sides of pan. Let cakes cool in pans 10 minutes, then unmold onto wire racks and remove wax paper. Invert cakes again and let cool completely. Fill and frost with Marzipan Buttercream. Gently press coconut onto top and sides of cake.

83   MARZIPAN BUTTERCREAM
Prep: 10 minutes   Cook: none   Makes: 3 cups

1½ sticks (6 ounces) butter, softened	1 teaspoon vanilla extract
	½ teaspoon almond extract
⅓ cup almond paste	2 to 3 tablespoons milk
3 cups sifted powdered sugar	

In a small bowl, beat butter and almond paste with an electric mixer on medium-high speed until very light and fluffy and completely smooth, about 5 minutes. Gradually beat in 1½ cups powdered sugar, vanilla, and

almond extract. Alternately add remaining 1½ cups sugar and 2 tablespoons milk, beating until smooth after each addition. Beat 1 minute
longer, adding remaining 1 tablespoon milk if necessary, until smooth and
spreadable.

84   GRAHAM CRACKER-NUT TORTE
Prep: 20 minutes   Bake: 38 to 45 minutes   Serves: 10 to 12

1 cup walnuts
¾ cup plus 2 tablespoons
   sugar
1 cup graham cracker crumbs
1 teaspoon baking powder
¼ teaspoon cinnamon
   Pinch of salt

6 large eggs, separated, at
   room temperature
   Sweetened Whipped Cream
   (page 265) or Espresso
   Whipped Cream (page
   213)
½ cup apricot preserves
   Shaved chocolate

1. Preheat oven to 350°F. Grease three 9-inch round cake pans. Line bottoms with wax paper; grease paper. Dust pans with flour; tap out excess.
Spread out walnuts on a small baking sheet. Bake 8 to 10 minutes, or until
nuts are lightly browned and fragrant. Transfer to a plate and let cool. In a
food processor, process nuts and 2 tablespoons sugar until finely ground.
In a medium bowl, combine nut mixture, graham cracker crumbs, baking
powder, cinnamon, and salt.

2. In a large bowl, beat egg whites with an electric mixer on medium speed
until soft peaks form when beaters are lifted. Gradually add ½ cup sugar,
1 tablespoon at a time, and continue to beat until peaks are stiff but not dry.

3. In another bowl, beat egg yolks with an electric mixer until light and
lemon colored. Gradually beat in remaining ¼ cup sugar until mixture is
very thick.

4. With a rubber spatula, gently fold ¼ of whites into yolk mixture, then
gently fold in crumb mixture. Fold in remaining whites just until blended.
Turn into prepared pans.

5. Bake 30 to 35 minutes, or until a cake tester inserted in center comes out
clean and top of cake springs back when lightly touched. Let cakes cool in
pans 10 minutes, then unmold onto wire racks and remove wax paper.
Invert cakes again and let cool completely.

6. Arrange 1 cake layer on a serving plate and spread with ⅓ of Sweetened
or Espresso Whipped Cream. Add second cake layer. In a small saucepan,
heat apricot preserves over low heat until melted. Strain through a fine
sieve into a small bowl, then spread over top of second layer. Top with
remaining cake layer and spread top and sides of cake with remaining
whipped cream. Decorate sides with shaved chocolate.

85 BERRIES 'N' CREAM BLITZ TORTE
Prep: 15 minutes   Bake: 38 to 45 minutes   Serves: 12

This perfect summer party cake is an unusual combination of crunchy almond meringue and buttery cake layers baked right on top of each other.

½ cup slivered blanched
  almonds
1 cup plus 1 tablespoon
  granulated sugar
1 stick (4 ounces) butter,
  softened
1 teaspoon vanilla extract
4 large eggs, separated, at
  room temperature
1 cup sifted cake flour
1 teaspoon baking powder

Pinch of salt
⅓ cup milk
¼ cup powdered sugar
¼ teaspoon almond extract
Blitz Cream Filling
  (recipe follows)
2 to 3 cups fresh assorted fruit:
  raspberries, blueberries,
  blackberries, sliced
  peaches, and/or
  nectarines

1. Preheat oven to 350°F. Spread out almonds on a small baking sheet. Bake 8 to 10 minutes, or until nuts are lightly browned and fragrant. Transfer to a plate and let cool. In a food processor, finely grind nuts with 1 tablespoon granulated sugar. Grease two 9-inch round cake pans. Line bottoms with wax paper; grease paper. Dust pans with flour; tap out excess.

2. In a large bowl, beat butter with an electric mixer on medium speed until smooth and creamy. Gradually add ½ cup granulated sugar and continue to beat until light and fluffy, about 2 minutes. Beat in vanilla. Add egg yolks, 1 at a time, beating well after each addition.

3. Sift together cake flour, baking powder, and salt. With mixer on low speed, alternately add flour mixture and milk to butter mixture, beginning and ending with flour and beating just until blended. Turn batter into prepared pans.

4. Sift together remaining ½ cup granulated sugar and the powdered sugar. In a small bowl, beat egg whites with an electric mixer on medium speed until soft peaks form. Gradually add sugar mixture and continue to beat until peaks are stiff but not dry. Beat in almond extract. Divide meringue evenly between prepared pans, then gently spread over batter to edge of pan to cover. Sprinkle ground almonds evenly over meringue.

5. Bake 30 to 35 minutes, or until meringue is golden brown and feels dry to the touch. Let cakes cool completely in pans on wire racks. Invert 1 cake layer, meringue side down, onto a serving plate and remove pan and wax paper. Spread top with Blitz Cream Filling. Unmold remaining cake layer, remove wax paper, and arrange on top of filling, meringue side up. Serve with assorted fruit on the side.

86   BLITZ CREAM FILLING
Prep: 5 minutes   Cook: none   Makes: 2½ cups

1 cup heavy cream	2 tablespoons sour cream
¼ cup powdered sugar	½ teaspoon vanilla extract

In a large mixer bowl, beat heavy cream, powdered sugar, sour cream, and vanilla with an electric mixer on medium speed until soft peaks form.

87   CHERRY CHIP CAKE
Prep: 20 minutes   Bake: 38 to 45 minutes   Serves: 8 to 10

Pretty and pink, this was my favorite birthday cake when I was a child.

1 cup walnuts	¾ cup milk
2½ cups cake flour	1 teaspoon vanilla extract
1¼ cups granulated sugar	4 large egg whites, at room
1 tablespoon baking powder	temperature
½ teaspoon salt	1 (3-ounce) package cream
1½ sticks (6 ounces) butter, softened	cheese, softened
1 (5-ounce) jar maraschino cherries, drained and finely chopped, liquid reserved	2 cups sifted powdered sugar

1. Preheat oven to 350°F. Spread out walnuts on a small baking sheet. Bake 8 to 10 minutes, or until nuts are lightly browned and fragrant. Transfer to a plate and let cool, then finely chop. Grease two 8-inch round cake pans. Line bottoms with wax paper; grease paper. Dust pans with flour; tap out excess.

2. In a large bowl, sift together cake flour, granulated sugar, baking powder, and salt. Cut up 1 stick of butter and beat into flour mixture with an electric mixer on low speed until crumbly. In a small bowl, combine ¼ cup cherry liquid with milk and vanilla. Add to flour mixture, increase speed to medium, and beat just until smooth. Add egg whites and beat 2 minutes longer. Stir in ½ cup chopped cherries. Turn batter into prepared pans.

3. Bake 30 to 35 minutes, or until a cake tester inserted in center comes out clean. Let cakes cool in pans 10 minutes, then unmold onto wire racks and remove wax paper. Invert cakes again and let cool completely.

4. In a small bowl, beat remaining ½ stick butter and cream cheese with an electric mixer on medium-high speed until light and fluffy. Gradually beat in 1 cup powdered sugar. Alternately add remaining 1 cup powdered sugar and remaining 2 tablespoons cherry liquid, beating until smooth after each addition. Beat in remaining 2 tablespoons chopped cherries, then beat until light and fluffy, about 1 minute longer. Fill and frost cake with cherry frosting. Gently press chopped toasted walnuts around sides of cake.

88 RASPBERRY PRINCESS CAKE
Prep: 20 minutes   Bake: 35 to 40 minutes   Serves: 12

Perfect for the bride, a sweet sixteen party, or a graduation reception, this cake features white chocolate layers topped with a ruby red raspberry buttercream.

4 ounces imported white
   chocolate, chopped
½ cup boiling water
½ cup milk
1 stick (4 ounces) butter,
   softened
1⅓ cups sugar
½ teaspoon vanilla extract
5 large eggs, separated, at
   room temperature

2½ cups cake flour
2 teaspoons baking powder
¼ teaspoon salt
   Raspberry Meringue
    Buttercream (page 71)
   Fresh raspberries and
    shaved white chocolate

1. Preheat oven to 350°F. Grease two 9-inch round cake pans. Line bottoms with wax paper; grease paper. Dust pans with flour; tap out excess. In a small glass bowl, combine white chocolate and boiling water and whisk until completely smooth. Whisk in milk.

2. In a large bowl, beat together butter and sugar with an electric mixer on medium speed until light and fluffy, about 2 minutes. Beat in vanilla. Add egg yolks, 1 at a time, beating well after each addition.

3. Sift together cake flour, baking powder, and salt. With mixer on low speed, alternately add flour and white chocolate mixture to butter mixture, beginning and ending with flour, and beat just until blended.

4. In a medium bowl, beat egg whites with an electric mixer with clean beaters on medium speed until stiff but not dry peaks form when beaters are lifted. With a rubber spatula, gently fold beaten whites into batter. Turn into prepared pans.

5. Bake 35 to 40 minutes, or until a cake tester inserted in center comes out clean. Let cakes cool in pans 10 minutes, then unmold onto wire racks and remove wax paper. Invert cakes again and let cool completely. Fill and frost cake with Raspberry Meringue Buttercream. Decorate top with fresh raspberries and shaved white chocolate.

89 RASPBERRY MERINGUE BUTTERCREAM
Prep: 15 minutes   Cook: 15 to 16 minutes   Makes: 4 cups

This is a wonderful frosting for any festive occasion, perfect with any white or golden layer cake.

1 (10-ounce) package frozen raspberries in syrup, thawed
1¼ cups sugar
2 tablespoons fresh lemon juice

5 large egg whites, at room temperature
½ teaspoon vanilla extract
3 sticks (12 ounces) unsalted butter, at room temperature, cut up

1. In a food processor or blender, puree raspberries with syrup. Strain through a fine sieve into a small nonreactive saucepan to remove seeds. Bring puree to a boil, then reduce heat and simmer until reduced to ½ cup, about 10 minutes. Let cool.

2. In a small saucepan, bring 1 cup sugar, lemon juice, and 2 tablespoons water to a boil over medium-high heat, stirring to dissolve sugar. Boil without stirring until syrup reaches 240°F on a candy thermometer or forms a soft ball, 5 to 6 minutes.

3. Meanwhile, in a large bowl, beat egg whites with an electric mixer on medium speed until soft peaks form. Add remaining ¼ cup sugar, 1 tablespoon at a time, and beat until stiff peaks form. Gradually pour in boiling syrup in a thin stream. Increase mixer speed to high and beat until meringue is thick and glossy and completely cooled, about 8 minutes. Beat in vanilla.

4. In another large bowl, beat butter with an electric mixer on medium-high speed until smooth and creamy. Beat in meringue, ¼ cup at a time, blending well after each addition. Gradually add raspberry puree and beat 2 minutes longer, or until the buttercream is light and spreadable.

90   MERINGUE-NUT ICE CREAM TORTE

Prep: 15 minutes   Bake: 2 hours 8 to 10 minutes   Freeze: 2½ hours
Serves: 12 to 14

Serve with chocolate-dipped strawberries for added elegance.

¾ cup pecans
¾ cup slivered blanched
   almonds
1¼ cups granulated sugar
1½ teaspoons instant coffee
   powder
¼ teaspoon cinnamon
6 large egg whites, at room
   temperature
2 teaspoons vanilla extract
¼ teaspoon cream of tartar

Pinch of salt
2 pints premium vanilla ice
   cream
1 pint premium coffee ice
   cream
1 cup heavy cream
2 tablespoons powdered
   sugar
Super Fudge Sauce (page
   205)

1. Preheat oven to 350°F. Spread out pecans and almonds on a small baking sheet. Bake 8 to 10 minutes, or until nuts are lightly browned and fragrant. Transfer to a plate and let cool. In a food processor, process nuts, ¾ cup granulated sugar, coffee powder, and cinnamon until finely ground.

2. Reduce oven temperature to 250°F. Line 2 large cookie sheets with parchment paper. Trace two 8-inch circles on each sheet.

3. In a large bowl, beat egg whites with an electric mixer on medium-low speed until foamy, about 4 to 5 minutes. Gradually increasing speed to medium, add vanilla, cream of tartar, and salt. Add remaining ½ cup sugar, 1 tablespoon at a time, beating well after each addition. When all sugar is incorporated, continue beating at medium speed until mixture is stiff and glossy, about 3 minutes longer.

4. With a rubber spatula, fold ⅓ of nut mixture into beaten whites. Repeat twice more with remaining nuts just until blended. Divide meringue into quarters and spoon into center of each outlined circle. With a spatula, spread meringue evenly to fill each circle.

5. Bake until meringues are dry to the touch, about 2 hours, switching positions of cookie sheets after 1 hour. With a large metal spatula, transfer meringues to wire racks. Let cool completely.

6. Place vanilla and coffee ice creams in refrigerator to slightly soften, about 20 minutes. Place 1 meringue on serving plate. Spread with 1 pint vanilla ice cream. Add second meringue layer and spread with coffee ice cream. Add third meringue and spread with remaining pint of vanilla ice cream. Top with remaining meringue. Freeze cake until firm, 2 hours or overnight.

7. In a large bowl, beat cream with an electric mixer until soft peaks form. Add powdered sugar and beat until stiff. Frost top and sides of cake with whipped cream. Freeze until ready to serve, 30 minutes or overnight. Serve with Super Fudge Sauce.

91   GINGER BLACKOUT CAKE

Prep: 15 minutes   Bake: 30 to 35 minutes   Serves: 12

1¾ cups flour
1⅓ cups sugar
½ cup unsweetened cocoa
   powder
1 teaspoon ground ginger
1 teaspoon baking soda
½ teaspoon baking powder
¼ teaspoon salt
1½ sticks (6 ounces) butter,
   softened and cut up

1½ cups buttermilk
2 large eggs
2 tablespoons unsulphured
   molasses
1 teaspoon vanilla extract
   Richly Chocolate Whipped
   Cream (recipe follows)
   Shaved chocolate

1. Preheat oven to 350°F. Grease three 8-inch round cake pans. Line bottoms with wax paper; grease paper. Dust pans with flour; tap out excess.

2. In a large bowl, sift together flour, sugar, cocoa powder, ginger, baking soda, baking powder, and salt. Beat in butter with an electric mixer on low speed until mixture is crumbly. Add buttermilk, eggs, molasses, and vanilla. Increase speed to medium and beat 3 minutes. Turn into prepared pans.

3. Bake 30 to 35 minutes, or until a cake tester inserted in center comes out clean and top of cake springs back when lightly touched. Let layers cool in pans 10 minutes, then unmold onto wire racks and remove wax paper. Invert cakes again and let cool completely. Fill and frost cake with Richly Chocolate Whipped Cream. Decorate top and sides with shaved chocolate.

92   RICHLY CHOCOLATE WHIPPED CREAM

Prep: 10 minutes   Cook: 1½ minutes   Makes: 2½ cups

Melted chocolate gives this whipped cream frosting just the right texture for spreading.

4 ounces semisweet
   chocolate, chopped
1 cup heavy cream

2 tablespoons powdered
   sugar
½ teaspoon vanilla extract

1. In a medium glass bowl, combine chocolate and 2 tablespoons water. Microwave on Medium 1½ minutes, or until water is hot. Whisk until completely smooth. Let cool.

2. In a large bowl, beat cream and powdered sugar with an electric mixer until stiff. Beat in vanilla. With a rubber spatula, fold in cooled chocolate mixture just until blended.

93 SWEETHEART CHOCOLATE-RASPBERRY CAKE

Prep: 20 minutes   Bake: 35 to 40 minutes   Serves: 10 to 12

Chocolate is always a favorite way to say "I love you," and this heart-shaped creation boasts the richest fudge topping ever.

3 (1-ounce) squares
   unsweetened chocolate,
   chopped
1 stick (4 ounces) butter, cut
   up
2 tablespoons raspberry
   liqueur or crème de cassis
4 large eggs, separated, at
   room temperature

1¼ cups sugar
½ teaspoon vanilla extract
½ cup flour
¼ teaspoon salt
   Raspberry Ganache
   (page 75)
½ pint fresh raspberries

1. Preheat oven to 350°F. Grease a 9-inch heart-shaped or springform pan. Line bottom with wax paper and trim to fit; grease paper. Dust pan with flour; tap out excess.

2. In a medium glass bowl, combine chocolate and butter. Microwave on Medium 2 to 2½ minutes, or until butter is melted. Whisk until completely smooth. Let cool to lukewarm, then whisk in liqueur.

3. In a large bowl, beat egg yolks with an electric mixer until light. Gradually beat in ¾ cup sugar until thick and lemon colored, 3 minutes. Beat in chocolate mixture and vanilla.

4. Sift together flour and salt. With mixer on low speed, add flour mixture to chocolate mixture just until blended. In another medium bowl, beat egg whites with an electric mixer with clean beaters on medium speed to soft peaks. Gradually beat in remaining ½ cup sugar and continue to beat until stiff peaks form. With a rubber spatula, gently fold ⅓ of beaten whites into chocolate mixture. Repeat twice more with remaining whites just until blended. Turn into prepared pan.

5. Bake 35 to 40 minutes, or until top of cake springs back when lightly touched. Let cake cool in pan 15 minutes. Unmold onto a wire rack, remove wax paper, and let cool completely. Spread top of cake with Raspberry Ganache, then decorate with fresh raspberries.

94 RASPBERRY GANACHE
Prep: 3 minutes   Cook: 1 to 2 minutes   Chill: 1 hour
Makes: 1½ cups

6 ounces semisweet or
    bittersweet chocolate,
    cut up
½ cup heavy cream
1 tablespoon butter, cut up

¼ cup seedless raspberry
    preserves
1 tablespoon raspberry
    liqueur or crème de cassis

In a food processor, process chocolate until finely chopped. In a small saucepan, heat cream to a boil over medium heat until boiling, 1 to 2 minutes. With machine on, pour hot cream through feed tube and process 15 seconds, or until chocolate is melted. Add butter and process to blend. Add raspberry preserves and liqueur and process 10 seconds longer, or until filling is smooth. Transfer to a bowl, cover, and refrigerate until thickened, stirring occasionally, 1 hour.

95 FIRECRACKER SPUD 'N' SPICE CAKE
Prep: 20 minutes   Bake: 30 to 35 minutes   Serves: 12

1½ sticks (6 ounces) butter,
    softened
1 cup granulated sugar
¾ cup packed brown sugar
2 large eggs
1 cup cold mashed potatoes
1 teaspoon vanilla extract
2 cups flour
2 teaspoons cinnamon
1 teaspoon baking powder

1 teaspoon baking soda
½ teaspoon salt
¼ teaspoon ground cloves
⅛ teaspoon ground red pepper
1 cup buttermilk
   Cinnamon Buttercream
    (page 76)
½ cup red cinnamon candies
    (red-hots)

1. Preheat oven to 350°F. Grease two 8-inch round cake pans. Line bottoms with wax paper; grease paper. Dust pans with flour; tap out excess.

2. In a large bowl, beat together butter, granulated sugar, and brown sugar with an electric mixer on medium speed until light and fluffy, about 2 minutes. Add eggs, 1 at a time, beating well after each addition. Beat in mashed potatoes and vanilla.

3. Sift together flour, cinnamon, baking powder, baking soda, salt, cloves, and red pepper. With mixer on low speed, alternately add flour mixture and buttermilk to butter mixture, beginning and ending with flour, and beat just until blended. Turn batter into prepared pans.

4. Bake 30 to 35 minutes, or until a cake tester inserted in center comes out clean and top of cake springs back when lightly touched. Let cool in pans 10 minutes, then unmold cakes onto wire racks and remove wax paper. Invert cakes again and let cool completely. Fill and frost with Cinnamon Buttercream. Gently press red cinnamon candies on top and sides of cake.

96 CINNAMON BUTTERCREAM
Prep: 5 minutes   Cook: none   Makes: 1½ cups

4 tablespoons butter, softened
1 (3-ounce) package cream
   cheese, softened

1 teaspoon vanilla extract
2 cups sifted powdered sugar
½ teaspoon cinnamon

In a small bowl, beat together butter and cream cheese with an electric mixer until light and fluffy, about 2 minutes. Beat in vanilla. Gradually beat in powdered sugar and cinnamon and beat 1 minute longer for desired spreading consistency.

97 SORBET 'N' CREAM ANGEL CAKE
Prep: 15 minutes   Bake: 5 to 8 minutes   Freeze: 6 hours
Serves: 12 to 14

While I've chosen orange, you can use any flavor sorbet and cream ice cream for this easy dessert.

5 tablespoons orange-flavored
   liqueur
2 tablespoons light corn syrup
   Classic Angel Food Cake
   (page 124)

2 pints orange sorbet and
   cream ice cream
1 cup flaked coconut
1 cup heavy cream
2 tablespoons powdered
   sugar

1. In a small bowl, combine 3 tablespoons liqueur, corn syrup, and 3 tablespoons water until blended.

2. Loosen angel food cake and remove from tube pan. (Clean pan before assembling cake.) With a long serrated knife, split cake crosswise into 3 even layers.

3. Place 1 pint ice cream in refrigerator to soften slightly, about 20 minutes. Place smallest cake layer, cut side up, in bottom of tube pan. Brush with 2 tablespoons liqueur mixture. Quickly spread top with softened ice cream, top with center layer of cake, and brush top with another 2 tablespoons liqueur mixture. Freeze until firm, about 1 hour.

4. Soften remaining 1 pint ice cream and spread over top of center cake layer. Brush cut side of remaining top cake layer with remaining liqueur mixture and place, cut side down, on top of ice cream. Cover tightly and freeze until firm, 6 hours or overnight.

5. Preheat oven to 350°F. Spread out coconut on a small baking sheet. Bake 5 to 8 minutes, or until lightly toasted and golden. Let cool. In a large bowl, beat cream with an electric mixer until soft peaks form. Beat in powdered sugar and remaining 2 tablespoons orange liqueur.

6. To unmold cake, run a long sharp knife around side of pan and invert onto a platter. Frost top and sides of cake with whipped cream. Gently press on toasted coconut. Freeze until ready to serve, 30 minutes or overnight.

98 BEE-STING HONEY FUDGE CAKE
Prep: 20 minutes   Bake: 40 to 45 minutes   Serves: 12

10⅔ tablespoons (⅔ cup) butter, softened
1 cup sugar
¾ cup honey
1 teaspoon vanilla extract
2 large eggs
4 (1-ounce) squares unsweetened chocolate, melted and cooled

2¼ cups flour
1 teaspoon baking powder
1 teaspoon baking soda
½ teaspoon salt
1 cup milk
Fluffy Honey Frosting (recipe follows)

1. Preheat oven to 350°F. Grease two 9-inch round cake pans. Line bottoms with wax paper; grease paper. Dust pans with flour; tap out excess.

2. In a large bowl, beat together butter and sugar with an electric mixer on medium speed until light and fluffy, about 2 minutes. Beat in honey and vanilla until smooth. Add eggs, 1 at a time, beating well after each addition. Beat in melted chocolate until blended.

3. Sift together flour, baking powder, baking soda, and salt. With mixer on low speed, alternately add flour mixture and milk to butter mixture, beginning and ending with flour, just until blended. Turn batter into prepared pans.

4. Bake 40 to 45 minutes, or until a cake tester inserted in center comes out clean. Let cakes cool in pans 10 minutes, then unmold onto wire racks and remove wax paper. Invert cakes again and let cool completely. Fill and frost cake with Fluffy Honey Frosting.

99 FLUFFY HONEY FROSTING
Prep: 5 minutes   Cook: 7 minutes   Makes: 5 cups

3 large egg whites
1½ cups sugar

¼ cup honey
½ teaspoon cream of tartar

1. In top of a large double boiler over simmering water, combine egg whites, sugar, ⅓ cup water, honey, and cream of tartar. Beat with a handheld electric mixer on high speed 7 minutes, or until soft but firm peaks form when beaters are lifted.

2. Remove from heat and transfer to a large bowl. Continue to beat until icing is very stiff and cooled, about 5 minutes longer.

100 GATEAU MOCHA

Prep: 50 minutes   Bake: 35 to 40 minutes   Chill: 1 hour
Serves: 12 to 14

This elegant party cake features genoise—the most delicate of sponge cakes—brushed with a sugar syrup and frosted with satiny buttercream.

¾ **cup hazelnuts**
1½ **sticks (6 ounces) butter, cut up**
6 **large eggs**
1 **cup granulated sugar**
1½ **teaspoons vanilla extract**
½ **teaspoon grated orange zest**
1¼ **cups cake flour**
Pinch of salt

¼ **cup hazelnut-flavored liqueur or brandy**
Chocolate Meringue Buttercream (page 79)
1 **teaspoon instant espresso powder**
¾ **cup heavy cream**
3 **tablespoons powdered sugar**

1. Preheat oven to 350°F. Grease two 9-inch round cake pans. Line bottoms with wax paper; grease paper. Dust pans with flour; tap out excess. Arrange hazelnuts on a small cookie sheet. Bake 15 minutes, or until nuts are lightly browned and dark skins are cracked. Rub warm nuts in a terrycloth towel to remove as much of skins as possible. Let cool, then chop.

2. In a small saucepan, melt butter over low heat. Skim foam off top and pour ½ cup clarified butter (clear liquid) into a measuring cup.

3. In a large bowl, whisk together eggs and ¾ cup granulated sugar to blend. Set over a saucepan of simmering—not boiling—water and gently whisk until mixture is warm (110 to 120°F) and sugar is completely dissolved, 3 to 5 minutes. Remove from heat and immediately beat with an electric mixer on medium-high speed until mixture is tripled in volume and forms a ribbon when beaters are lifted, 5 to 10 minutes. Reduce speed to medium and beat in vanilla and orange zest.

4. Sift together cake flour and salt. Sift ⅓ of flour over egg mixture; carefully fold in with a rubber spatula. Repeat twice more with remaining flour until just blended. Gradually drizzle clarified butter in a thin stream into batter, folding gently with a rubber spatula until just incorporated (do not overmix). Turn batter into prepared pans.

5. Bake 20 to 25 minutes, or until a cake tester inserted in center comes out clean. Let cakes cool in pans 10 minutes, then unmold onto wire racks and remove wax paper. Invert cakes again and let cool completely.

6. In a small saucepan, combine ½ cup water and remaining ¼ cup granulated sugar. Bring to a boil, reduce heat, and simmer 1 minute, stirring, until sugar is dissolved. Let cool, then stir in 2 tablespoons of liqueur.

7. With a long serrated knife, split each cake horizontally into 2 even layers. Brush cut sides of cakes with syrup. Place 1 cake layer, cut side up, on a serving plate and spread top with ¾ cup Chocolate Meringue Buttercream. Repeat 2 more times with 2 more cake layers and 1½ cups more buttercream. Top with remaining cake layer, cut side down. Frost top and sides of cake with remaining buttercream. Cover cake loosely and refrigerate 1 hour, or overnight.

8. In a large bowl, dissolve espresso powder in remaining 2 tablespoons liqueur. Add cream and powdered sugar and beat with an electric mixer until stiff. Uncover cake and frost top and sides with whipped cream. Gently press hazelnuts around sides of cake.

101 CHOCOLATE MERINGUE BUTTERCREAM
Prep: 15 minutes   Cook: 5 to 6 minutes   Makes: 4 cups

1¼ cups sugar
5 large egg whites, at room temperature
3 sticks (12 ounces) butter, at room temperature
1 teaspoon vanilla extract

4 ounces semisweet or bittersweet chocolate, melted and cooled
2 ounces semisweet or bittersweet chocolate, grated

1. In a small saucepan, cook 1 cup sugar and ¼ cup water over medium-high heat until sugar is dissolved and syrup reaches 240°F on a candy thermometer or forms a soft ball, 5 to 6 minutes.

2. Meanwhile, in a large bowl, beat egg whites with an electric mixer on medium speed until soft peaks form. Add remaining ¼ cup sugar, 1 tablespoon at a time, and beat until stiff peaks form. Gradually pour in boiling syrup in a thin stream. Increase mixer speed to high and beat until meringue is thick and glossy and completely cooled, about 8 minutes.

3. In another large bowl, beat butter with an electric mixer on medium-high speed until smooth and creamy. Beat in meringue, ¼ cup at a time, blending well after each addition, and beat 2 minutes longer, or until the buttercream is light and spreadable. Beat in vanilla.

4. In a small bowl, fold together 1 cup buttercream and melted, cooled chocolate until smooth. Beat into remaining buttercream until blended, then fold in grated chocolate.

102   ITALIAN MARSALA MASCARPONE CAKE

Prep: 35 minutes   Bake: 40 to 45 minutes   Chill: 6 hours
Serves: 12

This delicate sponge cake is a simple delight after a special dinner. Serve with additional berries, if desired, and Amaretti cookies.

5 **large egg yolks, at room temperature**
½ **cup plus 2 tablespoons granulated sugar**
2 **teaspoons grated orange zest**
1 **teaspoon vanilla extract**
1 **cup cake flour, sifted**
6 **large egg whites, at room temperature**

Pinch of salt
⅓ **cup marsala wine**
⅓ **cup amber rum**
   Mascarpone Cream (page 81)
½ **pint fresh raspberries**
   Powdered sugar

1. Preheat oven to 350°F. In a large bowl, beat egg yolks with an electric mixer on high speed until very thick and lemon colored. Gradually add ½ cup sugar, 1 tablespoon at a time, beating well after each addition, until mixture is tripled in volume, about 3 minutes. Reduce speed to medium-low and beat in orange zest, vanilla, and cake flour just until blended.

2. In a large clean bowl, beat egg whites and salt with an electric mixer with clean beaters on medium-low speed until foamy. Increase speed to medium. Gradually add remaining 2 tablespoons sugar, 1 teaspoon at a time, beating well after each addition. Continue beating on medium speed until mixture holds stiff peaks when beaters are lifted, about 3 minutes longer. With a rubber spatula, fold ⅓ of whites into yolk mixture, then fold in remaining whites until well blended.

3. Turn batter into an ungreased 9-inch springform pan. Bake 40 to 45 minutes, or until a cake tester inserted in center comes out clean and cake springs back when touched gently. Let cool completely on a wire rack.

4. Run a sharp knife around edge of pan and remove springform side of pan. In a small bowl, combine marsala and rum. With a long serrated knife, split cake crosswise into 3 even layers. Keeping 1 cake layer attached to bottom of springform pan, brush cut side with 3 tablespoons marsala-rum mixture and spread with half (1½ cups) Mascarpone Cream. Sprinkle top with half of raspberries.

5. Brush 1 cut side of center cake layer with another 3 tablespoons marsala mixture and arrange on top of fruit. Spread with remaining Mascarpone Cream and sprinkle with remaining berries. Brush cut side of top cake layer with remaining marsala mixture and place, cut side down, on top of filling. Reattach springform side of pan. Cover pan loosely and refrigerate 6 hours, or overnight.

6. Just before serving, remove side of springform and dust top of cake with powdered sugar.

103 MASCARPONE CREAM

Prep: 10 minutes   Cook: 5 minutes   Chill: 1 hour   Makes: 3 cups

This divine custard cream, a must served with fresh fruit, is also fantastic as a tart filling.

3 large egg yolks	1¼ cups milk
½ cup powdered sugar	½ teaspoon vanilla extract
Pinch of salt	8 ounces mascarpone cheese
¼ cup flour	

1. In a medium bowl, whisk egg yolks, ¼ cup powdered sugar, and salt until light and pale. Whisk in flour until smooth.

2. In a medium saucepan, heat milk until small bubbles appear around edge of pan. Gradually whisk hot milk into yolk mixture. Return custard to saucepan. Bring to boil over medium heat, whisking constantly. Boil gently, whisking, 1 minute. (Custard will be thick.) Remove from heat and blend in vanilla. Transfer to a clean bowl. Cover and refrigerate until cold, about 1 hour.

3. Beat mascarpone and remaining ¼ cup powdered sugar with an electric mixer until light and fluffy. Gradually beat in chilled custard, ¼ cup at a time, until filling is light and fluffy.

104   BIG AND BEAUTIFUL POPPY-CHOCOLATE CHIP CAKE

Prep: 20 minutes   Bake: 25 to 30 minutes   Serves: 12

This big kid party cake is for chocolate chip lovers only, with the extra bonus of crunchy poppyseeds and a satiny candy bar icing.

1½ sticks (6 ounces) butter, softened
1¾ cups sugar
6 large egg whites
1 teaspoon vanilla extract
2½ cups cake flour
1 teaspoon baking powder
1 teaspoon baking soda

½ teaspoon salt
2 tablespoons poppyseeds
1 cup sour cream
¾ cup miniature semisweet chocolate chips
Milk Chocolate Bar Frosting (recipe follows)

1. Preheat oven to 350°F. Grease three 8-inch round cake pans. Line bottoms with wax paper; grease paper. Dust pans with flour; tap out excess.

2. In a large bowl, beat together butter and sugar with an electric mixer on medium speed until smooth and creamy. Add egg whites and vanilla. Increase speed to high and beat until thick and fluffy, about 2 minutes longer.

3. Sift together cake flour, baking powder, baking soda, and salt. Stir in poppyseeds. With mixer on low speed, alternately add flour mixture and sour cream to butter mixture, beginning and ending with flour, just until blended. Stir in ½ cup chocolate chips. Turn batter into prepared pans.

4. Bake 25 to 30 minutes, or until a cake tester inserted in center comes out clean. Let cakes cool in pans 10 minutes, then unmold onto wire racks and remove wax paper. Invert cakes again and let cool completely. Fill and frost cake with Milk Chocolate Bar Frosting. Decorate top with remaining ¼ cup chocolate chips.

105   MILK CHOCOLATE BAR FROSTING

Prep: 10 minutes   Cook: 2½ to 3 minutes   Makes: 3½ cups

This big candy bar frosting gets its extra hit of fudge flavor from cocoa powder.

1 (7-ounce) bar milk chocolate, cut up
1 stick (4 ounces) butter, softened
2 to 3 tablespoons milk

½ teaspoon vanilla extract
2 cups powdered sugar
¼ cup unsweetened cocoa powder

1. In a medium glass bowl, microwave chocolate on Medium 2½ to 3 minutes, or until softened. Stir until smooth and let cool completely.

2. Beat butter with an electric mixer on medium-high speed until smooth and creamy. Beat in melted chocolate to blend, then beat in 2 tablespoons milk and vanilla.

3. Sift together powdered sugar and cocoa powder. Gradually beat into creamed chocolate mixture until frosting is light and fluffy, about 1 minute longer, adding a bit more milk if necessary.

---

106 CHOCOLATE AVALANCHE

Prep: 25 minutes   Cook: 5 minutes   Bake: 25 to 30 minutes
Chill: 30 minutes   Serves: 16 to 20

This giant flourless cake owes its rise and fall to fluffy beaten eggs and sugar. Since it is packed with chocolate, be sure not to overbake this cake; you want to maintain its moist, soufflé-like texture.

8 ounces semisweet
   chocolate, chopped
6 (1-ounce) squares
   unsweetened chocolate,
   chopped
2 sticks (8 ounces) butter, cut
   up
2 teaspoons instant espresso
   powder

¼ cup dark rum or bourbon
1 teaspoon vanilla extract
9 large eggs, separated, at
   room temperature
1 cup granulated sugar
   Powdered sugar
   Classic Custard Sauce (page
   84)

1. Preheat oven to 350°F. Grease a 10-inch springform pan. Dust with flour; tap out excess. In a large double boiler over simmering water, combine semisweet chocolate, unsweetened chocolate, butter, and espresso powder. Cook, stirring, until melted and smooth, about 5 minutes. Remove from heat and cool to lukewarm, stirring occasionally, about 15 minutes. Stir in rum and vanilla.

2. In a large bowl, beat together egg yolks and ¾ cup granulated sugar with an electric mixer on medium-high speed until thick and lemon colored and mixture forms a ribbon when beaters are lifted. With a rubber spatula, gently fold in chocolate mixture until blended.

3. In another large clean bowl, beat egg whites with an electric mixer and clean beaters on medium speed until foamy. Gradually beat in remaining ¼ cup granulated sugar and continue to beat to soft peaks, about 3 minutes. Gently fold ⅓ of whites into chocolate mixture. Repeat twice more with remaining whites just until blended. Turn into prepared pan.

4. Bake 25 to 30 minutes, or until cake is barely set in center. Let cool completely in pan on a wire rack. Refrigerate at least 30 minutes, or overnight. (If refrigerated overnight, let stand at room temperature 30 minutes before serving.) Dust top with powdered sugar and serve with Classic Custard Sauce.

107 CLASSIC CUSTARD SAUCE

Prep: 10 minutes   Cook: 5 minutes   Chill: 1 hour   Makes: 2 cups

¾ cup heavy cream
¾ cup milk
1 vanilla bean, split
   lengthwise, or 2
   teaspoons vanilla extract

4 large egg yolks
⅓ cup sugar

1. In a medium saucepan, bring cream, milk, and vanilla bean to a boil. In a medium bowl, whisk egg yolks and sugar until smooth. Gradually whisk in hot milk mixture. Return to pan and cook over medium heat, stirring, until custard has thickened slightly and coats the back of a spoon, about 3 minutes. (Do not boil.)

2. Strain custard through a fine sieve into a medium bowl. Remove vanilla bean and scrape out seeds; add seeds to cream and discard pod. (If using vanilla extract, whisk into strained custard to blend.) Refrigerate until chilled, 1 hour.

Chapter 4

Big Kid, Little Kid Cupcakes

Bite-sized and fun to eat, plain or fancy but always festive, a cupcake is a cake that's perfect for any occasion. Fast and easy to fix, many with just a bowl and a whisk, cupcakes were made with the kid in all of us in mind. Short and sweet to bake, cooled and frosted in a flash, cupcakes are versatile, just as comfortable iced with your favorite frosting or plain, dusted with powdered sugar, or brushed with a simple stirred glaze. For birthdays, bake sales, buffets, and after-school snacks, cupcakes are perfectly portioned.

The only pan you'll need for cupcakes is a muffin pan. Recipes were tested in standard medium-sized muffin cups between 2½ and 3 inches in diameter. These are available in 6- or 12-cup sizes. For best results, select pans made of heavy-gauge metal, which can be purchased at a very modest cost. Although the muffin cups can be greased with solid vegetable shortening or vegetable cooking spray, I'm a big fan of paper or foil cupcake liners. Fluted and available in a wide assortment of colors and patterns, cupcake liners add a whimsical visual touch to your cakes. They also make unmolding and cleanup a breeze and help retain moisture so that the cupcakes stay fresh longer.

To allow room for cupcakes to rise while baking, each muffin cup should be filled between half and two-thirds full of batter. For larger numbers of cupcakes, or if you have only one 6-cup muffin pan, the cakes can be baked in batches. Fill any unused muffin cups halfway with warm water during baking to keep the heat in the pan evenly distributed. Cupcakes are a bit fragile when they come out of the oven, so be sure to allow them to cool in the muffin pans for a few minutes before unmolding. Once completely cooled, if wrapped well they keep fresh at room temperature for up to 2 days. Cupcakes are also the perfect candidates for freezing, but keep them unfrosted until ready to serve.

One of the best parts of making cupcakes is decorating them. Start with a spread of your favorite frosting, then leave the rest to your imagination. Chopped nuts, cake or cookie crumbs, colored sprinkles, toasted coconut, candy-coated chocolate candies, and chopped chocolate bars are just some of the readily available toppers to choose from. Classic Seven-Minute Icing is an easy choice for decorating. This icing requires no spreading; simply dip the top of your cupcake into the mixing bowl, then slowly twist it as you lift it from the bowl to form a high peak. Some favorite party cupcakes include chocolaty Tin Roof Cupcakes with Fluffy Peanut But-

ter Icing, pretty as a picture Sunshine Butterfly Cupcakes, and
Peppermint Angel Cupcakes with a delicate pink-tinted glaze.

Easy-to-fix cupcakes can also be designed for the sophisti-
cate. Arranged on a pretty platter, many can be served as part
of a fancy buffet of tempting sweets, or in an elegant picnic
basket. Part of this collection for grown-up tastes includes
Fresh Gingerbread Cupcakes with a tart lemon glaze, Little
Red Devil Cupcakes with sour cream, German Chocolate
Cupcakes with the renowned coconut pecan topping, and
Iced Cappuccino Cupcakes with our favorite coffee kick.

108 GERMAN CHOCOLATE CUPCAKES
Prep: 20 minutes   Bake: 20 minutes   Makes: 18

Here's one of your favorite chocolate cakes in just the right size for sharing. Light and delicate, these boast a touch of chocolate in both the fluffy
cake and the classic coconut pecan topping.

2 ounces sweet cooking
   chocolate, cut into small
   pieces
¼ cup boiling water
1 stick (4 ounces) butter,
   softened
¾ cup sugar
2 large eggs, separated, at
   room temperature

½ teaspoon vanilla extract
1 cup cake flour
½ teaspoon baking soda
¼ teaspoon salt
½ cup buttermilk
   German Coconut Pecan
   Topping (page 87)

1. In a medium bowl, whisk together chocolate and boiling water until
chocolate melts. Let cool.

2. Preheat oven to 350°F. In a large bowl, beat together butter and sugar
with an electric mixer on medium-high speed until light and fluffy, about 2
minutes. Add egg yolks, 1 at a time, beating well after each addition. Gradually beat in melted chocolate and vanilla until smooth.

3. Sift together cake flour, baking soda, and salt. With mixer on low speed,
alternately add flour mixture and buttermilk to chocolate mixture, beginning and ending with flour, and beat just until blended. In another bowl,
beat egg whites with an electric mixer with clean beaters until stiff peaks
form when beaters are lifted. With a rubber spatula, fold beaten whites into
chocolate batter.

4. Divide batter evenly among 18 paper-lined muffin cups 2½ or 3 inches in
diameter. Bake 20 minutes, or until cupcakes spring back when touched
lightly in center. Let cool in pans 5 minutes, then remove to a wire rack,
right side up, to cool completely. Spread tops with German Coconut Pecan
Topping.

109 GERMAN COCONUT PECAN TOPPING
Prep: 10 minutes   Cook: 5 minutes   Makes: 2 cups

¾ cup evaporated milk
⅔ cup sugar
2 large egg yolks, lightly
    beaten
2 tablespoons butter, cut up
½ teaspoon vanilla extract

2 ounces sweet cooking
    chocolate, cut into small
    pieces
1½ cups flaked coconut
1 cup chopped pecans

1. In a medium saucepan, whisk together evaporated milk, sugar, and egg yolks until smooth, then stir in butter. Cook over medium heat, stirring constantly, until butter has melted and mixture is thickened, about 5 minutes. (Do not let boil.)

2. Remove from heat and stir in vanilla and chocolate until chocolate melts. Stir in coconut and pecans. Let cool.

110 BERRY 'N' ALMOND SWIRL CUPCAKES
Prep: 20 minutes   Bake: 28 to 32 minutes   Makes: 12

Have your cake and eat your jam too. These sweet treasures are just great with any of your favorite preserves.

½ cup sliced almonds
½ cup granulated sugar
⅓ cup butter, melted
½ cup milk
1 large egg
¼ teaspoon vanilla extract
¼ teaspoon almond extract

1 cup flour
½ teaspoon baking powder
½ teaspoon baking soda
¼ teaspoon salt
¼ cup seedless raspberry jam
Powdered sugar

1. Preheat oven to 350°F. Spread out almonds on a small baking sheet. Bake 8 to 10 minutes, until nuts are lightly browned and fragrant. Transfer to a plate and let cool. In a food processor, finely grind almonds and ¼ cup of the granulated sugar.

2. In a large bowl, whisk together melted butter, milk, remaining ¼ cup granulated sugar, egg, vanilla, and almond extract until smooth. Sift together flour, baking powder, baking soda, and salt. Whisk flour mixture into butter mixture until smooth. Stir in ground almonds.

3. Divide batter evenly among 12 paper-lined muffin cups 2½ or 3 inches in diameter. Spoon 1 scant teaspoon jam onto center of each cupcake. Swirl a thin knife or toothpick through batter to marbleize.

4. Bake 20 to 22 minutes, or until a cake tester inserted in a cupcake comes out clean and tops of cupcakes are golden. Let cool in pans 5 minutes, then remove to wire racks right side up to cool completely. Sift a dusting of powdered sugar over tops of cupcakes.

111 LITTLE RED DEVIL CUPCAKES
Prep: 15 minutes   Bake: 18 to 20 minutes   Makes: 24

Sour cream gives these dark cocoa cupcakes their famous red hue and makes the icing smooth as satin.

1 cup milk	1½ cups sugar
1 teaspoon instant coffee powder (optional)	2 large eggs
	1¾ cups flour
⅔ cup unsweetened cocoa powder	1 teaspoon baking soda
	½ teaspoon baking powder
½ cup sour cream	¼ teaspoon salt
1½ teaspoons vanilla extract	Red Devil Icing (recipe
1½ sticks (6 ounces) butter, softened	follows)

1. In a medium glass bowl, combine milk and coffee powder. Microwave on High 2 to 2½ minutes, or until milk is very hot and coffee is dissolved. Whisk in cocoa powder until smooth, then sour cream and vanilla. Let cool.

2. In a large bowl, beat together butter and sugar with an electric mixer on medium-high speed until light and fluffy, about 2 minutes. Beat in eggs, 1 at a time, until smooth and creamy.

3. Sift together flour, baking soda, baking powder, and salt. With mixer on low speed, alternately add flour and chocolate mixture to butter mixture, beginning and ending with flour, and beat just until blended.

4. Divide batter evenly among 24 paper-lined muffin cups 2½ or 3 inches in diameter. Bake 18 to 20 minutes, or until a cake tester inserted in a cupcake comes out clean. Let cool in pans 5 minutes; remove to a wire rack right side up to cool completely. Frost tops of cupcakes with Red Devil Icing.

112 RED DEVIL ICING
Prep: 10 minutes   Cook: 2½ to 3 minutes   Makes: 2 cups

This all-purpose icing is guaranteed to become one of your favorites. It is a perfect partner to any chocolate cupcake or layer cake.

4 (1-ounce) squares unsweetened chocolate, cut up	2 cups sifted powdered sugar
	1½ teaspoons vanilla extract
	⅓ cup sour cream
4 tablespoons butter, cut up	

1. In a small glass bowl, combine chocolate and butter. Microwave on Medium 2½ to 3 minutes, or until butter is melted. Whisk butter and chocolate together until completely smooth.

2. Transfer chocolate mixture to a large bowl. Beat in 1 cup powdered sugar and vanilla with an electric mixer on medium speed. Beat in sour cream, then remaining 1 cup powdered sugar until smooth and frosting is a spreadable consistency, about 1 minute longer.

113 TIN ROOF CUPCAKES
Prep: 15 minutes   Bake: 20 minutes   Makes: 18

These cupcakes are modeled after an old-fashioned chocolate and peanut butter ice cream sundae called a Tin Roof Sundae.

3 (1-ounce) squares
    unsweetened chocolate,
    chopped
1 stick (4 ounces) butter,
    softened
¾ cup granulated sugar
½ cup packed brown sugar
2 large eggs
1 teaspoon vanilla extract
	1¾ cups flour
	1 teaspoon baking powder
	½ teaspoon baking soda
	¼ teaspoon salt
	1 cup milk
	Fluffy Peanut Butter Icing
	    (recipe follows)
	⅓ cup finely chopped honey-
	    roasted peanuts

1. Preheat oven to 350°F. In a small glass bowl, microwave chocolate on Medium 2½ to 3 minutes, or until softened. Stir until completely smooth.

2. In a medium bowl, beat together butter, granulated sugar, and brown sugar with an electric mixer on medium-high speed until light and fluffy. Add eggs, 1 at a time, beating until just blended after each addition. Beat in melted chocolate and vanilla.

3. Sift together flour, baking powder, baking soda, and salt. With mixer on low speed, alternately add flour mixture and milk to chocolate mixture, beginning and ending with flour and beat just until blended.

4. Divide batter evenly among 18 paper-lined muffin cups 2½ or 3 inches in diameter. Bake 20 minutes, or until a cake tester inserted in a cupcake comes out clean. Let cool in pans 5 minutes, then remove to a wire rack, right side up, to cool completely. Frost tops of cupcakes with Fluffy Peanut Butter Icing and sprinkle with honey-roasted peanuts.

114 FLUFFY PEANUT BUTTER ICING
Prep: 5 minutes   Cook: none   Makes: 2 cups

A melt-in-your-mouth icing made for peanut butter lovers.

1 stick (4 ounces) butter,
    softened
4 ounces cream cheese,
    softened
	¾ cup smooth peanut butter
	1½ teaspoons vanilla extract
	2 cups sifted powdered sugar

In a large bowl, beat together butter and cream cheese with an electric mixer on medium-high speed until light and fluffy. Beat in peanut butter and vanilla until smooth. With mixer on low speed, gradually beat in powdered sugar to a spreading consistency.

115 OLD-FASHIONED PEANUT BUTTER FUDGE CUPCAKES

Prep: 20 minutes   Bake: 22 to 24 minutes   Makes: 24

Here's the ultimate cupcake for kids—a triple peanut delight perfect with vanilla ice cream.

⅔ cup smooth or chunky
   peanut butter
6 tablespoons butter, softened
1¼ cups packed dark brown
   sugar
2 large eggs
1½ teaspoons vanilla extract

2 cups flour
1 tablespoon baking powder
¼ teaspoon salt
1 cup milk
½ cup peanut butter chips
  Peanut Butter Fudge
  Frosting (recipe follows)

1. Preheat oven to 350°F. In a medium bowl, beat together peanut butter and butter with an electric mixer on medium-high speed until light and fluffy. Gradually beat in brown sugar until smooth. Add eggs, 1 at a time, beating well after each addition. Beat in vanilla.

2. Sift together flour, baking powder, and salt. With mixer on low speed, alternately add flour mixture and milk to peanut butter mixture, beginning and ending with flour, and beat just until blended. Stir in peanut butter chips.

3. Divide batter evenly among 24 paper-lined muffin cups 2½ or 3 inches in diameter. Bake 22 to 24 minutes, or until a cake tester inserted in a cupcake comes out clean. Let cool in pans 5 minutes, then remove to a wire rack right side up to cool completely. Frost tops of cupcakes with Peanut Butter Fudge Frosting.

116 PEANUT BUTTER FUDGE FROSTING

Prep: 15 minutes   Cook: 2 to 2½ minutes   Makes: 2 cups

Chocolate and peanut butter are a winning combination in this easy frosting.

1 (1-ounce) square
   unsweetened chocolate
¼ cup smooth or chunky
   peanut butter

4 tablespoons butter, softened
1 teaspoon vanilla extract
2 cups sifted powdered sugar
2 to 3 tablespoons milk

1. In a small glass bowl, microwave chocolate on Medium 2 to 2½ minutes, or until softened, then stir until completely smooth. Let cool slightly.

2. In a medium bowl, beat together peanut butter and butter with an electric mixer on medium-high speed until light and fluffy. Beat in melted chocolate and vanilla until smooth.

3. Gradually beat in 1 cup powdered sugar. Alternately add remaining 1 cup powdered sugar and 2 tablespoons milk, beating until smooth after each addition. Add remaining 1 tablespoon milk if necessary for desired spreading consistency, then beat about 1 minute longer.

117   SUGAR 'N' SPICE CUPCAKES
Prep: 10 minutes   Bake: 18 to 20 minutes   Makes: 12

Here's a one-bowl cupcake with a creamy melt-in-your-mouth spice icing.

⅓ **cup butter, melted**	½ **teaspoon baking powder**
½ **cup buttermilk**	½ **teaspoon baking soda**
1 **large egg**	¼ **teaspoon salt**
½ **teaspoon vanilla extract**	**Pinch of grated nutmeg**
1 **cup flour**	**Pinch of ground cloves**
⅔ **cup sugar**	**Cinnamon Butter Icing**
½ **teaspoon cinnamon**	**(recipe follows)**

1. Preheat oven to 350°F. In a large bowl, whisk together butter, buttermilk, egg, and vanilla until smooth.

2. Sift together flour, sugar, cinnamon, baking powder, baking soda, salt, nutmeg, and cloves. Whisk into buttermilk mixture until smooth.

3. Divide batter evenly among 12 paper-lined muffin cups 2½ or 3 inches in diameter. Bake 18 to 20 minutes, or until a cake tester inserted in a cupcake comes out clean. Let cool in pans 5 minutes, then remove to a wire rack right side up to cool completely. Spread tops of cupcakes with Cinnamon Butter Icing.

118   CINNAMON BUTTER ICING
Prep: 5 minutes   Cook: none   Makes: 1½ cups

Sugar and spice and everything nice—a creamy topping perfect for any cake.

4 **tablespoons butter, softened**	½ **teaspoon cinnamon**
1 **(3-ounce) package cream**	1 **teaspoon vanilla extract**
cheese, softened	2 **tablespoons heavy cream**
2 **cups sifted powdered sugar**	

1. In a small bowl, beat together butter and cream cheese with an electric mixer until light and fluffy. Gradually beat in 1 cup powdered sugar until smooth. Beat in cinnamon and vanilla.

2. Alternately add remaining 1 cup powdered sugar and cream, beating until smooth after each addition. Beat 1 minute longer, until spreadable.

119   SUNSHINE BUTTERFLY CUPCAKES
Prep: 20 minutes   Bake: 18 to 20 minutes   Makes: 18

These pretty little cupcakes are perfect for a little girl's birthday party. Have fun sprinkling the tops with colored sugar.

1 stick (4 ounces) butter, softened	½ cup fresh orange juice
1 cup sugar	½ cup sour cream
2 large eggs	1½ teaspoons grated orange zest
2 cups flour	½ teaspoon vanilla extract
1½ teaspoons baking powder	Classic Cream Cheese Frosting (recipe follows)
½ teaspoon baking soda	Colored sugar
½ teaspoon salt	

1. Preheat oven to 350°F. In a large bowl, beat together butter and sugar with an electric mixer on medium-high speed until light and fluffy, about 2 minutes. Beat in eggs, 1 at a time, beating well after each addition until smooth.

2. Sift together flour, baking powder, baking soda, and salt. In a small bowl, stir together orange juice, sour cream, orange zest, and vanilla. On low speed, add flour mixture and sour cream mixture alternately to butter mixture, beginning and ending with flour, and beat just until blended.

3. Divide batter evenly among 18 paper-lined muffin cups 2½ or 3 inches in diameter. Bake 18 to 20 minutes, or until a cake tester inserted in a cupcake comes out clean. Let cool in pans 5 minutes, then remove to a wire rack right side up to cool completely.

4. With a serrated knife, cut top off each cupcake right above paper liner. Cut each circle in half crosswise. Spoon 1 tablespoon Classic Cream Cheese Frosting over each cupcake. Arrange 2 halves of each circle, cut sides down, on top of icing at a slight angle to form a V shape for butterfly wings. Spoon additional frosting in center of V for butterfly body, then sprinkle with colored sugar.

120   CLASSIC CREAM CHEESE FROSTING
Prep: 10 minutes   Cook: none   Makes: 2¼ cups

Soft, billowy, and creamy, this frosting is a classic standby to spread on your favorite cake or cupcake.

1 (8-ounce) package cream cheese, softened	1 teaspoon vanilla extract
4 tablespoons butter, softened	½ teaspoon grated orange zest
	3 cups sifted powdered sugar

In a large bowl, beat together cream cheese, butter, vanilla, and orange zest with an electric mixer on medium-high speed until light and fluffy, about 2 minutes. Gradually beat in powdered sugar to a spreading consistency.

121 PEPPERMINT ANGEL CUPCAKES
Prep: 15 minutes   Bake: 18 to 20 minutes   Makes: 18

These downy white cupcakes with a pretty pink peppermint glaze are another surefire party favorite.

1 stick (4 ounces) butter,
   softened
1 cup plus 2 tablespoons
   sugar
1 teaspoon vanilla extract
¼ teaspoon peppermint extract
2 cups cake flour
2 teaspoons baking powder
½ teaspoon salt

¾ cup milk
¼ cup plus 2 tablespoons
   crushed peppermint
   candies
4 large egg whites, at room
   temperature
   Pink Peppermint Glaze
   (recipe follows)

1. Preheat oven to 350°F. In a large bowl, beat together butter and 1 cup sugar with an electric mixer on medium-high speed until light and fluffy, about 2 minutes. Beat in vanilla and peppermint extract.

2. Sift together cake flour, baking powder, and salt. With mixer on low speed, alternately add flour mixture and milk to butter mixture, beginning and ending with flour, and beat just until blended. Stir in ¼ cup crushed peppermint candies.

3. In a small clean bowl, beat egg whites with an electric mixer with clean beaters on medium speed until soft peaks form. Gradually beat in remaining 2 tablespoons sugar, then continue to beat until stiff. With a rubber spatula, gently fold ⅓ of beaten whites into batter, then repeat with remaining whites just until blended.

4. Divide batter evenly among 18 paper-lined muffin cups 2½ or 3 inches in diameter. Bake 18 to 20 minutes, or until a cake tester inserted in a cupcake comes out clean. Let cool in pans 5 minutes, then remove to a wire rack right side up to cool completely. Spread Pink Peppermint Glaze over tops of cupcakes and sprinkle with remaining 2 tablespoons peppermint candies. Let stand 30 minutes, or until glaze is set.

122 PINK PEPPERMINT GLAZE
Prep: 5 minutes   Cook: none   Makes: ⅔ cup

1¾ cups sifted powdered sugar
2 teaspoons light corn syrup
2 tablespoons hot water

¼ teaspoon peppermint extract
1 to 2 drops of red food
   coloring

In a small bowl, whisk together powdered sugar, corn syrup, water, and peppermint extract until smooth. Add food coloring, 1 drop at a time, until icing is pink.

123   CHUNKY MONKEY CUPCAKES
Prep: 15 minutes   Bake: 20 to 22 minutes   Makes: 24

1 stick (4 ounces) butter,
    softened
½ cup plus 2 tablespoons
    packed brown sugar
½ cup granulated sugar
3 very ripe bananas, mashed
    (about 1½ cups)
2 large eggs
1 teaspoon vanilla extract

2 cups flour
½ teaspoon baking powder
½ teaspoon baking soda
½ teaspoon salt
½ cup buttermilk
6 ounces (1 cup) semisweet
    chocolate chips
½ cup chopped walnuts
½ teaspoon cinnamon

1. Preheat oven to 350°F. In a large bowl, beat together butter, ½ cup brown sugar, and granulated sugar with an electric mixer on medium-high speed until light and fluffy. Beat in bananas, then eggs, 1 at a time, beating well after each addition. Beat in vanilla.

2. Sift together flour, baking powder, baking soda, and salt. With mixer on low speed, alternately add flour mixture and buttermilk to banana mixture, beginning and ending with flour, and beat just until blended. Stir in chocolate chips.

3. Divide batter evenly among 24 paper-lined muffin cups 2½ or 3 inches in diameter. In a small bowl, combine walnuts and cinnamon with remaining 2 tablespoons brown sugar and sprinkle over tops of cupcakes.

4. Bake 20 to 22 minutes, or until a cake tester inserted in a cupcake comes out clean. Let cool in pans 5 minutes, then remove to a wire rack right side up to cool completely.

124   BATTER-UP BUTTERSCOTCH CUPCAKES
Prep: 25 minutes   Bake: 18 to 20 minutes   Makes: 18

These dark brown sugar cupcakes are topped off with an easy-as-you-please creamy butterscotch chip icing.

6 tablespoons butter, softened
¾ cup packed dark brown
    sugar
1 large egg
1 teaspoon vanilla extract
1¼ cups flour

¾ teaspoon baking powder
¾ teaspoon baking soda
½ teaspoon salt
⅔ cup buttermilk
¾ cup butterscotch chips
2 tablespoons heavy cream

1. Preheat oven to 350°F. In a large bowl, beat together butter and brown sugar with an electric mixer on medium-high speed until light and fluffy, about 2 minutes. Beat in egg, then vanilla until smooth.

2. Sift together flour, baking powder, baking soda, and salt. With mixer on low speed, alternately add flour mixture and buttermilk to butter mixture, beginning and ending with flour, and beat until just blended.

3. Divide batter evenly among 18 paper-lined muffin cups 2½ or 3 inches in diameter. Bake 18 to 20 minutes, or until a cake tester inserted in a cupcake comes out clean. Let cool in pans 5 minutes, then remove to a wire rack right side up to cool completely.

4. In a small glass bowl, combine butterscotch chips and heavy cream. Microwave on Medium 1½ to 2 minutes, or until chips have softened. Whisk until completely smooth. Let cool, then spread evenly over tops of cupcakes.

125   ICED CAPPUCCINO CUPCAKES
Prep: 15 minutes   Bake: 22 to 23 minutes   Makes: 18

This sophisticated cupcake features the finest flavors of the espresso bar.

1   stick (4 ounces) butter, softened
1¼ cups sugar
2   large eggs
¼   cup milk
1½ teaspoons instant espresso powder
½   cup sour cream

¼   cup coffee-flavored liqueur
1   teaspoon vanilla extract
2   cups flour
1   teaspoon baking powder
1   teaspoon baking soda
½   teaspoon salt
⅛   teaspoon cinnamon
    Espresso Glaze (page 25)

1. Preheat oven to 350°F. In a large bowl, beat together butter and sugar with an electric mixer on medium-high speed until light and fluffy, about 2 minutes. Beat in eggs, 1 at a time, beating well after each addition, until smooth.

2. In a small glass bowl, combine milk and espresso powder. Microwave on High 1 minute, or until milk is very hot and espresso is dissolved. Whisk in sour cream, coffee liqueur, and vanilla until smooth.

3. Sift together flour, baking powder, baking soda, salt, and cinnamon. With mixer on low speed, alternately add flour mixture and espresso mixture to butter mixture, beginning and ending with flour, and beat just until blended.

4. Divide batter evenly among 18 paper-lined muffin cups 2½ or 3 inches in diameter. Bake 22 to 23 minutes, or until a cake tester inserted in a cupcake comes out clean. Let cool in pans 5 minutes, then remove to a wire rack right side up to cool completely. Spread tops of cupcakes with Espresso Glaze.

126 COCONUT CREAM BLACK-BOTTOM CUPCAKES

Prep: 15 minutes   Bake: 18 to 20 minutes   Makes: 14

A cupcake classic, each one of these little chocolate gems is brimming with miniature chips and filled with a creamy coconut surprise in the center.

1½ cups flour	2 large eggs
1 cup sugar	1½ teaspoons vanilla extract
⅓ cup unsweetened cocoa powder	1 teaspoon cider vinegar
1 teaspoon baking soda	⅔ cup miniature semisweet chocolate chips
½ teaspoon salt	2 (3-ounce) packages cream cheese, softened
1 cup milk	½ cup flaked coconut
⅓ cup vegetable oil	

1. Preheat oven to 350°F. In a large bowl, sift together flour, ¾ cup sugar, cocoa powder, baking soda, and salt. Whisk in milk, oil, 1 egg, 1 teaspoon vanilla, and vinegar until smooth. Stir in miniature chocolate chips.

2. Divide batter evenly among 14 paper-lined muffin cups 2½ or 3 inches in diameter.

3. To make filling, in a medium bowl, beat together cream cheese and remaining ¼ cup sugar with an electric mixer on medium speed until light and fluffy. Beat in remaining egg and remaining ½ teaspoon vanilla until smooth. Stir in coconut.

4. Spoon 1 scant tablespoon cream cheese filling onto center of each cupcake. Bake 18 to 20 minutes, or until a cake tester inserted into edge of cupcake comes out clean. Let cool in pans 5 minutes, then remove cupcakes to a wire rack, right side up, to cool completely.

127 FRESH GINGERBREAD CUPCAKES

Prep: 20 minutes   Bake: 18 to 20 minutes   Makes: 12

If you can't wait to try one, these spicy cakes are wonderful served warm, spread with a tart and translucent lemon glaze.

4 tablespoons butter, softened	½ teaspoon cinnamon
⅓ cup granulated sugar	¼ teaspoon salt
2 teaspoons freshly grated ginger	Pinch of ground cloves
1 large egg	½ cup unsulphured molasses
1¼ cups flour	½ cup boiling water
1 teaspoon baking soda	½ cup sifted powdered sugar
	2 teaspoons fresh lemon juice

1. Preheat oven to 350°F. In a large bowl, beat together butter, sugar, and ginger with an electric mixer on medium-high speed until light and fluffy, about 2 minutes. Beat in egg until smooth.

2. Sift together flour, baking soda, cinnamon, salt, and cloves. In a small bowl, stir together molasses and boiling water. With mixer on low speed, alternately add flour mixture and molasses to butter mixture, beginning and ending with flour, and beat just until blended.

3. Divide batter evenly among 12 paper-lined muffin cups 2½ or 3 inches in diameter. Bake 18 to 20 minutes, or until a cake tester inserted in a cupcake comes out clean. Let cool in pans 5 minutes, then remove to a wire rack right side up.

4. In a small bowl, whisk together powdered sugar and lemon juice until smooth. Spread glaze over tops of warm cupcakes. Serve warm or at room temperature.

128   COFFEE CAKE STREUSEL CUPCAKES
Prep: 15 minutes   Bake: 23 to 25 minutes   Makes: 18

These miniature sour cream coffee cakes are perfect for brunch.

1 stick (4 ounces) butter,
   softened
¾ cup sugar
2 large eggs
1 teaspoon vanilla extract
2 cups flour

1 teaspoon baking powder
1 teaspoon baking soda
¼ teaspoon salt
1 cup sour cream
Chocolate Chip Streusel
   (recipe follows)

1. Preheat oven to 350°F. In a large bowl, beat together butter and sugar on medium-high speed with an electric mixer until light and fluffy, about 2 minutes. Beat in eggs, 1 at a time, beating well after each addition. Beat in vanilla.

2. Sift together flour, baking powder, baking soda, and salt. With mixer on low speed, alternately add flour mixture and sour cream to butter mixture, beginning and ending with flour, and beat just until blended.

3. Spoon half of batter (2 cups) evenly among 18 paper-lined muffin cups 2½ or 3 inches in diameter. Sprinkle tops with ½ cup Chocolate Chip Streusel. Add remaining batter and sprinkle with remaining streusel.

4. Bake 23 to 25 minutes, or until a cake tester inserted in a cupcake comes out clean. Let cool in pans 5 minutes, then remove to a wire rack right side up to cool completely.

129   CHOCOLATE CHIP STREUSEL
Prep: 5 minutes   Cook: none   Makes: 1 cup

⅓ cup packed brown sugar
1 teaspoon cinnamon
1 tablespoon butter, melted

⅓ cup chopped walnuts
¼ cup miniature semisweet
   chocolate chips

In a medium bowl, combine sugar, cinnamon, and butter. Stir in nuts and chips.

Chapter 5

Mad About Cheesecake

What rich, creamy, smooth-as-satin cake is one of our all-time favorite desserts? Just say cheesecake. We've always loved the classics like New York-style cheesecake, dense with cream cheese and sour or heavy cream, or the lighter Italian variety prepared with ricotta or cottage cheese. But that's just the beginning, because there always appears to be a new flavor of cheesecake on the horizon, with new textures and toppings to tempt our sweetest fantasies: citrus, caramel, nut, fruit, and fudge swirl, to name just a few. Cheesecakes are made for company, and the bigger the crowd the better. When it's time to entertain and pull out all the stops, cheesecake is the hands-down favorite of dessert diehards—perfectly indulgent, perfectly do-ahead, and freezer-friendly.

Nothing is more magical than a perfect slice of luscious cheesecake, and once you master the simple technique of creating this creamy sensation, nothing is easier to prepare. For baking the perfect cheesecakes that are tall, handsome, and effortless to unmold, you'll need to begin with a springform pan. This is a round pan with a detachable bottom and straight sides between 2½ and 3 inches high. The expandable sides attach and release from the bottom of the pan with the aid of a metal clamp. Springform pans come in a variety of sizes; the majority of these recipes were tested in 8- and 9-inch-diameter pans. Some extra-large cheesecakes were prepared in 10-inch pans. Take care to bake your cheesecake in the correct size pan; 1 inch can make all the difference between success and a cake whose filling overflows, ending in an oven disaster.

Cheesecake crusts are also easy and offer a range of flavors. A simple buttery crumb crust is a favorite. Use whatever cookie strikes your fancy, chocolate or vanilla wafer, gingersnap or graham, and feel free to replace some of the crumbs with an equal amount of ground nuts for extra crunch. To release the cheesecake easily from the bottom of the springform pan for serving, I like to line the round base tightly with foil, then attach the sides of the pan before pressing in my crust ingredients. If prebaking your crust, be sure it is thoroughly cooled before adding the cheesecake filling; this will keep your crust moist, but not soggy.

For fillings prepared with cream cheese, it's best to use premium quality; never cream cheese labeled "imitation" or "whipped cream cheese," which will greatly alter the texture and volume of the cake. If you're looking for a lighter alternative, though, I have had success preparing these recipes with a reduced-fat Neufchâtel cheese as a substitute for cream cheese.

For a smooth, satiny cheesecake filling, always be sure to start with cream cheese that is very soft, then beat with an electric mixer on medium-high speed for at least 2 minutes, until creamy. The next step is to add the sugar gradually, frequently scraping the sides of the mixing bowl with a rubber spatula, until the mixture is thoroughly blended and completely smooth. This is the best way to avoid lumps, which are difficult to eliminate once they form. To avoid having the baked cheesecake crack by incorporating too much air into the batter, the next step is to reduce the mixer speed to medium. Add room-temperature eggs, one at a time, beating just until blended after each addition, then beat in any additional ingredients just until the batter is smooth.

A number of the cheesecakes in this collection were baked in a hot water bath (classically called a *bain-marie*), which I believe yields the creamiest filling and the least risk of cracking or sinking. The hot water provides a gentle and even distribution of heat. Always cover the entire outside of the springform with a double thickness of foil, preferably heavy-duty, to form a tight seal and prevent leaking. Fill your cheesecake as directed, then select a shallow pan at least 1 inch larger than the springform. I use a large roasting pan. Pour hot water into the larger pan until it reaches 1 inch up the side of the springform pan. I like to use a teapot or large liquid measure for this task, taking care not to pour any water into the batter.

A rule of thumb for all cheesecakes is to avoid the temptation of overbaking them. When a cheesecake is done, the top surface will appear slightly puffed and golden, the edges will be set, and the cake will jiggle slightly in the center. It's important to keep in mind that a cheesecake filling will solidify as it cools, and if any cracks appear they will reduce in size as the cake sinks slightly. Always cool a cheesecake completely on a wire rack before refrigerating. These cakes keep beautifully, covered and chilled, up to 3 days. If you want to freeze a cheesecake, cover the springform pan with plastic wrap, then foil, and freeze up to 1 month. Allow time to thaw in the refrigerator overnight before serving.

So what's so special about cheesecake? Just about everything when you have a choice of glorious Classic Whipped Cream Cheesecake, whimsical Malted Marble Cheesecake, refreshing Lemon Poppyseed Cheesecake, or Chocolate Ricotta or Chocolate Turtle Cheesecake with caramel and pecans to choose from.

130   CLASSIC WHIPPED CREAM CHEESECAKE

Prep: 20 minutes   Bake: 1 hour 25 to 30 minutes
Chill: 6 hours   Serves: 12

Whipped cream and fluffy beaten egg whites give this soufflé-style cheesecake an incredibly light and delicate texture. It is marvelous with fresh strawberries.

1 cup gingersnap cookie crumbs	1 tablespoon fresh lemon juice
½ cup finely chopped walnuts	1½ teaspoons grated lemon zest
2 tablespoons packed brown sugar	1 teaspoon vanilla extract
4 tablespoons butter, melted	Pinch of salt
3 (8-ounce) packages cream cheese, softened	4 large eggs, separated, at room temperature
1½ cups granulated sugar	½ cup heavy cream

1. Preheat oven to 350°F. To prepare crust, in a medium bowl combine gingersnap crumbs, walnuts, and brown sugar. Gradually work in melted butter until crumbs are evenly moistened. Press into bottom and 1 inch up sides of a well-greased 9-inch springform pan. Tightly cover outside of pan with a double thickness of aluminum foil. Bake until edges are lightly browned, about 10 minutes. Let cool completely on wire rack.

2. Reduce oven temperature to 325°F. In a large bowl, beat cream cheese with an electric mixer on medium-high speed until light and fluffy, about 2 minutes. Gradually beat in 1¼ cups granulated sugar and continue beating until completely smooth. Reduce speed to medium and beat in lemon juice, lemon zest, vanilla, and salt. Add egg yolks, 1 at a time, beating just until blended after each addition.

3. In another large clean bowl, beat egg whites with an electric mixer with clean beaters on medium speed until soft peaks form. Gradually add remaining ¼ cup sugar. Increase speed to medium-high and continue to beat until stiff but not dry peaks form when beaters are lifted. With a rubber spatula, gently fold ⅓ of whites into cheese mixture, then fold in remaining whites until just blended.

4. In same bowl used for whites, beat cream with an electric mixer and clean beaters until soft peaks form. Gently fold into cheese mixture.

5. Pour filling into prepared crust in pan and place in a larger baking pan. Place pan on an oven rack. Carefully pour enough hot water into larger pan to reach 1 inch up sides of springform pan. Bake 75 to 80 minutes, or until cake barely jiggles in center.

6. Remove cheesecake from water bath. Let cool on a wire rack and remove outside foil. Cover and refrigerate until chilled, 6 hours or overnight. Just before serving, run a sharp knife around edge of pan to loosen cake and remove springform side of pan.

131   THE PERFECT NEW YORK CHEESECAKE

Prep: 25 minutes   Bake: 1 hour 20 to 22 minutes
Chill: 7 hours   Serves: 16 to 20

This granddaddy of cheesecakes is distinguished by its buttery "wrap-around" lemon cookie crust and ultrarich filling. It is perfect for entertaining—wherever you live.

1   cup flour
2   cups sugar
2   teaspoons grated lemon zest
     Pinch of salt
1   stick (4 ounces) butter,
     softened and cut up
3   large egg yolks, at room
     temperature

5   (8-ounce) packages cream
     cheese, softened
1   teaspoon grated orange zest
1   teaspoon vanilla extract
5   large whole eggs, at room
     temperature
¼   cup heavy cream

1. To prepare crust, in a food processor combine flour, ¼ cup sugar, 1 teaspoon lemon zest, and salt. Process to blend, about 5 seconds. Stop machine; add butter, tossing gently until all pieces are coated with flour. Turn machine quickly on and off until mixture is in coarse crumbs. Add 1 egg yolk. Turn machine on and off 5 or 6 times, just until dough begins to hold together. (It should look coarse and crumbly but feel moist; do not let it mass together in processor.) Turn dough out onto a smooth surface and gather gently into a ball. Divide dough into 2 disks, one slightly larger than the other. Cover with plastic wrap and refrigerate 1 hour.

2. Preheat oven to 400°F. Roll smaller piece of dough between 2 sheets of lightly floured wax paper into a 9-inch circle. Remove top piece of paper and invert into well-greased bottom of a 9-inch springform pan. Remove remaining paper and press gently into pan. (Keep remaining dough refrigerated.) Bake 8 to 10 minutes, or until golden. Let cool completely on a wire rack.

3. Increase oven temperature to 500°F. In a large bowl, beat cream cheese with an electric mixer on medium-high speed until light and fluffy, about 2 minutes. Gradually beat in remaining 1¾ cups sugar and continue beating until completely smooth. Reduce speed to medium and beat in remaining 1 teaspoon lemon zest, orange zest, and vanilla. Add remaining 2 egg yolks, then whole eggs, 1 at a time, beating just until blended after each addition. Blend in cream.

4. Grease springform side of pan. Working with 1 tablespoon of remaining dough at a time, with lightly floured fingers, press dough around side of pan to form a ¼-inch-thick crust. Pour filling into prepared crust.

5. Bake 12 minutes. Reduce oven temperature to 200°F. Bake 60 minutes longer. Turn oven off and let cheesecake remain in oven with door ajar 30 minutes. Transfer cheesecake to a wire rack and let cool completely. Cover and refrigerate until chilled, 6 hours or overnight. Just before serving, run a sharp knife around edge of pan to loosen cake and remove springform side of pan.

132   MALTED MARBLE CHEESECAKE
Prep: 15 minutes   Bake: 1 hour 20 to 25 minutes
Chill: 6 hours   Serves: 12

Come celebrate your favorite soda fountain flavor with each creamy bite of this festive cheesecake. It will be a guaranteed winner for big and little kids alike.

1 cup chocolate cream
    sandwich cookie crumbs
1 cup plus 2 tablespoons
    sugar
3 tablespoons butter, melted
4 (8-ounce) packages cream
    cheese, softened
1 cup instant malted milk
    powder

2 teaspoons vanilla extract
4 large eggs, at room
    temperature
½ cup heavy cream
2 ounces semisweet
    chocolate, melted and
    cooled slightly

1. Preheat oven to 350°F. To prepare crust, in a medium bowl combine cookie crumbs and 2 tablespoons sugar. Gradually work in melted butter until crumbs are evenly moistened. Press into bottom of a well-greased 9-inch springform pan. Tightly cover outside of pan with a double thickness of aluminum foil. Bake until edges are lightly browned, about 10 minutes. Let cool completely on a wire rack.

2. In a large bowl, beat cream cheese with an electric mixer on medium-high speed until light and fluffy, about 2 minutes. Gradually beat in remaining 1 cup sugar, then blend in malted milk powder and vanilla until completely smooth. Add eggs, 1 at a time, beating just until blended after each addition. On low speed, beat in cream just until blended.

3. In a medium bowl, beat 2 cups batter and melted semisweet chocolate with an electric mixer on low speed until smooth. Turn remaining white batter into prepared crust and place in larger baking pan. Carefully spoon chocolate mixture over batter in pan. With a knife, swirl chocolate through white batter to marbleize.

4. Place nested pans on an oven rack. Pour enough hot water into larger pan to reach 1 inch up sides of springform pan. Bake 70 to 75 minutes, or until cake barely jiggles in center.

5. Remove cheesecake from water bath. Let cool completely on a wire rack and remove outside foil. Cover and refrigerate until chilled, 6 hours or overnight. Just before serving, run a sharp knife around edge of pan to loosen cake and remove springform side of pan.

133 FRESH STRAWBERRY-GLAZED MARZIPAN CHEESECAKE

Prep: 20 minutes   Bake: 1 hour 30 to 37 minutes
Chill: 7 hours   Serves: 12

A whipped almond paste filling gives fruit-topped cheesecake an extra-special flavor. This almond-flavored cake can also be served without the topping, accompanied by fresh sliced peaches, raspberries, or blueberries.

½ cup slivered blanched
   almonds
1 cup vanilla wafer cookie
   crumbs
2 tablespoons packed brown
   sugar
3 tablespoons butter, melted
3 (8-ounce) packages cream
   cheese, softened
½ cup almond paste

¾ cup granulated sugar
   Pinch of salt
1 cup sour cream
1 teaspoon grated lemon zest
½ teaspoon vanilla extract
6 large eggs, at room
   temperature
   Fresh Strawberry Glaze
   (page 105)
1½ pints fresh strawberries

1. Preheat oven to 350°F. To prepare crust, arrange almonds on a small cookie sheet. Bake 5 to 7 minutes, or until lightly toasted and fragrant. Let cool, then finely chop. Leave oven on. In a medium bowl, combine vanilla cookie crumbs, chopped almonds, and brown sugar. Gradually work in melted butter until crumbs are evenly moistened. Press into bottom and 1 inch up sides of a well-greased 9-inch springform pan. Tightly cover outside of pan with a double thickness of aluminum foil. Bake until edges are lightly browned, about 10 minutes. Let cool completely on a wire rack.

2. Reduce oven temperature to 325°F. In a large bowl, beat together cream cheese and almond paste with an electric mixer on medium-high speed until light and fluffy and completely smooth, about 5 minutes. Gradually beat in granulated sugar, 1 tablespoon at a time. Reduce speed to medium and beat in salt, sour cream, lemon zest, and vanilla. Add eggs, 1 at a time, beating just until blended after each addition. Turn filling into prepared crust in pan.

3. Place cheesecake in larger baking pan and place on an oven rack. Carefully pour enough hot water into larger pan to reach 1 inch up sides of springform pan. Bake 1 hour 15 to 20 minutes, or until cake barely jiggles in center.

4. Remove cheesecake from water bath. Let cool completely on a wire rack and remove outside foil. Cover and refrigerate until well chilled, 6 hours or overnight. Run a sharp knife around edge of pan to loosen cake and remove springform side of pan. About 1 hour before serving, arrange fresh strawberries pointed ends up on top of cheesecake. Brush berries with strawberry glaze, allowing excess to drip down sides of cake. Refrigerate 1 hour, or until glaze is set.

134   FRESH STRAWBERRY GLAZE
Prep: 5 minutes   Cook: 6 minutes
Makes: Topping for one 9-inch cheesecake

1 cup sliced fresh strawberries
¼ cup sugar
1 tablespoon fresh lemon
   juice

2 teaspoons cornstarch

1. In a small saucepan, combine sliced berries, sugar, and lemon juice. Cover and simmer over low heat 5 minutes.

2. In a small cup, dissolve cornstarch in 1 tablespoon water. Stir into simmering berries and cook uncovered, stirring occasionally, until thickened, about 1 minute.

3. Place strawberry mixture in a sieve set over a bowl. Strain, pressing against solids with back of a spoon. Discard solids and reserve clear glaze in bowl. Let glaze cool.

135   CRANBERRY TOPPING
Prep: 5 minutes   Cook: 11 to 12 minutes
Makes: Topping for one 9-inch cheesecake

1 cup sugar
1 (12-ounce) package fresh or
   thawed frozen
   cranberries

2 tablespoons cornstarch
½ teaspoon grated orange zest
1 tablespoon butter

1. In a medium nonreactive saucepan, combine sugar and ½ cup water. Bring to boil, reduce heat to medium, and simmer 5 minutes. Add cranberries, return to a simmer, and cook until berries begin to pop, 2 to 3 minutes. With a slotted spoon, skim off berries and remove to bowl. Boil liquid 3 minutes longer, or until syrup is slightly reduced.

2. In a small bowl, blend cornstarch with ¼ cup water until smooth. Stir into cranberry liquid. Add orange zest and return to a simmer. Cook, stirring occasionally, until thickened, about 1 minute. Remove from heat, stir in butter until melted, then gently stir in cranberries. Let cool completely before using as a topping.

136 CRANBERRY-GLAZED PUMPKIN SPICE CHEESECAKE

Prep: 20 minutes   Bake: 1 hour 25 to 30 minutes
Chill: 7 hours   Serves: 12

Here's the perfect do-ahead dessert for the holidays. The sweet and spicy cheesecake filling tastes just right when paired with its tart ruby-red cranberry topping.

1   cup gingersnap cookie
      crumbs
½   cup finely chopped pecans
1   cup plus 2 tablespoons
      packed dark brown sugar
4   tablespoons butter, melted
3   (8-ounce) packages cream
      cheese, softened
½   cup granulated sugar
1½ cups canned solid-pack
      pumpkin

½   cup heavy cream
1   teaspoon vanilla extract
1   teaspoon ground cinnamon
½   teaspoon ground ginger
¼   teaspoon ground allspice
4   large eggs, at room
      temperature
1   tablespoon cornstarch
      Cranberry Topping (page
      105)

1. Preheat oven to 350°F. To prepare crust, in a medium bowl combine gingersnap crumbs, pecans, and 2 tablespoons brown sugar. Gradually work in melted butter until crumbs are evenly moistened. Press into bottom and 1 inch up sides of a well-greased 9-inch springform pan. Tightly cover outside of pan with a double thickness of aluminum foil. Bake until edges are lightly browned, about 10 minutes. Let cool completely on wire rack. Leave oven on.

2. In a large bowl, beat cream cheese with an electric mixer on medium-high speed until light and fluffy, about 2 minutes. Gradually beat in granulated sugar, then remaining 1 cup brown sugar until completely smooth. Reduce speed to medium; beat in pumpkin, cream, vanilla, cinnamon, ginger, and allspice. Add eggs, 1 at a time, beating just until blended after each addition. Beat in cornstarch just until blended.

3. Pour filling into prepared crust in pan and place in a larger baking pan. Place on an oven rack. Carefully pour enough hot water into larger pan to reach 1 inch up sides of springform pan. Bake 75 to 80 minutes, or until cake barely jiggles in center.

4. Remove cheesecake from water bath. Let cool completely on a wire rack and remove outside foil. Cover and refrigerate until chilled, 6 hours or overnight. Run a sharp knife around edge of pan to loosen cake and remove springform side of pan. About 1 hour before serving, arrange Cranberry Topping on cheesecake. Refrigerate 1 hour, or until topping is set.

137   LEMON POPPYSEED CHEESECAKE

Prep: 15 minutes   Bake: 1 hour 15 to 20 minutes
Chill: 6 hours   Serves: 12 to 14

Fresh lemon and poppyseeds are a natural combination in this double layer cheesecake with a classic baked-on sour cream topping.

1 cup graham cracker cookie crumbs	2 tablespoons fresh lemon juice
2 tablespoons packed brown sugar	1½ teaspoons grated lemon zest
3 tablespoons butter, melted	1 teaspoon vanilla extract
3 (8-ounce) packages cream cheese	Pinch of salt
1½ cups plus 3 tablespoons granulated sugar	4 large eggs, at room temperature
2 tablespoons poppyseeds	½ cup heavy cream
	1 cup sour cream

1. Preheat oven to 350°F. To prepare crust, in a medium bowl combine graham cracker crumbs and brown sugar. Gradually work in melted butter until crumbs are evenly moistened. Press into bottom of a well-greased 9-inch springform pan. Tightly cover outside of pan with a double thickness of aluminum foil. Bake until edges are lightly browned, about 10 minutes. Let cool completely on a wire rack.

2. In a large bowl, beat cream cheese with an electric mixer on medium-high speed until light and fluffy, about 2 minutes. Gradually beat in 1½ cups granulated sugar and continue beating until completely smooth. Reduce speed to medium and beat in poppyseeds, lemon juice, lemon zest, vanilla, and salt. Add eggs, 1 at a time, beating just until blended after each addition. Beat in cream just until blended.

3. Pour filling into prepared crust in pan and place in a larger baking pan. Place pan on an oven rack. Carefully pour enough hot water into larger pan to reach 1 inch up sides of springform pan. Bake 60 to 65 minutes, or until cake barely jiggles in center.

4. Meanwhile, in a small bowl, whisk sour cream and remaining 3 tablespoons granulated sugar until smooth. Remove cheesecake from water bath and spread sour cream mixture evenly over top. Return to water bath and bake 5 minutes longer.

5. Remove cheesecake from water bath. Let cool completely on a wire rack and remove outside foil. Cover and refrigerate until chilled, 6 hours or overnight. Just before serving, run a sharp knife around edge of pan to loosen cake and remove springform side of pan.

138   HEAVENLY HAZELNUT CHEESECAKE
Prep: 20 minutes   Bake: 1 hour 38 to 55 minutes
Chill: 6½ hours   Serves: 16

Here's a totally sumptuous cream cheese and hazelnut filling sandwiched between a cocoa and nut crust and a velvety chocolate glaze.

1½ cups hazelnuts	2 tablespoons Frangelico or
1½ cups plus 6 tablespoons	other hazelnut-flavored
sugar	liqueur
¾ cup flour	1 teaspoon vanilla extract
3 tablespoons unsweetened	4 large eggs, at room
cocoa powder	temperature
6 tablespoons butter,	½ cup heavy cream
softened, cut up	Chocolate Glaze (page 109)
4 (8-ounce) packages cream	
cheese, softened	

1. Preheat oven to 350°F. To prepare crust, arrange hazelnuts on a small cookie sheet. Bake 10 to 15 minutes, or until nuts are lightly browned and dark skins are cracked. Leave oven on. Rub warm nuts in a terrycloth towel to remove as much of skins as possible. Let cool. In a food processor, finely grind ½ cup of nuts with 6 tablespoons sugar. Add flour and cocoa powder and process to blend. Add butter and pulse 4 to 5 times, until mixture resembles fine crumbs. Press into bottom of a well-greased 10-inch springform pan. Bake 18 to 20 minutes, or until crust is lightly colored and dry. Let cool completely on a wire rack. Tightly cover outside of pan with a double thickness of aluminum foil.

2. In a clean food processor bowl, process remaining 1 cup hazelnuts and ¼ cup sugar until finely ground.

3. In a large bowl, beat cream cheese with an electric mixer on medium-high speed until light and fluffy, 2 minutes. Gradually beat in remaining 1¼ cups sugar and continue beating until completely smooth. Reduce speed to medium and beat in hazelnut liqueur and vanilla. Add eggs, 1 at a time, beating just until blended after each addition. On low speed, beat in heavy cream just until blended. With a rubber spatula, fold in ground hazelnuts.

4. Pour filling into prepared crust in pan and place in larger baking pan. Place pan on an oven rack. Carefully pour enough hot water into larger pan to reach 1 inch up sides of springform pan. Bake 75 to 80 minutes, or until cake barely jiggles in center.

5. Remove cheesecake from water bath. Let cool completely on a wire rack and remove outside foil. Cover and refrigerate until chilled, 6 hours or overnight. About 30 minutes before serving, run a sharp knife around edge of pan to loosen cheesecake and remove springform side of pan. Spread top with Chocolate Glaze and refrigerate 30 minutes, or until glaze is set.

139   CHOCOLATE GLAZE
Prep: 5 minutes   Cook: 2 to 3 minutes   Makes: about ¾ cup

½ cup heavy cream
4 ounces semisweet or
   bittersweet chocolate,
   finely chopped

½ teaspoon vanilla extract

In a small saucepan, heat cream over medium-high heat until small bubbles appear around sides of pan, 2 to 3 minutes. Remove from heat. Whisk in chocolate and vanilla until smooth. Let cool to room temperature.

140   PRALINE BUTTERMILK CHEESECAKE
*Prep: 15 minutes   Bake: 1 hour 30 to 32 minutes   Chill: 6 hours
Serves: 16*

½ cup pecans
1 cup zwieback cookie
   crumbs
2 tablespoons granulated
   sugar
½ teaspoon cinnamon
4 tablespoons butter, melted
3 (8-ounce) packages cream
   cheese, softened

1½ cups packed brown sugar
   Praline Pecan Brittle (page
   261)
1½ teaspoons vanilla extract
   Pinch of salt
4 large eggs, at room
   temperature
¾ cup buttermilk
2 tablespoons flour

1. Preheat oven to 350°F. To prepare crust, arrange pecans on a small cookie sheet. Bake 5 to 7 minutes, or until lightly toasted and fragrant. Let cool, then finely chop. Leave oven on. In a medium bowl, combine zwieback crumbs, pecans, granulated sugar, and cinnamon. Gradually work in melted butter until crumbs are evenly moistened. Press into bottom and ½ inch up sides of a well-greased 9-inch springform pan. Tightly cover outside of pan with a double thickness of aluminum foil. Bake until edges are lightly browned, about 10 minutes. Let cool completely on a wire rack.

2. In a large bowl, beat cream cheese with an electric mixer on medium-high speed until light and fluffy, about 2 minutes. Gradually beat in brown sugar and continue beating until completely smooth. Reduce speed to medium and beat in Praline Pecan Brittle, vanilla, and salt. Add eggs, 1 at a time, beating just until blended after each addition. Beat in buttermilk, then flour until just blended.

3. Pour filling into prepared crust in pan and place in a larger baking pan. Place pan on an oven rack. Carefully pour enough hot water into larger pan to reach 1 inch up sides of springform pan. Bake 75 minutes, or until cake barely jiggles in center.

4. Remove cheesecake from water bath. Let cool completely on a wire rack and remove outside foil. Cover and refrigerate until chilled, 6 hours or overnight. Just before serving, run a sharp knife around edge of pan to loosen cake and remove springform side of pan.

141 CHOCOLATE RICOTTA CHEESECAKE
Prep: 15 minutes   Bake: 2 hours 10 minutes   Chill: 6 hours
Serves: 12 to 14

1½ cups chocolate wafer cookie
     crumbs
4   tablespoons butter, melted
6   ounces semisweet or
     bittersweet chocolate, cut
     up
1   teaspoon instant espresso
     powder
8   large eggs, at room
     temperature

1¾ cups sugar
2   teaspoons vanilla extract
     Pinch of salt
1   (3-pound) container whole-
     milk ricotta cheese
⅓ cup unsweetened cocoa
     powder
     Whipped cream and
     chocolate shavings

1. Preheat oven to 350°F. To prepare crust, in a medium bowl combine chocolate crumbs and melted butter until crumbs are evenly moistened. Press into bottom and 1 inch up sides of a well-greased 9-inch springform pan. Tightly cover outside of pan with a double thickness of aluminum foil. Bake until edges are lightly browned, about 10 minutes. Let cool completely on a wire rack. Leave oven on.

2. In a small glass bowl, microwave chocolate on Medium 2½ to 3 minutes, or until melted. Whisk in espresso powder until chocolate is smooth and espresso is dissolved. Let cool.

3. In a large bowl, whisk together eggs, sugar, vanilla, and salt until blended. Whisk in melted chocolate mixture to blend. In a food processor, puree ricotta, scraping down sides of bowl, until very smooth. Add cocoa powder to ricotta and process until blended. Whisk ricotta mixture into egg mixture until blended.

4. Pour filling into prepared crust in pan and place in a larger baking pan. Place pan on an oven rack. Carefully pour enough hot water into larger pan to reach 1 inch up sides of springform pan. Bake 2 hours, or until cake barely jiggles in center. Turn oven off. Let cheesecake cool in oven with door ajar 30 minutes.

5. Remove cheesecake from water bath. Let cool completely on a wire rack and remove outside foil. Cover and refrigerate until chilled, 6 hours or overnight. Just before serving, run a sharp knife around edge of pan to loosen cake and remove springform side of pan. Decorate top with whipped cream and chocolate shavings.

142   SWEET POTATO SPICE CHEESECAKE

Prep: 20 minutes   Bake: 1 hour 25 minutes   Chill: 6 hours
Serves: 12

Here's another holiday cheesecake. Canned solid-pack pumpkin can be substituted for the cooked mashed sweet potato.

1 cup gingersnap cookie crumbs	1 teaspoon grated orange zest
½ cup finely chopped pecans	Pinch of salt
2 tablespoons packed brown sugar	4 large eggs, at room temperature
4 tablespoons butter, melted	2 tablespoons flour
3 (8-ounce) packages cream cheese, softened	1 cup mashed cooked sweet potatoes, cooled
1½ cups granulated sugar	¾ teaspoon cinnamon
1 cup sour cream	½ teaspoon ground ginger
2 teaspoons vanilla extract	Pinch of ground cloves

1. Preheat oven to 350°F. To prepare crust, in a medium bowl combine gingersnap crumbs, pecans, and brown sugar. Gradually work in melted butter until crumbs are evenly moistened. Press into bottom of a well-greased 9-inch springform pan. Tightly cover outside of pan with a double thickness of aluminum foil. Bake until edges are lightly browned, about 10 minutes. Let cool completely on a wire rack. Leave oven on.

2. In a large bowl, beat cream cheese with an electric mixer on medium-high speed until light and fluffy, about 2 minutes. Gradually beat in granulated sugar and continue beating until completely smooth. Reduce speed to medium and beat in sour cream, vanilla, orange zest, and salt. On low speed, add eggs, 1 at a time, beating just until blended after each addition. Beat in flour.

3. In a small bowl, whisk 2 cups cream cheese mixture with sweet potatoes, cinnamon, ginger, and cloves until smooth. Turn remaining cream cheese mixture into prepared crust in pan and place in a larger baking pan. Drop sweet potato mixture in heaping tablespoons over filling in pan, swirling knife through batters to marbleize. Place pan on an oven rack. Carefully pour enough hot water into larger pan to reach 1 inch up sides of springform pan. Bake 1¼ hours, or until cake barely jiggles in center.

4. Remove cheesecake from water bath. Let cool completely on a wire rack and remove outside foil. Cover and refrigerate until chilled, 6 hours or overnight. Just before serving, run a sharp knife around edge of pan to loosen cake and remove springform side of pan.

143 CHOCOLATE TURTLE CHEESECAKE
Prep: 20 minutes   Cook: 5½ to 8 minutes
Bake: 1 hour 25 to 32 minutes   Chill: 6 hours   Serves: 16

1½ cups pecans
1½ cups graham cracker cookie
   crumbs
3 tablespoons packed brown
   sugar
½ teaspoon cinnamon
4 tablespoons butter, melted
12 ounces semisweet or
   bittersweet chocolate, cut
   up

⅓ cup hot brewed coffee
1 (14-ounce) package caramels
½ cup heavy cream
3 (8-ounce) packages cream
   cheese, softened
1 cup granulated sugar
4 large eggs, at room
   temperature
1 cup sour cream
1 teaspoon vanilla extract

1. Preheat oven to 350°F. To prepare crust, arrange pecans on a small cookie sheet. Bake 5 to 7 minutes, or until lightly toasted and fragrant. Let cool and finely chop. Leave oven on.

2. In a medium bowl, combine graham cracker crumbs, brown sugar, and cinnamon. Gradually work in melted butter until crumbs are evenly moistened. Press into bottom and 1 inch up sides of a well-greased 10-inch springform pan. Tightly cover outside of pan with a double thickness of aluminum foil. Bake until edges are lightly browned, about 10 minutes. Let cool completely on a wire rack.

3. In a small glass bowl, combine chocolate and coffee. Microwave on Medium 2½ to 3 minutes, or until chocolate is softened. Whisk chocolate and coffee together until smooth. Let cool.

4. In a large skillet, combine caramels and cream. Cook over medium-low heat, stirring often, until caramels are melted and mixture is smooth, 3 to 5 minutes. Pour into prepared crust. Sprinkle pecans on top and let cool.

5. In a large bowl, beat cream cheese with an electric mixer on medium-high speed until light and fluffy, about 2 minutes. Gradually beat in granulated sugar and continue beating until completely smooth. Reduce speed to medium and add eggs, 1 at a time, beating just until blended after each addition. On low speed, beat in chocolate mixture, then sour cream and vanilla until just blended.

6. Pour cheese filling over caramel pecan layer in pan and place in a larger baking pan. Place pan on an oven rack. Carefully pour enough hot water into larger pan to reach 1 inch up side of springform pan. Bake 70 to 75 minutes, or until cake barely jiggles in center.

7. Remove cheesecake from water bath. Let cool completely on a wire rack and remove outside foil. Cover and refrigerate until chilled, 6 hours or overnight. Just before serving, run a sharp knife around edge of pan to loosen cake and remove springform side of pan.

144   HONEY-NUT CRUNCH CHEESECAKE

Prep: 15 minutes   Bake: 1 hour 20 to 27 minutes
Chill: 6 hours   Serves: 12

Here's a smooth as satin but not too sweet honey filling. It's simply perfect with this walnut crust.

1½ cups walnuts
2 whole graham cracker
    cookies
¼ cup packed brown sugar
½ teaspoon cinnamon
4 tablespoons butter, melted
4 (8-ounce) packages cream
    cheese, softened
⅓ cup granulated sugar

¾ cup honey
½ cup sour cream
4 large eggs, at room
    temperature
1 tablespoon fresh lemon
    juice
1 teaspoon grated lemon zest
1 teaspoon grated orange zest
1 teaspoon vanilla extract

1. Preheat oven to 350°F. To prepare crust, arrange walnuts on a small cookie sheet. Bake 5 to 7 minutes, or until lightly toasted and fragrant. Let cool. Leave oven on. In a food processor, combine nuts with graham crackers, brown sugar, and cinnamon. Pulse 3 to 4 times, until mixture resembles coarse crumbs. Add melted butter and pulse until just combined and crumbs are medium fine. Press into bottom of a well-greased 9-inch springform pan and refrigerate while preparing filling.

2. In a large bowl, beat cream cheese with an electric mixer on medium-high speed until light and fluffy, about 2 minutes. Gradually beat in granulated sugar and continue beating until completely smooth. Reduce speed to medium and beat in honey and sour cream. Add eggs, 1 at a time, beating just until blended after each addition. On low speed, beat in lemon juice, lemon zest, orange zest, and vanilla.

3. Tightly cover outside of springform pan with a double thickness of aluminum foil. Pour filling into prepared crust in pan and place in a larger baking pan. Place pan on an oven rack. Carefully pour enough hot water into larger pan to reach 1 inch up sides of springform pan. Bake 75 to 80 minutes, or until cake barely jiggles in center.

4. Remove cheesecake from water bath. Let cool completely on a wire rack and remove outside foil. Cover and refrigerate until chilled, 6 hours or overnight. Just before serving, run a sharp knife around edge of pan to loosen cake and remove springform side of pan.

145 NO-BAKE MOCHA CHIP CHEESECAKE

Prep: 15 minutes   Freeze: 20 minutes   Cook: 4 minutes
Chill: 6 hours   Serves: 12

Keep your cool with this creamy coffee cheesecake. For a more sophisticated touch, substitute an equal amount of grated bittersweet chocolate for the miniature semisweet chocolate chips.

5 tablespoons butter, melted
2 tablespoons unsweetened
   cocoa powder
¾ cup plus 2 tablespoons
   sugar
1 tablespoon plus ½ teaspoon
   instant coffee powder
1½ cups vanilla wafer cookie
   crumbs
2 tablespoons coffee-flavored
   liqueur

1 (¼-ounce) envelope
   unflavored gelatin
3 large eggs, separated, at
   room temperature
1 cup half-and-half
1 teaspoon vanilla extract
2 (8-ounce) packages cream
   cheese, softened
½ cup miniature semisweet
   chocolate chips

1. To prepare crust, in a medium bowl stir melted butter, cocoa powder, 2 tablespoons sugar, and ½ teaspoon instant coffee powder until smooth. Stir in vanilla cookie crumbs until evenly moistened. Press into bottom of a 9-inch springform pan. Freeze crust while preparing filling.

2. In a cup, combine coffee liqueur and 2 tablespoons water. Sprinkle gelatin over top and let stand 5 minutes to soften. In a small heavy saucepan, whisk together egg yolks and remaining 1 tablespoon instant coffee; whisk in half-and-half until smooth. Cook over medium-low heat, stirring constantly, until coffee is dissolved and mixture thickens slightly and coats the back of a spoon, about 4 minutes. Remove from heat. Stir in softened gelatin mixture and vanilla until completely dissolved, about 2 minutes.

3. In a large bowl, beat cream cheese with an electric mixer on medium-high speed until light and fluffy, about 2 minutes. Gradually beat in ½ cup sugar and continue beating until completely smooth. Reduce speed to medium and beat in coffee mixture. Transfer to a large bowl and place in a larger bowl filled with ice water. Cool, stirring occasionally, until mixture mounds slightly when dropped from a spoon, about 15 minutes. (Or refrigerate, stirring occasionally, until partially set, 30 to 40 minutes.)

4. Meanwhile, in a large clean bowl, beat egg whites with an electric mixer with clean beaters to soft peaks. Gradually beat in remaining ¼ cup sugar until stiff peaks form. Remove gelatin mixture from ice water. With a rubber spatula, fold in beaten whites until blended, then gently fold in chocolate chips. Turn filling into prepared crust.

5. Cover and refrigerate until cheesecake is set, 6 hours or overnight. Just before serving, run a sharp knife around edge of pan to loosen cake and remove springform side of pan.

146 OLD-FASHIONED BLUEBERRY RIPPLE CHEESECAKE

Prep: 15 minutes   Bake: 1 hour 5 to 10 minutes
Chill: 6 hours   Serves: 12

This cheesecake is a summery treat, wonderful with extra fresh berries and sweetened whipped cream.

1 cup fresh or thawed frozen
  blueberries
2 tablespoons granulated
  sugar
1 teaspoon cornstarch
⅛ teaspoon cinnamon
2 tablespoons plus 2
  teaspoons fresh lemon
  juice
1 cup graham cracker crumbs
2 tablespoons packed brown
  sugar

3 tablespoons butter, melted
3 (8-ounce) packages cream
  cheese, softened
1 (14-ounce) can sweetened
  condensed milk
1 teaspoon grated lemon zest
1 teaspoon vanilla extract
3 large eggs, at room
  temperature

1. In a medium nonreactive saucepan, combine blueberries, granulated sugar, cornstarch, and cinnamon. Bring to boil over medium heat, stirring; boil 1 minute. Transfer to a blender or food processor and puree with 2 teaspoons lemon juice until smooth. Let cool.

2. Preheat oven to 350°F. To prepare crust, in a medium bowl, combine graham cracker crumbs and brown sugar. Gradually work in melted butter until crumbs are evenly moistened. Press into bottom of a greased 9-inch springform pan. Bake until edges are lightly browned, about 10 minutes. Let cool completely on a wire rack.

3. Reduce oven temperature to 300°F. In a large bowl, beat cream cheese with an electric mixer on medium-high speed until light and fluffy, about 2 minutes. Gradually beat in condensed milk and remaining 2 tablespoons lemon juice, lemon zest, and vanilla until completely smooth. Reduce speed to medium and add eggs, 1 at a time, beating just until blended after each addition.

4. Pour batter into prepared crust. Carefully drizzle blueberry puree over batter. Swirl knife through batter to marbleize. Bake 55 to 60 minutes, or until cake barely jiggles in center.

5. Let cool completely on a wire rack. Cover and refrigerate 6 hours or overnight. Just before serving, run a sharp knife around edge of pan to loosen cake and remove springform side of pan.

147 CINNAMON-APPLE CHEESECAKE
Prep: 15 minutes   Bake: 1 hour 30 to 35 minutes
Chill: 7 hours   Serves: 12

¾ cup cinnamon graham
  cracker cookie crumbs
¼ cup finely chopped walnuts
1 tablespoon firmly packed
  brown sugar
2 tablespoons butter, melted
1 cup cream-style cottage
  cheese
2 (8-ounce) packages cream
  cheese, softened
1¼ cups granulated sugar

1 tablespoon fresh lemon
  juice
½ teaspoon grated lemon zest
1 teaspoon vanilla extract
¼ teaspoon cinnamon
  Pinch of salt
4 large eggs, at room
  temperature
1 cup sour cream
  Cinnamon Red-Hot Apple
  Topping (page 117)

1. Preheat oven to 350°F. To prepare crust, in a medium bowl combine graham cracker crumbs, walnuts, and brown sugar. Gradually work in melted butter until crumbs are evenly moistened. Press into bottom of a well-greased 8-inch springform pan. Tightly cover outside of pan with a double thickness of aluminum foil. Bake until edges are lightly browned, about 10 minutes. Let cool completely on a wire rack.

2. In a food processor, puree cottage cheese until smooth. In a large bowl, beat cream cheese with an electric mixer on medium-high speed until light and fluffy, about 2 minutes. Gradually beat in granulated sugar and continue beating until completely smooth. Reduce speed to medium and beat in pureed cottage cheese, lemon juice, lemon zest, vanilla, cinnamon, and salt. Add eggs, 1 at a time, beating just until blended after each addition. Beat in sour cream just until smooth.

3. Pour filling into prepared crust in pan and place in a larger baking pan. Place pan on an oven rack. Carefully pour enough hot water into larger pan to reach 1 inch up side of springform pan. Bake 80 to 85 minutes, or until cake barely jiggles in center.

4. Remove cheesecake from water bath. Let cool completely on a wire rack and remove outside foil. Cover and refrigerate until chilled, 6 hours or overnight. Run a sharp knife around edge of pan to loosen cake and remove springform side of pan. About 1 hour before serving, arrange Cinnamon Red-Hot Apple Topping on cheesecake. Refrigerate 1 hour longer, or until topping is set.

148 CINNAMON RED-HOT APPLE TOPPING

Prep: 10 minutes   Cook: 11 minutes   Makes: Topping for one 8-inch cheesecake

3 peeled Golden or Red
   Delicious apples, cut into
   8 wedges each
2 tablespoons tiny red
   cinnamon candies
   (red-hots)

1 teaspoon fresh lemon juice
2 tablespoons butter
2 tablespoons packed brown
   sugar

1. In a medium bowl, toss apples with cinnamon candies and lemon juice.

2. In a large skillet, melt butter over medium-low heat. Stir in brown sugar, then apple mixture. Cook, stirring occasionally, until apples are tender and candies are melted, about 10 minutes. With a slotted spoon, transfer apples to a bowl; reserve syrup remaining in pan. Boil syrup 1 minute longer, or until slightly thickened. Let apples and syrup cool separately.

3. Starting along outside edge, arrange apples on top of cheesecake in concentric circles. Brush reserved syrup over fruit.

Chapter 6

All Cakes Light and Beautiful

Light, lighter, lightest—here are the cakes that
defy the laws of gravity. Soft and tender, these sponge, chiffon, roulade, and angel food cakes need only a wisp of air and
beaten eggs to rise to magnificent heights. They can be a bit
indulgent—roulades filled with flavored whipped cream or a
rich lemon curd, or frosted chiffon cakes packed with chocolate chips or coconut. But the beauty of these light cakes is that
they're just as special served unadorned. Angel food cake is
the best cake offering that is naturally low in fat and cholesterol. Yet served simply with a dusting of sugar and fresh berries, it still looks and feels sumptuous.

Briefly defined, sponge cakes contain no solid fat,
such as butter, have less flour than butter cakes, and are prepared with whole eggs. Roulades are sponge cakes baked in
shallow jelly-roll pans, then rolled up with a filling of whipped
cream, ice cream, or jam. Chiffon cakes have a similar composition to sponge cakes but they contain oil, which makes them
especially rich and moist. Angel food cakes are the lightest
cakes of all; they are prepared strictly with egg whites only
and no added fat. Because of their delicacy, these cakes should
be sliced with a long serrated knife using a gentle seesawing
action.

The main thing all these cakes have in common is
that much of their volume relies on properly beaten egg
whites. This is best accomplished with an electric mixer. Recipes in this chapter are written with a range of time for beating
the egg whites, keeping in mind that when using hand-held
models, beating whites will take a bit longer. Whether your
mixer is hand-held or standing, be sure to use the whisk
attachment for preparing these air-raised cakes. Here are
some other pointers to keep in mind when beating egg whites:

1. Always have your whites at room temperature;
they will whip up to a greater volume. It is easier to separate
the eggs when they are chilled. After making sure there are no
traces of egg yolk, let the whites stand at room temperature for
about 30 minutes before beating.

2. Make sure your bowl and electric beaters are
completely clean.

3. To build the strongest foundation, always
begin beating the egg whites at medium-low speed (or low
speed on a hand-held mixer). When the whites are foamy, salt
or cream of tartar can be added as a stabilizer.

4. Gradually increase the mixer speed to medium
and continue to beat until the whites form soft peaks when the

beaters are lifted. At this point, the whites are very moist and still somewhat translucent. At this stage sugar can be added, very gradually, sprinkled over the whites 1 tablespoon at a time.

5. Continue to beat at either medium or medium-high speed (or high speed on a hand-held mixer) until very firm peaks form when the beaters are lifted. The whites should appear white and glossy, moist and smooth. The ridges in the bowl will be well defined, and the peaks will stand straight up when tested with a spatula. Be careful not to overbeat the egg whites at this stage, or they will become dry, tighten, and form lumps when incorporated into the batter, which will cause the cake to deflate.

Sponge cakes rely on beaten egg yolks as well, whipped with sugar until light and thickened. It's important to start with the yolks at room temperature, then beat on high speed until thick and lemon colored. Gradually beat in the sugar and continue to beat until the mixture is pale and thick. It should form a ribbon, falling back on itself in the mixing bowl when the beaters are lifted.

Folding the beaten egg whites and dry ingredients together is the second critical technique when preparing these light cakes. To fold dry ingredients, always sift them first to aerate and eliminate any lumps. Start with a small amount of the ingredient you want to fold, one-quarter or one-third of the whites or flour mixture, and sift or spoon on top of the batter. Use a rubber spatula and gently cut through the center of the two mixtures, reaching down to the bottom of the mixing bowl; then twist the spatula slightly and bring it up along the side of the bowl. Repeat this process, giving the bowl a quarter turn with each fold, until the mixtures are just blended. Once the batter is assembled it starts to lose volume, so immediately spoon into the prepared pan and bake.

Angel food cakes, chiffon cakes, and many sponge cakes are baked in ungreased tube pans. The dry surface enables the batter to rise and cling to the sides of the pan as it bakes for maximum volume. The tube in the pan's center allows heat to penetrate the middle of the cake for even baking. Many of these cakes are cooled upside down to prevent shrinking. If your tube pan has metal feet or the inner tube is higher than the rim, simply invert directly on the countertop. Otherwise, immediately invert the tube over the neck of a bottle or inverted metal funnel. Allow the cake to cool completely before removing it from the pan. These cakes can be suspended overnight and once turned out, they can be wrapped and stored at room temperature for several days.

Now it's time to let your handy mixer do the work and whip up the easiest sky-high cakes imaginable. Start with a Classic Angel Food Cake or flavor it with chocolate, hazelnuts, spicy whole wheat, or a lemony glaze. Chiffon cakes are here in new and delightful flavors: Banana Poppyseed, tropical Coconut Colada, spiked with rum, and Mocha Marble, with a fudgy mocha glaze. Fragrant with fresh lime, Lovely Lime Daffodil Cake is an old-fashioned blend of angel food and yellow sponge batter. And get the sponge cake rolling with a Mexican Chocolate Cream Roll or Lemon-Coconut Roulade.

149 SPICED WHOLE WHEAT ANGEL CAKE
Prep: 25 minutes   Bake: 40 to 45 minutes   Stand: 30 minutes
Serves: 12

Whole wheat flour adds a nutty touch to this light spice cake.

½ cup cake flour
½ cup whole wheat flour
1½ cups sugar
1 teaspoon cinnamon
   Pinch of ground allspice
12 large egg whites, at room
   temperature

1½ teaspoons cream of tartar
½ teaspoon salt
1 teaspoon grated orange zest
   Fresh Orange Glaze (recipe
   follows)

1. Preheat oven to 375°F. Sift together cake flour, whole wheat flour, ¾ cup sugar, cinnamon, and allspice 3 times.

2. In a large bowl, beat egg whites with an electric mixer on medium-low speed until foamy, 2 to 3 minutes. Increase speed to medium and add cream of tartar and salt. Gradually add remaining ¾ cup sugar, 1 tablespoon at a time, beating well after each addition. When all sugar is incorporated, continue beating on medium speed until mixture holds very firm peaks when beaters are lifted, 3 to 5 minutes longer. (Do not overbeat.) Beat in orange zest.

3. Sift ⅓ of flour mixture over whites; carefully fold in with a rubber spatula. Repeat twice more with remaining flour just until blended. Turn batter into an ungreased 10-inch tube pan. Gently run a knife through batter to remove any large air pockets.

4. Bake 40 to 45 minutes, until top of cake springs back when pressed with fingertip. Immediately invert pan onto a funnel or bottle. Let cool completely. To loosen, run metal spatula or knife around sides of pan and tube. Invert to unmold. Turn cake right side up. Spread Fresh Orange Glaze over top. Let stand 30 minutes, or until glaze hardens.

FRESH ORANGE GLAZE
Makes: ⅓ cup

1 cup sifted powdered sugar
¼ teaspoon grated orange zest

1 to 2 tablespoons fresh
   orange juice

In a small bowl, whisk together sugar, orange zest, and 1 tablespoon orange juice. Add remaining 1 tablespoon orange juice as needed to make a thick glaze.

150 HAZELNUT PRALINE ANGEL FOOD CAKE

Prep: 20 minutes   Bake: 50 to 60 minutes   Serves: 12

Golden flecked, with a delicate crunch, angel food cake doesn't get any sweeter than this. Feel free to substitute blanched slivered almonds and almond liqueur for the hazelnuts.

⅓ cup hazelnuts	1 tablespoon Frangelico or
1¾ cups sugar	other hazelnut liqueur
1 cup cake flour	1 teaspoon vanilla extract
12 large egg whites, at room	1½ teaspoons cream of tartar
temperature	½ teaspoon salt

1. Preheat oven to 375°F. To prepare praline, arrange hazelnuts on a small cookie sheet. Bake 10 to 15 minutes, or until nuts are lightly browned and dark skins are cracked. Rub warm nuts in a terrycloth towel to remove as much of skins as possible. Let cool. Line a cookie sheet with foil and oil lightly. In a small saucepan, cook ¼ cup sugar over medium heat, swirling pan occasionally, until sugar melts and turns a deep amber color, about 5 minutes. (Do not stir.) Add hazelnuts and swirl pan to coat nuts. Immediately pour hot mixture onto prepared cookie sheet. Let cool completely. Peel off foil, transfer praline to a food processor, and process until finely ground.

2. Sift together cake flour and ¾ cup sugar 3 times. In a large bowl, beat egg whites with an electric mixer on medium-low speed until foamy, 2 to 3 minutes. Increase speed to medium and add liqueur, vanilla, cream of tartar, and salt. Gradually add remaining ¾ cup sugar, 1 tablespoon at a time, beating well after each addition. When all sugar is incorporated, continue beating on medium speed until mixture holds very firm peaks when beaters are lifted, 3 to 5 minutes longer. (Do not overbeat.)

3. Sift ⅓ of flour mixture over whites; carefully fold in with a rubber spatula. Repeat twice more with remaining flour just until blended, then fold in hazelnut praline. Turn batter into an ungreased 10-inch tube pan. Gently run a knife through batter to remove any large air pockets.

4. Bake 40 to 45 minutes, or until top of cake springs back when pressed with fingertip. Immediately invert pan onto a funnel or bottle. Let cool completely. To loosen, run metal spatula or knife around sides of pan and tube. Invert to unmold. Turn cake right side up.

151 BLACK AND WHITE ANGEL CLOUD CAKE
Prep: 30 minutes   Bake: 40 to 45 minutes   Serves: 12

¾ cup plus 2 tablespoons cake flour
1½ cups granulated sugar
3 tablespoons unsweetened cocoa powder
2 tablespoons powdered sugar

12 large egg whites, at room temperature
2 teaspoons vanilla extract
1½ teaspoons cream of tartar
½ teaspoon salt
1 ounce semisweet or bittersweet chocolate, grated

1. Preheat oven to 375°F. In a medium bowl, sift together cake flour and ¾ cup granulated sugar 3 times. In another bowl, sift together cocoa powder and powdered sugar.

2. In a large bowl, beat egg whites with an electric mixer on medium-low speed until foamy, 2 to 3 minutes. Increase speed to medium and add vanilla, cream of tartar, and salt. Gradually add remaining ¾ cup granulated sugar, 1 tablespoon at a time, beating well after each addition. When all sugar is incorporated, continue beating on medium speed until mixture holds very firm peaks when beaters are lifted, 3 to 5 minutes longer. (Do not overbeat.)

3. Sift ⅓ of the sifted cake flour-granulated sugar mixture over beaten egg whites; carefully fold in with a rubber spatula. Repeat twice more with remaining flour just until blended. Turn half of batter into another bowl. Sift cocoa mixture over top and carefully fold with a spatula until just blended. Fold in grated chocolate.

4. Scoop 3 large spoonfuls of remaining white batter 2 inches apart in an ungreased 10-inch tube pan. Place 3 large spoonfuls chocolate batter in between white batter scoops. Gently run a knife through batters to remove any large air pockets.

5. Bake 40 to 45 minutes, or until top of cake springs back when pressed with fingertip. Immediately invert pan onto a funnel or bottle. Let cool completely. To loosen, run metal spatula or knife around sides of pan and tube. Invert to unmold. Turn cake right side up.

152 COCONUT COLADA CHIFFON CAKE
Prep: 25 minutes   Bake: 1 hour 10 to 15 minutes   Serves: 12

For a real party dessert, dress up this cake even more with a scoop of vanilla ice cream and hot fudge sauce on each serving.

2 cups cake flour	½ cup cream of coconut
1¼ cups sugar	¼ cup dark rum
1 tablespoon baking powder	1 teaspoon vanilla extract
1 teaspoon salt	1 cup flaked coconut
5 large egg yolks, at room temperature	8 large egg whites, at room temperature
½ cup vegetable oil	½ teaspoon cream of tartar

1. Preheat oven to 325°F. In a large bowl, sift together cake flour, sugar, baking powder, and salt. With back of a spoon or a measuring cup, make a wide well in center of flour mixture.

2. In a medium bowl, whisk together egg yolks, oil, cream of coconut, rum, and vanilla until smooth. Stir in coconut. Pour into center of flour mixture. Gradually whisk liquid ingredients into flour until blended.

3. In a large bowl, beat egg whites with an electric mixer on medium speed until foamy. Add cream of tartar. Gradually increasing speed to medium-high, continue beating until whites are stiff but not dry, 3 to 4 minutes. With a rubber spatula, gently fold ⅓ of whites into coconut mixture. Repeat twice more with remaining whites until just blended. Turn batter into an ungreased 10-inch tube pan.

4. Bake 1 hour 10 to 15 minutes, or until a cake tester inserted halfway between tube and side of pan comes out clean and cake springs back when touched gently. Immediately invert pan onto a funnel or bottle. Let cool completely. To loosen, run a metal spatula or knife around sides of pan and tube. Invert to unmold. Turn cake right side up.

153 CLASSIC ANGEL FOOD CAKE
Prep: 25 minutes   Bake: 40 to 45 minutes   Serves: 12

Here is the ultimate air-raised cake. The secret to success: Take your time and gradually beat the egg whites and sugar on medium speed for the most tender crumb ever.

1 cup cake flour	1½ teaspoons vanilla extract
1½ cups sugar	½ teaspoon almond extract
12 large egg whites, at room temperature	1½ teaspoons cream of tartar
	½ teaspoon salt

1. Preheat oven to 375°F. Sift together cake flour and ¾ cup sugar 3 times.

2. In a large bowl, beat egg whites with an electric mixer on medium-low speed until foamy, 2 to 3 minutes. Increase speed to medium and add vanilla, almond extract, cream of tartar, and salt. Gradually add remaining

¾ cup sugar, 1 tablespoon at a time, beating well after each addition. When all sugar is incorporated, continue beating on medium speed until mixture holds very firm peaks when beaters are lifted, 3 to 5 minutes longer. (Do not overbeat.)

3. Sift ⅓ of flour mixture over whites; carefully fold in with a rubber spatula. Repeat twice more with remaining flour just until blended. Turn batter into an ungreased 10-inch tube pan. Gently run a knife through batter to remove any large air pockets.

4. Bake 40 to 45 minutes, or until top of cake springs back when pressed with fingertip. Immediately invert pan onto a funnel or bottle. Let cool completely. To loosen, run metal spatula or knife around sides of pan and tube. Invert to unmold. Turn cake right side up.

154   BANANA POPPYSEED CHIFFON CAKE
Prep: 25 minutes   Bake: 60 to 65 minutes   Serves: 12

Moist, ripe bananas are a natural flavor for chiffon cake, and poppyseeds add an unexpected crunch.

2 cups cake flour	1 cup ripe mashed bananas
¾ cup packed dark brown sugar	5 large egg yolks, at room temperature
½ cup plus 2 tablespoons granulated sugar	½ cup vegetable oil
1 tablespoon baking powder	1 teaspoon vanilla extract
1 teaspoon salt	8 large egg whites, at room temperature
¼ teaspoon mace	½ teaspoon cream of tartar
2 tablespoons poppyseeds	

1. Preheat oven to 325°F. In a large bowl, sift together cake flour, brown sugar, ½ cup granulated sugar, baking powder, salt, and mace. Stir in poppyseeds. With back of a spoon or a measuring cup, make a wide well in center.

2. In a medium bowl, whisk together bananas, egg yolks, vegetable oil, and vanilla. Pour into center of flour mixture. Gradually whisk liquid ingredients into flour until smooth.

3. In a large bowl, beat egg whites with an electric mixer on medium speed until foamy. Add cream of tartar and beat until soft peaks form. Gradually add remaining 2 tablespoons sugar and continue to beat on medium speed until whites are stiff but not dry, 3 to 4 minutes. With a rubber spatula, gently fold ⅓ of whites into banana mixture. Repeat twice more with remaining whites until just blended. Turn batter into an ungreased 10-inch tube pan.

4. Bake 60 to 65 minutes, or until a cake tester inserted halfway between tube and side of pan comes out clean and cake springs back when touched gently. Immediately invert pan onto a funnel or bottle. Let cool completely. To loosen, run metal spatula or knife around sides of pan and tube. Invert to unmold. Turn cake right side up.

155   CITRUS LIGHT CHIFFON CAKE
Prep: 25 minutes   Bake: 55 to 60 minutes
Stand: 30 minutes   Serves: 12

Here's the ultimate chiffon cake, extra-tall and packed with citrus flavor. Olive oil adds to its distinctive taste. For a low-cholesterol version, simply omit the egg yolks.

2 cups cake flour
1⅓ cups plus 3 tablespoons sugar
1 tablespoon baking powder
1 teaspoon salt
5 large egg yolks, at room temperature
¾ cup fresh orange juice
½ cup olive oil
2 tablespoons fresh lemon juice

1 tablespoon grated orange zest
2 teaspoons grated lemon zest
12 large egg whites, at room temperature
½ teaspoon cream of tartar
Golden Citrus Glaze (recipe follows)

1. Preheat oven to 325°F. In a large bowl, sift together cake flour, 1⅓ cups sugar, baking powder, and salt. With back of a spoon or a measuring cup, make a wide well in center of flour mixture.

2. In a medium bowl, whisk together egg yolks, orange juice, oil, lemon juice, orange zest, and lemon zest. Pour into center of flour mixture. Gradually whisk liquid ingredients into flour until smooth.

3. In a large bowl, beat egg whites with an electric mixer on medium speed until foamy. Add cream of tartar and beat until soft peaks form. Gradually add remaining 3 tablespoons sugar and continue to beat at medium speed until whites are stiff but not dry, 6 to 8 minutes. With a rubber spatula, gently fold ⅓ of whites into citrus mixture. Repeat twice more with remaining whites until just blended. Turn batter into an ungreased 10-inch tube pan.

4. Bake 55 to 60 minutes, or until a cake tester inserted halfway between tube and side of pan comes out clean and cake springs back when touched gently. Immediately invert pan onto a funnel or bottle. Let cool completely. To loosen, run a metal spatula or knife around sides of pan and tube. Invert to unmold. Turn cake right side up. Spread top with Golden Citrus Glaze. Let stand 30 minutes, or until glaze hardens.

GOLDEN CITRUS GLAZE
Makes: ⅓ cup

1 cup sifted powdered sugar
1 tablespoon fresh orange juice

1 tablespoon fresh lemon juice
½ teaspoon grated orange zest

In a small bowl, whisk together powdered sugar, orange juice, lemon juice, and orange zest until smooth.

156   GRAPEFRUIT-GINGER GLOW CHIFFON CAKE

Prep: 35 minutes   Bake: 50 to 55 minutes   Stand: 30 minutes
Serves: 12

Use fresh pink grapefruit if it is available. It will give the cake a lovely pale rose hue.

2 cups cake flour	½ cup vegetable oil
1¼ cups sugar	¾ cup fresh grapefruit juice
1 tablespoon baking powder	1 tablespoon grated grapefruit
1 teaspoon salt	zest
1 teaspoon ground ginger	8 large egg whites, at room
¼ teaspoon cinnamon	temperature
5 large egg yolks, at room	½ teaspoon cream of tartar
temperature	Grapefruit Glow Glaze
	(recipe follows)

1. Preheat oven to 325°F. In a large bowl, sift together cake flour, sugar, baking powder, salt, ginger, and cinnamon. With back of a spoon or a measuring cup, make a wide well in center of flour mixture.

2. In a medium bowl, whisk together egg yolks, oil, grapefruit juice, and grapefruit zest. Pour into center of flour mixture. Gradually whisk liquid ingredients into flour until smooth.

3. In a large bowl, beat egg whites with an electric mixer on medium speed until foamy. Add cream of tartar. Increase speed to medium-high and continue beating until whites are stiff but not dry, 3 to 5 minutes. With a rubber spatula, gradually fold grapefruit mixture into beaten whites, pouring in a thin, steady stream. Turn batter into an ungreased 10-inch tube pan.

4. Bake 50 to 55 minutes, or until cake tester inserted halfway between tube and side of pan comes out clean and cake springs back when touched gently. Immediately invert pan onto a funnel or bottle. Let cool completely. To loosen, run a metal spatula or knife around sides of pan and tube. Invert to unmold. Turn cake right side up. Spread top with Grapefruit Glow Glaze. Let stand 30 minutes, or until glaze hardens.

GRAPEFRUIT GLOW GLAZE
Makes: ⅓ cup

1 cup sifted powdered sugar	Pinch of ground ginger
½ teaspoon grated grapefruit	1 to 2 tablespoons fresh
zest	grapefruit juice

In a small bowl, whisk together powdered sugar, grapefruit zest, ginger, and 1 tablespoon grapefruit juice. Add remaining 1 tablespoon juice as needed to make a thick glaze.

157   MOCHA MARBLE CHIFFON CAKE
Prep: 35 minutes   Bake: 1 hour 10 to 15 minutes
Stand: 30 minutes   Serves: 12

2 (1-ounce) squares
  unsweetened chocolate,
  chopped
1⅔ cups plus 2 tablespoons
  sugar
2 cups cake flour
1 tablespoon baking powder
1 teaspoon salt
5 large egg yolks, at room
  temperature

½ cup vegetable oil
½ cup strongly brewed coffee
¼ cup coffee-flavored liqueur
1 teaspoon vanilla extract
8 large egg whites, at room
  temperature
½ teaspoon cream of tartar
  Mocha Fudge Glaze (recipe
  follows)

1. Preheat oven to 325°F. In a medium bowl, combine chocolate, 2 tablespoons sugar, and ¼ cup water. Microwave on Medium 2 to 3 minutes, or until water is hot. Whisk until chocolate is melted and sugar is dissolved. Let cool.

2. In a large bowl, sift together cake flour, remaining 1⅔ cups sugar, baking powder, and salt. With back of a spoon or a measuring cup, make a wide well in center of flour mixture.

3. In a medium bowl, whisk together egg yolks, oil, coffee, coffee liqueur, and vanilla. Pour into center of flour mixture. Gradually whisk liquid ingredients into flour until smooth.

4. In a large bowl, beat egg whites with an electric mixer on medium speed until foamy . Add cream of tartar. Increase speed to medium-high and continue beating until whites are stiff but not dry, 3 to 5 minutes. With a rubber spatula, gradually fold coffee mixture into beaten whites, pouring in a thin, steady stream.

5. Gently fold ⅓ of coffee batter into cooled chocolate mixture. Turn half the remaining coffee batter into an ungreased 10-inch tube pan. Pour half chocolate batter on top, then repeat process with remaining batters. With a long thin knife or metal spatula, swirl gently through batters to marbleize.

6. Bake 1 hour 10 to 15 minutes, or until a cake tester inserted halfway between tube and side of pan comes out clean and cake springs back when touched gently. Immediately invert pan onto a funnel or bottle. Let cool completely. To loosen, run a metal spatula or knife around sides of pan and tube. Invert to unmold. Turn cake right side up. Spread top of cake with Mocha Fudge Glaze. Let stand 30 minutes, or until glaze is set.

MOCHA FUDGE GLAZE
Makes: ¾ cup

⅓ cup heavy cream
2 tablespoons coffee-flavored
   liqueur

4 ounces semisweet
   chocolate, cut into small
   pieces

1. In a small bowl, combine cream and liqueur. Microwave on High 1 minute, or until cream comes to a boil.

2. Add chocolate and let stand 1 minute. Whisk until chocolate is melted and glaze is completely smooth. Let cool slightly.

---

158   APRICOT GOLD CHIFFON CAKE
Prep: 40 minutes   Cook: 10 to 15 minutes
Bake: 70 to 75 minutes   Serves: 12

The rich flavor of moist dried apricots and apricot brandy gives this chiffon cake a deep, almost buttery fruit taste.

½ cup (3 ounces) packed dried
   apricots
¼ cup apricot brandy or
   brandy
2 cups cake flour
1½ cups plus 2 tablespoons
   sugar
1 tablespoon baking powder

1 teaspoon salt
5 large egg yolks, at room
   temperature
½ cup vegetable oil
1 teaspoon vanilla extract
8 large egg whites, at room
   temperature
½ teaspoon cream of tartar

1. In a small saucepan, simmer apricots in 1 cup water until very soft, 10 to 15 minutes. Transfer apricots and liquid to a food processor and puree with brandy until smooth. Let cool. (You should have 1 cup puree.)

2. Preheat oven to 325°F. In a large bowl, sift together cake flour, 1½ cups sugar, baking powder, and salt. With back of a spoon or a measuring cup, make a wide well in center of flour mixture.

3. In a medium bowl, whisk together egg yolks, oil, apricot puree, and vanilla. Pour into center of flour mixture. Gradually whisk liquid ingredients into flour until smooth.

4. In a large bowl, beat egg whites with an electric mixer on medium speed until foamy. Add cream of tartar. Gradually add remaining 2 tablespoons sugar and continue to beat on medium speed until whites are stiff but not dry, 3 to 5 minutes. With a rubber spatula, gently fold ⅓ of whites into apricot mixture. Repeat twice more with remaining whites just until blended. Turn batter into an ungreased 10-inch tube pan.

5. Bake 70 to 75 minutes, or until cake tester inserted halfway between tube and side of pan comes out clean and cake springs back when touched gently. Immediately invert pan onto a funnel or bottle. Let cool completely. To loosen, run a metal spatula or knife around sides of pan and tube. Invert to unmold. Turn cake right side up.

159   RASPBERRY-AMARETTO CHIFFON CAKE
Prep: 25 minutes   Bake: 55 to 60 minutes   Serves: 12

1 (10-ounce) package frozen
   raspberries in syrup,
   thawed
2 cups cake flour
1¼ cups sugar
1 tablespoon baking powder
1 teaspoon salt
5 large egg yolks, at room
   temperature

½ cup vegetable oil
¼ cup amaretto liqueur
½ teaspoon vanilla extract
½ teaspoon almond extract
8 large egg whites, at room
   temperature
½ teaspoon cream of tartar
Raspberry-Amaretto Cream
   (recipe follows)

1. Preheat oven to 325°F. In a blender or food processor, puree raspberries with syrup. Set a fine sieve over a small bowl and strain puree, pressing against solids to remove seeds. Measure out ¾ cup puree. (Reserve remaining ¼ cup puree for Raspberry-Amaretto Cream.)

2. In a large bowl, sift together cake flour, sugar, baking powder, and salt. With back of a spoon or a measuring cup, make a wide well in center of flour mixture.

3. In a medium bowl, whisk together egg yolks, oil, ¾ cup raspberry puree, amaretto, vanilla, and almond extract. Pour into center of flour mixture. Gradually whisk liquid ingredients into flour until smooth.

4. In a large bowl, beat egg whites with an electric mixer on medium speed until foamy. Add cream of tartar. Increase speed to medium-high and continue beating until whites are stiff but not dry, 3 to 5 minutes. With a rubber spatula, gently fold ⅓ of whites into raspberry mixture. Repeat twice more with remaining whites just until blended. Turn batter into an ungreased 10-inch tube pan.

5. Bake 55 to 60 minutes, or until a cake tester inserted halfway between tube and side of pan comes out clean and cake springs back when touched gently. Immediately invert pan onto a funnel or bottle. Let cool completely. To loosen, run a metal spatula or knife around sides of pan and tube. Invert to unmold. Turn cake right side up. Serve with Raspberry-Amaretto Cream.

RASPBERRY-AMARETTO CREAM
Makes: 3 cups

1 cup heavy cream
2 tablespoons powdered
   sugar
2 tablespoons amaretto

¼ cup raspberry puree
   (reserved from Step 1 of
   Raspberry-Amaretto
   Chiffon Cake, above)

In a large bowl, beat cream, powdered sugar, and amaretto with an electric mixer until stiff peaks form. With a rubber spatula, gently fold in raspberry puree.

160 TANGERINE SUNSHINE SPONGE CAKE

Prep: 30 minutes   Bake: 40 to 45 minutes   Serves: 10 to 12

Sweet tangerines star in this fluffy cake and give it a special citrus flavor, but if they are unavailable, fresh oranges work beautifully, too.

8 large eggs, separated, at room temperature	1 cup sifted cake flour
1¼ cups sugar	1 teaspoon cream of tartar
¼ cup fresh tangerine juice	¼ teaspoon salt
1 tablespoon grated tangerine zest	Tangerine Buttercream (recipe follows)

1. Preheat oven to 325°F. In a large bowl, beat egg yolks with an electric mixer on high speed until very thick and lemon colored. Gradually add ¾ cup sugar, 1 tablespoon at a time, beating well after each addition, until mixture is very thick and tripled in volume, about 4 minutes. Reduce speed to medium-low; beat in tangerine juice and zest, then flour, just until blended.

2. In another large bowl, beat egg whites with an electric mixer with clean beaters on medium-low speed until foamy. Increase speed to medium and add cream of tartar and salt. Gradually add remaining ½ cup sugar, 1 table-spoon at a time, beating well after each addition. When all sugar is incorporated, continue beating on medium speed until mixture holds stiff peaks when beaters are lifted, about 3 minutes. (Do not overbeat.) With a rubber spatula, fold ⅓ of whites into tangerine mixture, then fold in remaining whites until well blended. Turn batter into an ungreased 10-inch tube pan.

3. Bake 40 to 45 minutes, or until cake tester inserted halfway between tube and side of pan comes out clean and cake springs back when touched gently. Immediately invert pan onto a funnel or bottle. Let cool completely. To loosen, run metal spatula or knife around sides of pan and tube. Invert pan over a serving plate and remove pan. Frost top and sides of cake with Tangerine Buttercream.

TANGERINE BUTTERCREAM
Makes: 2 cups

1½ sticks (6 ounces) butter, softened	2 teaspoons grated tangerine zest
2¼ cups sifted powdered sugar	
2 to 3 tablespoons fresh tangerine juice	

In a small bowl, beat butter with an electric mixer until smooth and creamy. Gradually beat in 1 cup powdered sugar, 2 tablespoons tangerine juice, and tangerine zest until smooth. Add remaining 1¼ cups sugar and 1 table-spoon juice, then continue to beat until light and fluffy.

161 MEXICAN CHOCOLATE CREAM ROLL
Prep: 45 minutes   Bake: 23 to 27 minutes   Chill: 30 minutes
Serves: 12

The flourless chocolate roll is a light cake classic, and this totally decadent version features the south-of-the-border flavors of coffee, toasted almonds, and cinnamon.

⅓ cup slivered blanched almonds
½ cup plus 2 tablespoons granulated sugar
¼ teaspoon cinnamon
6 ounces semisweet or bittersweet chocolate, cut into small pieces
⅓ cup strongly brewed coffee

6 large eggs, separated, at room temperature
Pinch of salt
2 tablespoons powdered sugar
2 tablespoons unsweetened cocoa powder
Coffee Cream Filling (recipe follows)

1. Preheat oven to 350°F. Spread out almonds on a small baking sheet. Bake 8 to 10 minutes, or until nuts are lightly browned and fragrant. Transfer to a plate and let cool. Transfer to a food processor and process with 2 tablespoons granulated sugar and cinnamon until finely ground.

2. Grease a 10½ x 15½-inch jelly-roll pan and line with wax paper; grease paper. Dust pan with flour; tap out excess.

3. In a small glass bowl, combine chocolate and coffee. Microwave on Medium 1½ to 2 minutes, or until coffee is very hot. Stir until chocolate is melted, then let cool completely.

4. In a large bowl, beat egg yolks with an electric mixer on high speed until thick and lemon colored, 3 minutes. Gradually beat in remaining ½ cup granulated sugar; beat 5 minutes longer, or until pale and thick and tripled in volume. With a rubber spatula, fold in chocolate mixture, then nuts just until blended.

5. In another large bowl, beat egg whites and salt with an electric mixer with clean beaters on medium-low speed until foamy. Increase speed to medium and continue to beat until stiff, about 3 minutes. Gently fold ⅓ of whites into chocolate mixture, then fold in remaining whites. Gently spread batter evenly in prepared pan.

6. Bake 15 to 17 minutes, or until cake is beginning to pull back from sides of pan. Meanwhile, sift powdered sugar and cocoa over a clean kitchen towel. Immediately invert cake onto towel and remove pan. Let cool about 1 hour.

7. Carefully peel wax paper off cake and spread Coffee Cream Filling evenly over top. Using kitchen towel as a guide, roll cake up from one long end and transfer, seam side down, to a serving platter. Refrigerate until filling is firm, at least 30 minutes. Just before serving, dust top of cake with additional cocoa and powdered sugar.

COFFEE CREAM FILLING
Makes: 2 cups

1 teaspoon unflavored gelatin
¼ cup coffee-flavored liqueur
1 cup heavy cream

2 tablespoons powdered
   sugar
1 teaspoon vanilla extract

1. In a small saucepan, sprinkle gelatin over liqueur. Stir gently and let stand 2 minutes to soften. Cook over low heat, stirring constantly, until gelatin is completely dissolved, 2 to 3 minutes. Remove from heat and let cool completely.

2. In a large bowl, beat cream with an electric mixer on medium speed until soft peaks form. Gradually beat in gelatin mixture in a thin, steady stream, then beat in powdered sugar and vanilla. Continue to beat just until firm peaks form. Cover and refrigerate for 1 to 2 hours before using, until set.

---

162 CHOCOLATE-CHOCOLATE CHIP CHIFFON CAKE
Prep: 25 minutes   Bake: 1 hour 25 to 30 minutes   Serves: 12

1½ cups cake flour
1¾ cups sugar
½ cup unsweetened cocoa
   powder
1 tablespoon baking powder
1 teaspoon salt
5 large egg yolks, at room
   temperature

½ cup vegetable oil
2 teaspoons vanilla extract
¾ cup miniature semisweet
   chocolate chips
8 large egg whites, at room
   temperature
½ teaspoon cream of tartar

1. Preheat oven to 325°F. In a large bowl, sift together cake flour, sugar, cocoa powder, baking powder, and salt. With back of a spoon or a measuring cup, make a wide well in center of flour mixture.

2. In a medium bowl, whisk together egg yolks, oil, ¾ cup water, and vanilla. Pour into center of flour mixture. Gradually whisk liquid ingredients into flour until smooth. Stir in ½ cup chocolate chips.

3. In a large bowl, beat egg whites with an electric mixer on medium speed until foamy. Add cream of tartar. Increase speed to medium-high and continue beating until whites are stiff but not dry, 3 to 5 minutes. Gently fold ⅓ of whites into chocolate mixture with a rubber spatula. Repeat twice more with remaining whites just until blended. Turn batter into an ungreased 10-inch tube pan. Sprinkle remaining ¼ cup chocolate chips over top.

4. Bake 1 hour 25 to 30 minutes, or until cake springs back when touched gently. Immediately invert pan onto a funnel or bottle. Let cool completely. To loosen, run metal spatula or knife around sides of pan and tube. Invert to unmold. Turn cake right side up.

163   TOASTED PECAN ROLL WITH SPICED WHIPPED CREAM

Prep: 25 minutes   Bake: 33 to 40 minutes   Serves: 8 to 10

1 cup pecans	1 teaspoon vanilla extract
¾ cup plus 2 tablespoons sugar	Pinch of salt
½ teaspoon baking powder	Powdered sugar
Pinch of ground cloves	Spiced Whipped Cream
6 large eggs, separated, at room temperature	(recipe follows)

1. Preheat oven to 350°F. Spread out pecans on a small baking sheet. Bake 8 to 10 minutes, or until nuts are lightly browned and fragrant. Transfer to a plate and let cool. In a food processor, combine pecans, 2 tablespoons granulated sugar, baking powder, and cloves. Process until very finely ground.

2. Grease a 10½ x 15½-inch jelly-roll pan and line with wax paper; grease paper. Dust pan with flour; tap out excess.

3. In a large bowl, beat egg yolks with an electric mixer on high speed until thick and lemon colored, about 3 minutes. Gradually beat in ½ cup granulated sugar; beat 5 minutes longer, or until pale and thick and tripled in volume. Stir in vanilla and salt. With a rubber spatula, fold in nut mixture until well combined.

4. In another large bowl, beat egg whites with clean beaters on medium-low speed until soft peaks form. Increase speed to medium and gradually add remaining ¼ cup granulated sugar, 1 tablespoon at a time, beating well after each addition. Continue beating on medium speed until mixture holds stiff peaks when beaters are lifted, about 3 minutes. Gently fold ⅓ of whites into pecan mixture, then fold in remaining whites. Gently spread batter evenly in prepared pan.

5. Bake 25 to 30 minutes, or until a cake tester inserted in center comes out clean. Meanwhile, sift powdered sugar lightly over a kitchen towel. Run a knife around sides of pan and immediately invert cake onto towel, remove pan, and carefully peel off wax paper. Roll up cake with towel from a long side. Place seam side down on wire rack. Let cool completely.

6. Just before serving, unroll cake and spread Spiced Whipped Cream evenly over top. Reroll cake and place on a serving platter, seam side down. Dust top with additional powdered sugar.

SPICED WHIPPED CREAM
Makes: 2 cups

1 cup heavy cream
⅓ cup powdered sugar
1 tablespoon brandy or dark rum

½ teaspoon vanilla extract
¼ teaspoon cinnamon

In a large bowl, beat cream with an electric mixer on high speed until soft peaks form. Add powdered sugar, brandy, vanilla, and cinnamon and continue to beat until stiff. Cover and refrigerate for up to 2 hours before serving.

164 LEMON-COCONUT ROULADE
Prep: 35 minutes   Bake: 10 to 12 minutes   Chill: 30 minutes
Serves: 8 to 10

5 large eggs, separated, at room temperature
½ cup plus 2 tablespoons granulated sugar
1 teaspoon vanilla extract
Pinch of salt

½ cup flaked coconut
⅔ cup cake flour
Powdered sugar
½ cup heavy cream
1 cup Classic Lemon Curd (page 217)

1. Preheat oven to 375°F. Grease a 10½ x 15½-inch jelly-roll pan and line with wax paper; grease paper. Dust pan with flour; tap out excess.

2. In a large bowl, beat egg yolks with an electric mixer on high speed until thick and lemon colored, 3 minutes. Gradually beat in ½ cup sugar; beat 3 minutes longer, or until pale and thick and tripled in volume. Reduce speed to low and beat in vanilla and salt. With a rubber spatula, fold in coconut.

3. In another large bowl, beat egg whites with an electric mixer with clean beaters on medium-low speed until soft peaks form. Increase speed to medium and gradually beat in remaining 2 tablespoons sugar; continue to beat to stiff peaks, about 2 minutes. Gently fold ⅓ of whites into coconut mixture. Sift ⅓ cup cake flour over top and gently fold in. Repeat process with another third of whites and remaining ⅓ cup cake flour. Fold in remaining whites until just blended. Gently spread batter evenly in prepared pan.

4. Bake 10 to 12 minutes, or until cake is beginning to pull back from sides of pan. Meanwhile, sift powdered sugar lightly over a kitchen towel. Immediately loosen cake from sides of pan and invert it onto towel. Remove pan and carefully peel off wax paper. Roll up cake with towel from a long side. Place seam side down on wire lack. Let cool completely.

5. In a small bowl, beat cream with an electric mixer until stiff. In a large bowl, whisk 1 cup Classic Lemon Curd to soften, then fold in whipped cream. Unroll cake and spread lemon filling evenly over top. Reroll cake and place on a serving platter, seam side down. Refrigerate 30 minutes. Dust top with additional powdered sugar just before serving.

165 OLD-FASHIONED BLACK RASPBERRY JAM ROLL

Prep: 25 minutes   Bake: 10 to 12 minutes   Serves: 8

This classic sponge roll can host a variety of fillings: your favorite seedless jam, whipped cream, or even softened ice cream.

⅓ cup flour
⅓ cup cornstarch
½ teaspoon salt
5 large eggs, separated, at room temperature
⅛ teaspoon cream of tartar

½ cup granulated sugar
1 teaspoon vanilla extract
Powdered sugar
¾ cup seedless black raspberry jam
Whipped cream

1. Preheat oven to 400°F. Grease a 10½ x 15½-inch jelly-roll pan and line with wax paper; grease paper. Dust pan with flour; tap out excess. Sift together flour, cornstarch, and salt.

2. In a large bowl, beat egg whites with an electric mixer on medium-low speed until foamy. Increase speed to medium and add cream of tartar. Gradually add granulated sugar, 1 tablespoon at a time, beating well after each addition. When all sugar is incorporated, continue beating on medium speed until mixture holds stiff peaks when beaters are lifted, about 2 minutes.

3. In another large bowl, beat egg yolks with an electric mixer on high speed until thick and lemon colored, 2 to 3 minutes. Beat in vanilla. With a rubber spatula, gently fold in beaten egg whites just until blended. Sift flour mixture over top, then fold just to combine. Gently spread batter evenly in prepared pan.

4. Bake 10 to 12 minutes, or until cake is lightly browned on top and center springs back when gently touched. Meanwhile, sift powdered sugar sparingly over a clean kitchen towel. Run a knife around sides of pan and immediately invert cake onto towel, remove pan, and peel off wax paper. Roll up cake with towel from a long side. Let stand 1 minute, then unroll to let steam escape. Reroll with towel and place seam side down on a large wire rack to cool completely.

5. Just before serving, unroll cake and spread jam evenly over cake. Reroll and place on a serving platter, seam side down. Dust top with additional powdered sugar and serve with whipped cream.

166 LOVELY LIME DAFFODIL CAKE
Prep: 35 minutes   Bake: 35 to 40 minutes   Stand: 30 minutes
Serves: 10 to 12

Here's an old-fashioned cake that's a pretty combination of white angel food and golden sponge cake batters. Fresh lime juice and zest add a refreshing new taste.

10 large egg whites	3 to 4 tablespoons fresh lime
½ teaspoon cream of tartar	juice
¼ teaspoon salt	1 tablespoon plus 1 teaspoon
1¼ cups granulated sugar	grated lime zest
1¼ cups sifted cake flour	1 cup sifted powdered sugar
6 large egg yolks	

1. Preheat oven to 350°F. In a large bowl, beat egg whites with an electric mixer on medium-low speed until foamy. Increase speed to medium and add cream of tartar and salt. Gradually add granulated sugar, 1 tablespoon at a time, beating well after each addition, and continue beating on medium speed until mixture holds stiff peaks when beaters are lifted, about 3 minutes.

2. Transfer half of beaten egg whites to a medium bowl. Sift ¾ cup cake flour over top, then fold gently with a rubber spatula until just blended. (Reserve remaining beaten egg whites in original mixing bowl.)

3. In a small bowl, beat egg yolks with an electric mixer on high speed until thick and lemon colored. Stir in 2 tablespoons lime juice and 1 tablespoon lime zest, then sift remaining ½ cup cake flour over top and fold gently in with rubber spatula to blend. Gently fold egg yolk mixture into reserved beaten egg whites. Alternately spoon yellow and white batters into an ungreased 10-inch tube pan. Gently run a knife through batters to remove any large air pockets.

4. Bake 35 to 40 minutes, or until a cake tester inserted halfway between tube and side of pan comes out clean and cake springs back when touched gently. Immediately invert pan onto a funnel or bottle. Let cool completely.

5. To loosen, run a metal spatula or knife around sides of pan and tube. Invert cake onto a serving plate. In a small bowl, whisk powdered sugar with remaining 1 teaspoon lime zest and 1 tablespoon lime juice. Add remaining 1 tablespoon juice as needed to make a thick glaze. Spread glaze over top of cake. Let stand 30 minutes, or until glaze hardens.

167   DEEP CHOCOLATE ANGEL FOOD CAKE
Prep: 25 minutes   Bake: 40 to 45 minutes   Serves: 12

This angel food cake has a double dose of great chocolate flavor, but it loses none of its lightness, thanks to sifted cocoa powder and finely grated chocolate.

⅔ cup cake flour
⅓ cup unsweetened cocoa
    powder
1½ cups sugar
1½ teaspoons instant espresso
    powder
12 large egg whites, at room
    temperature

2 teaspoons vanilla extract
1½ teaspoons cream of tartar
½ teaspoon salt
2 ounces semisweet or
    bittersweet chocolate,
    grated

1. Preheat oven to 375°F. Sift together cake flour, cocoa powder, ¾ cup sugar, and espresso powder 3 times.

2. In a large bowl, beat egg whites with an electric mixer on medium-low speed until foamy, 2 to 3 minutes. Increase speed to medium and add vanilla, cream of tartar, and salt. Gradually add remaining ¾ cup sugar, 1 tablespoon at a time, beating well after each addition. When all sugar is incorporated, continue beating on medium speed until mixture holds very firm peaks when beaters are lifted, 3 to 5 minutes longer. (Do not overbeat.)

3. Sift ⅓ of flour mixture over whites; carefully fold in with a rubber spatula. Repeat twice more with remaining flour just until blended, then gently fold in grated chocolate. Turn batter into an ungreased 10-inch tube pan. Gently run a knife through batter to remove any large air pockets.

4. Bake 40 to 45 minutes, or until top of cake springs back when pressed with fingertip. Immediately invert pan onto a funnel or bottle. Let cool completely. To loosen, run metal spatula or knife around sides of pan and tube. Invert to unmold. Turn cake right side up.

Chapter 7

Shortcut Cakes

How can you beat a cake that's ready to bake in no time flat? What cake can be whipped up simply in one bowl? What cake doesn't need a minute of baking at all? Here's a collection of convenience cakes created with ease in mind, a collection that tackles that age-old problem of what to bake when you want a fabulous tasting cake in a flash.

The best cakes from one bowl can start with a cake mix or can be prepared from scratch. You won't be spending time creaming butter for One-Bowl Chocolate Buttermilk Cake and Applesauce Raisin Cake. Easy as 1-2-3, first the dry ingredients are combined in a bowl, then butter is added until crumbly, finally the liquid ingredients are added to blend and voilà—you've got a great snacking cake.

Quick-as-a-mix cakes can be plain or fancy, and this collection comes up with some new flavor sensations. Some favorites include beautiful bundt cakes for entertaining, such as Whiskey Cream Bundt Cake, Sherried Spice Cake, southern Ambrosia Bundt Cake with orange and coconut, and Shortcut Caraway Seed Cake. Other cakes like Fudgy Candy Bar Cake squares, Speedy Soda Pop Cake packed with citrus, and the all-time favorite Cookies 'n' Cream Bundt Cake are perfect for kids. Take note that some recipes specify that cake mixes without pudding added must be used, so check the box before getting ready to bake.

Lazy Daisy Caramel Cake and Chocolate Date Cake owe their speed to the saucepan. Nana's Lemon Icebox Cake, Chocolate Malted Icebox Cake, and Triple-Layer Macaroon Toffee Ice Cream Cake have prepared cookies and cake as layers, are beautifully do-ahead, and require no baking. Now there's no room left for excuses, so just have fun. With these shortcut recipes at the ready, anytime is the right time to bake a cake!

168 LAZY DAISY CARAMEL CAKE

Prep: 10 minutes   Cook: 2 to 3 minutes   Bake: 27 to 33 minutes
Serves: 9

This hot milk sponge cake is a convenience classic. It packs perfectly in a picnic basket.

½ cup milk
1 tablespoon butter
2 large eggs
1 cup sugar
1 teaspoon vanilla extract

1 cup flour
1 teaspoon baking powder
¼ teaspoon salt
Cinnamon Caramel
   Topping (recipe follows)

1. Preheat oven to 350°F. Grease an 8-inch square baking pan. Dust with flour; tap out excess. In a small saucepan, heat milk and butter over medium-low heat until milk is hot and butter is melted, 2 to 3 minutes.

2. Meanwhile, in a large bowl, beat eggs with an electric mixer on medium-high speed until thick and lemon colored. Gradually beat in sugar and beat until mixture has doubled in volume, about 2 minutes longer. Beat in vanilla.

3. Sift together flour, baking powder, and salt. With mixer on low speed, alternately add flour and hot milk mixture to butter mixture, beginning and ending with flour, and beat just until blended. Turn batter into prepared pan.

4. Bake 25 to 30 minutes, or until a cake tester inserted in center comes out clean. Remove cake from oven and let stand 5 minutes.

5. Preheat broiler. Spread Cinnamon Caramel Topping over top of hot cake. Broil 5 inches from heat until brown and bubbly, 2 to 3 minutes. Let cool completely on a wire rack before serving.

CINNAMON CARAMEL TOPPING
Makes: 1 cup

4 tablespoons butter, cut up
¼ cup heavy cream
½ cup packed dark brown
   sugar

½ teaspoon cinnamon
½ cup flaked coconut
½ cup chopped walnuts

In a small saucepan, combine butter, cream, brown sugar, and cinnamon. Cook over medium heat, stirring, until butter is melted and topping is smooth, 3 to 5 minutes. Stir in coconut and walnuts.

169   CHOCOLATE MALTED ICEBOX CAKE

Prep: 5 minutes   Bake: none   Chill: 4 to 6 hours   Serves: 12

Here's a fun variation on the classic cookies and whipped cream cake we all love.

2 cups heavy cream
1 cup instant malted milk
   powder
¼ cup powdered sugar

1½ teaspoons vanilla extract
1 (8½-ounce) package
   chocolate wafers

1. In a large bowl, beat cream with an electric mixer on medium speed until soft peaks form. Gradually add malted milk powder and powdered sugar. Continue to beat until malted milk powder is dissolved and cream forms stiff peaks when beaters are lifted, about 1 minute longer. Beat in vanilla.

2. Spread one side of each chocolate wafer with malted cream. Make 2 equal stacks of cookies. On a serving plate, arrange stacks on sides, parallel to each other. Frost with remaining cream. Refrigerate until chocolate wafers have softened, 4 to 6 hours. To serve, cut in diagonal slices.

170   CRAZY DEVIL CAKE

Prep: 10 minutes   Bake: 25 to 30 minutes   Serves: 9

A cake that goes by many names—Wacky Cake, Three-Hole Cake, Mixed-Up Cake—this flash-in-the-pan version is extremely rich and fudgy thanks to a dollop of good old sour cream.

1½ cups flour
1 cup sugar
⅓ cup unsweetened cocoa
   powder
1 teaspoon baking soda
¼ teaspoon salt

⅓ cup vegetable oil
2 teaspoons cider vinegar
1½ teaspoons vanilla extract
½ cup sour cream
   Red Devil Icing (page 88) or
   whipped cream

1. Preheat oven to 350°F. Grease an 8-inch square cake pan. Dust with flour; tap out excess.

2. In a medium bowl, combine flour, sugar, cocoa powder, baking soda, and salt; sift into prepared cake pan. Make 3 holes—1 large, 1 medium, and 1 small—in dry ingredients. Add oil to large hole, vinegar to medium hole, and vanilla to small hole. In a small bowl, whisk together sour cream and ½ cup water; pour over all. Stir well with whisk to blend. Scrape down sides of dish with a rubber spatula.

3. Bake 25 to 30 minutes, or until a cake tester inserted in center comes out clean. Let cake cool in pan. Frost top with Red Devil Icing or serve plain with whipped cream.

171 SHORTCUT CARAWAY SEED CAKE
Prep: 10 minutes   Bake: 50 to 55 minutes   Serves: 12

This quick fix from a cake mix has all the elegance of an English pound cake, thanks to a touch of brandy and caraway seeds.

1 (18.25-ounce) package white
   or yellow cake mix
1 cup sour cream
3 large eggs
⅓ cup vegetable oil
2 tablespoons brandy

2 tablespoons fresh lemon
   juice
2 teaspoons caraway seeds
2 teaspoons grated lemon zest
½ teaspoon mace

1. Preheat oven to 350°F. Grease a 10-cup bundt pan. Dust with flour; tap out excess.

2. In a large bowl, combine cake mix, sour cream, eggs, oil, brandy, lemon juice, caraway seeds, lemon zest, and mace. Beat with an electric mixer on low speed to blend. Increase speed to high and beat until batter is completely smooth, about 2 minutes longer. Turn into prepared pan.

3. Bake 50 to 55 minutes, or until a cake tester inserted in center comes out clean. Let cake cool in pan 25 minutes, then unmold onto a wire rack to cool completely.

172 DEVIL-MINT BROWNIE PUDDING CAKE
Prep: 15 minutes   Bake: 30 to 35 minutes   Serves: 6

1 cup flour
½ cup granulated sugar
½ cup unsweetened cocoa
   powder
2 teaspoons baking powder
¼ teaspoon salt
½ cup milk
2 tablespoons butter, melted

1 teaspoon vanilla extract
½ cup mint semisweet
   chocolate chips
½ cup packed brown sugar
½ cup chopped walnuts
1¾ cups boiling water
   Peppermint or vanilla ice
   cream

1. Preheat oven to 350°F. In a large bowl, sift together flour, granulated sugar, ¼ cup cocoa powder, baking powder, and salt. Whisk in milk, melted butter, and vanilla until smooth. Stir in mint chocolate chips. Spread batter in an ungreased 9-inch square glass baking pan.

2. In a medium bowl, mix together brown sugar and remaining ¼ cup cocoa powder; stir in walnuts. Sprinkle over batter in pan. Place pan on oven rack and gently pour boiling water evenly over all.

3. Bake 30 to 35 minutes, or until cake looks firm and begins to pull away from sides of pan. Let cool in pan 10 minutes. Cut into squares and serve warm with sauce from bottom of pan and ice cream.

173   QUICK-MIX SPICED CRUMBLE CAKE
Prep: 15 minutes   Bake: 25 to 30 minutes   Serves: 9

2 cups flour
1 cup packed brown sugar
1 teaspoon cinnamon
½ teaspoon grated nutmeg
½ teaspoon salt
⅛ teaspoon ground cloves

1 stick (4 ounces) butter, cut up
1 cup buttermilk
1 teaspoon baking soda
1 large egg
1 teaspoon vanilla extract

1. Preheat oven to 350°F. Grease a 9-inch square baking pan. Dust with flour; tap out excess.

2. In a medium bowl, sift together flour, brown sugar, cinnamon, nutmeg, salt, and cloves. With pastry blender or 2 knives, cut in butter until mixture resembles fine crumbs. Set aside 1 cup crumb mixture for topping.

3. In a small bowl, whisk together buttermilk and baking soda until soda is dissolved. Whisk in egg and vanilla. Stir into remaining crumb mixture just until blended. (Batter will not be smooth.) Turn batter into prepared pan and sprinkle reserved 1 cup crumbs over top.

4. Bake 25 to 30 minutes, or until a cake tester inserted in center comes out clean. Serve warm or let cool completely on a wire rack.

174   WHISKEY CREAM BUNDT CAKE
Prep: 10 minutes   Bake: 55 to 60 minutes   Serves: 12 to 14

For the best results, bake this one-bowl cake a day ahead to allow the rich liqueur and mocha flavors to develop.

2 cups granulated sugar
1¾ cups flour
¾ cup unsweetened cocoa powder
2 teaspoons baking powder
1 teaspoon baking soda
½ teaspoon salt

2 large eggs
1 cup Irish cream liqueur
1 cup brewed coffee
½ cup vegetable oil
1½ teaspoons vanilla extract
Powdered sugar

1. Preheat oven to 350°F. Grease a 10-cup bundt pan. Dust with flour; tap out excess.

2. In a large bowl, sift together granulated sugar, flour, cocoa powder, baking powder, baking soda, and salt. Beat in eggs, liqueur, coffee, oil, and vanilla with an electric mixer on low speed to blend. Increase speed to medium-high and beat until completely smooth, about 2 minutes longer. Turn into prepared pan.

3. Bake 55 to 60 minutes, or until a cake tester inserted in center comes out clean. Let cake cool in pan 10 minutes, then unmold onto a wire rack to cool completely. Just before serving, sift powdered sugar over top of cake.

175   BLACK MAGIC 1-2-3-4 CAKE
Prep: 15 minutes   Bake: 60 to 65 minutes   Serves: 12

Here's the easiest marble cake ever! Easy as 1-2-3. Step 4 is when the chocolate batter settles into the yellow batter and creates a lovely swirl pattern in each buttery slice.

2 sticks (8 ounces) butter, softened	1 tablespoon baking powder
2 cups sugar	½ teaspoon salt
1½ teaspoons vanilla extract	1 cup milk
4 large eggs, at room temperature	4 ounces semisweet chocolate, melted and cooled
3 cups sifted cake flour	

1. Preheat oven to 350°F. Grease a 10-inch tube pan. Dust with flour; tap out excess.

2. In a large bowl, beat butter with an electric mixer on medium speed until smooth and creamy. Gradually beat in sugar, 1 tablespoon at a time, until very light and fluffy, about 3 minutes. Beat in vanilla. Add eggs, 1 at a time, beating well after each addition.

3. Sift together cake flour, baking powder, and salt. With mixer on low speed, alternately add flour mixture and milk to butter mixture, beginning and ending with flour, and beat just until blended.

4. In a medium bowl, gently fold half (about 3 cups) of batter and melted chocolate together with a rubber spatula until blended. Turn remaining yellow batter into prepared pan; spoon chocolate batter on top.

5. Bake 60 to 65 minutes, or until a cake tester inserted in center comes out clean. Let cake cool in pan 25 minutes, then unmold onto a wire rack to cool completely.

176   SPEEDY SODA POP CAKE
*Prep: 10 minutes   Bake: 55 to 60 minutes   Stand: 30 minutes
Serves: 12*

Lemon-lime soda gives this cake an extra citrusy boost, and no one will ever guess the secret ingredient.

1 (18.25-ounce) package white cake mix	2 tablespoons fresh lemon juice
1 cup plus 2 tablespoons 7-Up or other lemon-lime soda	2 tablespoons fresh lime juice
3 large eggs	1½ teaspoons grated lemon zest
⅓ cup vegetable oil	1½ teaspoons grated lime zest
	1¾ cups sifted powdered sugar

1. Preheat oven to 350°F. Grease a 10-cup bundt pan. Dust with flour; tap out excess.

2. In a large bowl, combine cake mix, 1 cup lemon-lime soda, eggs, oil, lemon juice, lime juice, 1 teaspoon lemon zest, and 1 teaspoon lime zest. Beat with an electric mixer on low speed to blend. Increase speed to high and beat until completely smooth, about 2 minutes longer. Turn into prepared pan.

3. Bake 55 to 60 minutes, or until a cake tester inserted in center comes out clean. Let cake cool in pan 25 minutes, then unmold onto a wire rack to cool completely.

4. In a medium bowl, whisk together powdered sugar, remaining 2 tablespoons soda, and remaining ½ teaspoon each lemon zest and lime zest until smooth. Drizzle over top of cake. Let stand 30 minutes, or until icing hardens.

177 TRIPLE-LAYER MACAROON TOFFEE ICE CREAM CAKE

Prep: 15 minutes   Freeze: 8 hours   Bake: none   Serves: 16 to 20

This ice cream cake has been an all-time favorite of my mother's for entertaining for years. For best flavor, use premium ice cream.

1 (11-ounce) package coconut macaroon cookies, crumbled (4 cups)
1 quart coffee ice cream
Espresso Super Fudge Sauce (page 205) or favorite prepared chocolate sauce

1 quart chocolate ice cream
6 (1.4-ounce) packages chocolate-covered English toffee candy bars (such as Heath Bars), chopped
1 quart vanilla ice cream

1. Press 2 cups macaroon crumbs into bottom of a 10-inch springform pan. Place coffee ice cream in refrigerator to slightly soften, about 20 minutes. Quickly spread over macaroon crust and drizzle 2 tablespoons Espresso Super Fudge Sauce over ice cream. Freeze until firm, about 1 hour.

2. Place chocolate ice cream in refrigerator to slightly soften, about 20 minutes. Quickly spread onto coffee layer and drizzle top with another 2 tablespoons fudge sauce. Sprinkle with remaining 2 cups macaroons and ⅔ cup chopped toffee candy. Freeze 1 hour.

3. Place vanilla ice cream in refrigerator to slightly soften, about 20 minutes. Spread on top of chocolate layer, drizzle on another 2 tablespoons fudge sauce, and sprinkle with remaining toffee candy. Cover top of cake and freeze 6 hours or overnight.

4. To serve, uncover cake and refrigerate 20 minutes. Remove springform side of pan. Serve with remaining Espresso Super Fudge Sauce, warmed if desired.

178   FUDGY CANDY BAR CAKE
Prep: 10 minutes   Bake: 45 to 50 minutes   Serves: 12

There's no candy bar in this dessert, but it is a tribute to my favorite candy bar, which has a rich, gooey caramel center studded with chocolate chips and pecans. No frosting is required for this chocolate treat.

1 (18.25-ounce) package devil's food cake mix	1 (14-ounce) package caramels
1 cup buttermilk	¾ cup heavy cream
3 large eggs	6 ounces (1 cup) semisweet chocolate chips
⅓ cup vegetable oil	1 cup chopped pecans

1. Preheat oven to 350°F. In a large bowl, combine cake mix, buttermilk, eggs, and oil. Beat with an electric mixer on low speed to blend. Increase speed to high and beat until completely smooth, about 2 minutes longer. Turn half of batter (about 2½ cups) into a well-greased 13 x 9-inch baking pan. (Reserve remaining batter in bowl.) Bake 20 minutes.

2. Meanwhile, in a large skillet, combine caramels and cream. Heat over medium-low heat, stirring often, until caramels are melted and mixture is smooth, 8 to 10 minutes.

3. Remove cake and pour caramel mixture over baked cake layer, then sprinkle on chocolate chips and pecans. Spoon remaining batter over top; spread with a spatula to cover caramel filling.

4. Bake 25 to 30 minutes longer, or until cake springs back when lightly touched in center. Let cool completely on a wire rack.

179   BUTTERMILK PECAN CRUNCH CAKE
Prep: 10 minutes   Bake: 50 to 55 minutes   Serves: 24

Here one package of cake mix makes two snacking loaves, tender buttermilk cakes surrounded by a crunchy pecan-praline crust. To serve, cut into thin slices with a serrated knife.

1½ sticks (6 ounces) butter, softened	1 cup buttermilk
1 cup packed brown sugar	3 large eggs
½ cup flour	⅓ cup vegetable oil
2 cups finely chopped pecans	½ teaspoon grated nutmeg
1 (18.25-ounce) package yellow cake mix	

1. Preheat oven to 375°F. In a large bowl, beat together butter and brown sugar with an electric mixer on medium-high speed until light and fluffy, about 2 minutes. Reduce speed to low and beat in flour just until blended. Stir in pecans. Divide crumb mixture in half and spoon into 2 well-greased 9 x 5 x 3-inch loaf pans. With lightly floured fingers, press crumb mixture along bottom and ¾ up sides of each pan, forming an even crust.

2. In a large bowl, combine cake mix, buttermilk, eggs, oil, and nutmeg. Beat with an electric mixer on low speed to blend. Increase speed to high and beat until completely smooth, about 2 minutes longer. Turn into prepared pans.

3. Bake 50 to 55 minutes, or until a cake tester inserted in center comes out clean. Let cakes cool in pans 10 minutes, then carefully loosen cakes from pans with a metal spatula and unmold onto wire racks to cool completely.

180   NANA'S LEMON ICEBOX CAKE
Prep: 15 minutes   Cook: 6 minutes   Chill: 6 hours   Serves: 8 to 10

This cake was a favorite citrus dessert of my friend Jean Galton's grandmother.

1 (¼-ounce) envelope
   unflavored gelatin
5 large eggs, separated, at
   room temperature
1 cup sugar
⅔ cup fresh lemon juice

1 tablespoon grated lemon
   zest
16 ladyfingers, split
½ cup heavy cream
   Whipped cream and fresh
   strawberries

1. In a cup, sprinkle gelatin over ¼ cup water and let stand 5 minutes to soften.

2. In a double boiler, whisk together egg yolks, ¾ cup sugar, lemon juice, and lemon zest. Place over simmering water and cook, stirring often, until mixture thickens slightly and coats back of a spoon, about 6 minutes. Remove from heat and stir in softened gelatin mixture until completely dissolved, about 2 minutes. Transfer to a large bowl and let stand, stirring occasionally, until completely cool. Meanwhile, cover bottom and sides of a 9-inch springform pan with ladyfingers, cut sides in.

3. In a large bowl, beat egg whites with an electric mixer on medium speed until soft peaks form. Gradually add remaining ¼ cup sugar and continue to beat on medium speed until stiff peaks form when beaters are lifted. With a rubber spatula, fold egg whites into lemon mixture until blended.

4. In same mixer bowl, beat ½ cup heavy cream with an electric mixer to soft peaks, then gently fold into lemon mixture. Turn into prepared pan; cover top loosely and refrigerate until set, 6 hours or overnight. Uncover and remove springform side of pan. Decorate top of cake with whipped cream and strawberries.

181 ONE-BOWL APPLESAUCE RAISIN CAKE
Prep: 10 minutes   Bake: 43 to 50 minutes   Serves: 12

Applesauce makes this fast-fix cake very moist. Use the cinnamon-flavored variety for an extra hint of spiciness.

¾ cup chopped walnuts or
   pecans
2 cups flour
1 cup sugar
2 tablespoons unsweetened
   cocoa powder
2 teaspoons baking soda
1½ teaspoons cinnamon
½ teaspoon ground ginger
½ teaspoon grated nutmeg

½ teaspoon salt
   Pinch of ground cloves
1 stick (4 ounces) butter, cut
   up and softened
1 (15-ounce) jar applesauce
2 large eggs
¾ cup raisins
   Maple Whipped Cream
   (page 251)

1. Preheat oven to 350°F. Grease a 13 x 9-inch baking pan. Dust with flour; tap out excess. Arrange nuts on a small cookie sheet. Bake 8 to 10 minutes, or until nuts are lightly browned and fragrant. Transfer to a plate and let cool, then coarsely chop.

2. In a large bowl, sift together flour, sugar, cocoa powder, baking soda, cinnamon, ginger, nutmeg, salt, and cloves. Beat in butter with an electric mixer on low speed until mixture is crumbly. Add applesauce and eggs. Increase speed to medium and beat until smooth, 2 to 3 minutes. Stir in nuts and raisins. Turn batter into prepared pan.

3. Bake 35 to 40 minutes, or until a cake tester inserted in center comes out clean. Let cake cool in pan on a wire rack. Cut into squares and serve with Maple Whipped Cream.

182 TART LEMON PUDDING CAKE
Prep: 10 minutes   Bake: 40 to 45 minutes   Serves: 6

Assembled in minutes, this is a wonderful dessert with fresh strawberries.

1 cup sugar
3 tablespoons flour
⅛ teaspoon salt
⅓ cup fresh lemon juice
3 tablespoons butter, melted

1½ teaspoons grated lemon zest
3 large eggs, separated, at
   room temperature
1¼ cups milk
   Sweetened whipped cream

1. Preheat oven to 350°F. Grease a 1½-quart glass baking dish about 9 inches square. In a medium bowl, sift together ¾ cup sugar with flour and salt. Whisk in lemon juice, melted butter, lemon zest, and egg yolks until well blended. Whisk in milk.

2. In a small bowl, beat egg whites with an electric mixer on high speed until soft peaks form. Gradually add remaining 1/4 cup sugar and continue to beat until stiff. With a rubber spatula, gently fold whites into lemon mixture. Turn batter into prepared dish.

3. Set dish in a larger baking pan and fill outer pan with 1 inch hot water. Bake 40 to 45 minutes, or until top is lightly browned and set. Remove cake from water bath and serve warm or cold with sweetened whipped cream.

183 ONE-BOWL CHOCOLATE BUTTERMILK CAKE

Prep: 10 minutes Bake: 35 to 40 minutes Serves: 12

Here's a cake that's made for a party. Kids will love the chocolate chip icing, but this cake is also delicious served plain.

1 3/4 cups flour
1 1/2 cups sugar
2/3 cup unsweetened cocoa powder
1 teaspoon baking soda
1/2 teaspoon baking powder
1/4 teaspoon salt
1 1/2 sticks (6 ounces) butter, cut up and softened
1 1/2 cups buttermilk
2 large eggs
1 teaspoon vanilla extract
Fluffy Chip Frosting (recipe follows)

1. Preheat oven to 350°F. In a large bowl, sift together flour, sugar, cocoa powder, baking soda, baking powder, and salt. Beat in butter with an electric mixer on low speed until mixture is crumbly. Add buttermilk, eggs, and vanilla. Increase speed to medium and beat until completely smooth, 2 to 3 minutes. Turn into a well-greased 13 x 9-inch baking pan.

2. Bake 35 to 40 minutes, or until a cake tester inserted in center comes out clean. Let cake cool in pan on a wire rack. Frost top with Fluffy Chip Frosting.

184 FLUFFY CHIP FROSTING

Prep: 5 minutes Cook: 3 to 4 minutes Makes: 1 cup

1 large egg white
1/2 cup sugar
1 tablespoon light corn syrup
1/8 teaspoon cream of tartar
1 teaspoon vanilla extract
1/4 cup miniature semisweet chocolate chips

1. In top of a large double boiler over simmering water, combine egg white, sugar, 2 tablespoons water, corn syrup, and cream of tartar. Beat with a hand-held electric mixer on high speed 3 to 4 minutes, or until soft but firm peaks form when beaters are lifted.

2. Remove from heat and beat in vanilla. Continue to beat until icing is very stiff, about 3 minutes longer. With a rubber spatula, fold in chocolate chips.

185 PRALINE PINEAPPLE SHEET CAKE
Prep: 10 minutes   Bake: 40 to 45 minutes   Serves: 12

Here's the easiest version of pineapple upside-down cake ever! It's perfect for a crowd.

1 cup packed brown sugar	1 (8-ounce) can crushed
1 stick (4 ounces) butter, cut	pineapple in juice
up	1 (6-ounce) can unsweetened
⅓ cup heavy cream	pineapple juice
1 cup chopped pecans	3 large eggs
1 (18.25-ounce) package	⅓ cup vegetable oil
yellow cake mix	

1. Preheat oven to 350°F. In a small saucepan, combine brown sugar, butter, and cream. Cook over low heat, stirring, until butter is melted and sugar dissolved, 6 to 8 minutes. Pour into a lightly greased 13 x 9-inch baking pan. Sprinkle chopped pecans evenly over top.

2. In a large bowl, combine cake mix, crushed pineapple, pineapple juice, eggs, and oil. Beat with an electric mixer on low speed to blend. Increase speed to high and beat until completely blended, about 2 minutes longer. Carefully spoon batter over pecan mixture.

3. Bake 40 to 45 minutes, or until a cake tester inserted in center comes out clean. Let cake cool in pan 10 minutes, then unmold onto a wire rack to cool completely.

186 CHOCOLATE DATE CAKE
Prep: 15 minutes   Bake: 30 to 35 minutes   Serves: 12

Dates add moistness to this dark, fudgy cake. The batter is completely prepared in a saucepan.

1 cup whole pitted dates,	¼ cup unsweetened cocoa
coarsely chopped	powder
1 stick (4 ounces) butter, cut	½ teaspoon salt
up	6 ounces (1 cup) semisweet
1 cup sugar	chocolate chips
1 teaspoon baking soda	½ cup chopped walnuts
1 large egg, lightly beaten	Whipped cream or vanilla
1 teaspoon vanilla extract	ice cream
1½ cups flour	

1. Preheat oven to 350°F. In a medium saucepan, bring dates and 1 cup water to a boil over medium heat. Remove from heat. Add butter and sugar and stir until sugar is dissolved and butter is melted, 2 to 3 minutes. Stir in baking soda until dissolved. Blend in egg and vanilla.

2. Sift together flour, cocoa powder, and salt. Stir into date mixture along with ½ cup chocolate chips and the walnuts. Turn into a well-greased 13 x 9-inch baking pan. Sprinkle remaining ½ cup chocolate chips over top.

3. Bake 30 to 35 minutes, or until a cake tester inserted in center of cake comes out barely clean. Let cool completely on a wire rack and serve with whipped cream or ice cream.

187   SHERRIED SPICE CAKE
Prep: 10 minutes   Bake: 45 to 50 minutes   Serves: 12

This recipe is from my dear friend Reva Weinshenker, and it's a favorite cake of her husband, Ray. While still warm, this cake is brushed with a powdered sugar icing, which turns into a lovely translucent glaze when it cools.

4 **large eggs**	1 **(3¼-ounce) package instant**
1 **(18.25-ounce) yellow cake**	**vanilla pudding and pie**
mix (without pudding	**filling mix**
included)	1 **teaspoon grated nutmeg**
¾ **cup dry sherry**	**Sherry-Bourbon Icing**
¾ **cup vegetable oil**	**(recipe follows)**

1. Preheat oven to 350°F. Grease a 10-cup bundt pan. Dust with flour; tap out excess.

2. In a large bowl, beat eggs with an electric mixer on medium speed until foamy and slightly thickened, about 2 minutes. Add cake mix, sherry, oil, pudding mix, and nutmeg. Beat on high speed until completely smooth, about 2 minutes longer. Turn into prepared pan.

3. Bake 45 to 50 minutes, or until a cake tester inserted in center comes out clean. Let cake cool in pan 15 minutes, then unmold onto a wire rack placed over a large sheet of wax paper or foil. Gently prick cake all over with a fork. Gradually brush Sherry-Bourbon Icing all over hot cake until absorbed. Let cool completely.

188   SHERRY-BOURBON ICING
Prep: 5 minutes   Cook: none   Makes: ¾ cup

2 **cups sifted powdered sugar**	2 **tablespoons bourbon**
2 **tablespoons dry sherry**	

In a medium bowl, whisk together powdered sugar, sherry, and bourbon until smooth.

189   QUICK COCOA-OATMEAL CAKE
Prep: 10 minutes   Bake: 35 to 40 minutes   Serves: 12

Here is a cake that is not too sweet and slightly chewy, thanks to the old-fashioned oats.

1⅓ cups boiling water	1½ teaspoons vanilla extract
1 cup old-fashioned rolled oats	1 cup flour
1 teaspoon instant coffee powder	½ cup unsweetened cocoa powder
1 stick (4 ounces) butter, softened	1 teaspoon baking soda
1½ cups sugar	½ teaspoon salt
2 large eggs	6 ounces (1 cup) semisweet chocolate chips

1. In a medium heatproof bowl, pour boiling water over oats. Stir in coffee powder until dissolved. Let cool to lukewarm, about 20 minutes, stirring occasionally.

2. Preheat oven to 350°F. In a large bowl, beat together butter and sugar with an electric mixer on medium speed until smooth and creamy, about 2 minutes. Add eggs, 1 at a time, beating well after each addition. Beat in vanilla, then stir in oat mixture.

3. Sift together flour, cocoa powder, baking soda, and salt. On low speed, add to butter mixture, beating just until blended. Stir in ½ cup chocolate chips. Turn batter into a well-greased 13 x 9-inch baking pan. Sprinkle top evenly with remaining ½ cup chips.

4. Bake 35 to 40 minutes, or until a cake tester inserted in center comes out clean. Let cool completely on a wire rack before serving.

190   AMBROSIA BUNDT CAKE
Prep: 15 minutes   Bake: 60 to 65 minutes   Serves: 12

Inspired by one of the South's favorite desserts, this buttery cake studded with moist coconut features both fresh orange juice and orange zest, the flavorful colored part of the skin.

1 (18.25-ounce) white cake mix (without pudding included)	1 (3¼-ounce) package instant vanilla pudding and pie filling mix
1 cup fresh orange juice	2 teaspoons coconut extract
2 teaspoons grated orange zest	1 cup flaked coconut
4 large eggs	Powdered sugar
⅓ cup vegetable oil	

1. Preheat oven to 350°F. Grease a 10-cup bundt pan. Dust with flour; tap out excess.

2. In a large bowl, combine cake mix, orange juice, orange zest, eggs, oil, pudding mix, and coconut extract. Beat with an electric mixer on low speed to blend. Increase speed to high and beat until completely blended, about 2 minutes longer. Stir in flaked coconut. Turn into prepared pan.

3. Bake 60 to 65 minutes, or until a cake tester inserted in center comes out clean. Let cake cool in pan 25 minutes, then unmold onto a wire rack to cool completely. Dust top with powdered sugar before serving.

191   COOKIES 'N' CREAM BUNDT CAKE
Prep: 10 minutes   Bake: 1 hour 5 to 10 minutes
Stand: 30 minutes   Serves: 12 to 14

All this cake needs is a scoop of cookies 'n' cream ice cream!

1 (18.25-ounce) white or yellow cake mix (without pudding included)
1 cup sour cream
4 large eggs
½ cup vegetable oil
1 (3¼-ounce) package instant vanilla pudding and pie filling mix

14 cream-filled sandwich cookies, coarsely chopped, or 2 cups cream sandwich cookie crumbs
Mocha Fudge Glaze (page 129)

1. Preheat oven to 350°F. Grease a 12-cup bundt pan. Dust with flour; tap out excess.

2. In a large bowl, combine cake mix, sour cream, eggs, oil, pudding mix, and ¼ cup water. Beat with an electric mixer on low speed to blend. Increase speed to high and beat until completely smooth, about 2 minutes longer.

3. Spread ⅓ (2 cups) batter into prepared pan. Sprinkle with half the cookie crumbs (1 cup) and spread with half the remaining batter. Repeat process with remaining filling and batter.

4. Bake 65 to 70 minutes, or until a cake tester inserted in center comes out clean. Let cake cool in pan 25 minutes, then unmold onto rack to cool completely. Drizzle top with Chocolate Fudge Glaze and let stand 30 minutes, or until glaze sets.

192 CHOCOLATE SAUERKRAUT CAKE
Prep: 10 minutes   Bake: 35 to 40 minutes   Serves: 12

Bakers have always kept the sauerkraut a secret ingredient in this old-fashioned chocolate cake. All you'll taste is the rich chocolate flavor enhanced by buttermilk and coffee.

1 **(18.25-ounce) package
 devil's food cake mix**
1 **(8-ounce) can sauerkraut,
 rinsed well, drained, and
 finely chopped**
¾ **cup buttermilk**

½ **cup brewed coffee**
3 **large eggs**
½ **cup vegetable oil**
 **Fluffy Fudge Frosting
 (page 53) or Red Devil
 Icing (page 88)**

1. Preheat oven to 350°F. Grease two 9-inch round cake pans. Line bottoms with wax paper; grease paper. Dust pans with flour; tap out excess.

2. In a large bowl, combine cake mix, sauerkraut, buttermilk, coffee, eggs, and oil. Beat with an electric mixer on low speed to blend. Increase speed to high and beat until completely blended, about 2 minutes longer. Turn batter into prepared pans.

3. Bake 35 to 40 minutes, or until a cake tester inserted in center comes out clean. Let cakes cool in pans 10 minutes, then unmold onto wire racks and remove wax paper. Invert cakes again and let cool completely. Fill and frost cake with Fluffy Fudge Frosting or Red Devil Icing.

Chapter 8

It's All in the Crust

I'm fanatical about homemade pie crusts and love
every step involved in creating them. But when talking about
pie making with both novice and expert cooks, quite often I
hear the lament that crusts can be both daunting and intimidating to make. In some cases this is understandable, because
the composition of the pastry dough is a delicate balance of the
correct blending of fat and flour, the quantity of liquid used,
and the amount the dough is handled. But don't be afraid!
With the aid of a food processor, electric mixer, or hand-held
pastry blender, flaky pie crusts can be assembled in minutes.
Once you master the basic techniques, all of which involve
simple steps, making perfect pastry is possible for everyone.

Mixing the perfect pastry: When blending the fat and
flour, handle no more than necessary. For the beginning pie
crust maker, I would recommend using a hand-held pastry
blender, made of several metal loops attached to a handle. Be
sure to use cold butter or other fats where applicable. After
cutting in the fat, small particles should be visible, evenly
coated with flour. The mixture should feel light and dry, not
greasy. When baked, these bits of fat will melt and steam
within the layers of flour, creating a flaky, tender crust.

For all the pie and tart pastries, I've given a range
of amounts of liquid to incorporate into the dough. Always
make sure your liquid is cold, and if you are using water, chill
it down with a few ice cubes. It's also important to remember
that too much liquid will produce a tough crust, while too little
will cause your crust to be dry and brittle when you roll it out.
The amount of liquid will depend on the moisture content of
the flour and the temperature of the kitchen. Always start
with the minimum amount of liquid and add only enough
more to hold the dough together before forming into a disk.
This pastry disk should feel smooth and pliable, not sticky. If
your dough feels dry and crumbly to the touch after the maximum amount of liquid has been added, add a few drops more
at a time until the desired texture is reached.

Rolling out the perfect pastry: Start with a smooth
working surface: marble, wood, or Formica. Always refrigerate the dough before rolling to chill the particles of fat and prevent them from blending too easily with the flour. If you
refrigerate your pastry longer than 1 hour, though, let it stand
10 to 15 minutes at room temperature before rolling so that it
will be malleable. For best results, do not roll out pastry
directly on the countertop; rather, place the pastry between

two lightly floured sheets of wax paper or plastic wrap or cover your rolling pin with a cotton sock and roll the pastry directly on a floured pastry cloth. In both cases, the pastry will be much easier to rotate and you won't need as much flour for rolling; extra flour can make pastry tough. Start with your rolling pin positioned at the center, then begin to roll away from you toward the outside edge of the pastry disk in all directions. Lift the rolling pin when you reach the outer edge to prevent the rim from becoming too thin. Rotate the dough a quarter turn at a time and repeat, keeping the shape a circle and sprinkling the pastry with a light dusting of flour if it becomes sticky. Be careful not to apply more pressure than is necessary when rolling or fitting the pastry into your pie plate or tart pan, because stretching the dough will cause your pastry to shrink when it is baked.

   Fluting pie pastry: Another part of pie making I love is creating a fluted pie edge. A simple raised pastry flute is functional as well as decorative. It helps prevent the filling from overflowing in a single crust pie and seals the top and bottom crust in a double crust pie. A simple press of fork tines is the easiest edge to execute and best for pies with a shallow filling. Just form an even, raised dough edge around the rim of a pie pan or trim the dough edge even with the edge of the pie pan. Dip the tines of a fork in flour and gently press around the inside edge of the dough. (This can also be done with the rounded side of a spoon.) For a simple scalloped flute, form an even, ¾-inch-high dough edge around the rim of the pie pan. Place your right index finger on the outside of the pie rim. Press the dough in toward the center of the pie pan while pressing out from the center of the pie plate with your left thumb and index finger, to form a V shape. Repeat this process all around the edge of the pie.

   Many single pie crusts in this book use the technique called "blind baking." This technique of partially or fully baking a pie crust before it is filled prevents the crust from slipping or shrinking during baking and makes the bottom crust crisp and flaky. After the bottom of a pastry shell has been pricked and frozen until hard, I line the pastry with a double thickness of foil and weigh it down with metal pie weights, dried beans, or raw rice. Bake as directed until the edges of the pie shell are set. Remove the foil and weights and continue to bake until the crust is golden, keeping the weights, beans, or rice, because they can be used again and again. If the pastry puffs up during baking, prick it again with a fork. After removing your pie shell or a baked pie from the oven, be sure to let it cool completely on a wire rack before filling.

   In a pinch, store-bought pie and crumb crusts can be substituted. For many of the recipes tested, the quantity of pie filling is amply generous. As a rule of thumb, I would recommend purchasing deep-dish size pie shells and following the manufacturer's directions for baking when applicable.

193   FLAKY PASTRY
Prep: 20 minutes   Chill: 1 hour   Makes: 1 single or double 9- or 10-inch pie crust

Here's the never-fail pie pastry all others are judged by. It can easily be prepared by hand, in the food processor, or with an electric mixer.

SINGLE CRUST PIE

1½ cups flour
¼ teaspoon salt
½ cup solid vegetable
    shortening
3 to 4 tablespoons ice water

DOUBLE CRUST PIE

2 cups flour
½ teaspoon salt
¾ cup solid vegetable
    shortening
5 to 6 tablespoons ice water

HAND METHOD: In a medium bowl, combine flour and salt. Add shortening and toss gently until all pieces are coated with flour. With pastry blender or 2 knives, cut in shortening until mixture resembles fine crumbs. Add ice water, 1 tablespoon at a time, drizzling over flour mixture, then tossing vigorously with a fork, just until dough begins to hold together. (It will look coarse and crumbly, but feel moist.) Turn dough out onto a work surface and gather gently into a ball. (For a double crust pie, shape dough into 2 balls, one slightly larger than the other.) Tightly wrap dough in plastic wrap and flatten into 1 or 2 disks. Refrigerate 1 hour or overnight.

FOOD PROCESSOR METHOD: In a food processor, combine flour and salt. Process to blend, about 5 seconds. Add shortening, then turn machine quickly on and off until mixture is in coarse crumbs. Sprinkle top of flour mixture with 1 tablespoon ice water. Turn machine on and off 2 or 3 times. Repeat process with remaining ice water as needed, 1 tablespoon at a time, following each addition of water by 2 quick pulses, just until dough begins to hold together. (Dough will be in fine crumbs and will begin to stick to food processor blade. It will look crumbly, but feel moist.) Turn dough out onto smooth surface and gather gently into a ball. (For a double crust pie, shape dough into 2 balls, one slightly larger than the other.) Tightly wrap dough in plastic wrap and flatten into 1 or 2 disks. Refrigerate 1 hour or overnight.

ELECTRIC MIXER METHOD: In a large bowl, combine flour and salt with an electric mixer paddle attachment on low speed. Blend in shortening until mixture resembles coarse crumbs, about 1 minute. Add ice water, 1 tablespoon at a time, just until dough begins to hold together. (Dough will begin to stick to the mixer paddle. It will look crumbly but feel moist.) Turn dough out onto a work surface and gather gently into a ball. (For a double crust pie, shape dough into 2 balls, one slightly larger than the other.) Tightly wrap dough in plastic wrap and flatten into 1 or 2 disks. Refrigerate 1 hour or overnight.

194 UNBAKED PIE SHELL
Prep: 10 minutes   Bake: none   Makes: one 9- or 10-inch pie shell

Flaky Pastry for a Single
Crust Pie (page 157)

On a lightly floured surface, roll out pastry disk into a ⅛-inch-thick round. Fold in half and ease gently into a 9- or 10-inch pie pan. Unfold dough, letting pastry overhang edge. Trim overhanging pastry to 1 inch. Fold under and flute.

195 PARTIALLY BAKED PIE SHELL
Prep: 10 minutes   Freeze: 20 minutes   Bake: 19 to 20 minutes
Makes: 1 single 9- or 10-inch partially baked pie crust for a single crust
pie

Flaky Pastry for a Single
Crust Pie (page 157)

1. Preheat oven to 425°F. On a lightly floured surface, roll out pastry ⅛ inch thick. Fold in half and ease gently into a 9- or 10-inch pie pan. Unfold dough. Trim overhanging pastry to 1 inch. Fold under and flute. Freeze until firm, about 20 minutes.

2. Tear 2 sheets of aluminum foil slightly larger than pie pan. Press foil, shiny side down, into frozen pie shell, turning back ends of foil to cover fluted pastry edge. Fill pie pan halfway with pie weights, dry beans, or uncooked rice. Bake 12 minutes, until edge of pastry is set and lightly colored. Remove foil and beans. If pastry puffs, prick with a fork. Bake 7 to 8 minutes longer, until crust is dry and just beginning to turn golden. Transfer to a wire rack and let cool completely before filling.

196 FULLY BAKED PIE SHELL
Prep: 10 minutes   Freeze: 20 minutes   Bake: 25 to 27 minutes
Makes: 1 single 9- or 10-inch fully baked crust for a single crust pie

Flaky Pastry for a Single
Crust Pie (page 157)

1. Preheat oven to 425°F. On a lightly floured surface, roll out pastry ⅛ inch thick. Fold in half and ease gently into a 9- or 10-inch pie pan. Unfold dough. Trim overhanging pastry to 1 inch. Fold under and flute. Prick bottom of pie shell with tines of a fork at ½-inch intervals. Freeze until firm, about 20 minutes.

2. Tear 2 sheets of aluminum foil slightly larger than pie pan. Press foil, shiny side down, into frozen pie shell, turning back the ends of foil to cover fluted pastry edge. Fill pie pan halfway with pie weights, dry beans, or uncooked rice. Bake 12 minutes, until edge of pastry is set and lightly colored. Remove foil and beans. (Reserve beans for your next pastry.) Bake 13 to 15 minutes longer, or until bottom and sides of crust are golden brown. Transfer to a wire rack and let cool completely before filling.

197   MOSTLY BUTTER PASTRY

Prep: 10 minutes   Chill: 1 hour
Makes: 1 single or double 9- or 10-inch pie crust

This pastry is the best of both worlds—it's superflaky thanks to the shortening, and boasts the rich buttery flavor we all love.

SINGLE CRUST PIE

- 1½ cups flour
- ¼ teaspoon salt
- 6 tablespoons cold butter, cut up
- 3 tablespoons solid vegetable shortening
- 3 to 4 tablespoons ice water

DOUBLE CRUST PIE

- 2 cups flour
- ½ teaspoon salt
- 1 stick (4 ounces) cold butter, cut up
- 3 tablespoons solid vegetable shortening
- 5 to 6 tablespoons ice water

1. In a medium bowl, combine flour and salt. Add butter and shortening, tossing gently until all pieces are coated with flour. With pastry blender or 2 knives, or in food processor or electric mixer, cut in butter and shortening until mixture resembles fine crumbs. Add ice water, 1 tablespoon at a time, drizzling over flour mixture, then tossing vigorously with a fork or pulsing or beating very briefly, just until dough begins to hold together. (It will look coarse and crumbly, but feel moist.)

2. Turn dough out onto smooth surface and gather gently into a ball. (For a double crust pie, shape dough into 2 balls, one slightly larger than the other.) Tightly wrap dough in plastic wrap and flatten into 1 or 2 disks. Refrigerate 1 hour or overnight.

198   NUTTY GRAHAM CRACKER CRUST

Prep: 10 minutes   Bake: 13 to 17 minutes
Makes: 1 (9-inch) crumb crust

The mellow flavors of graham cracker crumbs and toasted walnuts are a natural combination.

- ½ cup walnuts
- 1 cup graham cracker crumbs
- 2 tablespoons packed brown sugar
- 4 tablespoons butter, melted

1. Preheat oven to 350°F. Arrange walnuts on a small cookie sheet. Bake 5 to 7 minutes, or until lightly toasted and fragrant. Cool and finely chop.

2. In a medium bowl, combine graham cracker crumbs, brown sugar, and nuts. Stir in butter, tossing until mixture is evenly moistened. Press crumb mixture evenly over bottom and sides of a 9-inch pie pan. Bake 8 to 10 minutes, or until crumbs are lightly toasted. Cool completely on a wire rack before filling.

199   OLD-FASHIONED VINEGAR PASTRY

Prep: 20 minutes   Chill: 1 hour
Makes: 1 single or double 9- or 10-inch pie crust

You'd never know by tasting this pastry that there was vinegar in it. It only takes a small amount to give you a very flaky crust.

SINGLE CRUST PIE

1½ cups flour
¼ teaspoon salt
6 tablespoons cold butter, cut up
3 tablespoons solid vegetable shortening
2 teaspoons distilled white vinegar
3 to 4 tablespoons ice water

DOUBLE CRUST PIE

2 cups flour
½ teaspoon salt
1 stick (4 ounces) cold butter, cut up
3 tablespoons solid vegetable shortening
1 tablespoon distilled white vinegar
4 to 5 tablespoons ice water

1. In a medium bowl, combine flour and salt. Add butter and shortening, tossing gently until all pieces are coated with flour. With pastry blender or 2 knives, or in a food processor or electric mixer, cut in butter until mixture resembles fine crumbs.

2. In a cup, combine vinegar with 1 tablespoon ice water. Drizzle over flour mixture and toss with a fork or pulse or beat very briefly. Add remaining ice water, 1 tablespoon at a time, mixing as before, just until dough begins to hold together. (It will look coarse and crumbly, but feel moist.)

3. Turn dough out onto smooth surface and gather gently into a ball. (For a double crust pie, shape dough into 2 balls, one slightly larger than the other.) Tightly wrap dough in plastic wrap and flatten into 1 or 2 disks. Refrigerate 1 hour or overnight.

200   GRAHAM CRACKER CRUMB CRUST

Prep: 10 minutes   Bake: 8 to 10 minutes
Makes: 1 (9-inch) crumb crust

Here's the granddaddy of all crumb crusts, perfect for any custard or chiffon pie.

1½ cups graham cracker crumbs
2 tablespoons sugar

½ teaspoon ground allspice
5 tablespoons butter, melted

Preheat oven to 350°F. In a medium bowl, combine graham cracker crumbs, sugar, and allspice. Stir in butter and toss until mixture is evenly moistened. Press crumb mixture evenly over bottom and sides of a 9-inch pie pan. Bake 8 to 10 minutes, or until crumbs are lightly toasted. Cool completely on a wire rack before filling.

201   CHOCOLATE WAFER CRUST
Prep: 5 minutes   Bake: 8 to 10 minutes   Makes: 1 (9-inch) pie crust

This pie crust loves chocolate fillings of all kinds—custard, chiffon, or ice cream.

1½ cups chocolate wafer cookie crumbs

4 tablespoons butter, melted

Preheat oven to 350°F. In a medium bowl, combine cookie crumbs and butter and toss until mixture is evenly moistened. Press crumb mixture evenly over bottom and sides of a 9-inch pie pan. Bake 8 to 10 minutes, or until crumbs are lightly toasted. Cool completely on a wire rack before filling.

202   FLAKY CITRUS PASTRY
Prep: 15 minutes   Chill: 1 hour
Makes: 1 single or double 9- or 10-inch pie crust

Here's an all-purpose pie pastry that has the subtle flavor of orange, a surefire winner for all your favorite fruit pies.

SINGLE CRUST PIE

1½ cups flour
1 tablespoon sugar
1½ teaspoons grated orange zest
¼ teaspoon salt
½ cup solid vegetable
  shortening
1 tablespoon fresh orange
  juice
2 to 3 tablespoons ice water

DOUBLE CRUST PIE

2 cups flour
2 tablespoons sugar
2 teaspoons grated orange zest
½ teaspoon salt
¾ cup solid vegetable
  shortening
2 tablespoons fresh orange
  juice
3 to 4 tablespoons ice water

1. In a medium bowl, combine flour, sugar, orange zest, and salt. Add shortening, tossing gently until all pieces are coated with flour. With pastry blender or 2 knives, or in a food processor or electric mixer, cut in shortening until mixture resembles fine crumbs. In a cup, combine orange juice with 1 tablespoon ice water. Drizzle over flour mixture and toss with a fork. Add remaining ice water, 1 tablespoon at a time, and toss vigorously with a fork or pulse or beat very briefly, just until dough begins to hold together. (It will look coarse and crumbly, but feel moist.)

2. Turn dough out onto smooth surface and gather gently into a ball. (For a double crust pie, shape dough into 2 balls, one slightly larger than the other.) Tightly wrap dough in plastic wrap and flatten into 1 or 2 disks. Refrigerate 1 hour or overnight.

203   WHOLE WHEAT PASTRY
Prep: 20 minutes   Chill: 1 hour
Makes: 1 single or double 9- or 10-inch pie crust

A blend of whole wheat and all-purpose flours gives this pastry crust a nutty flavor that is wonderful in apple and other fall fruit pies.

SINGLE CRUST PIE

1¼ cups all-purpose flour
¼ cup whole wheat flour
1 tablespoon sugar
¼ teaspoon salt
½ cup solid vegetable
   shortening
3 to 4 tablespoons ice water

DOUBLE CRUST PIE

1⅔ cups all-purpose flour
⅓ cup whole wheat flour
2 tablespoons sugar
½ teaspoon salt
¾ cup solid vegetable
   shortening
5 to 6 tablespoons ice water

1. In a medium bowl, combine all-purpose flour, whole wheat flour, sugar, and salt. Add shortening, tossing gently until all pieces are coated with flour mixture. With pastry blender or 2 knives, or in a food processor or electric mixer, cut in shortening until mixture resembles fine crumbs. Add ice water, 1 tablespoon at a time, drizzling over flour mixture; then toss vigorously with a fork or pulse or beat very briefly, just until dough begins to hold together. (It will look coarse and crumbly, but feel moist.)

2. Turn dough out onto smooth surface and gather gently into a ball. (For a double crust pie, shape dough into 2 balls, one slightly larger than the other.) Tightly wrap dough in plastic wrap and flatten into 1 or 2 disks. Refrigerate 1 hour or overnight.

204   ALMOND-AMARETTI COOKIE CRUST
Prep: 10 minutes   Bake: 13 to 17 minutes
Makes: 1 (9-inch) crumb crust

This sophisticated crumb crust is an elegant and versatile base for cream or fruit pies.

⅓ cup blanched slivered
   almonds
1½ cups (3 ounces) amaretti
   cookies

1 cup premium butter wafer
   or vanilla cookies
⅓ cup butter, melted

1. Preheat oven to 350°F. Arrange almonds on a small cookie sheet. Bake 5 to 7 minutes, or until lightly toasted and fragrant. Cool.

2. In a food processor, process cookies and nuts until finely ground and transfer to a medium bowl. Stir in butter, tossing until mixture is evenly moistened. Press crumb mixture evenly over bottom and sides of a 9-inch pie pan. Bake 8 to 10 minutes, or until crumbs are lightly toasted. Cool completely on a wire rack before filling.

205 BUTTERY VANILLA NUT CRUMB CRUST

Prep: 10 minutes   Bake: 13 to 17 minutes
Makes: 1 (9-inch) pie crust

The addition of toasted nuts gives this crust an extra-rich flavor. Spice things up by adding ½ teaspoon cinnamon to the crumbs.

½ cup pecans or walnuts
1¼ cups premium butter wafer
  or vanilla cookie crumbs

5 tablespoons butter,
  melted

1. Preheat oven to 350°F. Arrange nuts on a small cookie sheet. Bake 5 to 7 minutes, or until lightly toasted and fragrant. Cool and finely chop.

2. In a medium bowl, combine cookie crumbs and nuts. Stir in butter, tossing until mixture is evenly moistened. Press crumb mixture evenly over bottom and sides of a 9-inch pie pan. Bake 8 to 10 minutes, or until crumbs are lightly toasted. Cool completely on a wire rack before filling.

206 SOUR CREAM PASTRY

Prep: 10 minutes   Chill: 1 hour
Makes: 1 single or double 9- or 10-inch pie crust

This pastry is a snap to make. It's rich, tender, and wonderful with berry pie fillings.

SINGLE CRUST PIE

1½ cups flour
¼ teaspoon salt
⅓ cup solid vegetable
  shortening
¼ cup sour cream
3 to 4 tablespoons ice water

DOUBLE CRUST PIE

2 cups flour
½ teaspoon salt
½ cup solid vegetable
  shortening
¼ cup sour cream
5 to 6 tablespoons ice water

1. In a medium bowl, combine flour and salt. Add shortening and sour cream, tossing gently until all pieces are coated with flour. With pastry blender or 2 knives, or in a food processor or electric mixer, cut in shortening until mixture resembles fine crumbs. Add ice water, 1 tablespoon at a time, drizzling over flour mixture; then toss vigorously with a fork or pulse or beat very briefly, just until dough begins to hold together. (It will look coarse and crumbly, but feel moist.)

2. Turn dough out onto smooth surface and gather gently into a ball. (For a double crust pie, shape dough into 2 balls, one slightly larger than the other.) Tightly wrap dough in plastic wrap and flatten into 1 or 2 disks. Refrigerate 1 hour or overnight.

207 CRISPY OIL PASTRY

Prep: 10 minutes   Chill: 1 hour
Makes: 1 (9-inch) single or double pie crust

This "stir-it-up" pastry has two advantages—it's low in cholesterol and can be prepared with any mild-tasting oil—vegetable, canola, or olive.

SINGLE CRUST PIE

1½ **cups flour**
½ **teaspoon sugar**
¼ **teaspoon salt**
⅓ **cup vegetable oil**
2 **to 3 tablespoons ice water**

DOUBLE CRUST PIE

2 **cups flour**
¾ **teaspoon sugar**
½ **teaspoon salt**
½ **cup vegetable oil**
3 **to 4 tablespoons ice water**

1. In a medium bowl, combine flour, sugar, and salt. Gradually add oil, tossing with a fork, until mixture resembles fine crumbs.

2. Add ice water, 1 tablespoon at a time, drizzling over flour mixture, then tossing vigorously with a fork, just until dough begins to hold together. (It will look coarse and crumbly, but feel moist.) Turn dough out onto a smooth surface and gather gently into a ball, then flatten into a round disk. (For double crust pie pastry, shape dough into 2 disks, one slightly larger than the other.) Cover and refrigerate 1 hour or overnight.

SINGLE CRUST PIE:

Between 2 sheets of lightly floured wax paper, roll dough into a 12-inch circle. (Patch any cracks by gently pressing dough together with lightly floured fingers or piecing together with excess dough.) Carefully peel off top sheet wax paper, then gently invert pastry over pie pan and peel off remaining paper. Gently press pastry with fingertips along bottom and up edge of pan; trim and flute edge.

DOUBLE CRUST PIE:

Between 2 sheets of lightly floured wax paper, roll larger piece of dough into a 12-inch circle. (Patch any cracks by gently pressing dough together with lightly floured fingers or piecing together with excess dough.) Peel off top sheet wax paper, then gently invert pastry over pie pan and peel off remaining paper. Gently press pastry with fingertips along bottom and up edge of pan. Trim overhanging edge of pastry ½ inch from rim of pan. Roll smaller pastry disk between 2 sheets of wax paper as directed above into a 10-inch circle. Cut slits for steam into top crust and place over filling in pie plate. Fold and roll top edge under lower edge, pressing to seal. Flute edges.

208 CLASSIC LARD PASTRY
Prep: 10 minutes   Chill: 1 hour
Makes: 1 (9- or 10-inch) single or double pie crust

This old-fashioned pastry is total indulgence. Lard, a high-fat shortening, produces the flakiest of crusts. Be sure the lard has a fresh scent before using and keep any unused portion refrigerated.

SINGLE CRUST PIE

- 1½ cups flour
- ¼ teaspoon salt
- ½ cup chilled lard, cut up
- 1 large egg yolk
- 2 teaspoons distilled white vinegar or fresh lemon juice
- 2 to 3 tablespoons ice water

DOUBLE CRUST PIE

- 2 cups flour
- ½ teaspoon salt
- ¾ cup chilled lard, cut up
- 1 large egg yolk
- 1 tablespoon vinegar or fresh lemon juice
- 4 to 5 tablespoons ice water

1. In a medium bowl, combine flour and salt. Add lard, tossing gently until all pieces are coated with flour. With pastry blender or 2 knives, or in a food processor or electric mixer, cut in lard until mixture resembles fine crumbs.

2. In a cup, beat egg yolk, vinegar, and 1 tablespoon ice water together. Drizzle over flour mixture and toss with a fork. Add remaining ice water, 1 tablespoon at a time, tossing vigorously with a fork or pulsing or beating very briefly, just until dough begins to hold together. (It will look coarse and crumbly, but feel moist.)

3. Turn dough out onto smooth surface and gather gently into a ball. (For a double crust pie, shape dough into 2 balls, one slightly larger than the other.) Tightly wrap dough in plastic wrap and flatten into 1 or 2 disks. Refrigerate 1 hour or overnight.

209 GINGERSNAP CRUMB CRUST
Prep: 10 minutes   Bake: 8 to 10 minutes
Makes: 1 (9-inch) crumb crust

Here's a crumb crust with spice fans in mind.

- 1½ cups gingersnap cookie crumbs
- ⅛ teaspoon cinnamon or ground allspice
- 4 tablespoons butter, melted

Preheat oven to 350°F. In a medium bowl, combine cookie crumbs and allspice. Stir in butter, tossing until mixture is evenly moistened. Press crumb mixture evenly over bottom and sides of a 9-inch pie pan. Bake 8 to 10 minutes, or until crumbs are lightly toasted. Cool completely on a wire rack before filling.

210 CREAM CHEESE PASTRY
Prep: 10 minutes   Chill: 1 hour
Makes: 1 (9- or 10-inch) single or double pie crust

This tender crust is perfect with all fruit pies. Be sure the cream cheese is thoroughly chilled before preparing this pastry.

SINGLE CRUST PIE

1¼ cups flour
¼ teaspoon salt
1 (3-ounce) package cream cheese, cut up
½ cup solid vegetable shortening
2 tablespoons ice water

DOUBLE CRUST PIE

1¾ cups flour
½ teaspoon salt
4 ounces cream cheese, cut up
⅔ cup solid vegetable shortening
2 to 3 tablespoons ice water

1. In medium bowl, combine flour and salt. Add cream cheese and shortening, tossing gently until all pieces are coated with flour. With pastry blender or 2 knives, or in a food processor or electric mixer, cut in cream cheese mixture until mixture resembles fine crumbs. Add ice water, 1 tablespoon at a time, drizzling over flour mixture; then toss vigorously with a fork or pulse or beat very briefly, just until dough begins to hold together. (It will look coarse and crumbly, but feel moist.)

2. Turn dough out onto smooth surface and gather gently into a ball. (For a double crust pie, shape dough into 2 balls, one slightly larger than the other.) Tightly wrap dough in plastic wrap and flatten into 1 or 2 disks. Refrigerate 1 hour or overnight.

211 BUTTERY VANILLA WAFER CRUMB CRUST
Prep: 10 minutes   Bake: 8 to 10 minutes
Makes: 1 (9-inch) pie crust

This delicate crumb crust filled with fresh fruit says springtime.

1½ cups premium butter wafer or vanilla cookie crumbs

4 tablespoons butter, melted

Preheat oven to 350°F. In a medium bowl, combine cookie crumbs and butter and toss until mixture is evenly moistened. Press crumb mixture evenly over bottom and sides of a 9-inch pie pan. Bake 8 to 10 minutes, or until crumbs are lightly toasted. Cool completely on a wire rack before filling.

212   IOWA PRIDE PIE PASTRY MIX
Prep: 10 minutes   Chill: 1 hour   Makes: 8 cups

Here's a recipe for do-ahead pie mix that can be refrigerated up to six weeks! When ready to bake, all you add is ice water, then whip up a home-made crust in no time flat.

6 cups flour
1½ teaspoons salt

2 cups solid vegetable
   shortening

PASTRY MIX:
In a large bowl, combine flour and salt. Add shortening, tossing until all pieces are coated with flour. With pastry blender or 2 knives, cut in shortening until mixture resembles fine crumbs. Transfer to a covered container. Use immediately or refrigerate up to 6 weeks

SINGLE CRUST PIE:
In a large bowl, measure 1¾ cups pastry mix. Add 3 to 4 tablespoons ice water, 1 tablespoon at a time, drizzling over flour mixture, then tossing vigorously with a fork just until dough begins to hold together. (It will look coarse and crumbly, but feel moist.) Turn dough out onto smooth surface and gather gently into a ball. Wrap dough in plastic wrap and flatten into a disk. Refrigerate 1 hour or overnight.

DOUBLE CRUST PIE:
In a large bowl, measure 2¾ cups pastry mix. Add 4 to 5 tablespoons ice water, 1 tablespoon at a time, drizzling over flour mixture, then tossing vigorously with a fork just until dough begins to hold together. (It will look coarse and crumbly, but feel moist.) Turn dough out onto smooth surface and gather gently into 2 balls, one slightly larger than the other. Wrap dough in plastic wrap and flatten into 2 disks. Refrigerate 1 hour or overnight.

213 SUGAR 'N' SPICE PASTRY
Prep: 10 minutes   Chill: 1 hour
Makes: 1 single or double 9- or 10-inch pie crust

Made for apples and pears, this sweet and spicy pie pastry is also perfect with pumpkin, squash, and sweet potato fillings for the holidays.

SINGLE CRUST PIE

1½ cups flour
 3 tablespoons packed brown
    sugar
 ¾ teaspoon cinnamon
 ¼ teaspoon salt
 6 tablespoons cold butter,
    cut up
 3 tablespoons solid vegetable
    shortening
 3 to 4 tablespoons ice water

DOUBLE CRUST PIE

 2 cups flour
 ¼ cup packed brown sugar
 1 teaspoon cinnamon
 ½ teaspoon salt
 1 stick (4 ounces) cold butter,
    cut up
 3 tablespoons solid vegetable
    shortening
 5 to 6 tablespoons ice water

1. In a medium bowl, combine flour, brown sugar, cinnamon, and salt. Add butter and shortening, tossing gently until all pieces are coated with flour. With pastry blender or 2 knives, or in a food processor or electric mixer, cut in butter and shortening until mixture resembles fine crumbs. Add ice water, 1 tablespoon at a time, drizzling over flour mixture; then toss vigorously with a fork or pulse or beat very briefly, just until dough begins to hold together. (It will look coarse and crumbly, but feel moist.)

2. Turn dough out onto smooth surface and gather gently into a ball. (For a double crust pie, shape dough into 2 balls, one slightly larger than the other.) Tightly wrap dough in plastic wrap and flatten into 1 or 2 disks. Refrigerate 1 hour or overnight.

Chapter 9

Farm-Fresh Fruit Pies

For every season there is a fruit, and with all those cherries, berries, apricots, apples, and pears to choose from, baking fresh fruit pies can be a wondrous treat all year long. With this in mind, it's important to remember that more often than not in pie making, you should select fresh fruit when it is ready and ripe—it can make all the difference. Seeking out expensive but flavorless fresh peaches in November simply will not result in the same juicy pie you'd prepare with the bushels of juicy native peaches available in July. So whether it's a tart, crisp apple in winter, a sweet golden apricot, nectarine, or bubbly berry filling in summer, every fresh fruit pie has its special season. And to catch all those sticky juices from bubbling all over your oven, remember as a precaution to bake fruit pies on a baking sheet.

As a substitute for fresh, some fruits freeze beautifully for pie fillings, especially berries. Simply arrange a supply of your favorites—blueberries, raspberries, strawberries, or cherries—about ½ inch apart on cookie sheets, then freeze until completely firm. Transfer frozen fruit to freezerproof bags or containers. When ready to use, simply add the frozen berries, unthawed, to your pie filling and bake as directed.

For the best fresh peach and nectarine pies, always start with peeled fruit. Select only fully ripe fruit. With a small sharp knife, remove the stem of the fruit and, with the tip of the knife, score the opposite end. Bring a large saucepan of water to a boil and drop in a few pieces of fruit at a time for 30 to 60 seconds. Immediately remove the fruit with a slotted spoon and transfer to a bowl filled with ice water. The skins should slip off instantly. Remove pits and slice as desired.

Double crusted, lattice-, or streusel-topped, fruit pies are the pie baker's pride and joy. So go ahead and show off fresh fruit's summer glory with Raspberry Rhubarb Streusel Pie, Blueberry Buckle Sour Cream Pie, or a plain Old-Fashioned Peach Pie. Or take away the first signs of autumn's chill with Classic Dutch Apple Pie, Plum Crumb Pie with ginger, or ruby-red Concord Grape and Pear Pie with all its fabulous fruit juices. Now every season is just right for pie baking!

A SEASON FOR EVERY FRUIT

Apples: Pie's favorite fruit! With their multitude of varieties, apples are available year-round, but peak season's best ranges from September through November. Here are the preferred varieties for baking:

Baldwin: October to April. Bright red mottled skin, streaked with yellow, mildly tart.

Cortland: September to early spring. Smooth, shiny red skin, sweet-tart flavor.

Golden Delicious: September to early June. Golden yellow skin, tangy, juicy, and sweet. Holds its shape well in baking.

Granny Smith: Year-round availability. Bright green skin, firm texture. Moderately tart.

Greening: October to March. Yellowish green, firm. Tart, juicy, and crisp.

Jonathan: September through early spring. Yellow with bright red streaks. Crisp and juicy, sweet and slightly tart.

McIntosh: September through April. Shiny red skin with streaks of green and yellow. Tart-sweet and juicy.

Newtown Pippin: September through midspring. Greenish yellow, firm, and slightly tart.

Northern Spy: October through March. Bright red with yellow streaks. Very juicy, moderately tart.

Rome Beauty: October through May. Deep red skin with yellow or green markings. Mild flavor, retains its shape well in baking.

Stayman: October to early April. Buffed red skin with streaking. Crisp, juicy, and slightly tart.

Winesap: November through May. Deep red skin, juicy, and firm. Moderately tart, rich flavor.

York Imperial: September to May. Red with yellow streaks, off-white flesh. Moderately tart and firm.

Apricots: Peak season is June through July. Select plump, fragrant, firm fruit with a uniform golden color. Rinse briefly. When properly ripe and cut in half, pit should remove easily.

Blackberries: Peak season ranges from May through August. Look for plump, jet black berries with no evidence of mold. Discard any leaves or stems. Do not wash until ready to use, then gently rinse under cold running water; leave to dry on single layer of paper toweling.

Blueberries: Peak season end of May through October. Select blueberries that are uniform in size and firm with a blue-black hue. Discard any shriveled, moldy berries, leaves, or stems. Do not wash until ready to use, then rinse briefly under cold running water: leave to dry on single layer of paper toweling.

Tart Cherries: Peak season late June through early July. Look for a bright red color, stems intact, and firm skin without blemishes. Rinse briefly, then remove pits with a cherry pitter (set over a colander if cherries are very juicy).

Sweet Cherries: Peak season May through August. These cherries should be firm with a dark purplish hue. Rinse briefly, then remove pits with a cherry pitter.

Nectarines: Although this tree fruit is available from spring through September, its peak season is July to August. When ripe, nectarines should be fragrant and slightly firm with a bright red golden hue.

Peaches: Peak season end of May to October. Ripe peaches are fragrant and give slightly when flesh is pressed with fingertip. Avoid bruises or green spots.

Pears: Peak season August through early spring. Yellow and red Bartletts, Anjou, Comice, and the firm-textured Bosc are great for pie baking. Choose pears with a smooth skin, spicy fragrance, and juicy interior.

Plums: With a multitude of varieties available, plums can readily be found from May to October. Red, purple, green, or yellow fresh plums should have a smooth, unblemished skin whose flesh should give slightly when pressed with fingertip. Rinse briefly, remove pits, and cut as desired.

Raspberries: Now more readily available fresh year-round, peak red raspberries have two growing seasons ranging from May through November. Choose berries with a vibrant red color and no evidence of mold. Handle with care. If they need to be rinsed, do not do so until ready to use, then rinse briefly under cold running water; leave to dry on single layer of paper toweling.

Rhubarb: Peak season April to June. Look for crisp, fresh-looking stalks with a bright red color. Rinse stalks, trim ends, and discard leaves before cutting into pieces.

Strawberries: Now more readily available fresh year-round, peak season strawberries are found in May through early July. Choose brightly colored medium-sized berries with their green stems attached. Do not wash until ready to use, then rinse briefly under cold running water; immediately blot dry on paper towels.

214 MOM'S APPLE PIE

Prep: 35 minutes   Bake: 60 to 65 minutes   Serves: 8

Here's the ultimate classic fruit pie. I love it served warm with vanilla ice cream. If you want a more butterscotch flavor in the filling, simply substitute an equal amount of packed brown sugar for the granulated.

⅔ cup sugar
3 tablespoons flour
1 teaspoon cinnamon
¼ teaspoon grated nutmeg
¼ teaspoon salt
3 pounds tart apples, peeled and cut into ¾-inch-thick wedges

1 tablespoon fresh lemon juice
Mostly Butter Pastry for 9-inch double crust pie (page 159)
2 tablespoons butter, cut up

1. Preheat oven to 450°F. In a large bowl, combine sugar, flour, cinnamon, nutmeg, and salt. Stir in apples and lemon juice, tossing to coat.

2. On a lightly floured surface, roll out larger pastry disk into a ⅛-inch-thick round. Fold in half and ease gently into a 9-inch pie pan. Unfold dough, letting pastry overhang edge. Trim pastry 1 inch from rim of pan. Spoon filling into pie shell and dot with butter.

3. Roll out remaining pastry disk into a ⅛-inch-thick round; place on top of pie. Fold edge of top pastry over lower pastry; flute. Cut vents for steam.

4. Place pie on a cookie sheet and bake 10 minutes. Reduce oven temperature to 375°F. Bake 50 to 55 minutes longer, or until filling is bubbly and crust is golden brown. Transfer to a wire rack. Serve warm or at room temperature.

215 WISCONSIN APPLE CHEESE PIE

Prep: 25 minutes   Bake: 70 to 75 minutes   Serves: 8

This heartland pie features a golden Cheddar cheese pastry crust, proving once again that fruit and cheese are a perfect combination.

⅔ cup packed brown sugar
3 tablespoons flour
1 teaspoon cinnamon
¼ teaspoon grated nutmeg
¼ teaspoon salt
Pinch of ground cloves
3 pounds tart apples, peeled and cut into ¾-inch-thick wedges

2 teaspoons fresh lemon juice
Flaky Cheddar Pastry (recipe follows)
2 tablespoons butter, cut up

1. Preheat oven to 450°F. In a large bowl, combine brown sugar, flour, cinnamon, nutmeg, salt, and cloves. Stir in apples and lemon juice, tossing to coat.

2. On a lightly floured surface, roll out larger pastry disk into a ⅛-inch-thick round. Fold in half and ease gently into a 9-inch pie pan. Unfold dough, letting pastry overhang edge. Trim pastry 1 inch from rim of pan. Spoon filling into pie shell and dot with butter.

3. Roll out remaining pastry disk into a ⅛-inch-thick round; place on top of pie. Fold edge of top pastry over lower pastry; flute. Cut vents for steam.

4. Place pie on a cookie sheet and bake 10 minutes. Reduce oven temperature to 375°F. Bake 60 to 65 minutes longer, or until filling is bubbly and crust is golden brown. Transfer to a wire rack. Serve warm or at room temperature.

216 FLAKY CHEDDAR PASTRY
Prep: 10 minutes   Chill: 1 hour   Makes: 1 double 9-inch pie crust

For maximum flavor, choose sharp Cheddar cheese. Once the pie is baked, the cheese will form golden streaks throughout this rich crust.

2 cups flour	1 cup shredded sharp
½ teaspoon salt	Cheddar cheese
Pinch of ground red pepper	6 to 8 tablespoons ice water
⅔ cup solid vegetable	
shortening	

1. In a medium bowl, combine flour, salt, and red pepper. With a pastry blender or 2 knives, or in a food processor or electric mixer, cut in shortening until mixture resembles fine crumbs. Stir in cheese. Add ice water, 1 tablespoon at a time, drizzling over flour mixture, then tossing vigorously with a fork or pulsing or beating very briefly, just until dough begins to hold together. (It will look coarse and crumbly, but feel moist.)

2. Turn dough out onto work surface and gather gently into 2 balls, one slightly larger than the other. Flatten into 2 disks and wrap tightly in plastic wrap. Refrigerate 1 hour or overnight.

217   CLASSIC DUTCH APPLE PIE
Prep: 25 minutes   Bake: 65 to 70 minutes   Serves: 8

This custard-style apple pie has been a farm favorite for generations.

⅔ cup sugar
3 tablespoons flour
1 teaspoon cinnamon
¼ teaspoon ground ginger
¼ teaspoon salt
3 pounds tart apples, peeled
  and cut into ¾-inch-thick
  wedges

2 teaspoons fresh lemon juice
Flaky Pastry for a 9-inch
  double crust pie (page
  157)
2 tablespoons butter,
  cut up
½ cup heavy cream

1. Preheat oven to 450°F. In a large bowl, combine sugar, flour, cinnamon, ginger, and salt. Stir in apples and lemon juice, tossing to coat.

2. On a lightly floured surface, roll out larger pastry disk into a ⅛-inch-thick round. Fold in half and ease gently into a 9-inch pie pan. Unfold dough, letting pastry overhang edge. Trim pastry 1 inch from rim of pan. Spoon filling into pie shell and dot with butter.

3. Roll out remaining pastry disk into a ⅛-inch-thick round; place on top of pie. Fold edge of top pastry over lower pastry; flute. Cut vents for steam.

4. Place pie on a cookie sheet and bake 10 minutes. Reduce oven temperature to 375°F. Bake 45 to 50 minutes longer, or until apples are tender when tested with a small sharp knife. Carefully pour cream into a steam vent. Bake another 10 minutes, or until filling is bubbly and crust is golden. Transfer to a wire rack. Serve warm or at room temperature.

218   GOLDEN APPLE-PURPLE PLUM PIE
Prep: 25 minutes   Bake: 45 to 50 minutes   Serves: 8

This bottom crust pie is a cinch to assemble, and there's no fluting required.

Mostly Butter Pastry for
  9-inch double crust pie
  (page 159)
½ cup plus 1 tablespoon sugar
½ teaspoon cinnamon
Pinch of salt
1½ pounds Italian purple
  plums, pitted and
  quartered

1 pound Golden Delicious
  apples, peeled and thinly
  sliced
2 teaspoons fresh lemon juice
2 tablespoons butter,
  cut up
1 tablespoon heavy cream or
  milk

1. Preheat oven to 400°F. On a lightly floured surface, roll out dough into a 14-inch circle about ⅛ inch thick. Fold in half and ease gently into a 9-inch pie pan; unfold dough, letting pastry edge overhang sides of pan.

2. In a large bowl, combine ½ cup sugar, cinnamon, and salt. Stir in plums, apples, and lemon juice, tossing to coat.

3. Turn filling into pie shell and dot with butter. Fold overhanging pastry along sides of pie plate to partially enclose the fruit, pleating gently as you go. Brush pastry border with cream. Sprinkle remaining 1 tablespoon sugar over top of pie.

4. Bake 45 to 50 minutes, or until fruit is bubbly in center and crust is golden. Let cool completely on a wire rack.

219 APPLE PEAR PIE WITH CARDAMOM STREUSEL

Prep: 25 minutes   Freeze: 20 minutes
Bake: 55 to 60 minutes   Serves: 8

Ginger preserves are a wonderful addition to this apple pie filling and the ground cardamom in the streusel topping adds an extra kick of spice.

1 (9-inch) Unbaked Pie Shell (page 158)
½ cup sugar
3 tablespoons flour
¼ cup ginger or apricot preserves
2 tablespoons fresh lemon juice

2 pounds tart apples, peeled and thickly sliced
1 pound pears, peeled and thickly sliced
Cardamom Streusel (recipe follows)

1. Preheat oven to 425°F. Freeze pastry shell 20 minutes, or until firm.

2. In a large bowl, combine sugar and flour. Stir in preserves and lemon juice. Fold in apples and pears with a rubber spatula. Turn filling into pie shell. Sprinkle Cardamom Streusel evenly over top of pie.

3. Place pie on a cookie sheet and bake 15 minutes. Reduce oven temperature to 375°F. Bake 40 to 45 minutes longer, or until filling is bubbly in center. Let cool completely on a wire rack.

CARDAMOM STREUSEL
Makes: 1¼ cups

1 stick (4 ounces) butter, softened
½ cup packed brown sugar

1 teaspoon grated lemon zest
½ teaspoon ground cardamom
1 cup flour

In a medium bowl, beat butter and brown sugar with an electric mixer until light and fluffy. Beat in lemon zest and cardamom. With mixer on low speed, gradually beat in flour just until crumbly.

220 BLACKBERRY-APPLE SPICE PIE
Prep: 25 minutes   Bake: 55 to 60 minutes   Serves: 8

This pie is divine served warm with a pitcher of cream. It's great with a mix of favorite tart apples and with Golden Delicious, too.

¾ cup sugar
3 tablespoons flour
1 tablespoon cornstarch
  Pinch of salt
1½ pounds tart apples, peeled
   and diced (4 cups)
2 cups fresh or frozen
  blackberries

2 teaspoons fresh lemon juice
  Sugar 'n' Spice Pastry for a
  9-inch double crust pie
  (page 168)
2 tablespoons butter,
  cut up
  Vanilla ice cream or
  whipped cream

1. Preheat oven to 425°F. In a large bowl, combine sugar, flour, cornstarch, and salt. Gently stir in apples, blackberries, and lemon juice.

2. On a lightly floured surface, roll out larger pastry disk into a ⅛-inch-thick round. Fold in half and ease gently into a 9-inch pie pan. Unfold dough, letting pastry overhang edge. Trim pastry 1 inch from rim of pan. Spoon filling into pie shell and dot with butter.

3. Roll out remaining pastry disk into a ⅛-inch-thick round; place on top of pie. Fold edge of top pastry over lower pastry; flute. Cut vents for steam.

4. Place pie on a cookie sheet and bake 15 minutes. Reduce oven temperature to 350°F. Bake 40 to 45 minutes longer, or until filling is bubbly in center and crust is golden. Let cool completely on a wire rack. Serve with ice cream or whipped cream.

221 TRUE BLUE BERRY PIE
Prep: 20 minutes   Bake: 60 to 65 minutes   Serves: 8

⅔ cup plus 1 tablespoon sugar
¼ cup flour
¼ teaspoon cinnamon
  Pinch of ground allspice
5 cups fresh or frozen
  blueberries
2 tablespoons fresh lemon
  juice

½ teaspoon grated lemon zest
  Flaky Pastry for a 9-inch
  double crust pie (page
  157)
2 tablespoons butter, cut up
1 tablespoon heavy cream or
  milk
  Vanilla ice cream

1. Preheat oven to 450°F. In a large bowl, combine ⅔ cup sugar, flour, cinnamon, and allspice. Gently stir in blueberries, lemon juice, and lemon zest.

2. On a lightly floured surface, roll out larger pastry disk into a ⅛-inch-thick round. Fold in half and ease gently into a 9-inch pie pan. Unfold dough, letting pastry overhang edge. Trim pastry 1 inch from rim of pan. Spoon filling into pie shell and dot with butter.

3. Roll out remaining pastry disk into a ⅛-inch-thick round; place on top of pie. Fold edge of top pastry over lower pastry; flute. Cut vents for steam. Brush top of pie with cream; sprinkle on remaining 1 tablespoon sugar.

4. Place pie on cookie sheet and bake 20 minutes. Reduce oven temperature to 375°F. Bake 40 to 45 minutes longer, or until filling is bubbly in center. Transfer to a wire rack. Serve warm with vanilla ice cream.

222 BING CHERRY PIE
Prep: 40 minutes   Bake: 60 to 65 minutes   Serves: 8

Dark, sweet Bing cherries make a wonderful pie filling; this version features a delicate dusting of almond sugar.

⅔ **cup plus 1 tablespoon sugar**
3 tablespoons cornstarch
6 cups pitted sweet fresh cherries
1 tablespoon fresh lemon juice
⅛ **teaspoon almond extract**
Flaky Pastry for a 9-inch double crust pie (page 157)

2 tablespoons butter, cut up
1 tablespoon blanched almonds
1 large egg white, lightly beaten
Vanilla ice cream

1. Preheat oven to 425°F. In a large bowl, mix ⅔ cup sugar and cornstarch. Gently stir in cherries, lemon juice, and almond extract.

2. On a lightly floured surface, roll out larger pastry disk into a ⅛-inch-thick round. Fold in half and ease gently into a 9-inch pie pan. Unfold dough, letting pastry overhang edge. Trim pastry 1 inch from rim of pan. Spoon filling into pie shell and dot with butter.

3. Roll out remaining pastry disk into a ⅛-inch-thick round; place on top of pie. Fold edge of top pastry over lower pastry; flute. Cut vents for steam.

4. In a food processor, process almonds and remaining 1 tablespoon sugar until finely ground. Brush top of pie with egg white; sprinkle with almond-sugar mixture.

5. Place pie on a cookie sheet and bake 15 minutes. Reduce oven temperature to 375°F. Bake 45 to 50 minutes longer, or until crust is golden and filling is bubbly in center. Transfer to a wire rack. Serve warm or at room temperature with vanilla ice cream.

223 BLUEBERRY BUCKLE SOUR CREAM PIE
Prep: 15 minutes   Bake: 40 to 45 minutes   Serves: 8

Call this a "Dutch-style" blueberry pie. The berries and sour cream custard are perfect together topped off with a buttery brown sugar streusel.

3 tablespoons flour	½ teaspoon vanilla extract
½ cup sugar	2 cups fresh blueberries
⅛ teaspoon grated nutmeg	1 (9-inch) Partially Baked Pie
Pinch of salt	Shell (page 157)
1 cup sour cream	Butter Buckle Topping
1 large egg	(recipe follows)

1. Preheat oven to 400°F. In a large bowl, combine flour, sugar, nutmeg, and salt. Whisk in sour cream, egg, and vanilla until smooth. Stir in blueberries.

2. Turn filling into partially baked crust. Sprinkle Butter Buckle Topping evenly over top of pie.

3. Place pie on cookie sheet. Bake 40 to 45 minutes, or until filling is just set in center and topping is golden. Let cool completely on a wire rack.

BUTTER BUCKLE TOPPING
Makes: 1¼ cups

⅓ cup flour	3 tablespoons butter, cut up
⅓ cup packed brown sugar	½ cup chopped pecans

In a medium bowl, combine flour and brown sugar. With a pastry blender or 2 knives, cut in butter until mixture resembles fine crumbs. Stir in pecans.

224 FRESH APRICOT PIE
Prep: 30 minutes   Bake: 50 to 55 minutes   Serves: 8

There's no substitute for the just-picked flavor of fresh apricots. Any fruit brandy is terrific here, or just use 1 tablespoon fresh lemon juice.

2 pounds (16 medium) fresh	3 tablespoons quick-cooking
apricots, halved and	tapioca
pitted	¼ teaspoon salt
2 tablespoons apricot brandy	Mostly Butter Pastry for a
½ teaspoon vanilla extract	9-inch double crust pie
½ cup granulated sugar	(page 159)
½ cup packed brown sugar	2 tablespoons butter, cut up

1. Preheat oven to 450°F. In a large bowl, combine apricots, apricot brandy, and vanilla. In another bowl, combine granulated sugar, brown sugar, tapioca, and salt. Gently stir apricots into sugar mixture. Let stand 15 minutes, stirring occasionally.

2. On a lightly floured surface, roll out larger pastry disk into a ⅛-inch-thick round. Fold in half and ease gently into a 9-inch pie pan. Unfold dough, letting pastry overhang edge. Trim pastry 1 inch from rim of pan. Spoon filling into pie shell and dot with butter.

3. Roll out remaining pastry disk into a ⅛-inch-thick round. Cut into ¾-inch-wide strips and arrange in a lattice pattern on top of filling. Fold edge of bottom pastry up over ends of strips, building a high edge. Seal and flute.

4. Place pie on a cookie sheet and bake 10 minutes. Reduce oven temperature to 375°F. Bake 40 to 45 minutes longer, until center is bubbly and crust is golden brown. Let cool completely on a wire rack.

---

225 DEEP-DISH BUTTERSCOTCH BLUEBERRY-PEACH PIE

Prep: 25 minutes   Bake: 60 to 65 minutes   Serves: 8

Here's a gorgeous fresh fruit pie packed with thickly sliced peaches, blueberries, and brown sugar. A 9-inch deep-dish pie plate is just perfect for those generous portions.

¾ **cup packed brown sugar**
3 **tablespoons cornstarch**
   Pinch of salt
2 **pounds ripe peaches, peeled and thickly sliced (4 cups)**
1 **pint fresh blueberries**
1 **tablespoon fresh lemon juice**

½ **teaspoon grated lemon zest**
½ **teaspoon vanilla extract**
   Mostly Butter Pastry for a 9-inch double crust pie (page 159)
2 **tablespoons butter, cut up**

1. Preheat oven to 450°F. In a large bowl, combine brown sugar, cornstarch, and salt. Gently stir in peaches, blueberries, lemon juice, lemon zest, and vanilla, tossing to coat.

2. On a lightly floured surface, roll out larger pastry disk into a ⅛-inch-thick round. Fold in half and ease gently into a 9-inch pie pan. Unfold dough, letting pastry overhang edge. Trim pastry 1 inch from rim of pan. Spoon filling into pie shell and dot with butter.

3. Roll out remaining pastry disk into a ⅛-inch-thick round; place on top of pie. Fold edge of top pastry over lower pastry; flute. Cut vents for steam.

4. Place pie on a cookie sheet and bake 15 minutes. Reduce oven temperature to 375°F. Bake 45 to 50 minutes longer, or until filling is bubbly in center. Let cool completely on a wire rack.

226   FRESH SOUR CHERRY CRISSCROSS PIE
Prep: 25 minutes   Bake: 55 to 60 minutes   Serves: 8

Bright red sour cherries are only available from late June through July, so snatch them up and bake this summer beauty while they last.

1 cup sugar
3 tablespoons cornstarch
⅛ teaspoon cinnamon
    Pinch of salt
5 cups pitted fresh or frozen
    sour cherries
1 tablespoon fresh lemon
    juice

½ teaspoon grated lemon
    zest
    Mostly Butter Pastry for a
    9-inch double crust pie
    (page 159)
2 tablespoons butter,
    cut up

1. Preheat oven to 425°F. In a large bowl, combine sugar, cornstarch, cinnamon, and salt. Stir in cherries, lemon juice, and lemon zest.

2. On a lightly floured surface, roll out larger pastry disk into a ⅛-inch-thick round. Fold in half and ease gently into a 9-inch pie pan. Unfold dough, letting pastry overhang edge. Spoon cherry filling into pie shell and dot with butter.

3. Roll out remaining pastry disk into a ⅛-inch-thick round. Cut into ¾-inch-wide strips and arrange in a lattice pattern on top of filling. Fold edge of bottom pastry up over ends of strips, building a high edge. Seal and flute.

4. Place pie on a cookie sheet and bake 15 minutes. Reduce oven temperature to 375°F. Bake 40 to 45 minutes longer, or until filling is bubbly in center and crust is golden. Transfer to a wire rack. Serve warm or at room temperature.

227   BERRY CHERRY MARZIPAN CRUMB PIE
Prep: 30 minutes   Freeze: 20 minutes
Bake: 60 to 65 minutes   Serves: 8

1 (9-inch) Unbaked Pie Shell
    (page 158)
¾ cup sugar
3 tablespoons cornstarch
4 cups pitted fresh sweet
    cherries

2 cups fresh raspberries,
    blueberries, or
    blackberries
1 tablespoon fresh lemon
    juice
    Marzipan Crumb Topping
    (recipe follows)

1. Preheat oven to 425°F. Freeze pie shell 20 minutes, or until firm.

2. In a large bowl, combine sugar and cornstarch. Gently stir in cherries, berries, and lemon juice. Turn filling into pie shell. Sprinkle Marzipan Crumb Topping evenly over top of pie.

3. Place pie on a cookie sheet and bake 15 minutes. Reduce oven temperature to 375°F. Bake 45 to 50 minutes longer, or until filling is bubbly in center. Let cool completely on a wire rack.

MARZIPAN CRUMB TOPPING
Makes: ¾ cup

4 tablespoons butter, softened
¼ cup packed brown sugar
¼ cup almond paste

½ teaspoon grated lemon zest
½ cup flour

In a small bowl, beat butter, brown sugar, almond paste, and lemon zest with an electric mixer until smooth. With mixer on low speed, gradually beat in flour just until crumbly.

---

228 TART CHERRY-SWEET BERRY PIE
Prep: 25 minutes   Bake: 50 to 55 minutes   Serves: 8

¾ cup plus 1 tablespoon sugar
3 tablespoons quick-cooking
 tapioca
 Pinch of salt
2 cups pitted fresh or frozen
 sour cherries
2 cups fresh or frozen
 raspberries

1 tablespoon fresh lemon
 juice
 Sour Cream Pastry for a
 9-inch double crust pie
 (page 163)
1 tablespoon butter, cut up
1 tablespoon heavy cream or
 milk

1. Preheat oven to 425°F. In a large bowl, combine ¾ cup sugar, tapioca, and salt. Stir in cherries, raspberries, and lemon juice. Let stand 15 minutes, stirring occasionally.

2. On a lightly floured surface, roll out larger pastry disk into a ⅛-inch-thick round. Fold in half and ease gently into a 9-inch pie pan. Unfold dough, letting pastry overhang edge. Trim pastry 1 inch from rim of pan. Spoon filling into pie shell and dot with butter.

3. Roll out remaining pastry disk into a ⅛-inch-thick round; place on top of pie. Fold edge of top pastry over lower pastry; flute. Cut vents from steam. Brush top of pie with cream; sprinkle on remaining 1 tablespoon sugar.

4. Place pie on cookie sheet and bake 15 minutes. Reduce oven temperature to 375°F. Bake 35 to 40 minutes longer, or until filling is bubbly in center and crust is golden. Transfer to a wire rack. Serve warm or at room temperature.

229 OLD-FASHIONED PEACH PIE
Prep: 20 minutes   Bake: 55 to 60 minutes   Serves: 8

Juicy ripe peaches are essential for this pie. For easy peeling, drop a few peaches in boiling water for 30 seconds, remove with a slotted spoon, then plunge into a bowl of ice water. The skins will slip off instantly.

⅓ cup granulated sugar
⅓ cup packed brown sugar
¼ cup flour
½ teaspoon cinnamon
¼ teaspoon grated nutmeg
⅛ teaspoon salt
3 pounds ripe peaches, peeled and thickly sliced

1 tablespoon fresh lemon juice
Cream Cheese Pastry for a 9-inch double crust pie (page 166)
2 tablespoons butter, cut up

1. Preheat oven to 425°F. In a large bowl, combine granulated sugar, brown sugar, flour, cinnamon, nutmeg, and salt. Stir in peaches and lemon juice.

2. On a lightly floured surface, roll out larger pastry disk into a ⅛-inch-thick round. Fold in half and ease gently into a 9-inch pie pan. Unfold dough, letting pastry overhang edge. Trim pastry 1 inch from rim of pan. Spoon filling into pie shell and dot with butter.

3. Roll out remaining pastry disk into a ⅛-inch-thick round. Cut into ¾-inch-wide strips and arrange in a lattice pattern on top of filling. Fold edge of bottom pastry up over ends of strips, building a high edge. Seal and flute.

4. Place pie on a cookie sheet and bake 15 minutes. Reduce oven temperature to 375°F. Bake 40 to 45 minutes longer, or until filling is bubbly in center. Let cool completely on a wire rack.

230 CONCORD GRAPE AND PEAR PIE
Prep: 35 minutes   Bake: 55 to 60 minutes   Serves: 8

Sweet and juicy Concord grapes gives this fall pie a beautiful blue-black color.

4 cups Concord grapes (about 1½ pounds)
1 pound peeled pears, thickly sliced
⅔ cup sugar
3 tablespoons flour
2 teaspoons fresh lemon juice

½ teaspoon cinnamon
Pinch of salt
Flaky Pastry for a 9-inch double crust pie (page 157)
2 tablespoons butter, cut up

1. Preheat oven to 425°F. Wash and drain grapes. Pinching each grape between thumb and forefinger, squeeze out pulp and seeds into a saucepan. In a large bowl, combine grape skins and pears; set aside.

2. Bring pulp mixture to boil over medium heat, stirring constantly. Cook 3 minutes, or until pulp is dissolved. Strain pulp through a sieve to remove seeds; combine with pears and grape skins in bowl. Stir in sugar, flour, lemon juice, cinnamon, and salt.

3. On a lightly floured surface, roll out larger pastry disk into a ⅛-inch-thick round. Fold in half and ease gently into a 9-inch pie pan. Unfold dough, letting pastry overhang edge. Trim pastry 1 inch from rim of pan. Spoon filling into pie shell and dot with butter.

4. Roll out remaining pastry disk into a ⅛-inch-thick round; place on top of pie. Fold edge of top pastry over lower pastry; flute. Cut vents for steam.

5. Place pie on a cookie sheet and bake 25 minutes. Reduce oven temperature to 375°F. Bake 30 to 35 minutes longer, or until filling is bubbly in center and crust is golden. Let cool completely on wire rack.

231 PLUM CRUMB PIE

Prep: 20 minutes   Freeze: 20 minutes   Bake: 60 to 65 minutes
Serves: 8

Sweet juicy plums tossed with orange marmalade are topped off with a gingery crumble topping.

1 (9-inch) Unbaked Pie Shell (page 158)	6 cups sliced plums
⅔ cup sugar	⅓ cup orange marmalade
3 tablespoons quick-cooking tapioca	1 teaspoon fresh lemon juice
¼ teaspoon salt	Ginger Crumb Topping (recipe follows)

1. Preheat oven to 425°F. Freeze pastry shell 20 minutes, or until firm.

2. In a large bowl, combine sugar, tapioca, and salt. Stir in plums, marmalade, and lemon juice. Let stand 15 minutes, stirring occasionally.

3. Turn filling into pie shell. Sprinkle Ginger Crumb Topping evenly over top of pie. Place pie on a cookie sheet and bake 10 minutes. Reduce oven temperature to 375°F. Bake 50 to 55 minutes longer, or until filling is bubbly in center. Let cool completely on a wire rack.

GINGER CRUMB TOPPING
Makes: ¾ cup

½ cup flour	½ teaspoon cinnamon
⅓ cup packed brown sugar	4 tablespoons butter, cut up
½ teaspoon ground ginger	

In a medium bowl, combine flour, brown sugar, ginger, and cinnamon. With a pastry blender or 2 knives, cut in butter until mixture resembles fine crumbs.

232 BLUSHING PEACH BUCKLE PIE
Prep: 25 minutes   Freeze: 20 minutes   Bake: 55 to 60 minutes
Serves: 8

Raspberries gives this peach pie a rosy blush. Toasted hazelnuts make the buckle topping distinctive, but feel free to substitute toasted almonds if you prefer.

1 (9-inch) Unbaked Pie Shell (page 157)
⅔ cup sugar
3 tablespoons quick-cooking tapioca
½ teaspoon cinnamon
⅛ teaspoon mace
Pinch of salt

2 pounds ripe peaches, peeled and thickly sliced (4 cups)
2 cups fresh or frozen raspberries
1 tablespoon fresh lemon juice
Hazelnut Buckle Topping (recipe follows)

1. Preheat oven to 425°F. Freeze pie shell 20 minutes, or until firm.

2. In a large bowl, combine sugar, tapioca, cinnamon, mace, and salt. Stir in peaches, raspberries, and lemon juice. Let stand 15 minutes, stirring occasionally.

3. Turn filling into pie shell. Sprinkle Hazelnut Buckle Topping evenly over top of pie. Place pie on a cookie sheet and bake 15 minutes. Reduce oven temperature to 375°F. Bake 40 to 45 minutes longer, or until filling is bubbly in center. Let cool completely on wire rack.

HAZELNUT BUCKLE TOPPING
Makes: 1½ cups

½ cup hazelnuts or blanched almonds
½ cup flour

½ cup packed brown sugar
½ teaspoon cinnamon
5 tablespoons butter, cut up

1. Preheat oven to 350°F. Spread out hazelnuts or almonds on a small baking sheet. Bake 10 minutes, or until hazelnuts are lightly browned and dark skins are cracked. Rub warm hazelnuts in a terrycloth towel to remove as much of skins as possible. Let cool, then finely chop.

2. In a medium bowl, combine flour, brown sugar, and cinnamon. With a pastry blender or 2 knives, cut in butter until mixture resembles fine crumbs. Stir in chopped hazelnuts.

233   NECTARINE-VANILLA BEAN PIE
Prep: 35 minutes   Bake: 55 to 60 minutes   Serves: 8

Whole vanilla bean adds a special sweetness to this fruit pie. This cream filling is also lovely with fresh peeled peaches in place of the nectarines.

⅔ cup plus 1 tablespoon heavy
   cream
½ vanilla bean, split
   lengthwise, or 1 teaspoon
   vanilla extract
1 large egg
½ cup plus 1 tablespoon sugar
2 tablespoons flour
⅛ teaspoon grated nutmeg
   Pinch of salt

6 cups peeled and thickly
   sliced nectarines (about
   3 pounds)
1 tablespoon fresh lemon
   juice
   Mostly Butter Pastry for a
   9-inch double crust pie
   (page 159)

1. Preheat oven to 425°F. In a small saucepan, heat ⅔ cup cream and vanilla bean over medium-low heat until cream is very hot and small bubbles appear around edges of pan. Remove from heat, cover, and let stand 15 minutes. Remove vanilla bean and scrape out seeds; add seeds to cream and discard pod. Stir occasionally until cool, about 10 minutes. Whisk in egg. (If using vanilla extract, simply beat with cream and egg until blended.)

2. In a large bowl, combine ½ cup sugar, flour, nutmeg, and salt. Stir in nectarines and lemon juice, tossing to coat.

3. On a lightly floured surface, roll out larger pastry disk into a ⅛-inch-thick round. Fold in half and ease gently into a 9-inch pie pan. Unfold dough, letting pastry overhang edge. Trim pastry 1 inch from rim of pan. Turn nectarine filling into pie shell; pour vanilla custard over fruit.

4. Roll out remaining pastry disk into a ⅛-inch-thick round; place on top of pie. Fold edge of top pastry over lower pastry; flute. Cut vents for steam. Brush top of pie with remaining 1 tablespoon cream; sprinkle on remaining 1 tablespoon sugar.

5. Place pie on a cookie sheet and bake 15 minutes. Reduce oven temperature to 375°F. Bake 40 to 45 minutes longer, or until filling is bubbly in center and crust is golden. Transfer to a wire rack. Serve warm or at room temperature.

234   RED RASPBERRY-GREEN APPLE PIE
Prep: 25 minutes   Bake: 55 to 60 minutes   Serves: 8

Red raspberries give this tart apple pie a rosy blush, perfect with bright green Granny Smith apples.

¾ cup plus 1 tablespoon sugar
⅓ cup flour
1 teaspoon cinnamon
⅛ teaspoon grated nutmeg
⅛ teaspoon salt
2 pounds tart apples, peeled and cut into ¾-inch-thick wedges
2 cups fresh or frozen raspberries

2 teaspoons fresh lemon juice
Old-Fashioned Vinegar
Pastry for a 9-inch double crust pie (page 160)
2 tablespoons butter, cut up
1 tablespoon heavy cream or milk
Vanilla ice cream

1. Preheat oven to 450°F. In a large bowl, combine ¾ cup sugar, flour, cinnamon, nutmeg, and salt. Gently stir in apples, raspberries, and lemon juice, tossing to coat.

2. On a lightly floured surface, roll out larger pastry disk into a ⅛-inch-thick round. Fold in half and ease gently into a 9-inch pie pan. Unfold dough, letting pastry overhang edge. Trim pastry 1 inch from rim of pan. Spoon filling into pie shell and dot with butter.

3. Roll remaining pastry disk into a ⅛-inch-thick round; place on top of pie. Fold edge of top pastry over lower pastry; flute. Cut vents for steam. Brush top crust with cream; sprinkle on remaining 1 tablespoon sugar.

4. Place pie on a cookie sheet and bake 15 minutes. Reduce oven temperature to 375°F. Bake 40 to 45 minutes longer, or until apples are tender when tested with a small sharp knife in center. Let cool completely on a wire rack. Serve with vanilla ice cream.

235   RASPBERRY RHUBARB STREUSEL PIE
Prep: 20 minutes   Freeze: 20 minutes   Bake: 55 to 60 minutes   Serves: 8

This ruby red tart and sweet fruit filling nestles under a crunchy brown sugar-oat streusel.

1 (9-inch) Unbaked Pie Shell (page 158)
1¼ cups sugar
¼ cup quick-cooking tapioca
Pinch of salt
1¼ pounds fresh rhubarb, cut into ½-inch pieces (4 cups)

½ teaspoon vanilla extract
2 cups fresh or frozen raspberries
Brown Sugar Streusel (recipe follows)

1. Preheat oven to 425°F. Freeze pastry shell 20 minutes, or until firm.

2. In a large bowl, combine sugar, tapioca, and salt. Stir in rhubarb and vanilla. Let stand 15 minutes, stirring occasionally.

3. Add raspberries to filling and gently mix. Turn filling into pie shell. Sprinkle Brown Sugar Streusel evenly over top of pie.

4. Place pie on a cookie sheet and bake 10 minutes. Reduce oven temperature to 350°F. Bake 45 to 50 minutes longer, or until filling is bubbly in center. Let cool completely on a wire rack.

BROWN SUGAR STREUSEL
Makes: 1⅓ cups

½ **cup packed brown sugar**
½ **cup flour**

3 **tablespoons butter, cut up**
½ **cup old-fashioned oats**

In a medium bowl, combine brown sugar and flour. With a pastry blender or 2 knives, cut in butter until mixture resembles fine crumbs. Stir in oats.

---

236   STRAWBERRY-RHUBARB LATTICE PIE
Prep: 25 minutes   Bake: 60 to 65 minutes   Serves: 8

When the farm stands reopen to celebrate the rites of spring, it's time to take advantage of a bumper crop of strawberries and rhubarb. There's no better way to do it than with this juicy fruit pie.

1¼ **cups sugar**
⅓ **cup flour**
¼ **teaspoon cinnamon**
   Pinch of salt
1 **pound fresh rhubarb, cut into ½-inch pieces (3 cups)**
1 **pint fresh whole strawberries, hulled and cut in half**

1 **tablespoon fresh lemon juice**
   Flaky Pastry for a 9-inch double crust pie (page 157)
2 **tablespoons butter, cut up**

1. Preheat oven to 425°F. In a large bowl, combine sugar, flour, cinnamon, and salt. Stir in rhubarb, strawberries, and lemon juice.

2. On a lightly floured surface, roll out larger pastry disk into a ⅛-inch-thick round. Fold in half and ease gently into a 9-inch pie pan. Unfold dough, letting pastry overhang edge. Trim pastry 1 inch from rim of pan. Spoon filling into pie shell and dot with butter.

3. Roll out remaining pastry disk into a ⅛-inch-thick round. Cut into ¾-inch-wide strips and arrange in a lattice pattern on top of filling. Fold edge of bottom pastry up over ends of strips, building a high edge. Seal and flute.

4. Place pie on a cookie sheet and bake 15 minutes. Reduce oven temperature to 350°F. Bake 45 to 50 minutes longer, or until filling is bubbly in center. Let cool completely on a wire rack before serving.

237   CLASSIC SOUR CREAM-CINNAMON CRUMBLE APPLE PIE

Prep: 30 minutes   Freeze: 20 minutes   Bake: 60 to 65 minutes
Serves: 8

This fruit filling is not too sweet, and my friend Ray loved a leftover slice for breakfast! It's just perfect with a spicy cinnamon crumble topping.

1 **(9-inch) Unbaked Pie Shell (page 158)**	2 **teaspoons fresh lemon juice**
⅓ **cup sugar**	1 **teaspoon vanilla extract**
2 **tablespoons flour**	2 **pounds tart apples, peeled**
¼ **teaspoon grated nutmeg**	**and cut into ¾-inch-thick**
Pinch of salt	**wedges**
1 **cup sour cream**	**Cinnamon Crumble**
1 **large egg, lightly beaten**	**Topping (recipe follows)**

1. Preheat oven to 425°F. Freeze pastry shell 20 minutes, or until firm.

2. In a large bowl, combine sugar, flour, nutmeg, and salt. Whisk in sour cream, egg, lemon juice, and vanilla until smooth. Stir in apples. Turn filling into pie shell. Sprinkle Cinnamon Crumble Topping evenly over top of pie.

3. Place pie on a cookie sheet and bake 20 minutes. Reduce oven temperature to 350°F. Bake 40 to 45 minutes longer, or until apples are tender when tested with a small sharp knife. Let cool completely on a wire rack.

CINNAMON CRUMBLE TOPPING
Makes: 1¼ cups

½ **cup flour**	5 **tablespoons butter, cut up**
½ **cup packed brown sugar**	½ **cup chopped walnuts**
1 **teaspoon cinnamon**	

In a medium bowl, combine flour, brown sugar, and cinnamon. With a pastry blender or 2 knives, cut in butter until mixture resembles fine crumbs. Stir in walnuts.

238 FARMHAND'S GREEN TOMATO-APPLE PIE

Prep: 35 minutes   Bake: 50 to 55 minutes   Serves: 8

Remember, tomatoes are a fruit and in this pie we've picked the tomato before it's ripe. The special tart flavor of green tomatoes paired with apples is a farm pie favorite.

3 medium green tomatoes
½ cup plus 1 tablespoon granulated sugar
½ cup packed brown sugar
3 tablespoons flour
1 teaspoon cinnamon
¼ teaspoon grated nutmeg
⅛ teaspoon salt
⅛ teaspoon freshly ground pepper

3 cups thinly sliced peeled tart apples
1 tablespoon fresh lemon juice
Mostly Butter Pastry for a 9-inch double crust pie (page 159)
2 tablespoons butter, cut up
1 tablespoon heavy cream or milk

1. Preheat oven to 425 °F. In a large saucepan, bring 6 cups water to a boil. Add green tomatoes, remove from heat, and let stand for 2 to 3 minutes, then remove with a slotted spoon and plunge into a bowl of ice water. With a small sharp knife, peel off skins and thinly slice tomatoes. (There should be 2 cups.)

2. In a large bowl, combine ½ cup granulated sugar, brown sugar, flour, cinnamon, nutmeg, salt, and pepper. Stir in sliced green tomatoes, apples, and lemon juice.

3. On a lightly floured surface, roll out larger pastry disk into a ⅛-inch-thick round. Fold in half and ease gently into a 9-inch pie pan. Unfold dough, letting pastry overhang edge. Trim pastry 1 inch from rim of pan. Spoon filling into pie shell and dot with butter.

4. Roll out remaining pastry disk into a ⅛-inch-thick round; place on top of pie. Fold edge of top pastry over lower pastry; flute. Cut vents for steam. Brush top of pie with cream; sprinkle on remaining 1 tablespoon granulated sugar.

5. Place pie on a cookie sheet and bake 15 minutes. Reduce oven temperature to 375°F. Bake 35 to 40 minutes longer, or until filling is bubbly in center and crust is golden. Let cool completely on a wire rack.

239   CIDER BARREL APPLE CRUMB PIE

Prep: 30 minutes   Bake: 40 to 45 minutes   Serves: 8

Fresh apple cider spiked with a hint of cinnamon and orange zest sets this apple pie apart from all the rest. This filling is also a treat paired with Flaky Cheddar Pastry (page 173).

3   **pounds peeled tart apples, cut into ¾-inch-thick wedges**
⅔   **cup sugar**
¾   **cup apple cider**
2   **tablespoons cornstarch**
1   **tablespoon butter**
½   **teaspoon cinnamon**

½   **teaspoon grated orange zest**
    Pinch of grated nutmeg
1   **(9-inch) Partially Baked Pie Shell (page 158)**
    Pecan Crumb Topping (recipe follows)

1. Preheat oven to 425°F. In a large skillet, combine apples, sugar, and ½ cup cider. Bring to simmer over medium heat; cover and cook 5 minutes. In small bowl, dissolve cornstarch in remaining ¼ cup cider; stir into apple mixture. Bring to a boil and cook 2 minutes. Stir in butter, cinnamon, orange zest, and nutmeg. Remove from heat and let cool.

2. Turn filling into pastry shell. Sprinkle Pecan Crumb Topping evenly over top of pie. Place pie on a cookie sheet and bake 15 minutes. Reduce oven temperature to 375°F. Bake 25 to 30 minutes longer, or until filling is bubbly in center. Let cool completely on a wire rack.

PECAN CRUMB TOPPING
Makes: 1¼ cups

½   **cup flour**
⅓   **cup packed brown sugar**
½   **teaspoon cinnamon**

⅛   **teaspoon ground cloves**
4   **tablespoons butter, cut up**
½   **cup chopped pecans**

In a medium bowl, combine flour, brown sugar, cinnamon, and cloves. With a pastry blender or 2 knives, cut in butter until mixture resembles fine crumbs. Stir in pecans.

Chapter 10

The Best No-Bake Pies

  Chiffon and ice cream pies are perfect no-bake party pies. Completely do-ahead, each one is ready and waiting in your fridge overnight or in the freezer for weeks until it's time to entertain. Gorgeous to look at—filled with big, billowy mounds of fruit-infused chiffon, or layered with your favorite ice cream, nuts, and candies—every one of these pie beauties is a showstopper, guaranteed to wow your guests. Best of all, they're a breeze to make, fresh and fabulous tasting, and not one requires a moment of baking.

  These pies start with a crisp crumb crust, prepared with an assortment of crushed cookies tossed with butter and nuts for extra crunch. I think crumb crusts taste best when toasted. Bake your crumb crusts as directed in the "It's All in the Crust" chapter (page 155) or use the microwave. Always start with a microwaveproof pie pan, preferably made of glass. For plain crumb crusts, prepare as directed and microwave on High 1 to 1½ minutes, rotating the pie plate every 30 seconds, or until the crumbs are lightly toasted. For nut crumb crusts, first toast the nuts by arranging them on a small glass plate. Microwave on High for 1 to 1½ minutes, stirring the nuts every 30 seconds, or until fragrant. Let cool. Then prepare the nut crumb crust as directed. Microwave on High 1 to 1½ minutes, rotating the pie plate every 30 seconds, or until crumbs are lightly toasted. Cool crumb crusts completely on a wire rack before filling.

  Chiffon pie pointers: Set with gelatin and lightened by beaten egg whites and whipped cream, chiffon is the most delicate filling for do-ahead pies. For a completely smooth filling, dissolving the gelatin correctly is a crucial first step. Always start by sprinkling the gelatin over cold liquid, then let the mixture stand 5 minutes to allow the granules to soften. When heating, stir constantly with a spatula, 2 to 3 minutes. To make sure the gelatin is completely dissolved, run your finger along the surface of the spatula. It should feel absolutely smooth. If there are still granules, continue to heat another minute. At this point, I transfer the dissolved gelatin mixture to a large metal bowl placed over another bowl of ice water. This is the fastest way to get a chiffon filling to gel. First the mixture needs to chill until it mounds slightly when dropped from a spoon. Stir the mixture occasionally until it begins to thicken and take on the consistency of unbeaten egg whites. If you take a spoonful and it forms a dollop when dropped back into the bowl, it's ready. (If your mixture becomes overchilled and too firm, simply whisk until smooth or place in a bowl of hot water for about 1 minute to melt, then chill again.) The gelatin mixture can also be chilled in the refrigerator, but it takes a bit more time.

The light and airy texture of chiffon-filled pies depends on the beaten egg whites and heavy cream. When whipping egg whites, always remember to begin with a clean mixing bowl and beaters. The egg whites should be at room temperature, and there should be no sign of egg yolk. If your filling has whipped cream as well, it helps to chill the mixing bowl and beaters first. This can be done simply by placing the utensils in the freezer for 5 minutes. Beat the cream until stiff peaks form when the beaters are raised. Be careful not to overbeat, though, or the cream will become grainy. When folding beaten egg whites and whipped cream into the gelatin mixture, spoon the beaten whites or cream on top of the gelatin mixture. Using a rubber spatula, gently lift the gelatin mixture over the beaten whites or cream, rotating the bowl until just blended. Once your pie shell is filled, the filling then needs to be chilled at least 4 hours to set. If it is refrigerated overnight, cover the filling loosely with plastic wrap.

Fabulous ice cream pies: Although these ice cream pies were designed with specific flavors in mind, feel free to mix and match with whatever taste combinations suit your fancy. Here are some tips to fill your pie crust in a flash:

For the most even job with the least amount of melting, I found the best way to soften ice cream for pie fillings is in the refrigerator. Keep in mind that if you use a premium versus a store-bought brand of ice cream, it will have a higher density and will take a little longer to soften. On average, a premium ice cream takes 30 minutes in the refrigerator to soften; store-bought, about 20 minutes.

When filling a pie crust, apply the softened ice cream in layers, using an ice cream scoop or sturdy spoon, instead of trying to press down on a single large block of ice cream. To store, cover the top surface of the ice cream filling directly with wax paper, then wrap your pie in heavy-duty freezer wrap or foil. Store ice cream pies in the back of the freezer where it's coldest. They can be prepared ahead up to 2 weeks. Serving your pie is a bit easier if you let it soften slightly first. Simply unwrap, decorate if desired, then refrigerate about 15 minutes.

So now it's time to chill out with some of the best no-bake creations in a crust. The classic chiffons are here with a twist: Triple Mint Grasshopper Pie, Sour Cream Lemon Chiffon Pie, Raspberry Margarita Chiffon Pie. And fast from the freezer come Honey Crunch-Chocolate Chunk Peanut Butter Pie and Frozen Mississippi Mud Pie, both perfect with your favorite hot fudge sauce.

240   PASSIONFRUIT SATIN CHIFFON PIE

Prep: 20 minutes   Cook: 5 to 7 minutes   Chill: 4 hours   Serves: 8

Fresh passionfruit is available March through September, and it's definitely worth seeking out for this gorgeous pie. Choose fully ripe fruit with a deep purple skin and a dimpled surface.

10 fresh passionfruit or ½ cup
    frozen passionfruit
    puree, thawed
1 (¼-ounce) envelope
    unflavored gelatin
4 large eggs, separated, at
    room temperature
¾ cup sugar
2 tablespoons fresh lime juice

½ teaspoon grated lime zest
½ cup heavy cream
1 Buttery Vanilla Nut Crumb
    Crust (page 163) or 1 (6-
    ounce) prepared vanilla
    cookie or graham cracker
    crumb crust
    Whipped cream and fresh
    raspberries

1. Cut each fresh passionfruit in half and scoop out pulp and seeds with a spoon. Transfer to a fine sieve set over a bowl; strain pulp through sieve, pressing with back of spoon. Discard seeds. You should have ½ cup passionfruit puree.

2. In a cup, sprinkle gelatin over ¼ cup water; let stand 5 minutes to soften.

3. In a medium saucepan, whisk together egg yolks and ½ cup sugar. Whisk in passionfruit puree and lime juice until smooth. Cook over medium heat, stirring constantly, until mixture thickens and coats back of a spoon, 5 to 7 minutes.

4. Remove from heat and stir in softened gelatin and lime zest until gelatin is completely dissolved, about 2 minutes. Transfer mixture to a large bowl and place in a larger bowl filled with ice water. Let cool, stirring occasionally, until mixture mounds slightly when dropped from spoon, 8 to 10 minutes. (Or refrigerate, stirring occasionally, until partially set, 30 to 40 minutes.)

5. Meanwhile, in a large bowl, beat egg whites with an electric mixer on medium speed to soft peaks. Gradually add remaining ¼ cup sugar. Increase mixer speed to medium-high and continue to beat until stiff peaks form when beaters are lifted. Remove partially set gelatin mixture from ice water. With a rubber spatula, fold in beaten whites until blended.

6. In another bowl, beat cream with an electric mixer until stiff. Fold into passionfruit mixture. Turn filling into Buttery Vanilla Nut Crumb Crust. Cover and refrigerate until filling is set, several hours or overnight. Uncover, decorate top with whipped cream, and garnish with fresh raspberries.

241   BUTTERSCOTCH PUMPKIN CHIFFON PIE

Prep: 30 minutes   Cook: 4 to 6 minutes   Chill: 4 hours   Serves: 8

The dark brown sugar and a touch of molasses, combined with warm spices, make this chiffon pie a comfort classic.

1 (¼-ounce) envelope unflavored gelatin
4 large eggs, separated, at room temperature
¾ cup packed dark brown sugar
1¼ cups canned solid-pack pumpkin
½ cup heavy cream
2 tablespoons unsulphured molasses

1 teaspoon cinnamon
½ teaspoon ground ginger
Pinch of ground allspice
¼ teaspoon salt
¼ cup granulated sugar
1 Gingersnap Crumb Crust (page 165) or 1 (6-ounce) prepared graham cracker crumb crust
Whipped cream

1. In a cup, sprinkle gelatin over ¼ cup water; let stand 5 minutes to soften.

2. In a medium saucepan, whisk egg yolks and brown sugar until smooth. Add pumpkin, heavy cream, molasses, cinnamon, ginger, allspice, and salt and blend well. Cook over medium heat, stirring constantly, until mixture comes to a boil, 4 to 6 minutes. Remove from heat and stir in softened gelatin until completely dissolved, about 2 minutes. Transfer mixture to a large bowl and place in a larger bowl filled with ice water. Let cool, stirring occasionally, until mixture mounds slightly when dropped from spoon, about 15 minutes. (Or refrigerate, stirring occasionally, until partially set, 30 to 40 minutes.)

3. Meanwhile, in a large bowl, beat egg whites with an electric mixer on medium speed to soft peaks. Gradually add granulated sugar. Increase mixer speed to medium-high and continue to beat until stiff peaks form when beaters are lifted. Remove partially set pumpkin mixture from ice water. With a rubber spatula, fold in beaten egg whites until blended.

4. Turn filling into Gingersnap Crumb Crust. Cover loosely and refrigerate until filling is set, 4 hours or overnight. Uncover and decorate top with whipped cream.

242 SOUR CREAM LEMON CHIFFON PIE

Prep: 30 minutes   Cook: 6 to 8 minutes   Chill: 4 hours   Serves: 8

1 (¼-ounce) envelope
  unflavored gelatin
1 cup sugar
  Pinch of salt
4 large eggs, separated, at
  room temperature
⅔ cup sour cream
½ cup fresh lemon juice

1 tablespoon grated lemon
  zest
  Graham Cracker Crumb
  Crust (page 160) or 1 (6-
  ounce) prepared graham
  cracker crumb crust
  Sweetened Whipped Cream
  (page 265)

1. In a medium saucepan, combine gelatin, ½ cup sugar, and salt. Whisk in egg yolks, sour cream, and lemon juice. Let stand 3 minutes. Cook over medium heat, stirring constantly, until gelatin is completely dissolved and mixture is thick enough to coat back of a spoon, 6 to 8 minutes. Remove from heat and stir in lemon zest.

2. Transfer mixture to a large bowl and place in a larger bowl filled with ice water. Let cool, stirring occasionally, until mixture mounds slightly when dropped from a spoon, about 10 to 12 minutes. (Or refrigerate, stirring occasionally, until partially set, 30 to 40 minutes.)

3. Meanwhile, in a large bowl, beat egg whites with an electric mixer on medium speed to soft peaks. Gradually beat in remaining ½ cup sugar until stiff peaks form when beaters are lifted. Remove partially set gelatin mixture from ice water. With a rubber spatula, fold in beaten whites until blended.

4. Turn filling into Graham Cracker Crumb Crust. Cover loosely and refrigerate until filling is set, 4 hours or overnight. Uncover and decorate top with Sweetened Whipped Cream.

243 RASPBERRY MARGARITA CHIFFON PIE
Prep: 20 minutes   Cook: 6 to 8 minutes   Chill: 4 hours   Serves: 8

3 cups fresh or frozen
   raspberries, thawed
1 (¼-ounce) envelope
   unflavored gelatin
¼ cup fresh lime juice
4 large eggs, separated, at
   room temperature
¾ cup sugar
2 tablespoons tequila
2 tablespoons orange-flavored
   liqueur

½ teaspoon grated lime zest
½ cup heavy cream
   Graham Cracker Crumb
   Crust (page 160) or 1 (6-
   ounce) prepared graham
   cracker crumb crust
   Margarita Whipped Cream
   (recipe follows)
8 lime slices

1. In a blender or food processor, puree raspberries. Strain into a bowl through a fine sieve to yield 1 cup puree; discard seeds. In a cup, sprinkle gelatin over lime juice and stir gently; let stand 5 minutes to soften.

2. In a small heavy saucepan, whisk together egg yolks, ½ cup sugar, and 2 tablespoons water until smooth. Cook over medium-low heat, stirring constantly, until mixture thickens slightly and coats back of a spoon, about 6 minutes. Remove from heat and stir in softened gelatin mixture. Stir until gelatin is completely dissolved, about 2 minutes. Stir in raspberry puree, tequila, orange liqueur, and lime zest. Transfer mixture to a large bowl and place in a larger bowl filled with ice water. Let cool, stirring occasionally, until mixture mounds slightly when dropped from spoon, 12 to 15 minutes. (Or refrigerate, stirring occasionally, until partially set, 30 to 40 minutes.)

3. Meanwhile, in a large bowl, beat egg whites with an electric mixer on medium speed to soft peaks. Gradually beat in remaining ¼ cup sugar until stiff peaks form when beaters are lifted. Remove partially set gelatin mixture from ice water. With a rubber spatula, fold in beaten whites until blended.

4. In another bowl, beat cream with an electric mixer until soft peaks form. Fold into gelatin mixture. Turn filling into Graham Cracker Crumb Crust. Cover loosely and refrigerate until filling is set, 4 hours or overnight. Uncover and decorate top with Margarita Whipped Cream and lime slices.

MARGARITA WHIPPED CREAM
Makes: 2½ cups

1 cup heavy cream
¼ cup powdered sugar
2 tablespoons orange-flavored
   liqueur

1 tablespoon tequila
½ teaspoon grated lime zest

In a large bowl, beat cream and powdered sugar with an electric mixer until soft peaks form. Add orange liqueur, tequila, and lime zest and continue to beat to stiff peaks.

244 MEXICAN CHOCOLATE CHIFFON PIE
Prep: 20 minutes   Cook: 6 to 8 minutes   Chill: 4 hours   Serves: 8

1 (¼-ounce) envelope
  unflavored gelatin
1 cup milk
3 large eggs, separated, at
  room temperature
1 cup sugar
½ teaspoon cinnamon
  Pinch of salt
3 (1-ounce) squares
  unsweetened chocolate,
  finely chopped

3 tablespoons Kahlúa liqueur
½ cup heavy cream
  Chocolate Wafer Crust
  (page 161) or 1 (6-ounce)
  prepared chocolate cookie
  crumb crust
  Sweetened Whipped Cream
  (page 265)
  Shaved chocolate

1. In a heavy medium saucepan, sprinkle gelatin over milk; let stand 5 minutes to soften. In a small bowl, whisk egg yolks, ¾ cup sugar, cinnamon, and salt until smooth. Whisk yolk mixture into softened gelatin to blend. Cook over medium heat, stirring constantly, until gelatin is completely dissolved and mixture is thick enough to coat back of a spoon, 6 to 8 minutes.

2. Remove from heat and stir in chocolate until melted. Stir in Kahlúa. Transfer mixture to a large bowl and place in a larger bowl filled with ice water. Let cool, stirring occasionally, until mixture mounds slightly when dropped from spoon, about 10 minutes. (Or refrigerate, stirring occasionally, until partially set, 30 to 40 minutes.)

3. Meanwhile, in a large bowl, beat egg whites with an electric mixer on medium speed to soft peaks. Gradually beat in remaining ¼ cup sugar. Increase mixer speed to medium-high and continue to beat until stiff peaks form when beaters are lifted. Remove partially set gelatin mixture from ice water. With a rubber spatula, fold in beaten egg whites until blended.

4. In another bowl, beat cream with an electric mixer until stiff. Fold into chocolate mixture. Turn filling into Chocolate Wafer Crust. Cover loosely and refrigerate until filling is set, 4 hours or overnight. Uncover and decorate top with Sweetened Whipped Cream and shaved chocolate.

245   STRAWBERRY ALMOND CHIFFON PIE
Prep: 20 minutes   Cook: 10 minutes   Chill: 4 hours   Serves: 8

2 (10-ounce) packages frozen
  strawberries in light
  syrup, thawed
1 (¼-ounce) envelope plus 1
  teaspoon unflavored
  gelatin
1 tablespoon fresh lemon
  juice
3 large egg whites, at room
  temperature
½ cup sugar

¼ teaspoon almond extract
½ cup heavy cream
1 Almond-Amaretti Cookie
  Crust (page 162) or 1 (6-
  ounce) prepared vanilla
  cookie or graham cracker
  crumb crust
¼ cup sliced almonds
Sweetened Whipped Cream
  (page 265)
Fresh whole strawberries

1. Strain syrup from strawberries through a fine sieve into a small saucepan. Sprinkle gelatin over syrup; let stand 5 minutes to soften. In a large bowl, crush berries with a potato masher or fork; stir in lemon juice.

2. Cook gelatin mixture over low heat until gelatin is completely dissolved, about 10 minutes. Stir syrup into crushed berries. Place bowl in a larger bowl filled with ice water. Let cool, stirring occasionally, until mixture mounds slightly when dropped from spoon, 3 to 5 minutes.

3. Meanwhile, in a large bowl, beat egg whites with an electric mixer on medium speed to soft peaks. Gradually add sugar and almond extract. Beat on medium-high speed until stiff peaks form when beaters are lifted. Remove partially set gelatin mixture from ice water. With a rubber spatula, fold in beaten whites until blended.

4. In another bowl, beat cream with an electric mixer until stiff. Fold into strawberry mixture. Turn filling into Almond-Amaretti Cookie Crust. Cover loosely and refrigerate until filling is set, 4 hours or overnight.

5. On a small glass plate, arrange almonds. Microwave on High 1 to 1½ minutes, stirring nuts every 30 seconds until lightly toasted. Let cool. Uncover pie and decorate top with Sweetened Whipped Cream, toasted almonds, and fresh whole strawberries.

246   SWEET MAPLE CHIFFON PIE
Prep: 30 minutes   Cook: 6 to 8 minutes   Chill: 4 hours   Serves: 8

1 (¼-ounce) envelope
  unflavored gelatin
4 large eggs, separated, at
  room temperature
1 cup pure maple syrup
  Pinch of salt
1 cup milk
1 teaspoon vanilla extract

¼ cup sugar
⅓ cup heavy cream
  Buttery Vanilla Nut Crumb
  Crust (page 163) or 1 (6-
  ounce) prepared vanilla
  cookie or graham cracker
  crumb crust

1. In a cup, sprinkle gelatin over ¼ cup water; let stand 5 minutes to soften.

2. In a small heavy saucepan, whisk together egg yolks, ⅔ cup maple syrup, and salt. Gradually whisk in milk until smooth. Cook over medium-low heat, stirring constantly, until mixture thickens slightly and coats back of a spoon, 6 to 8 minutes. Remove from heat, add softened gelatin mixture, and stir until completely dissolved, about 2 minutes. Stir in vanilla. Transfer mixture to a large bowl and place in a larger bowl filled with ice water. Let cool, stirring occasionally, until mixture mounds slightly when dropped from a spoon, about 15 minutes. (Or refrigerate, stirring occasionally, until partially set, 30 to 40 minutes.)

3. Meanwhile, in a large bowl, beat egg whites with an electric mixer on medium speed to soft peaks. Gradually beat in sugar. Increase mixer speed to medium-high and continue to beat until stiff peaks form when beaters are lifted. Remove partially set gelatin mixture from ice water. With a rubber spatula, fold in beaten whites until blended.

4. In another bowl, beat cream with an electric mixer until stiff. Fold into maple mixture. Turn filling into Buttery Vanilla Nut Crumb Crust. Cover loosely and refrigerate until filling is set, 4 hours or overnight. Cut pie into serving pieces. Serve with remaining ⅓ cup syrup.

---

247 FROZEN MISSISSIPPI MUD PIE

Prep: 20 minutes   Cook: none   Freeze: 5 hours   Serves: 10

2 pints vanilla ice cream
2 tablespoons bourbon
1 Chocolate Wafer Crust
   (page 161) or 1 (6-ounce)
   prepared chocolate cookie
   crumb crust

Bourbon Super Fudge Sauce
   (page 205)
⅔ cup chopped pecans
2 pints coffee ice cream
Sweetened Whipped Cream
   (page 265)

1. Place vanilla ice cream in refrigerator to soften slightly, 20 minutes. In a medium bowl, quickly blend ice cream with bourbon. Quickly spread ice cream mixture evenly over bottom of Chocolate Wafer Crust. Top with ½ cup Bourbon Super Fudge Sauce, then sprinkle on ⅓ cup chopped pecans. Freeze until firm, about 1 hour.

2. Place coffee ice cream in refrigerator to soften slightly, 20 minutes. Spoon on top of filling in pie shell, mounding slightly in center. Quickly spread another ½ cup Bourbon Super Fudge Sauce over ice cream and sprinkle remaining ⅓ cup pecans on top.

3. Cover loosely and freeze until firm, 4 hours or overnight. Uncover and decorate top with Sweetened Whipped Cream. Serve with remaining Bourbon Super Fudge Sauce, reheated until warm, if desired.

248   PEACH MELBA SORBET 'N' CREAM PIE
Prep: 35 minutes   Cook: none   Freeze: 6½ hours   Serves: 8

1 pint raspberry sorbet or sherbet
1 Almond-Amaretti Cookie Crust (page 162) or 1 (6-ounce) prepared vanilla cookie or graham cracker crumb crust

2 pints vanilla ice cream
1 cup peach preserves, chilled
1 pint orange sorbet or sherbet
Whipped cream
Red Raspberry Sauce (recipe follows)
Sliced fresh peaches

1. Place raspberry sorbet in refrigerator to soften slightly, 20 minutes. Spoon sorbet evenly over bottom of Almond-Amaretti Cookie Crust. Freeze until firm, about 1 hour.

2. Place vanilla ice cream in refrigerator to soften slightly, 20 minutes. In a medium bowl, quickly combine ice cream with preserves just to blend. Quickly spread over top of filling in pie shell, mounding slightly in center. Freeze until firm, 1 hour.

3. Place orange sorbet in refrigerator to soften slightly, 20 minutes. Quickly spread on top of peach layer. Cover loosely and freeze until firm, 4 hours or overnight.

4. One hour before serving, uncover pie and decorate top with whipped cream. Freeze 30 minutes, or until cream is firm. Just before serving, drizzle ¼ cup Red Raspberry Sauce over pie. Serve with remaining sauce and sliced peaches on the side.

249   RED RASPBERRY SAUCE
Prep: 5 minutes   Cook: none   Makes: 2 cups

2 (10-ounce) packages frozen raspberries in light syrup, thawed

2 tablespoons sugar

In a food processor or blender, puree raspberries until smooth. Transfer to a fine sieve set over a bowl; strain through sieve, pressing with back of spoon to remove seeds. Stir in sugar until dissolved.

250 FROZEN PISTACHIO-BLACKBERRY RIPPLE PIE

Prep: 20 minutes   Cook: 5 minutes   Freeze: 5 hours   Serves: 10

1 (12-ounce) bag frozen blackberries, thawed
½ cup sugar
1 tablespoon cornstarch
2 tablespoons butter, cut up
4 pints vanilla ice cream
⅔ cup finely chopped pistachio nuts
¼ cup amaretto liqueur

1 Almond-Amaretti Cookie Crust (page 162) or 1 (6-ounce) prepared vanilla cookie or graham cracker crumb crust
Sweetened Whipped Cream (page 265)
Chocolate shavings

1. In a blender or food processor, puree blackberries. Strain puree into a bowl through a fine sieve; discard seeds. In a small nonreactive saucepan, whisk together sugar and cornstarch; stir in blackberry puree. Bring to a boil over medium-low heat, stirring occasionally; boil 1 minute. Remove from heat and stir in butter until melted. Let cool.

2. Place 2 pints ice cream in refrigerator to soften slightly, about 20 minutes. In a medium bowl, quickly blend ice cream with ⅓ cup pistachios and 2 tablespoons amaretto liqueur. Spoon ice cream mixture evenly over bottom of pie crust. Quickly spread top with half the blackberry puree. Freeze until firm, about 1 hour.

3. Repeat process with remaining 2 pints vanilla ice cream blended with nuts and amaretto liqueur; then top with blackberry mixture. Cover loosely and freeze until firm, 4 hours or overnight. Uncover and decorate top with Sweetened Whipped Cream and chocolate shavings.

251   TRIPLE MINT GRASSHOPPER PIE

Prep: 20 minutes   Cook: 5 to 8 minutes   Chill: 4 hours   Serves: 8

This classic no-bake pie is made extra-minty thanks to grated mint candies and a mint chocolate wafer crust.

4 large eggs, separated, at
    room temperature
¾ cup milk
1 (¼-ounce) envelope
    unflavored gelatin
¾ cup sugar
    Pinch of salt
¼ cup green crème de menthe
    liqueur

3 tablespoons white crème de
    cacao liqueur
½ cup heavy cream
12 chocolate-covered mint
    candies
    Minty Chocolate Crumb
    Crust (page 203)
    Whipped cream

1. In a small saucepan, whisk together egg yolks and milk. Sprinkle gelatin over top; let stand 5 minutes to soften. Whisk in ½ cup sugar and salt. Cook over medium-low heat, stirring constantly, until gelatin is completely dissolved and mixture coats back of a spoon, 5 to 8 minutes. Remove from heat and stir in crème de menthe and crème de cacao liqueurs. Transfer mixture to a large bowl and place in a larger bowl filled with ice water. Let cool, stirring occasionally, until mixture mounds slightly when dropped from a spoon, about 15 minutes. (Or refrigerate, stirring occasionally, until partially set, 30 to 40 minutes.)

2. Meanwhile, in a large bowl, beat egg whites with an electric mixer on medium speed to soft peaks. Gradually add remaining ¼ cup sugar. Beat on medium-high speed until stiff peaks form when beaters are lifted. Remove partially set gelatin mixture from ice water. With a rubber spatula, fold in beaten egg whites until blended.

3. In another bowl, beat cream with an electric mixer until stiff. Fold into gelatin mixture. Using large holes of a standing grater, coarsely grate mint candies. Fold ½ cup grated mint candies into filling; turn into Minty Chocolate Crumb Crust. Cover loosely and refrigerate until filling is set, 4 hours or overnight.

4. Uncover pie and decorate with whipped cream. Sprinkle remaining grated mint candies on top.

252 MINTY CHOCOLATE CRUMB CRUST
Prep: 5 minutes   Cook: 2 to 2½ minutes   Freeze: 15 minutes
Makes: 1 (9-inch) crumb crust

This no-bake crust has a fabulous mint flavor, perfect for your favorite cream pie filling.

½ cup mint semisweet chocolate chips

2 tablespoons butter, cut up

1½ cups chocolate wafer cookie crumbs

1. In a medium glass bowl, combine mint chocolate chips and butter. Microwave on Medium 2 to 2½ minutes, or until chips are melted; stir until smooth.

2. Stir in cookie crumbs until mixture is evenly moistened. Press crumb mixture evenly over bottom and sides of a 9-inch glass pie pan. Freeze until firm, about 15 minutes.

253 HONEY CRUNCH-CHOCOLATE CHUNK PEANUT BUTTER PIE
Prep: 20 minutes   Cook: none   Freeze: 6 hours   Serves: 12

6 whole graham cracker cookies

½ cup honey-roasted peanuts

2 tablespoons packed brown sugar

½ cup honey peanut butter

2 tablespoons butter, melted

1 quart chocolate ice cream

6 (1.6-ounce) chocolate-covered peanut butter cup candies, coarsely chopped (about 2 cups)

1 quart butter brickle or vanilla ice cream

3 tablespoons crushed peanut brittle candy

Peanut Butter Super Fudge Sauce (page 205)

1. In a food processor, process graham crackers, peanuts, and brown sugar to fine crumbs. Add peanut butter and melted butter and process, turning machine quickly on and off, until crumbs are evenly moistened. Press into a greased 9-inch pie plate. Freeze until firm, about 1 hour.

2. Place chocolate ice cream in refrigerator to soften slightly, about 20 minutes. In a medium bowl, quickly blend ice cream and 1 cup chopped peanut butter cup candies. Spoon ice cream evenly over bottom of frozen pie crust. Freeze until firm, about 1 hour.

3. Meanwhile, place butter brickle or vanilla ice cream in refrigerator to soften slightly, about 20 minutes. In a medium bowl, quickly blend ice cream with remaining 1 cup peanut butter cup candies. Spoon on top of chocolate layer, mounding slightly in center. Sprinkle crushed peanut brittle candy on top. Cover loosely and freeze until firm, 4 hours or overnight. Uncover and serve with Peanut Butter Super Fudge Sauce.

254   FROZEN TIRAMISÙ PIE

Prep: 20 minutes   Cook: 5 minutes   Freeze: 5 hours   Serves: 10

This frosty version of the Italian classic has all the great tastes of mascarpone cheese, espresso, and chocolate.

2   pints premium coffee ice
    cream
    Buttery Vanilla Wafer
    Crumb Crust (page 163)
    or 1 (6-ounce) prepared
    vanilla cookie or graham
    cracker crumb crust
½   cup chocolate-coated coffee
    beans or mocha-flavored
    coffee-bean candies, or
    2 ounces semisweet
    chocolate, chopped

⅔   cup sugar
5   large egg whites, at room
    temperature
8   ounces mascarpone cheese
2   tablespoons brandy
1   tablespoon unsweetened
    cocoa powder
    Espresso Super Fudge Sauce
    (page 205)

1. Place ice cream in refrigerator to soften slightly, about 30 minutes. Spoon ice cream evenly over bottom of crumb crust. Sprinkle chocolate-coated coffee beans on top. Freeze until firm, about 1 hour.

2. In a medium saucepan, cook sugar and 3 tablespoons water over medium-high heat until sugar is dissolved and syrup reaches 240°F on a candy thermometer or forms a soft ball, about 5 minutes.

3. Meanwhile, in a large bowl, beat egg whites with an electric mixer on medium speed to soft peaks. Gradually pour in boiling syrup in a thin, steady stream. Increase mixer speed to medium-high and continue to beat until meringue is thick and glossy and cooled to lukewarm, 3 to 4 minutes.

4. In another large bowl, stir mascarpone cheese and brandy until blended. Gently fold one quarter of meringue into cheese mixture with a rubber spatula, then fold in remaining meringue. Spoon on top of ice cream shell, mounding slightly in center. Cover loosely and freeze until firm, 4 hours or overnight. Uncover and sift cocoa powder lightly over top. Serve with Espresso Super Fudge Sauce.

---

255   SUPER FUDGE ROCKY ROAD ICE CREAM PIE

Prep: 15 minutes   Cook: none   Freeze: 6½ hours   Serves: 12

2   (5½-ounce) packages
    brownie chocolate nut
    cookies, crushed (⅔
    cups)
4   tablespoons butter, melted

4   pints rocky road ice cream
1   cup Super Fudge Sauce,
    cooled (recipe follows)
1   (7-ounce) jar marshmallow
    cream

1. In a medium bowl, toss 2 cups crushed cookies and butter until mixture is evenly moistened. Press into a 9-inch pie plate. Freeze until firm, 1 hour.

2. Place 2 pints ice cream in refrigerator to soften slightly, 20 minutes. Spoon ice cream evenly over bottom of frozen pie crust. Quickly cover with ½ cup Super Fudge Sauce and sprinkle on remaining ⅔ cup crushed cookies. Freeze until firm, about 1 hour. Spread marshmallow cream over top; freeze 30 minutes longer.

3. Meanwhile, soften remaining 2 pints ice cream. Spoon on top of filling in pie shell, mounding slightly in center. Quickly spread with remaining ½ cup fudge sauce. Cover loosely and freeze until firm, 4 hours or overnight. Uncover and serve with remaining Super Fudge Sauce, reheated until warm, if desired.

256 SUPER FUDGE SAUCE
Prep: 5 minutes   Cook: 3 to 3½ minutes   Makes: 2 cups

Hot or cold, this is the ultimate chocolate sauce. And don't miss the flavor variations that follow.

4 (1-ounce) squares	**¾ cup heavy cream**
unsweetened chocolate,	**¼ cup light corn syrup**
coarsely chopped	**2 tablespoons butter, cut up**
½ cup packed brown sugar	**½ teaspoon vanilla extract**
¼ cup granulated sugar	

In a medium glass bowl, combine chocolate, brown sugar, granulated sugar, cream, and corn syrup. Microwave on High 3 to 3½ minutes, whisking every minute, or until mixture is bubbly and slightly thickened. Whisk in butter and vanilla until smooth.

Variations:

PEANUT BUTTER SUPER FUDGE SAUCE

Microwave Super Fudge Sauce as directed except omit butter. Stir in ⅓ cup smooth peanut butter until melted.

ESPRESSO SUPER FUDGE SAUCE

Prepare Super Fudge Sauce, adding 1 teaspoon instant espresso powder. Microwave as directed.

BOURBON SUPER FUDGE SAUCE

Microwave Super Fudge Sauce as directed. Stir in 3 tablespoons bourbon.

257   HONEY CREAM STRAWBERRY GLACÉ PIE

Prep: 30 minutes   Cook: 5 minutes   Chill: 2 to 3 hours   Serves: 8

For maximum fresh fruit flavor, serve this pie the day it's made.

2 (3-ounce) packages cream
   cheese, softened
¾ cup plus 2 tablespoons
   sugar
3 tablespoons honey
¼ teaspoon grated lemon zest
   Nutty Graham Cracker
   Crust (page 159) or 1 (6-
   ounce) prepared graham
   cracker crumb crust

6 cups whole fresh
   strawberries
2 tablespoons cornstarch
1 tablespoon fresh lemon
   juice

1. In a medium bowl, beat cream cheese, 2 tablespoons sugar, honey, and lemon zest with an electric mixer on medium speed until smooth. Spread along bottom of Nutty Graham Cracker Crust. Refrigerate.

2. In a medium bowl, crush 2 cups strawberries to yield 1 cup crushed berries. In a medium saucepan, thoroughly combine remaining ¾ cup sugar with cornstarch. Stir in crushed strawberries and 2 tablespoons water. Bring to boil over medium heat, stirring occasionally. Boil 1 minute. Remove from heat and stir in lemon juice. Place strawberry mixture in a sieve set over a bowl. Strain strawberry mixture, pressing against solids with back of a spoon; discard solids and reserve clear glaze in bowl.

3. Cut remaining 4 cups strawberries in half. Arrange, cut sides down, on top of cream cheese filling in concentric circles until surface of pie is filled. Pour strawberry glaze evenly over fruit. Refrigerate several hours, or until glaze is just set.

Chapter 11

A Tribute to Tarts

When you want to serve a pie with a continental touch and you want a sophisticated presentation, it's time to create a tart. Shallower than pies, open-faced, and wrapped in a rich all-butter pastry, tarts are easy to prepare and utterly elegant. Fresh fruit tarts filled with apples and pears or topped with colorful berries nestled in a velvety pastry cream are a European classic. Tarts also invite chocolate, whether they are filled with mousse, a fudgy brownie center, or simply brushed with melted chocolate and packed with berries. Thanks to a selection of do-ahead baked tart shells that you'll find at the end of this chapter, many of these tarts can be effortlessly assembled in minutes with dramatic results.

Tarts can be prepared in a variety of sizes, either large like a pie or miniaturized into individual tartlets. So if you're serious about tart baking, purchasing special tart pans, which are widely available at moderate cost, is a good investment. My favorite is a round metal tart pan with fluted sides and a removable bottom. Because tarts are served freestanding, this pan is best for unmolding. I also love the scalloped design the edge gives the baked tart shell. Recipes in this collection mostly call for pans between 9 and 10 inches in diameter, either of which will serve 8. In a pinch, you may substitute 9- or 10-inch cake pans with removable bottoms. Special occasion tarts come in slightly larger sizes, and for these I specify an 11-inch tart pan.

For individual tartlets, these recipes call for 4½-inch tartlet pans; you can substitute 6-ounce ovenproof custard cups, though they will not be as attractive. To do so, roll and cut the pastry as directed for tartlets. Simply invert the custard cups and drape the pastry over the backs. Trim the edges and pleat so the pastry fits snugly over the cup. Prick the pastry with a fork, transfer the cups to a cookie sheet, and bake as directed.

By definition, tart pastry is a bit richer than pie pastry, and this collection has both elegant basic crusts and some custom-designed for special fillings. Some pastries are more cookie-like, with the addition of egg yolk and cream. I prefer the taste of unsalted butter in my tart pastry, although salted can certainly be used. The technique for rolling tart pastry is the same as for pie pastry. Once you master the simple technique of preparing baked tart shells, they can be prepared up to a day ahead, wrapped tightly at room temperature, or frozen. They need little embellishment; I often brush them with melted chocolate or fruit preserves and top with fresh fruit, or fill them with lemon or lime curd and garnish with berries and whipped cream.

Be sure never to butter your tart pan, because with the removable bottom, the butter will leak during baking. After a tart bakes and cools, the sides of the pastry shell will pull away from the sides of the pan, making unmolding in most cases quite easy. If, however, your tart filling bubbles up during baking and spills over between the tart shell and the side of the pan, there might be a bit of sticking. Just allow the tart to cool slightly, then gently loosen the pastry shell from the pan with the tip of a small knife. For serving, you may serve the tart directly from the bottom disk or transfer it to a serving plate using a wide metal spatula.

One of the easiest ways to dress up a fruit tart is by brushing it with a glaze made from fruit preserves or jelly. Apricot or peach preserves are a good choice for lighter colored fruits, such as fresh apricots, apples, peaches, pears, or bananas. Red currant jelly brings out the best color in berries and plums. Heat ¼ cup of preserves or jelly in a saucepan or microwave until melted. (Strain preserves to remove any pieces of fruit.) Stir in 1 tablespoon of brandy, kirsch, or other fruit liqueur, if desired. Brush warm glaze over the tart and let stand until set. Any extra glaze can be covered and refrigerated, then rewarmed for your next tart.

Fruit tarts for the sophisticate include a Golden Apricot and Mascarpone Tart, French Apple and Pear Tart, or the classic Sour Cherry Linzer Tart. Or if chocolate and nuts strike your fancy, choose from Coconut Macadamia Pecan Tart, Espresso Brownie Tart with Espresso Whipped Cream, or Black and White Chocolate Mousse Tartlets. Each one is a pastry cart sensation!

258 FRENCH APPLE AND PEAR TART

Prep: 1 hour   Freeze: 20 minutes   Cook: 35 to 40 minutes
Bake: 62 to 69 minutes   Serves: 8 to 10

This double-fruit tart, perfect for entertaining, features a homemade apple-pear puree that can be prepared a day ahead.

Mostly Butter Pastry for a 9-inch single crust pie (page 159)
2½ pounds tart apples, peeled
1½ pounds ripe pears, peeled and chopped (4 cups)
3 tablespoons butter
¼ cup plus 2 teaspoons brandy

5 tablespoons sugar
½ vanilla bean, split lengthwise, or 1 teaspoon vanilla extract
½ teaspoon grated lemon zest
¼ teaspoon grated nutmeg
3 tablespoons apricot preserves

1. Preheat oven to 425°F. On a lightly floured surface, roll out pastry into a 14-inch circle. Fold pastry in half and ease gently into an 11-inch tart pan with removable bottom; unfold dough. Gently press pastry with fingertips along bottom and up sides of pan. Trim overhanging edge of pastry to 1 inch above edge of pan. Fold and roll pastry in over side of crust and gently press edge up to extend ¼ inch above side of pan. Prick bottom with a fork. Freeze 20 minutes.

2. Line frozen pastry shell with foil and fill with pie weights, dried beans, or uncooked rice. Bake 12 minutes. Remove foil and weights. Bake pastry 10 to 12 minutes longer, until lightly golden. Let cool completely on a wire rack.

3. Chop enough apples (about 1½ pounds) to equal 4 cups. Combine chopped apples in a large saucepan with pears and butter. Cover and cook over low heat, stirring occasionally, until fruit is very soft, about 20 minutes. Whisk until smooth. Stir in ¼ cup brandy, 3 tablespoons sugar, and vanilla bean. Increase heat to medium and cook uncovered until puree is very thick and reduced to 3 cups, 15 to 20 minutes. Carefully remove vanilla bean and scrape out seeds into pear-apple sauce. (If using vanilla extract, stir in until blended.) Let cool completely.

4. Reduce oven temperature to 375°F. Thinly slice remaining 1 pound apples (3 cups); toss in a bowl with remaining 2 tablespoons sugar, lemon zest, and nutmeg. Spread apple-pear puree in bottom of baked tart shell. Arrange apple slices, overlapping them slightly in concentric circles, over top. Bake 40 to 45 minutes, or until apple slices are tender. Let cool on a wire rack.

5. In small saucepan, heat apricot preserves and remaining 2 teaspoons brandy over medium heat until bubbly; strain through a fine sieve. Brush glaze evenly over cooled tart. Remove sides of pan and serve at room temperature.

259 GOLDEN APRICOT AND MASCARPONE TART

Prep: 25 minutes   Bake: none   Serves: 8

Take advantage of fresh apricots to prepare this glorious summer fruit tart.

8 ounces mascarpone cheese
2 tablespoons heavy cream
2 tablespoons powdered or granulated sugar
¼ teaspoon grated lemon zest
⅛ teaspoon almond extract

Ultimate Tart Shell (page 228)
6 fresh apricots, thinly sliced
3 tablespoons apricot preserves

1. In a small bowl, stir mascarpone, cream, sugar, lemon zest, and almond extract until smooth and spreadable. Spread filling in baked tart shell. Arrange sliced apricots on top.

2. In a small glass bowl, microwave preserves on High 45 seconds to 1 minute, or until melted. Strain through a fine sieve into a bowl. Immediately brush warm preserves over fruit; remove sides of pan. Serve immediately or chill up to 2 hours.

260 COUNTRYSIDE BLUEBERRY TART

Prep: 20 minutes   Bake: 35 to 40 minutes   Serves: 8

This simple buttermilk custard tart can be prepared with fresh raspberries or blackberries in place of the blueberries. The cornmeal pastry adds a delightful nutty flavor and crunch.

⅓ cup sugar
1 tablespoon flour
Pinch of salt
1 large whole egg
1 large egg yolk
1 cup buttermilk

2 tablespoons butter, melted and cooled slightly
¼ teaspoon grated lemon zest
1½ cups fresh blueberries
1 (9-inch) Cornmeal Tart Shell (page 211)

1. Preheat oven to 350°F. In a large bowl, combine sugar, flour, and salt. Whisk in egg and egg yolk until smooth. Beat in buttermilk, melted butter, and lemon zest until blended.

2. Arrange blueberries in an even layer in tart shell. Carefully pour buttermilk custard over fruit.

3. Bake 35 to 40 minutes, or until filling is just set in center. Let cool completely on a wire rack before removing sides of pan. Serve at room temperature.

261 CORNMEAL TART SHELL
Prep: 10 minutes   Chill: 1 hour   Freeze: 20 minutes
Bake: 26 to 28 minutes   Makes: 1 (9- or 10-inch) tart shell

1 cup flour
⅓ cup yellow cornmeal
2 tablespoons sugar
¼ teaspoon salt

1 stick (4 ounces) cold
   unsalted butter, cut up
1 large egg yolk
3 to 4 tablespoons ice water

1. In a medium bowl, combine flour, cornmeal, sugar, and salt. Add butter and toss gently until all pieces are coated with flour. With a pastry blender or 2 knives, cut in butter until mixture resembles fine crumbs.

2. In a cup, whisk together egg yolk and 1 tablespoon ice water until blended. Drizzle over flour mixture, then toss with a fork. Add remaining ice water, 1 tablespoon at a time as needed, tossing vigorously with a fork just until dough begins to hold together. Turn out onto a work surface and shape pastry into a ball, kneading lightly. Flatten into a disk, then wrap tightly in plastic wrap. Refrigerate 1 hour or overnight.

3. Preheat oven to 425°F. On a lightly floured surface, roll pastry into a ⅛-inch-thick round. Fold pastry in half and ease gently into a 9- or 10-inch tart pan with a removable bottom. Unfold dough and gently press pastry with fingertips along bottom and up edge of pan. Trim overhanging edge of pastry to 1 inch above edge of pan. Fold and roll pastry in, then gently press edge up to extend ¼ inch above side of pan. Freeze 20 minutes.

4. Tear 2 sheets of foil slightly larger than tart pan. Press foil, shiny side down, into frozen tart shell, turning back ends of foil to cover edge of pan. Fill tart pan with pie weights, uncooked beans, or rice. Bake 12 minutes. Remove foil and weights. Bake pastry 14 to 16 minutes longer, or until crust is a deep golden brown. Let cool completely on a wire rack. Remove sides of pan. Transfer to a serving plate before filling.

262 SOUR CHERRY LINZER TART

Prep: 15 minutes   Chill: 2 hours 20 minutes   Freeze: 20 minutes
Bake: 45 to 47 minutes   Serves: 8

This classic tart from Austria features a spicy hazelnut-almond pastry. Always prepared with a lattice top and filled with preserves, the tart can be spread with the traditional raspberry, or you can choose blackberry or apricot.

4 ounces hazelnuts	10 tablespoons butter, softened
4 ounces slivered blanched almonds	2 large egg yolks
⅔ cup granulated sugar	1 teaspoon grated lemon zest
1 cup flour	½ teaspoon vanilla extract
½ teaspoon cinnamon	1 (10- or 12-ounce) jar sour cherry preserves
¼ teaspoon ground ginger	2 tablespoons powdered sugar
¼ teaspoon salt	
Pinch of ground cloves	

1. Preheat oven to 350°F. Spread out hazelnuts on a small baking sheet. Bake 10 to 12 minutes, or until nuts are lightly browned and dark skins are cracked. Rub warm nuts in a terrycloth towel to remove as much of skins as possible. Let cool. In a food processor, process hazelnuts, almonds, and ⅓ cup granulated sugar until finely ground. In a medium bowl, combine nut-sugar mixture with flour, cinnamon, ginger, salt, and cloves.

2. In a large bowl, beat butter and remaining ⅓ cup granulated sugar with an electric mixer until light and fluffy. Beat in 1 egg yolk, lemon zest, and vanilla. With mixer on low speed, gradually add nut mixture until just blended. Turn dough out onto a work surface and gather gently into a ball, then shape dough into 2 balls, one slightly larger than the other. Wrap in plastic wrap and flatten into 2 disks. Refrigerate 2 hours, or overnight.

3. Roll larger piece dough between 2 sheets lightly floured wax paper into a 12-inch circle about ⅛ inch thick. Remove top sheet of wax paper and carefully drape pastry over a 9-inch tart pan with removable bottom. (If dough cracks, patch together with lightly floured fingers.) Refrigerate 20 minutes. Roll remaining pastry disk between 2 sheets of lightly floured wax paper into a 10-inch circle. Remove top sheet of wax paper and cut dough into 1-inch-wide strips. Freeze until firm, about 20 minutes.

4. Preheat oven to 400°F. Fill pastry shell with an even layer of sour cherry preserves. Carefully arrange frozen pastry strips on top in a lattice pattern; trim edges. In a small bowl, lightly beat remaining egg yolk with 1 teaspoon water; brush over lattice.

5. Place tart on a cookie sheet and bake 15 minutes. Reduce oven temperature to 350°F. Bake 20 to 25 minutes longer, or until pastry is golden brown and filling is bubbly. (If pastry browns too quickly, cover loosely with foil.) Let cool completely on a wire rack. Just before serving, remove sides of pan and sift powdered sugar over top.

263 ESPRESSO BROWNIE TART WITH ESPRESSO WHIPPED CREAM

Prep: 15 minutes   Bake: 31 to 35 minutes   Serves: 16

Brownies have never been so elegant! To keep the filling moist and fudgy, be sure not to overbake this tart.

1 cup walnuts or pecans	1½ cups sugar
¾ cup flour	3 large eggs
¾ cup unsweetened cocoa	2 teaspoons vanilla extract
powder	Rich 'n' Sweet Tart Shell
¼ teaspoon salt	(page 226)
1½ sticks (6 ounces) butter,	Espresso Whipped Cream
melted	(recipe follows)
1 teaspoon instant espresso	
powder	

1. Preheat oven to 350°F. Spread out nuts on a small baking sheet. Bake 8 to 10 minutes, until golden brown and fragrant. Let cool, then coarsely chop.

2. In a small bowl, sift together flour, cocoa powder, and salt. In a large bowl, whisk together melted butter and espresso powder; whisk in sugar until well blended. Add eggs, 1 at a time, beating well after each addition. Mix in vanilla. Whisk in dry ingredients just until blended. Pour filling into baked tart shell; sprinkle nuts on top.

3. Bake 23 to 25 minutes, or until a cake tester inserted in center of tart comes out barely clean. Let cool completely on a wire rack. Remove sides of pan and serve with Espresso Whipped Cream.

ESPRESSO WHIPPED CREAM
Makes: 2½ cups

This whipped topping is fabulous with any chocolate dessert. It can easily be doubled for a crowd.

1 tablespoon instant espresso	¼ cup powdered sugar
powder	½ teaspoon vanilla extract
1 cup heavy cream	

In a cup, combine espresso and 1 tablespoon very hot water, stirring until espresso is dissolved. In a large bowl, beat cream with an electric mixer until soft peaks form. Add sugar, dissolved espresso, and vanilla and continue to beat to stiff peaks.

264 GORGEOUS GINGER BERRY TART
Prep: 25 minutes   Bake: none   Chill: 2 hours   Serves: 8

The subtle taste of fresh ginger is a wonderful complement to this color-ful berry topping. This tart can also be prepared with sliced fresh peaches, nectarines, or plums, or filled with Classic Pastry Cream (page 224).

4 slices of peeled fresh ginger, each ¼ inch thick	1 tablespoon butter
1 cup milk	½ teaspoon vanilla extract
3 large egg yolks	⅓ cup heavy cream
⅓ cup sugar	Basic Tart Shell (page 226)
Pinch of salt	1½ pints assorted fresh
¼ cup flour	raspberries, blueberries, or strawberries

1. In a small saucepan, combine ginger and water to cover. Bring to boil and boil 30 seconds; drain. In a medium saucepan, bring milk and ginger to a simmer over medium heat. Remove pan from heat, cover, and let stand 20 minutes.

2. Meanwhile, in a medium bowl, whisk egg yolks, sugar, and salt until light and pale. Whisk in flour until smooth. Remove ginger from milk. Gradually whisk hot milk into egg yolks. Return custard to saucepan. Bring to boil over medium heat, whisking constantly. Boil gently, whisking, 1 minute. (Custard will be thick.) Remove from heat and whisk in butter and vanilla. Transfer to a clean bowl. Cover surface directly with wax paper or plastic wrap and refrigerate until cold, 2 hours or overnight.

3. Just before filling tart, whisk custard gently to soften. In a small bowl, beat cream with an electric mixer until stiff peaks form. With a rubber spat-ula, carefully fold cream into custard and spread evenly in baked tart shell. Arrange fruit decoratively over top; remove sides of pan. Serve immedi-ately or chill up to 2 hours.

265 COCONUT MACADAMIA PECAN TART
Prep: 15 minutes   Bake: 21 to 28 minutes   Serves: 8

This chewy nutty tart is packed with a double dose of coconut flavor in the creamy filling and crust, and a rum-spiked coconut whipped cream tops it all off.

1 (7-ounce) jar macadamia nuts	½ cup cream of coconut
1 cup pecans	5⅓ tablespoons (⅓ cup) butter, cut up
Basic Tart Shell (page 226)	Coconut Whipped Cream (recipe follows)
1 cup packed brown sugar	

1. Preheat oven to 350°F. Spread out macadamia nuts and pecans on a small baking sheet. Bake 6 to 8 minutes, until golden brown and fragrant. Let cool, then coarsely chop. Spread chopped nuts evenly over bottom of baked tart shell.

2. In a medium saucepan, combine brown sugar, cream of coconut, and butter. Bring to boil, stirring to dissolve sugar; boil 1 minute. Pour over nuts.

3. Bake 15 to 20 minutes, or just until filling bubbles along edge. Let cool completely on a wire rack. Remove sides of pan and serve with Coconut Whipped Cream.

COCONUT WHIPPED CREAM
Makes: 2 cups

⅓ cup flaked coconut
1 cup heavy cream
1 tablespoon dark rum

2 tablespoons powdered
  sugar

1. In a small skillet, toast coconut over medium heat, stirring constantly, until golden, about 3 minutes. Transfer to a small bowl and let cool.

2. In a large bowl, beat cream with an electric mixer until soft peaks form. Add rum and powdered sugar and continue to beat to stiff peaks. Gently fold in toasted coconut. Use at once or cover and refrigerate up to 2 hours before serving.

266 RED BEAUTY PLUM-HAZELNUT TART
Prep: 40 minutes   Bake: 50 to 57 minutes   Serves: 8

This tart is inspired by the classic French frangipane tart, which is prepared with ground almonds.

½ cup hazelnuts
1 tablespoon flour
4 tablespoons butter, softened
⅓ cup plus 1 tablespoon sugar
1 large egg

Pinch of salt
1 tablespoon hazelnut or
  almond liqueur
Lemon Tart Shell (page 227)
4 plums, thinly sliced

1. Preheat oven to 375°F. Spread out hazelnuts on a small baking sheet. Bake 10 to 12 minutes, or until nuts are lightly browned and dark skins are cracked. Rub warm nuts in a terrycloth towel to remove as much of skins as possible. Let cool. In a food processor, process hazelnuts and flour until finely ground. Transfer to a bowl.

2. In same food processor bowl, blend butter and ⅓ cup sugar until smooth. Add egg, salt, and liqueur; process to blend. Add ground hazelnut mixture and pulse until just combined.

3. Spread filling in baked tart shell. Arrange plum slices, overlapping slightly in concentric circles, over top. Sprinkle fruit with remaining 1 tablespoon sugar.

4. Bake 40 to 45 minutes, or until filling is puffed and golden. Let cool completely on a wire rack before removing sides of pan.

267 PEAR AND BLACK WALNUT TART
Prep: 40 minutes   Bake: 51 to 58 minutes   Cook: 1 minute
Serves: 8

½ cup black walnuts
1 tablespoon flour
4 tablespoons butter, softened
⅓ cup sugar
1 large egg
Pinch of salt
1 teaspoon vanilla extract

Ultimate Tart Shell (page 228)
1 (16-ounce) can pear halves in heavy syrup, drained and thinly sliced
3 tablespoons apricot preserves

1. Preheat oven to 375°F. Spread out walnuts on a small baking sheet. Bake 5 to 7 minutes, until golden brown and fragrant. Let cool.

2. In a food processor, finely grind walnuts with flour. Transfer to a bowl. In same food processor bowl, blend butter and sugar until smooth. Add egg, salt, and vanilla; process to blend. Add ground black walnut mixture and pulse until just combined.

3. Spread nut filling in baked tart shell. Pat pear slices dry on paper towels. Arrange slices, overlapping slightly in concentric circles, over top of filling. Bake 45 to 50 minutes, or until filling is puffed and golden. Let cool on a wire rack, then remove sides of pan.

4. In a small glass bowl, microwave preserves on High 45 seconds to 1 minute, or until melted. Strain preserves through a fine sieve into a cup. Brush while warm over fruit. Let tart stand until preserves have set, about 30 minutes.

268 CLASSIC LEMON CURD TART
Prep: 15 minutes   Chill: 2 hours   Bake: none   Serves: 8

This citrus tart is simplicity itself; it can also be prepared as individual tartlets. For a festive presentation, arrange the berries on top of the lemon curd filling.

Classic Lemon Curd (page 217)
Basic Tart Shell (page 226)
Whipped cream

1 pint assorted fresh berries: raspberries, blueberries, or blackberries

Spread Classic Lemon Curd evenly in baked tart shell. Decorate top with whipped cream and serve with fresh berries. Serve immediately or refrigerate up to 2 hours.

269   CLASSIC LEMON CURD

Prep: 15 minutes   Cook: 6 to 8 minutes   Chill: 2 hours
Makes: 2 cups

1   cup sugar
½   cup fresh lemon juice
2   large whole eggs
2   large egg yolks

1   stick (4 ounces) unsalted
    butter, cut up
1   tablespoon grated lemon
    zest

1. In a medium saucepan, cook sugar and lemon juice over medium heat, stirring occasionally, until sugar is dissolved, 2 to 3 minutes. In a medium bowl, whisk together whole eggs and egg yolks. Gradually whisk hot sugar syrup into eggs; return to saucepan. Cook over medium-low heat, stirring constantly, just until mixture thickens and coats back of a spoon, about 4 minutes. (Do not boil.) Remove from heat.

2. Whisk in butter, a few pieces at a time, until melted. Whisk in lemon zest. Transfer lemon curd to a bowl. Cover with plastic wrap, pressing directly onto top surface of filling to form a tight seal. Refrigerate until cold, 2 hours or overnight.

270   SUMMER BERRY-ALMOND TART

Prep: 20 minutes   Chill: 30 minutes   Bake: 30 to 35 minutes
Serves: 8

Prepared puff pastry and a speedy marzipan filling make this an easy and elegant tart that's perfect for summer entertaining.

1   sheet (half a 17¼-ounce
    package) frozen puff
    pastry, thawed
¼   cup almond paste
⅓   cup plus 2 tablespoons
    sugar
4   tablespoons butter, softened

1   large egg
1   teaspoon vanilla extract
1   teaspoon grated lemon zest
    Pinch of salt
2   cups fresh blackberries
2   cups fresh raspberries
½   cup sliced almonds

1. On a sheet of lightly floured wax paper, roll out puff pastry sheet to a 12 x 14-inch rectangle. Cut into a 12-inch square, reserving a 12 x 2-inch pastry strip. Transfer pastry square to a large well-greased cookie sheet. Cut reserved pastry strip lengthwise into four 12 x ½-inch strips. Brush edges of pastry square with water and set reserved pastry strips on top to form a border; press to seal. Refrigerate 30 minutes.

2. Preheat oven to 400°F. In a small bowl, beat almond paste, ⅓ cup sugar, and butter until smooth. Beat in egg, vanilla, lemon zest, and salt with an electric mixer until light and fluffy. Spread within borders of pastry square. Top with an even layer of blackberries and raspberries, then sprinkle with almonds and remaining 2 tablespoons sugar.

3. Bake 30 to 35 minutes, or until topping is golden brown. With a large metal spatula, slide tart onto a wire rack. Let cool.

271 PEAR AND PLUM PITHIVIERS

Prep: 10 minutes   Chill: 30 minutes   Freeze: 20 minutes
Bake: 40 to 45 minutes   Serves: 8

1 (17¼-ounce) package frozen
   puff pastry, thawed
Toasted Almond Pastry
   Cream (recipe follows)

2 medium plums, sliced
1 peeled ripe pear, quartered
1 large egg

1. Grease 1 large cookie sheet and line another with wax paper. On another sheet of lightly floured wax paper, roll 1 puff pastry sheet into a 10½-inch circle. Using a plate or lid as a guide, trim pastry with sharp knife to a 10-inch circle. Transfer pastry to greased cookie sheet. Roll remaining pastry to a 12½-inch circle; trim to 12 inches. Transfer 12-inch circle to wax paper-lined cookie sheet. With the wide end of a plain pastry tip, cut out a ½-inch round in center of pastry with a small sharp knife. Refrigerate both pastry circles 30 minutes.

2. Remove cookie sheet with 10-inch pastry circle from refrigerator. Spread Toasted Almond Pastry Cream over top, leaving a 1-inch border. Arrange an overlapping circle of plum slices along outer edge of pastry cream filling. Cut each pear quarter lengthwise into 4 slices. Arrange in center of filling in a circle with tapered ends facing center. Brush pastry border with water. Arrange remaining pastry circle over fruit; press edges together to seal. With blunt side of a small knife, press pastry edges at 1-inch intervals toward center to form a scalloped edge. Freeze 20 minutes.

3. Preheat oven to 425°F. In a cup, whisk egg and 1 tablespoon water; brush over top crust. With a small sharp knife, score top crust about ⅛ inch deep in a spoke pattern, beginning at center and curving down to scalloped edge.

4. Bake 10 minutes. Reduce oven temperature to 375°F. Bake 30 to 35 minutes longer, or until crust is golden brown. With a large metal spatula, slide pastry onto a wire rack. Let cool completely.

272 TOASTED ALMOND PASTRY CREAM

Prep: 10 minutes   Bake: 8 to 10 minutes   Cook: 3 to 4 minutes
Chill: 1 hour   Makes: 1⅔ cups

This is also a wonderful filling for almost any fresh fruit tart.

⅔ cup blanched almonds
½ cup plus 2 tablespoons
   sugar
1 cup milk
   Pinch of salt

2 large egg yolks
2 tablespoons cornstarch
2 tablespoons butter
½ teaspoon vanilla extract
¼ teaspoon almond extract

1. Preheat oven to 350°F. Spread out almonds on a small baking sheet. Bake 8 to 10 minutes, or until nuts are lightly browned and fragrant. Let cool. In a food processor, finely grind nuts with 2 tablespoons sugar.

2. In a medium saucepan, combine milk, 6 tablespoons sugar, and salt. Bring to a simmer, about 2 minutes. In a medium bowl, whisk egg yolks, remaining 2 tablespoons sugar, and cornstarch. Gradually whisk in hot milk mixture. Return to saucepan. Return to a boil and boil 1 minute longer. (Custard will become thick.) Remove from heat and whisk in vanilla and almond extract. Transfer to a clean bowl, cover surface with wax paper or plastic wrap, and refrigerate until cold, about 1 hour. Stir in ground almonds.

---

273   FIVE-SPICE APPLE CUSTARD TART
Prep: 30 minutes   Freeze: 20 minutes   Bake: 72 to 79 minutes
Serves: 8 to 10

Five-spice powder, most commonly used in Chinese cooking, is a blend of cinnamon, cloves, fennel seed, star anise, and Szechuan peppercorns. Combined with sweet cream and apples, it adds a delightful twist to this autumnal fruit tart.

Mostly Butter Pastry for a 9-inch single crust pie (page 159)
1 pound tart apples, peeled and sliced ⅛ inch thick
½ cup sugar
2 large egg yolks

1 teaspoon Chinese five-spice powder
Pinch of salt
2 tablespoons flour
1 cup heavy cream
½ teaspoon vanilla extract

1. Preheat oven to 425°F. On a lightly floured surface, roll out pastry into a 14-inch circle. Fold pastry in half and ease gently into an 11-inch tart pan with removable bottom; unfold dough. Gently press pastry with fingertips along bottom and up sides of pan. Trim overhanging edge of pastry to 1 inch above edge of pan. Fold and roll pastry in over side of crust and gently press edge up to extend ¼ inch above sides of pan. Freeze 20 minutes.

2. Line frozen pastry shell with foil and fill with pie weights, dried beans, or uncooked rice. Bake 12 minutes. Remove foil and weights. Bake pastry 10 to 12 minutes longer, until lightly golden. Let cool completely on a wire rack.

3. In a medium bowl, toss apple slices with 2 tablespoons sugar. Arrange apple slices, overlapping them slightly in concentric circles, in baked tart shell. Bake 20 minutes.

4. Meanwhile, in a small bowl, whisk together egg yolks, remaining 6 tablespoons sugar, five-spice powder, and salt. Whisk in flour until smooth, then stir in heavy cream and vanilla until blended. Carefully remove tart from oven. Reduce oven temperature to 375°F. Pour custard over apples. Bake 30 to 35 minutes longer, or until custard is just set. Let cool on a wire rack; remove sides of pan. Serve at room temperature.

274 RASPBERRY PINE NUT TART
Prep: 20 minutes   Bake: 30 to 37 minutes   Serves: 8

Thanks to the addition of toasted pine nuts, this almond paste filling is not too sweet, and it perfectly complements the fresh berries.

½ cup pine nuts
⅓ cup granulated sugar
5⅓ tablespoons (⅓ cup) butter, softened
¼ cup almond paste
1 large egg
1 teaspoon grated lemon zest

½ teaspoon vanilla extract
¼ teaspoon salt
Buttery Shortbread Tart Shell (recipe follows)
1½ pints fresh raspberries
Powdered sugar

1. Preheat oven to 350°F. Spread out pine nuts on a small baking sheet. Bake 5 to 7 minutes, or until nuts are lightly browned and fragrant. Transfer to a plate and let cool. Combine nuts and granulated sugar in food processor; process until finely ground.

2. In a medium bowl, beat butter and almond paste with an electric mixer until light and fluffy. Gradually add pine nut-sugar mixture and beat until well combined. Beat in egg, lemon zest, vanilla, and salt. Spread into baked Buttery Shortbread Tart Shell.

3. Bake 25 to 30 minutes, or until top of filling is golden. Let cool on wire rack.

4. Arrange raspberries in concentric circles on top of nut filling; remove side of pan. Sprinkle sifted powdered sugar over top.

275 BUTTERY SHORTBREAD TART SHELL
Prep: 10 minutes   Bake: 24 to 26 minutes
Makes: 1 (9-inch) tart shell

You won't need a rolling pin to prepare this delicate shortbread-style pastry.

10 tablespoons unsalted butter, softened
¼ cup plus 2 tablespoons powdered sugar

1 teaspoon vanilla extract
½ teaspoon grated lemon zest
1⅓ cups flour

1. Preheat oven to 350°F. In a large bowl, beat together butter, powdered sugar, vanilla, and lemon zest with an electric mixer on medium speed until light and fluffy, 1 to 2 minutes. Gradually add flour, beating until well combined.

2. With lightly floured fingers, press dough into a 9-inch tart pan with removable bottom. Prick bottom of pastry with a fork. Bake 24 to 26 minutes, or until golden. Let cool completely on a wire rack before filling.

276 CARAMEL GINGER WALNUT TART
Prep: 15 minutes   Bake: 8 to 10 minutes   Cook: 8 to 10 minutes
Stand: 1 hour   Serves: 12 to 14

Totally indulgent, candied ginger provides an unexpected burst of taste in this satiny caramel nut filling.

2 cups walnuts
¼ cup minced candied ginger
1 cup sugar
½ cup heavy cream
1½ sticks (6 ounces) butter, cut into 12 pieces

Rich 'n' Sweet Tart Shell
(page 226)
Chocolate Cognac Glaze
(recipe follows)

1. Preheat oven to 350°F. Spread out walnuts on a small baking sheet. Bake 8 to 10 minutes, or until golden brown and fragrant. Transfer to a plate and let cool, then coarsely chop. Transfer to a medium bowl and toss with candied ginger.

2. Place sugar in a large heavy skillet. Cook over medium-low heat, swirling pan occasionally, until sugar is melted and syrup is a deep amber color, 8 to 10 minutes (do not stir). Reduce heat to low. With a long-handled spoon, quickly and carefully stir in cream. (Mixture will bubble vigorously.) Add butter, 3 pieces at a time, stirring until smooth after each addition. Remove from heat. Stir in nuts and ginger. Immediately pour into baked tart shell; spread evenly. Let cool completely on a wire rack.

3. Spread warm Chocolate Cognac Glaze on top of cooled tart. Let stand 1 hour, or until chocolate is set. Remove sides of pan and serve at room temperature.

277 CHOCOLATE COGNAC GLAZE
Prep: 5 minutes   Cook: 1½ to 2 minutes   Makes: ½ cup

2 ounces semisweet or bittersweet chocolate, cut up
1 tablespoon butter

1 teaspoon light corn syrup
2 tablespoons heavy cream
1 tablespoon Cognac or brandy

1. In a small glass bowl, combine chocolate, butter, and corn syrup. Microwave on Medium 1 to 1½ minutes, or until butter is melted. Whisk until chocolate is melted and completely smooth. Keep warm.

2. In another small glass bowl, combine cream and Cognac. Microwave on High 30 seconds, or until cream is hot. Whisk cream into warm chocolate mixture until glaze is completely smooth. Use at once.

278   BLACK AND WHITE CHOCOLATE MOUSSE TARTLETS
Prep: 15 minutes   Stand: 25 minutes   Chill: 1 hour   Serves: 6

3 ounces bittersweet or
    semisweet chocolate,
    finely chopped
1 cup heavy cream
    Chocolate Tartlet Shells
    (recipe follows)

5 ounces imported white
    chocolate, finely chopped
2 tablespoons white crème de
    cacao liqueur
    Shaved white chocolate

1. In a small glass bowl, combine bittersweet chocolate and ¼ cup cream. Microwave on Medium 1½ to 2 minutes, or until cream is hot. Whisk until chocolate is melted and smooth. Let cool to room temperature, about 25 minutes. Spread 1 generous tablespoon bittersweet chocolate cream in bottom of each tart crust.

2. In a medium glass bowl, combine white chocolate, crème de cacao, and 1 tablespoon water. Microwave on Low 1½ to 2 minutes, or until liqueur and water are very hot. Whisk until white chocolate is completely melted.

3. In a medium bowl, beat remaining ¾ cup cream with an electric mixer until stiff. With a rubber spatula, gradually fold white chocolate mixture into whipped cream until blended. Spoon whipped cream into a large pastry bag fitted with a star tip. Pipe white chocolate mousse filling evenly among tart crusts.

4. Refrigerate until filling is firm, about 1 hour. Remove sides of pans and decorate with shaved white chocolate.

279   CHOCOLATE TARTLET SHELLS
Prep: 10 minutes   Chill: 1 hour   Freeze: 20 minutes
Bake: 14 to 16 minutes   Makes: 6 (4½-inch) tartlet shells

Be careful not to overbake this rich chocolate pastry; it will continue to cook as it cools.

1 stick (4 ounces) unsalted
    butter, softened
⅓ cup sugar
1 teaspoon vanilla extract

Pinch of salt
¼ cup unsweetened cocoa
    powder
1 cup flour

1. In a medium bowl, beat butter, sugar, vanilla, and salt with an electric mixer on medium speed until light and fluffy. Beat in cocoa powder until smooth. With mixer on low speed, gradually add flour until just blended. (Mixture will be crumbly.) Turn out onto a work surface and shape pastry into ball, kneading lightly if necessary. Flatten into 2 disks and wrap tightly in plastic wrap. Refrigerate 1 hour or overnight.

2. On a lightly floured surface, roll out 1 disk into a ⅛-inch-thick round. Cut into 3 (5½-inch) circles. Fit circles into 3 (4½-inch) tartlet pans with removable bottoms, gently pressing pastry with fingertips along bottom and up edges of pans. Trim overhanging edge of pastry to ½ inch above edge of pan. Fold and roll pastry in, then gently press edge up to extend ¼ inch above side of pan. (Patch any cracks in pastry with excess dough.) Prick bottoms of tartlet shells with a fork. Repeat process with remaining disk and 3 more tartlet pans. Freeze 20 minutes.

3. Preheat oven to 375°F. Arrange tartlet pans 2 inches apart on a large cookie sheet. Bake 14 to 16 minutes, or until pastry is dry and set along edges. (It may look slightly moist in center, but that's okay.) Let cool completely on a wire rack before filling.

280   QUEEN OF HEARTS STRAWBERRY TARTS
Prep: 10 minutes   Freeze: 20 minutes   Bake: 22 to 24 minutes
Serves: 6

These delicate little tarts, with a double dose of strawberry, are a pure delight.

1 **recipe pastry for Basic Tart Shell (page 226)**	**Classic Pastry Cream (page 224)**
¼ **cup strawberry preserves**	2 **pints fresh whole strawberries, hulled**
1 **tablespoon kirsch**	

1. Divide pastry disk in half. On a lightly floured surface, roll out 1 piece of dough into a ⅛-inch-thick round. Cut into 3 (5½-inch) circles. Fit circles into 3 (4½-inch) tartlet pans with removable bottoms, gently pressing pastry with fingertips along bottom and up edge of pans. Trim overhanging edge of pastry to ½ inch above edge of pan. Fold and roll pastry in, then gently press edge up to extend ¼ inch above side of pan. (Patch any cracks in pastry with excess dough.) Prick bottom of tartlet shells with a fork. Repeat process with remaining dough and 3 more tartlet pans. Freeze 20 minutes.

2. Preheat oven to 425°F. Tear 6 sheets of foil slightly larger than tartlet pans. Press foil, shiny side down, into frozen tartlet shells, turning back ends of foil to cover edges of pans. Fill tartlet pans with pie weights, uncooked beans, or rice. Arrange tartlet pans 2 inches apart on a large cookie sheet. Bake 12 minutes. Remove foil and weights. Bake pastry 10 to 12 minutes longer, until a deep golden brown. Let cool completely on a wire rack.

3. In a small bowl, combine strawberry preserves and kirsch; blend well. Spoon 1 tablespoon preserves mixture in bottom of each tart shell. Top each with a scant ¼ cup pastry cream. Place 1 whole strawberry in center of each tart. Cut remaining strawberries in half and arrange, cut sides down, in a circle around whole berry. Remove sides of pans. Serve tarts immediately or refrigerate up to 4 hours.

281   CLASSIC PASTRY CREAM

Prep: 5 minutes   Cook: 6 minutes   Chill: 2 hours   Makes: 1⅓ cups

This creamy filling is a sweet tradition with any of your favorite tarts.

1 cup milk	2 tablespoons flour
¼ cup sugar	1 tablespoon butter
3 large egg yolks	1 teaspoon vanilla extract

1. In a medium saucepan, bring milk and 2 tablespoons sugar just to a boil.

2. In a medium bowl, whisk egg yolks with remaining 2 tablespoons sugar until thick and lemon colored. Whisk in flour until smooth. Gradually whisk hot milk into egg yolks. Return custard to saucepan. Bring to a boil over medium heat, whisking constantly. Boil gently, whisking, 1 minute. (Custard will be thick.)

3. Remove from heat and whisk in butter and vanilla. Transfer to a clean bowl. Cover surface directly with wax paper or plastic wrap and refrigerate until cold, 2 hours or overnight.

282   TROPICAL LIME BRÛLÉE TARTLETS

Prep: 1 hour   Cook: 4 to 6 minutes   Broil: 1 minute
Chill: 2½ to 5 hours   Serves: 6

⅔ cup granulated sugar	1 tablespoon grated lime zest
½ cup fresh lime juice	¼ cup heavy cream
2 large whole eggs	1 ripe banana, thinly sliced
2 large egg yolks	Coconut Tartlet Shells (page
1 stick (4 ounces) unsalted	225)
butter, cut up	¼ cup packed brown sugar

1. In a medium saucepan, cook granulated sugar and lime juice over medium heat, stirring occasionally, until sugar is dissolved, 2 to 3 minutes. In a medium bowl, whisk together whole eggs and egg yolks. Gradually whisk hot sugar syrup into eggs; return to saucepan. Cook over medium-low heat, stirring constantly, just until mixture thickens and coats the back of a spoon, 2 to 3 minutes. (Do not boil.) Remove from heat.

2. Whisk in butter, a few pieces at a time, until melted. Whisk in lime zest. Transfer lime custard to a bowl. Cover with plastic wrap, pressing directly onto top surface of filling to form a tight seal. Refrigerate until cold, 2 hours or overnight.

3. Whisk lime custard gently to soften. In a small bowl, beat cream with an electric mixer until stiff peaks form. With a rubber spatula, carefully fold cream into lime custard.

4. Preheat broiler. Arrange banana slices in Coconut Tartlet Shells. Spoon lime mousse evenly over top of fruit; smooth tops. Sift 2 teaspoons brown sugar over each tartlet. Broil tartlets 4 inches from heat until sugar is melted and caramelized, about 1 minute. Refrigerate tartlets 30 minutes or up to 3 hours. Remove sides of pans before serving.

283 COCONUT TARTLET SHELLS
Prep: 10 minutes   Chill: 1 hour   Freeze: 20 minutes
Bake: 22 to 24 minutes   Makes: 6 (4½-inch) tartlet shells

I love this tart pastry with chocolate fillings, or brushed with melted bittersweet chocolate and filled with fresh berries. Lightly toast the coconut before preparing the pastry for a nuttier flavor.

1¼ cups flour	1 stick (4 ounces) cold
½ cup flaked coconut	unsalted butter, cut up
2 tablespoons sugar	1 teaspoon vanilla extract
Pinch of salt	3 to 4 tablespoons ice water

1. In a medium bowl, combine flour, coconut, sugar, and salt. Add butter and toss gently until all pieces are coated with flour. With a pastry blender or 2 knives, cut in butter until mixture resembles fine crumbs.

2. In a cup, mix vanilla and 1 tablespoon ice water. Drizzle over flour mixture, then toss with a fork. Add remaining ice water, 1 tablespoon at a time as needed, tossing vigorously with a fork just until dough begins to hold together. Turn out onto a work surface and shape pastry into ball, kneading lightly. Divide in half and flatten into 2 disks, then wrap each tightly in plastic wrap. Refrigerate 1 hour or overnight.

3. On a lightly floured surface, roll out 1 disk into a ⅛-inch-thick round. Cut into 3 (5½-inch) circles. Fit circles into 3 (4½-inch) tartlet pans with removable bottoms, gently pressing pastry with fingertips along bottom and up edge of pans. Trim overhanging edge of pastry to ½ inch above edge of pan. Fold and roll pastry in, then gently press edge up to extend ¼ inch above side of pan. (Patch any cracks in pastry with excess dough.) Prick bottoms of tartlet shells with a fork. Repeat process with remaining dough and 3 more tartlet pans. Freeze 20 minutes.

4. Preheat oven to 425°F. Tear 6 sheets of foil slightly larger than tartlet pans. Press foil, shiny side down, into frozen tartlet shells, turning back ends of foil to cover edge of pans. Fill tartlet pans with pie weights, uncooked beans, or rice. Arrange tartlet pans 2 inches apart on a large cookie sheet. Bake 12 minutes. Remove foil and weights. Bake pastry 10 to 12 minutes longer, until crust is a deep golden brown. Let cool completely on a wire rack before filling.

284 BASIC TART SHELL
Prep: 10 minutes   Chill: 1 hour   Freeze: 20 minutes
Bake: 26 to 28 minutes   Makes: 1 (9- or 10-inch) tart shell

This all-butter pastry is pure perfection with any tart filling. Be sure your cut-up butter is well chilled—I put it in the freezer for a few minutes before using.

1¼ cups flour
1 tablespoon sugar
Pinch of salt

1 stick (4 ounces) cold
   unsalted butter, cut up
3 to 4 tablespoons ice water

1. In a medium bowl, combine flour, sugar, and salt. Add butter and toss gently until all pieces are coated with flour. With a pastry blender or 2 knives, cut in butter until mixture resembles fine crumbs. Add ice water, 1 tablespoon at a time, drizzling over flour mixture, then tossing vigorously with a fork just until dough begins to hold together. On smooth surface, shape pastry into a ball, kneading lightly if necessary. Flatten into a disk, then wrap tightly in plastic wrap. Refrigerate 1 hour or overnight.

2. Preheat oven to 425°F. On a lightly floured surface, roll out pastry into a ⅛-inch-thick round. Fold pastry in half and ease gently into a 9- or 10-inch tart pan with a removable bottom. Unfold dough and gently press pastry with fingertips along bottom and up edge of pan. Trim overhanging edge of pastry to 1 inch above edge of pan. Fold and roll pastry in, then gently press edge up to extend ¼ inch above side of pan. Prick bottom with a fork. Freeze 20 minutes.

3. Tear 2 sheets of foil slightly larger than tart pan. Press the foil, shiny side down, into frozen tart shell, turning back the ends of foil to cover edge of pan. Fill tart pan with pie weights, uncooked beans, or rice. Bake 12 minutes. Remove foil and weights. Bake pastry 14 to 16 minutes longer, or until crust is a deep golden brown. Let cool completely on a wire rack. Remove sides of pan. Transfer to a serving plate before filling.

285 RICH 'N' SWEET TART SHELL
Prep: 10 minutes   Bake: 20 to 22 minutes
Makes: 1 (11-inch) tart shell

This pastry is great when you have larger fruit and nut tarts in mind.

10⅔ tablespoons (⅔ cup)
   unsalted butter, softened
½ cup powdered sugar
1 teaspoon vanilla extract

⅛ teaspoon salt
1 large egg yolk
1¾ cups flour

1. Preheat oven to 375°F. In a large bowl, beat butter, powdered sugar, vanilla, and salt with an electric mixer on medium speed until light and creamy. Beat in egg yolk until smooth.

2. With mixer on low speed, gradually add flour until butter is evenly distributed and dough is crumbly. With lightly floured fingers, press dough along bottom and sides of an 11-inch tart pan with a removable bottom. Prick bottom of pastry with fork. Bake 20 to 22 minutes, or until golden. Let cool completely on a wire rack before filling.

286 LEMON TART SHELL
Prep: 10 minutes   Chill: 1 hour   Freeze: 20 minutes
Bake: 26 to 28 minutes   Makes: 1 (9- or 10-inch) tart shell

This citrus tart pastry is particularly suited for fresh fruit fillings. Feel free to substitute fresh orange or lime juice and zest if desired.

1¼ **cups flour**
1 **tablespoon sugar**
½ **teaspoon grated lemon zest**
  Pinch of salt
1 **stick (4 ounces) cold**
  unsalted butter, cut up

1 **tablespoon fresh lemon**
  juice
3 **to 4 tablespoons ice water**

1. Combine flour, sugar, lemon zest, and salt in medium bowl. Add butter and toss gently until all pieces are coated with flour. With a pastry blender or 2 knives, cut in butter until mixture resembles fine crumbs.

2. In a cup, combine lemon juice and 1 tablespoon ice water. Drizzle over flour mixture, then toss with a fork. Add remaining ice water, 1 tablespoon at a time as needed, tossing vigorously with a fork just until dough begins to hold together. Turn out onto a work surface and shape pastry into a ball, kneading lightly. Flatten into a disk, then wrap tightly in plastic wrap. Refrigerate 1 hour or overnight.

3. Preheat oven to 425°F. On a lightly floured surface, roll out pastry into a ⅛-inch-thick round. Fold pastry in half and ease gently into a 9- or 10-inch tart pan with a removable bottom. Unfold dough and gently press pastry with fingertips along bottom and up edge of pan. Trim overhanging edge of pastry to 1 inch above edge of pan. Fold and roll pastry in, then gently press edge up to extend ¼ inch above side of pan. Prick bottom with a fork. Freeze 20 minutes.

4. Tear 2 sheets of foil slightly larger than tart pan. Press the foil, shiny side down, into frozen tart shell, turning back ends of foil to cover edge of pan. Fill tart pan with pie weights, uncooked beans, or rice. Bake 12 minutes. Remove foil and weights. Bake pastry 14 to 16 minutes longer, or until crust is a deep golden brown. Let cool completely on a wire rack. Remove sides of pan. Transfer to a serving plate before filling.

287 ULTIMATE TART SHELL

Prep: 10 minutes   Chill: 1 hour   Freeze: 20 minutes
Bake: 26 to 28 minutes   Makes: 1 (9- or 10-inch) tart shell

This rich tart pastry is extremely flaky and tender, thanks to the addition of an egg yolk and heavy cream.

1¼ cups flour
1 tablespoon sugar
Pinch of salt
1 stick (4 ounces) cold
    unsalted butter, cut up

1 large egg yolk
3 to 4 tablespoons heavy
    cream

1. In a medium bowl, combine flour, sugar, and salt. Add butter and toss gently until all pieces are coated with flour. With a pastry blender or 2 knives, cut in butter until mixture resembles fine crumbs.

2. In a small bowl, whisk together egg yolk and 3 tablespoons cream until blended. Drizzle over flour mixture, tossing vigorously with a fork just until dough begins to hold together, adding remaining 1 tablespoon cream if necessary. Turn out onto a work surface and shape pastry into ball, kneading lightly. Flatten into a disk, then wrap tightly in plastic wrap. Refrigerate 1 hour or overnight.

3. Preheat oven to 425°F. On a lightly floured surface, roll out pastry into a ⅛-inch-thick round. Fold pastry in half and ease gently into a 9- or 10-inch tart pan with a removable bottom. Unfold dough and gently press pastry with fingertips along bottom and up edge of pan. Trim overhanging edge of pastry to 1 inch above edge of pan. Fold and roll pastry in, then gently press edge up to extend ¼ inch above side of pan. Prick bottom with a fork. Freeze 20 minutes.

4. Tear 2 sheets of foil slightly larger than tart pan. Press the foil, shiny side down, into frozen tart shell, turning back the ends of foil to cover edge of pan. Fill tart pan with pie weights, uncooked beans, or rice. Bake 12 minutes. Remove foil and weights. Bake pastry 14 to 16 minutes longer, or until crust is a deep golden brown. Let cool completely on a wire rack. Remove sides of pan. Transfer to a serving plate before filling.

Chapter 12

Deep-Dish Spoon Pies

Here are the pies you can't wait to eat, warm and brimming with bubbly fruit, pies that love a bowl and spoon. These are our most American of pies, steeped in countryside tradition. Their single-crust topping goes by many names— deep-dish, cobbler, grunt, slump, buckle, and crisp—each and every one right at home served with a pitcher of cream or a scoop of vanilla ice cream. Spoon pies are among the easiest pies to make, so if you're a beginner pie baker, they're for you. Most toppings can be prepared in minutes, and there's no bottom crust to become soggy. Deep-dish spoon pies are simply the perfect comfort dessert, a wonderful finale to a casual supper or a fruitful wake-up call when served for breakfast or brunch.

Topped with your favorite flaky pastry for a single crust pie, deep-dish pies celebrate fruit's bounty, because you'll need double the amount of fruit of a regular pie to make them. Roll the flaky pastry as you would for any pie crust, making sure to cut vents in the pastry to allow steam to escape.

Cobblers—also called grunts, slumps, pandowdies, or spoon pies—have a rich biscuit topping. For the best baked biscuit, always make sure your fruit filling is hot when you add the topping, and bake the cobbler immediately. I prepare my fruit filling first, then cover and keep warm while assembling the biscuit. Some biscuit toppings can be dropped with a spoon over the filling; others are rolled or patted into a thick square and placed over the fruit in the baking dish. Like a flaky pastry pie dough, a tender biscuit relies on blending with a light touch. Always start with chilled butter, then cut in the flour and leavening, using a hand-held pastry blender or two knives, until the mixture resembles coarse crumbs. Add the liquid ingredients all at once, stirring vigorously with a spoon or rubber spatula just until the dough is moistened. Once the flour is incorporated, do not work the dough any more than is necessary. It's perfectly fine if the batter isn't completely smooth, because the small bits of butter will make your topping extra flaky.

With no rolling required, fruit crisps are the easiest of spoon pies, their streusel-style topping a simple toss of butter, flour, sugar, nuts, oats, and spices. Toppings for crisps can be prepared ahead, refrigerated, or even frozen, then sprinkled onto the fruit when you're ready to bake.

When you get ready to fix a spoon pie, feel free to mix and match toppings and fillings to whatever is available or strikes your fancy. Here is a seasonal selection that includes summertime Jumbleberry Oat Cobbler, Praline Peach and Sour Cherry Crisp, and a Deep-Dish Plum, Apricot, and Almond Pie. Or choose from soothing cold weather favorites like Buttery Apple-Parmesan Crisp or Apple-Pear Pandowdy with a classic cream biscuit.

288   PLUM GOOD RASPBERRY GRUNT
Prep: 15 minutes   Bake: 25 to 30 minutes   Serves: 6

Biscuit-topped deep-dish pies are called by many names, including this whimsical one. This old-fashioned "grunt" features an unusual ricotta biscuit topping.

¾ cup plus 2 tablespoons sugar	2 cups fresh or frozen raspberries
2 tablespoons cornstarch	2 teaspoons fresh lemon juice
1½ pounds purple plums, cut into ½-inch-thick slices (4 cups)	Sweet Ricotta Biscuit Topping (recipe follows) Vanilla ice cream

1. Preheat oven to 400°F. In a large saucepan, combine sugar and cornstarch. Stir in ⅓ cup water until well blended. Add plums and raspberries. Bring to a boil, stirring gently. Boil 1 minute. Stir in lemon juice. Turn filling into a 9-inch square baking pan. Keep hot.

2. Prepare Sweet Ricotta Biscuit Topping and arrange on top of filling. Bake 25 to 30 minutes, or until topping is golden and fruit is bubbly. Serve warm in shallow bowls with vanilla ice cream.

289   SWEET RICOTTA BISCUIT TOPPING
Prep: 10 minutes   Makes: Topping for one 9-inch square fruit cobbler

1½ cups flour	4 tablespoons butter, cut up
3 tablespoons sugar	½ cup ricotta or cream-style cottage cheese
2 teaspoons baking powder	
½ teaspoon grated lemon zest	3 tablespoons milk
¼ teaspoon grated nutmeg	⅛ teaspoon almond extract
¼ teaspoon salt	

1. In a medium bowl, combine flour, sugar, baking powder, lemon zest, nutmeg, and salt. With a pastry blender or 2 knives, cut in butter until mixture resembles fine crumbs; stir in ricotta. In a cup, combine milk and almond extract; stir into ricotta mixture. Knead gently in bowl until mixture just holds together.

2. On a lightly floured sheet of wax paper, gently stretch dough with a rolling pin or pat with lightly floured hands into a 9-inch square. Invert biscuit onto hot fruit filling and remove wax paper.

290 GOLDEN APPLE-DATE COBBLER
Prep: 20 minutes   Bake: 55 to 60 minutes   Serves: 6

This homey cobbler, topped with a whole wheat biscuit, is divine with any sweet apple. Chopped dates add a melt-in-your-mouth fruity flavor.

½ cup plus 1 tablespoon sugar
2 tablespoons flour
½ teaspoon cinnamon
¼ teaspoon ground allspice
   Pinch of salt
3 pounds Golden Delicious
   apples, peeled and
   thickly sliced

½ cup chopped dates
1 tablespoon fresh lemon
   juice
½ teaspoon grated lemon zest
2 tablespoons butter
   Whole Wheat Biscuit
   Topping (recipe follows)
¾ cup heavy cream

1. Preheat oven to 425°F. In a large bowl, combine ½ cup sugar, flour, cinnamon, allspice, and salt. Gently stir in apples, dates, lemon juice, and lemon zest.

2. Turn filling into a greased 9-inch square baking pan; dot with butter. Cover tightly with foil and bake 40 minutes.

3. Meanwhile, prepare Whole Wheat Biscuit Topping. Remove foil from pan and arrange biscuit on top of fruit. Brush with 1 tablespoon cream and sprinkle on remaining 1 tablespoon sugar. Bake 15 to 20 minutes longer, or until topping is golden and apples are tender when tested with a small sharp knife. Serve warm with a pitcher of remaining cream on the side.

291 WHOLE WHEAT BISCUIT TOPPING
Prep: 10 minutes   Bake: 5 minutes
Makes: Topping for one 9-inch square fruit cobbler

⅓ cup walnuts
¾ cup all-purpose flour
¾ cup whole wheat flour
2 tablespoons sugar

2 teaspoons baking powder
   Pinch of salt
6 tablespoons butter, cut up
6 tablespoons milk

1. Preheat oven to 425°F. Spread out walnuts on a small baking sheet. Bake about 5 minutes, or until nuts are lightly browned and fragrant. Let cool, then finely chop.

2. In a medium bowl, combine all-purpose flour, whole wheat flour, sugar, baking powder, and salt. With pastry blender or 2 knives, cut in butter until mixture resembles coarse crumbs. Stir in walnuts. Gradually add milk, drizzling over flour mixture, then tossing vigorously with a fork until dough begins to hold together. Knead gently in bowl until mixture just holds together.

3. On a lightly floured sheet of wax paper, gently stretch dough with a rolling pin or pat with lightly floured hands into a 9-inch square. Invert biscuit onto hot fruit filling and remove wax paper.

292 BIG MAC DEEP-DISH APPLE PIE
Prep: 25 minutes   Bake: 35 to 40 minutes   Serves: 8

Here's a pie perfect for a bumper crop supply of sweet McIntosh apples. Golden Delicious apples are also terrific in this filling.

½ cup packed brown sugar
¼ cup plus 1 tablespoon granulated sugar
3 tablespoons flour
¼ teaspoon grated nutmeg
⅛ teaspoon salt
4 pounds McIntosh apples, peeled and cut into ¾-inch-thick wedges

3 tablespoons tiny red cinnamon candies (red-hots)
1 tablespoon fresh lemon juice
½ teaspoon grated lemon zest
2 tablespoons butter, cut up
Flaky Pastry for a 9-inch single crust pie (page 157)
⅛ teaspoon cinnamon
1 tablespoon milk

1. Preheat oven to 425°F. In a large bowl, combine brown sugar, ¼ cup granulated sugar, flour, nutmeg, and salt. Add apples, red cinnamon candies, lemon juice, and lemon zest and stir gently to mix. Turn filling into a greased 9-inch square baking pan; dot with butter.

2. Roll pastry into a 13-inch square and trim edges with a small sharp knife. Fold pastry into quarters and unfold over fruit in baking pan. Cut steam vents in top. Fold and roll pastry under, just inside edge of pan, and flute. In a cup, combine remaining 1 tablespoon granulated sugar and cinnamon. Brush top of pie with milk, then sprinkle with cinnamon sugar.

3. Place pie on a cookie sheet and bake 20 minutes. Reduce oven temperature to 375°F. Bake 15 to 20 minutes longer, or until crust is golden and filling is bubbly in center. Let cool on a wire rack.

293 BUTTERY APPLE-PARMESAN CRISP
Prep: 25 minutes   Bake: 40 to 45 minutes   Serves: 6

¼ cup granulated sugar
1 teaspoon cinnamon
¼ teaspoon ground allspice
3 pounds tart apples, peeled and thickly sliced
1 tablespoon fresh lemon juice

¾ cup flour
¾ cup packed brown sugar
½ cup freshly grated Parmesan cheese
Pinch of ground red pepper
6 tablespoons butter, cut up
½ cup chopped pecans

1. Preheat oven to 425°F. In a large bowl, combine granulated sugar, cinnamon, and allspice. Add apples and lemon juice and toss to coat. Turn into a 9-inch square baking pan.

2. In another large bowl, combine flour, brown sugar, Parmesan cheese, and red pepper. With a pastry blender or 2 knives, cut in butter until mixture resembles fine crumbs. Stir in pecans. Sprinkle evenly over fruit.

3. Bake 15 minutes. Reduce oven temperature to 350°F. Bake 25 to 30 minutes longer, or until top is golden and fruit is bubbly. (If topping browns too quickly, cover loosely with foil.) Serve warm.

---

294   APPLE-PEAR PANDOWDY
Prep: 30 minutes   Bake: 25 to 30 minutes   Serves: 8

For this classic New England apple cobbler, pears have been added to the bubbly fruit filling and toasted pecans to the cream biscuit on top.

2 tablespoons butter	¼ teaspoon ground allspice
4 medium tart apples, peeled	Pinch of salt
and sliced ¼ inch thick	2 tablespoons brandy
4 medium pears, peeled and	¼ cup heavy cream
sliced ¼ inch thick	Pecan Pandowdy Topping
½ cup sugar	(recipe follows)
1 teaspoon cinnamon	

1. Preheat oven to 375°F. In a large skillet, melt butter over medium heat. Stir in apples and pears. Cook, stirring, 5 minutes, or until fruit is tender but retains its shape. Stir in sugar, cinnamon, allspice, and salt. Cook 1 minute, or until sugar is melted. Increase heat to high; stir in brandy and heavy cream. Cook until liquid thickens slightly, 1 minute longer.

2. Turn filling into a greased 9-inch square baking dish and arrange Pecan Pandowdy Topping over top. Bake 25 to 30 minutes, or until filling is bubbly and topping is puffed and golden. Serve warm.

---

295   PECAN PANDOWDY TOPPING
Prep: 10 minutes   Bake: 5 to 7 minutes
Makes: Topping for one 9-inch square fruit cobbler

½ cup pecans	Pinch of salt
1½ cups flour	4 tablespoons butter, cut up
3 tablespoons sugar	½ cup heavy cream
2 teaspoons baking powder	½ teaspoon vanilla extract

1. Preheat oven to 375°F. Spread out pecans on a small baking sheet. Bake 5 to 7 minutes, or until nuts are lightly browned and fragrant. Let cool, then finely chop.

2. In a medium bowl, combine flour, sugar, baking powder, and salt. With a pastry blender or 2 knives, cut in butter until mixture resembles fine crumbs; stir in pecans. In a small bowl, whisk cream and vanilla, then stir into dry ingredients until evenly moistened. Knead gently in bowl until mixture just holds together.

3. On a lightly floured sheet of wax paper, gently stretch dough with a rolling pin or pat with lightly floured hands into a 9-inch square, ¼ inch thick. Invert biscuit onto hot fruit filling and remove wax paper.

296 GINGERSNAP APPLE-PEAR BROWN BETTY

Prep: 20 minutes   Bake: 55 to 60 minutes   Serves: 6

6 slices of firm white
    sandwich bread
16 gingersnap cookies
5⅓ tablespoons (⅓ cup) butter,
    melted
⅓ cup granulated sugar
⅓ cup packed brown sugar
½ teaspoon grated lemon zest

½ teaspoon ground ginger
    Pinch of ground cloves
3 medium tart apples, peeled
    and thinly sliced
3 medium ripe pears, peeled
    and thinly sliced
1 tablespoon fresh lemon
    juice

1. Preheat oven to 400°F. In a food processor, process bread to fine crumbs. Transfer to a medium bowl. In same food processor bowl, grind gingersnap cookies to fine crumbs. Toss with bread crumbs and melted butter until mixture is evenly moistened.

2. In a medium bowl, combine granulated sugar, brown sugar, lemon zest, ginger, and cloves. In another bowl, toss apples and pears with lemon juice.

3. Sprinkle ½ cup crumb mixture over bottom of a 9-inch square baking dish. Top with one third of brown sugar and spice mixture, half of fruit, another third of sugar mixture, and another ½ cup crumbs. Repeat layering with remaining sugar and fruit and top with remaining crumbs.

4. Cover with foil and bake 25 minutes. Uncover and bake 30 to 35 minutes longer, or until crumbs are golden and fruit is tender. Serve warm or at room temperature.

297 GRANOLA CRUNCH APPLE CRISP

*Prep: 20 minutes   Cook: 3 to 5 minutes   Bake: 40 to 45 minutes
Serves: 6*

1 tablespoon sesame seeds
2 tablespoons granulated
    sugar
¼ teaspoon grated nutmeg
2½ pounds tart apples, peeled
    and thinly sliced
1 tablespoon fresh lemon
    juice
⅔ cup packed brown sugar
½ cup flour

½ teaspoon cinnamon
    Pinch of salt
4 tablespoons butter, cut up
2 tablespoons solid vegetable
    shortening
½ cup old-fashioned oats
¼ cup flaked coconut
¼ cup chopped almonds
    Vanilla frozen yogurt or ice
    cream

1. Preheat oven to 425°F. In a small dry skillet, cook sesame seeds over medium heat, stirring, until golden, 3 to 5 minutes. Let cool.

2. In a large bowl, combine granulated sugar and nutmeg. Add apples and lemon juice and toss to coat. Turn into an 8-inch square baking pan.

3. In another large bowl, combine brown sugar, flour, cinnamon, and salt. With a pastry blender or 2 knives, cut in butter and shortening until mixture resembles fine crumbs. Stir in oats, coconut, almonds, and toasted sesame seeds. Sprinkle evenly over fruit.

4. Bake 15 minutes. Reduce oven temperature to 350°F. Bake 25 to 30 minutes longer, or until top is golden and fruit is bubbly. (If topping browns too quickly, cover loosely with foil.) Serve warm with frozen yogurt.

298 CRANBERRY-APPLE CORNBREAD COBBLER
Prep: 20 minutes   Stand: 15 minutes   Bake: 55 to 60 minutes
Serves: 8

¾ cup sugar
3 tablespoons quick-cooking tapioca
1 teaspoon cinnamon
½ teaspoon grated lemon zest
3 pounds tart apples, peeled and thickly sliced
2 cups chopped fresh or frozen cranberries

¼ cup pure maple syrup
1 tablespoon fresh lemon juice
2 tablespoons butter, cut up
Sweet Cornbread Biscuit Topping (recipe follows)
Vanilla ice cream

1. Preheat oven to 425°F. In a large bowl, combine sugar, tapioca, cinnamon, and lemon zest. Gently stir in apples, cranberries, maple syrup, and lemon juice. Let stand 15 minutes, stirring occasionally.

2. Turn filling into a greased 9-inch square baking dish; dot with butter. Cover tightly with foil and bake 40 minutes.

3. Meanwhile, prepare Sweet Cornbread Biscuit Topping. Remove foil from pan and drop topping by generous tablespoonfuls onto hot apple filling. Bake 15 to 20 minutes longer, or until topping is golden and apples are tender when tested with a small sharp knife. Serve warm with vanilla ice cream and additional maple syrup.

299 SWEET CORNBREAD BISCUIT TOPPING
Prep: 5 minutes   Makes: Topping for one 9-inch square fruit cobbler

1 cup flour
½ cup yellow cornmeal
¼ cup sugar
2 teaspoons baking powder

¼ teaspoon cinnamon
⅛ teaspoon salt
4 tablespoons butter, cut up
½ cup heavy cream

In a medium bowl, combine flour, cornmeal, sugar, baking powder, cinnamon, and salt. With a pastry blender or 2 knives, cut in butter until mixture resembles coarse crumbs. Stir in cream until evenly moistened. Knead gently in bowl just until mixture holds together.

300 DEEP-DISH RED BERRY PIE
Prep: 20 minutes   Bake: 30 to 35 minutes   Serves: 8

For a triple berry treat, serve this luscious pie with strawberry ice cream.

1 cup sugar
⅓ cup cornstarch
½ teaspoon cinnamon
3 pints whole fresh
   strawberries, halved
2 cups fresh or frozen
   raspberries

1 tablespoon fresh lemon
   juice
2 tablespoons butter, cut up
   Flaky Pastry for a 9-inch
   single crust pie (page 157)

1. Preheat oven to 425°F. In a large bowl, combine sugar, cornstarch, and cinnamon. Gently stir in strawberries, raspberries, and lemon juice. Turn filling into a greased 9-inch square baking pan; dot with butter.

2. Roll pastry into a 13-inch square and trim edges with a small sharp knife. Fold pastry into quarters and unfold over fruit in baking pan. Cut steam vents in top. Fold and roll pastry under, just inside edge of pan, and flute. Place pie on a cookie sheet.

3. Bake 30 to 35 minutes, until crust is golden and filling is bubbly in center. Let cool on a wire rack.

301 BLACK 'N' BLUEBERRY PEACH CRISP
Prep: 25 minutes   Bake: 45 to 50 minutes   Serves: 6

This oat and nut crisp is also wonderful with nectarines. The combination of solid vegetable shortening and sweet butter in the streusel topping gives it extra crunch.

2 pounds ripe peaches, peeled
   and thickly sliced (5 cups)
1 cup fresh or frozen
   blackberries
1 cup fresh or frozen
   blueberries
1 tablespoon fresh lemon
   juice
1 teaspoon grated lemon zest
⅔ cup packed brown sugar

½ cup flour
½ teaspoon grated nutmeg
   Pinch of salt
4 tablespoons butter, cut up
2 tablespoon solid vegetable
   shortening
⅓ cup old-fashioned oats
⅓ cup chopped walnuts
   Vanilla ice cream

1. Preheat oven to 425°F. In a large bowl, combine peaches, blackberries, blueberries, lemon juice, and lemon zest. Turn into an 8-inch square baking pan.

2. In a medium bowl, combine brown sugar, flour, nutmeg, and salt. Mix well. With pastry blender or 2 knives, cut in butter and shortening until mixture resembles fine crumbs. Stir in oats and walnuts. Sprinkle evenly over fruit.

3. Bake 15 minutes. Reduce oven temperature to 350°F. Bake 30 to 35 minutes longer, or until top is golden and fruit is bubbly. Serve warm with vanilla ice cream.

302 NUTTY PLUM-RHUBARB COBBLER
Prep: 20 minutes   Bake: 25 to 30 minutes   Serves: 6

This rosy red fruit filling can also be prepared with frozen thawed rhubarb. Plums lend a subtle sweetness.

¾ **cup sugar**
2 **tablespoons cornstarch**
1½ **pounds purple plums, cut
    into ½-inch-thick slices**
½ **pound fresh rhubarb, thinly
    sliced**

2 **teaspoons fresh lemon juice**
 **Nutty Biscuit Topping
    (recipe follows)**

1. Preheat oven to 400°F. In a large saucepan, combine sugar and cornstarch. Stir in ½ cup water, then plums and rhubarb. Bring to a boil, stirring gently. Boil 1 minute. Stir in lemon juice. Turn filling into a 9-inch square baking pan. Cover to keep hot.

2. Prepare Nutty Biscuit Topping. Place on top of fruit. Bake 25 to 30 minutes, or until topping is golden and filling is bubbly. Serve warm.

303 NUTTY BISCUIT TOPPING
Prep: 15 minutes   Bake: 5 to 7 minutes
Makes: Topping for one 9-inch square fruit cobbler

⅓ **cup pecans**
1 **cup flour**
2 **tablespoons sugar**
1½ **teaspoons baking powder**

½ **teaspoon cinnamon**
¼ **teaspoon salt**
4 **tablespoons butter, cut up**
⅔ **cup heavy cream**

1. Preheat oven to 400°F. Spread out pecans on a small baking sheet. Bake 5 to 7 minutes, or until nuts are lightly browned and fragrant. Let cool, then finely chop.

2. In a medium bowl, combine flour, sugar, baking powder, cinnamon, and salt. With a pastry blender or 2 knives, cut in butter until mixture resembles coarse crumbs. Stir in pecans, then cream until just moistened. Knead gently in bowl just until mixture holds together.

3. On a lightly floured sheet of wax paper, gently stretch dough with a rolling pin or pat with lightly floured hands into a 9-inch square. Invert biscuit onto hot fruit filling and remove wax paper.

304 BLACKBERRY AND NECTARINE BUCKLE
Prep: 20 minutes   Bake: 30 to 35 minutes   Serves: 6

This deep-dish pie features a sweet cream biscuit that is prepared with self-rising flour. It's fast and fluffy, with a very tender crumb.

2 pounds nectarines, peeled
  and thickly sliced
2 cups fresh blackberries
1 tablespoon fresh lemon
  juice

¼ teaspoon grated lemon zest
¾ cup sugar
2 tablespoons butter, cut up
  Whipped Cream Biscuit
  Topping (recipe follows)

1. Preheat oven to 400°F. In a large bowl, combine nectarines, blackberries, lemon juice, and lemon zest. Gently stir in sugar. Turn filling into a 9-inch square baking pan or a 10-inch pie pan and dot with butter.

2. Prepare Whipped Cream Biscuit Topping and spoon on top of filling. Bake 30 to 35 minutes, or until topping is golden and fruit is bubbly. Serve warm in shallow bowls.

305 WHIPPED CREAM BISCUIT TOPPING
Prep: 5 minutes   Makes: Topping for one 10-inch round or 9-inch square fruit cobbler

1 cup self-rising flour
3 tablespoons sugar

1 cup heavy cream

1. In a medium bowl, combine self-rising flour and sugar. In a large bowl, beat cream with an electric mixer to stiff peaks.

2. Gently fold whipped cream into flour mixture with a rubber spatula just until blended and a soft dough forms. Drop by generous tablespoonfuls onto fruit filling.

306 JUMBLEBERRY OAT COBBLER
Prep: 15 minutes   Bake: 25 to 30 minutes   Serves: 6

¾ cup sugar
2 tablespoons quick-cooking
  tapioca
5 cups assorted fresh or frozen
  blackberries, blueberries,
  or raspberries

2 teaspoons fresh lemon juice
  Oaty Biscuit Topping (page
  239)

1. Preheat oven to 400°F. In a large saucepan, combine sugar and tapioca. Gradually stir in ⅔ cup water. Cook, stirring, until mixture comes to a boil. Add berries and cook 1 minute. Stir in lemon juice. Turn filling into a 9-inch deep-dish (1-quart) pie pan. Cover to keep hot.

2. Prepare Oaty Biscuit Topping and arrange on top of berry filling. Bake 25 to 30 minutes, or until topping is golden and filling is bubbly. Serve warm.

307   OATY BISCUIT TOPPING
Prep: 5 minutes   Makes: Topping for one 9-inch square fruit cobbler

Try toasting the oats in the preheated 400°F oven until golden, about 6 to 8 minutes. Let cool completely, then add to the biscuit topping for a wonderful nutty flavor.

1 cup flour	Pinch of grated nutmeg
2 tablespoons sugar	4 tablespoons butter, cut up
1½ teaspoons baking powder	½ cup old-fashioned oats
¼ teaspoon salt	⅔ cup heavy cream

1. In a medium bowl, combine flour, sugar, baking powder, salt, and nutmeg. With a pastry blender or 2 knives, cut in butter until mixture resembles coarse crumbs. Stir in oats, then cream until just moistened. Knead gently in bowl until mixture just holds together.

2. On a lightly floured sheet of wax paper, gently stretch dough with a rolling pin or pat with lightly floured hands into a 9-inch square. Invert biscuit onto hot fruit filling and remove wax paper.

308   PRALINE PEACH AND SOUR CHERRY CRISP
Prep: 25 minutes   Bake: 30 to 35 minutes   Serves: 6

If tart cherries are unavailable, sweet Bing cherries are a fine substitute.

⅓ cup granulated sugar	½ cup packed dark brown sugar
1 tablespoon cornstarch	⅓ cup flour
½ teaspoon cinnamon	Pinch of salt
⅛ teaspoon grated nutmeg	4 tablespoons butter, cut up
4 cups thickly sliced peeled peaches (about 2 pounds)	¾ cup chopped pecans
1 cup pitted fresh or frozen sour cherries	Vanilla ice cream
1 tablespoon fresh lemon juice	

1. Preheat oven to 375°F. In a large bowl, combine granulated sugar, cornstarch, cinnamon, and nutmeg. Stir in peaches, sour cherries, and lemon juice. Spoon into a greased 10-inch pie pan.

2. In a medium bowl, combine brown sugar, flour, and salt. With a pastry blender or 2 knives, cut in butter until mixture resembles coarse crumbs. Stir in pecans. Sprinkle evenly over fruit.

3. Bake 30 to 35 minutes, or until top is golden and fruit is bubbly. (If topping browns too quickly, cover loosely with foil.) Serve warm, with vanilla ice cream.

309 DEEP-DISH PLUM, APRICOT, AND ALMOND PIE

Prep: 25 minutes   Bake: 30 to 35 minutes   Serves: 8

Amaretto liqueur and a toasted almond pastry crust highlight this summery deep-dish pie.

¾ cup sugar
¼ cup flour
¼ teaspoon salt
4 cups thickly sliced fresh apricots
4 cups thickly sliced plums
2 tablespoons amaretto liqueur

1 tablespoon fresh lemon juice
⅛ teaspoon almond extract
2 tablespoons butter, cut up
Mostly Butter Pastry for a 9-inch single crust pie (page 159)

1. Preheat oven to 425°F. In a large bowl, combine sugar, flour, and salt. Gently stir in apricots, plums, amaretto, lemon juice, and almond extract. Turn filling into a greased 9-inch square baking pan; dot with butter.

2. Roll pastry into a 13-inch square and trim edges with a small sharp knife. Fold pastry into quarters and unfold over fruit in baking pan. Cut vents in top. Fold and roll pastry under, just inside edge of pan, and flute. Place pie on a cookie sheet.

3. Bake 30 to 35 minutes, or until crust is golden and filling is bubbly in center. Let cool on a wire rack.

---

310 BLACKBERRY BRAMBLE COBBLER

Prep: 15 minutes   Bake: 25 to 30 minutes   Serves: 6

Here's summer's best: A coal black bubbly fruit filling topped with a no-fuss buttermilk biscuit crown.

5 cups fresh or frozen blackberries
¾ cup sugar
2 tablespoons cornstarch
¼ teaspoon cinnamon

1 tablespoon fresh lemon juice
Buttermilk Biscuit Topping (recipe follows)
Vanilla ice cream

1. Preheat oven to 400°F. In a large saucepan, combine blackberries, sugar, ¼ cup water, cornstarch, and cinnamon. Bring to a boil, stirring gently. Boil 1 minute. Stir in lemon juice. Turn filling into an 9-inch square baking pan. Cover to keep hot.

2. Prepare Buttermilk Biscuit Topping and spoon on top of fruit. Bake 25 to 30 minutes, or until topping is golden and filling is bubbly. Serve warm with vanilla ice cream.

311 BUTTERMILK BISCUIT TOPPING

Prep: 5 minutes   Makes: Topping for one 9-inch square cobbler

1 cup flour
2 tablespoons sugar
1 teaspoon baking powder
½ teaspoon baking soda

⅛ teaspoon salt
4 tablespoons butter, cut up
½ cup buttermilk

In a medium bowl, combine flour, sugar, baking powder, baking soda, and salt. With a pastry blender or 2 knives, cut in butter until mixture resembles coarse crumbs. Stir in buttermilk until just moistened. Knead gently in bowl just until mixture holds together. Drop by generous tablespoonfuls onto fruit filling.

312 LEMON CORNBREAD BLUEBERRY COBBLER

Prep: 10 minutes   Bake: 25 to 30 minutes   Serves: 6

Cornmeal lends a golden color and crunch to this classic fruit cobbler. Use stone-ground yellow cornmeal for maximum taste.

5 cups fresh or frozen
   blueberries
⅔ cup sugar
2 tablespoons cornstarch

⅛ teaspoon grated nutmeg
2 teaspoons fresh lemon juice
Lemon Cornbread Topping
   (recipe follows)

1. Preheat oven to 400°F. In a large nonreactive saucepan, combine blueberries, sugar, 3 tablespoons water, cornstarch, and nutmeg. Bring to a boil, stirring gently. Boil 1 minute. Stir in lemon juice. Turn filling into a 9-inch square baking pan. Cover to keep hot.

2. Prepare Lemon Cornbread Topping. Drop by generous tablespoonfuls onto berry filling. Bake 25 to 30 minutes, or until topping is golden and filling is bubbly.

313 LEMON CORNBREAD TOPPING

Prep: 5 minutes   Cook: none
Makes: Topping for one 9-inch square cobbler

½ cup flour
½ cup yellow cornmeal
3 tablespoons sugar
1 teaspoon baking powder
½ teaspoon baking soda

¼ teaspoon grated lemon zest
¼ teaspoon salt
4 tablespoons butter, cut up
½ cup buttermilk

In a medium bowl, combine flour, cornmeal, sugar, baking powder, baking soda, lemon zest, and salt. With a pastry blender or 2 knives, cut in butter until mixture resembles coarse crumbs. Stir in buttermilk until just blended. Knead gently in bowl just until mixture holds together.

314 DOUBLE PEACH AND HAZELNUT COBBLER

Prep: 25 minutes   Bake: 25 to 30 minutes   Serves: 6

⅔ cup sugar
2 tablespoons cornstarch
½ teaspoon grated nutmeg
  Pinch of salt
¼ cup peach preserves
½ teaspoon grated lemon zest
3 pounds ripe peaches, peeled
  and thickly sliced (6 cups)

1 tablespoon Frangelico or
  other hazelnut liqueur
1 tablespoon butter
  Hazelnut Biscuit Topping
  (recipe follows)
  Peach or vanilla ice cream

1. Preheat oven to 400°F. In a large saucepan, combine sugar, cornstarch, nutmeg, and salt. Stir in ¼ cup water, peach preserves, and lemon zest until well blended. Fold in peaches. Bring to a boil, stirring gently. Boil 2 minutes. Remove from heat and stir in hazelnut liqueur and butter until butter melts. Turn filling into a 9-inch square baking pan. Cover to keep hot.

2. Prepare Hazelnut Biscuit Topping and arrange on top of filling. Bake 25 to 30 minutes, or until topping is golden and filling is bubbly. Serve warm with ice cream.

315 HAZELNUT BISCUIT TOPPING

Prep: 15 minutes   Bake: 15 minutes
Makes: Topping for one 9-inch square fruit cobbler

½ cup hazelnuts
2 tablespoons sugar
1 cup flour
1½ teaspoons baking powder

⅛ teaspoon salt
4 tablespoons butter, cut up
½ cup half-and-half
⅛ teaspoon vanilla extract

1. Preheat oven to 350°F. Spread out hazelnuts on a small baking sheet. Bake 15 minutes, or until nuts are lightly browned and dark skins are cracked. Rub warm nuts in a terrycloth towel to remove as much of skins as possible. Let cool.

2. In a food processor, process hazelnuts and sugar until finely ground. In a medium bowl, combine flour, ground nut mixture, baking powder, and salt. With a pastry blender or 2 knives, cut in butter until mixture resembles fine crumbs.

3. In a small bowl, combine half-and-half and vanilla. Stir into dry ingredients until moistened. Knead gently in bowl until mixture just holds together.

4. On a lightly floured sheet of wax paper, gently stretch dough with a rolling pin or pat with lightly floured hands into a 9-inch square. Invert biscuit onto hot fruit filling and remove wax paper.

316   PEAR-MAPLE CRUNCHY CRISP
Prep: 20 minutes   Bake: 40 to 45 minutes   Serves: 6

3 pounds ripe pears, peeled
and thinly sliced
(7 cups)
¼ cup pure maple syrup
1 tablespoon fresh lemon
juice
1 teaspoon grated lemon zest
⅔ cup packed brown sugar
¼ cup flour

¼ cup yellow cornmeal
½ teaspoon cinnamon
Pinch of salt
3 tablespoons butter, cut up
3 tablespoons solid vegetable
shortening
⅓ cup old-fashioned oats
⅓ cup finely chopped pecans
Vanilla ice cream

1. Preheat oven to 425°F. In a large bowl, combine pears, maple syrup, lemon juice, and lemon zest. Turn into an 8-inch square baking pan.

2. In another large bowl, combine brown sugar, flour, cornmeal, cinnamon, and salt. With a pastry blender or 2 knives, cut in butter and shortening until mixture resembles fine crumbs. Stir in oats and pecans; sprinkle evenly over fruit.

3. Bake 15 minutes. Reduce oven temperature to 350°F. Bake 25 to 30 minutes longer, or until top is golden and fruit is bubbly. Serve warm with vanilla ice cream.

Chapter 13

Holiday Pies

The holiday table at Thanksgiving time, laden
with turkey and all the trimmings, is a quintessential American tradition, yet perhaps no other part of that feast is more
eagerly awaited than dessert, when homemade pie takes center stage. Holidays are the time to serve an assortment of pies
—no problem with recipes like these, because many can be
prepared in advance.

If there's one variety of pie expected on your holiday table, it will be pumpkin. That's a pleasure for any pie
maker, because the filling is so easy to fix. I always use canned
pumpkin for my filling; the taste is fresh and spicy. But when
preparing these recipes, be sure to purchase solid-pack pumpkin rather than pumpkin pie filling, which contains sweeten-
ers and spices. I believe pumpkin filling tastes best the day it's
made, but the pie shell can be prepared ahead and frozen
unbaked or partially baked. If you're in a time crunch, pumpkin pies and other winter squash and sweet potato pies can be
baked completely a day ahead and refrigerated. The flavor
will be fine, but you'll sacrifice a crisp bottom crust. If refrigerating these pies, for maximum taste just allow them to stand at
room temperature a few hours before serving.

Pecan pie is another Thanksgiving favorite. Rich
and crunchy, this pie loses none of its flavor or texture if baked
a day ahead, covered, and kept at room temperature. Pecan
pies freeze beautifully, too. To thaw, simply allow the pie to
stand at room temperature for several hours, then recrisp in a
350°F oven for 10 to 15 minutes. Nuts are the star ingredient in
this filling and in many recipes, feel free to substitute walnuts
for pecans, or use a combination. Toasting brings out the best
flavor in nuts. I like to toast them in a 350°F oven for 8 to 10
minutes until lightly browned and fragrant, but watch them
carefully so they don't burn. Always cool nuts completely
before adding them to your filling.

Fruit fillings bring a touch of lightness and refresh-
ment to any selection of pies, and when we think of Thanksgiving, fresh cranberries are a must. When selecting
cranberries, look for firm, bright red berries; discard any shriveled or white cranberries. Luckily for the holidays, peak season is October through December, but for other times of the
year, keep in mind that tightly wrapped fresh cranberries can
be refrigerated for up to a month or frozen for up to a year.
Both fresh and unthawed frozen berries can be used interchangeably in these pies.

For pumpkin pie fans it's all here, from the classic

Brown Sugar Pumpkin Pie to a few choices with a twist, like Apple Butter-Pumpkin Pie with Pecan Crunch Topping, Rum-Raisin Pumpkin Pie, or a totally do-ahead Frozen Maple Sugar Pumpkin Mousse Pie. Nut lovers will dive into New England Cranberry-Pecan Pie, Sweet Potato Walnut pie, and an utterly decadent Espresso Pecan Fudge Pie laden with chocolate. For fruit tastes, choose from Upside-Down Apple-Pecan Pie or a gorgeous Cranberry-Pear Lattice Pie. Every one is a winner, pies so easy and delicious you'll want to bake them straight through Christmas and all winter long.

317 APPLE BUTTER-PUMPKIN PIE WITH PECAN CRUNCH TOPPING

Prep: 15 minutes　Freeze: 20 minutes　Bake: 45 to 50 minutes Broil: 1½ to 2 minutes　Serves: 8

1 (9-inch) Unbaked Pie Shell (page 158)	¾ teaspoon cinnamon
3 large eggs	½ teaspoon ground ginger
1 cup canned solid-pack pumpkin	½ teaspoon salt
1 cup apple butter	Pinch of ground allspice
½ cup sugar	1 cup heavy cream
	Pecan Crunch Topping (recipe follows)

1. Preheat oven to 375°F. Freeze pie shell 20 minutes.

2. In a large bowl, beat eggs lightly. Add pumpkin, apple butter, sugar, cinnamon, ginger, salt, and allspice and whisk until blended. Whisk in heavy cream until smooth. Turn filling into frozen pastry crust.

3. Bake 45 to 50 minutes, or until filling is just set. Let cool completely on a wire rack.

4. Preheat broiler. Sprinkle Pecan Crunch Topping evenly over top of pie. Cover edge of pastry crust with foil. Broil 7 inches from heat 1½ to 2 minutes, or until topping is golden and sugar is dissolved. Let pie cool slightly before serving.

PECAN CRUNCH TOPPING
Makes: Topping for one 9-inch pie

⅔ cup packed brown sugar　　　　¼ teaspoon grated nutmeg
3 tablespoons butter, melted　　　1 cup chopped pecans

In a medium bowl, combine brown sugar, butter, and nutmeg. Stir in chopped pecans.

318 BROWN SUGAR PUMPKIN PIE

Prep: 15 minutes   Bake: 50 to 55 minutes   Serves: 8

2 large eggs, lightly beaten
1 (16-ounce) can solid-pack
   pumpkin
¾ cup packed brown sugar
1 teaspoon cinnamon
½ teaspoon ground ginger
½ teaspoon salt

¼ teaspoon grated nutmeg
   Pinch of ground cloves
1 (12-ounce) can evaporated
   milk
1 (9-inch) Partially Baked Pie
   Shell (page 158)

1. Preheat oven to 425°F. In a large bowl, whisk together eggs, pumpkin, brown sugar, cinnamon, ginger, salt, nutmeg, and cloves. Gradually whisk in evaporated milk until smooth.

2. Turn filling into partially baked crust. Bake 10 minutes. Reduce oven temperature to 350°F. Bake 40 to 45 minutes longer, or until filling is just set. Let cool completely on a wire rack.

319 RUM-RAISIN PUMPKIN PIE

Prep: 10 minutes   Stand: 1 hour   Bake: 45 to 50 minutes   Serves: 8

Here's a pumpkin pie for the sophisticate. You can substitute an equal amount of brandy for the rum if you prefer.

½ cup golden raisins
¼ cup dark rum
3 large eggs
1½ cups canned solid-pack
   pumpkin
⅔ cup sugar
¾ teaspoon cinnamon
½ teaspoon salt

¼ teaspoon grated nutmeg
⅛ teaspoon ground cloves
1 cup half-and-half
1 (9-inch) Partially Baked Pie
   Shell (page 158)
   Maple Whipped Cream
   (page 251)

1. In a small bowl, combine raisins and rum. Let stand 1 hour, or overnight.

2. Preheat oven to 425°F. Drain raisins into a sieve set over a large bowl. Add eggs, pumpkin, sugar, cinnamon, salt, nutmeg, and cloves to rum in bowl and whisk to blend well. Gradually whisk in half-and-half until smooth.

3. Turn filling into partially baked crust. Sprinkle raisins on top. Bake 10 minutes. Reduce oven temperature to 350°F. Bake 35 to 40 minutes longer, or until filling is just set. Let cool on a wire rack. Serve with Maple Whipped Cream.

320 SPICED PUMPKIN CREAM CHEESE PIE
Prep: 20 minutes   Bake: 55 to 60 minutes   Serves: 8 to 10

1 (8-ounce) package cream
    cheese, softened
⅔ cup sugar
1 (16-ounce) can solid-pack
    pumpkin
½ cup heavy cream
⅓ cup honey
1½ teaspoons cinnamon
1 teaspoon grated orange zest
½ teaspoon ground ginger

½ teaspoon salt
¼ teaspoon ground allspice
    Pinch of freshly ground
    black pepper
3 large eggs
    Pecan Praline Crust (recipe
    follows)
    Maple Whipped Cream
    (page 251)

1. Preheat oven to 350°F. In a large bowl, beat cream cheese and sugar with an electric mixer on medium speed until light and fluffy. Beat in pumpkin, cream, honey, cinnamon, orange zest, ginger, salt, allspice, and pepper until smooth. With mixer on low speed, add eggs, 1 at a time, beating well after each addition. Pour filling into Pecan Praline Crust.

2. Bake 55 to 60 minutes, or until a cake tester inserted in center comes out clean. Let cool on a wire rack. Serve at room temperature or chilled, with Maple Whipped Cream.

321 PECAN PRALINE CRUST
Prep: 25 minutes   Chill: 1 hour   Freeze: 20 minutes
Bake: 33 to 37 minutes   Makes: 1 single 9-inch pie crust

This is a fabulous pie crust for cream pies, especially those with a banana or chocolate filling.

⅓ cup pecans
2 tablespoons packed brown
    sugar
1 cup flour

¼ teaspoon salt
6 tablespoons cold butter, cut
    up
2 to 3 tablespoons ice water

1. Preheat oven to 350°F. Spread out pecans on a small baking sheet. Bake 8 to 10 minutes, or until nuts are lightly browned and fragrant. Let cool.

2. In a food processor, process pecans and brown sugar until finely ground. Add flour and salt and pulse to mix. Add butter, then turn machine quickly on and off until mixture is in coarse crumbs. Sprinkle on 1 tablespoon water. Turn machine on and off 2 or 3 times. Repeat process with remaining ice water as needed, 1 tablespoon at a time, following each addition of water by 2 quick pulses, just until dough begins to hold together. (Dough will be in fine crumbs and will begin to stick to food processor blade. It will look crumbly but feel moist.) Turn dough out onto smooth surface and gather gently into a ball. Flatten ball into a disk and wrap tightly in plastic wrap. Refrigerate 1 hour or overnight.

3. On a lightly floured surface, roll out disk into ⅛-inch-thick round. Fold in half and ease gently into a 9-inch pie pan. Unfold dough, letting pastry overhang edge. Trim overhanging edge of pastry 1 inch from rim of pan. Fold pastry edge under the flute. Prick bottom of pie shell with a fork. Freeze 20 minutes, or until firm.

4. Preheat oven to 400°F. Line pie shell with foil; fill halfway with pie weights, dried beans, or rice. Bake 15 minutes, or until edge of pastry is set and lightly colored. Remove foil and weights. Bake 10 to 12 minutes longer, or until bottom and sides of crust are golden brown. Transfer to a wire rack and let cool completely before filling.

322   PECAN SHOOFLY PIE

Prep: 15 minutes   Freeze: 20 minutes   Bake: 54 to 60 minutes
Serves: 8

Shoofly pie, bursting with enough dark molasses and brown sugar to "shoo away the flies," is an American classic of Pennsylvania Dutch origin. To grace your holiday table, I've added toasted pecans to complement the sweet filling.

Flaky Pastry for a 9-inch
   single crust pie (page 157)
¾ cup flour
½ cup packed brown sugar
½ teaspoon cinnamon
¼ teaspoon ground ginger
¼ teaspoon grated nutmeg
¼ teaspoon salt

Pinch of ground cloves
4 tablespoons butter, cut up
⅔ cup chopped pecans
1 teaspoon baking soda
1 cup boiling water
1 cup unsulphured molasses
2 large eggs
Whipped cream

1. Roll pastry disk into a ⅛-inch-thick round. Fold in half and ease gently into a 9-inch pie pan. Unfold dough, letting pastry overhang edge. Trim overhanging edge of pastry 1 inch from rim of pan. Fold pastry edge under and flute. Freeze 20 minutes, or until firm.

2. Preheat oven to 425°F. Line pie shell with foil; fill halfway with pie weights. Bake 12 minutes, or until edge of pastry is set and lightly colored. Remove foil and weights. Bake 7 to 8 minutes longer, or until bottom and sides of crust are golden brown. Transfer to a wire rack and let cool completely.

3. Reduce oven temperature to 400°F. In a medium bowl, combine flour, brown sugar, cinnamon, ginger, nutmeg, salt, and cloves. With a pastry blender or two knives, cut in butter until mixture resembles fine crumbs. Stir in pecans.

4. In a large bowl, dissolve baking soda in ¼ cup boiling water. Whisk in molasses, eggs, and remaining ¾ cup boiling water until smooth. Turn into pastry crust. Sprinkle pecan mixture evenly over top of pie.

5. Bake 10 minutes. Reduce oven temperature to 350°F. Bake 25 to 30 minutes longer, or until filling is set and topping is golden. Let cool completely on a wire rack. Serve with whipped cream.

323   CREAMY RUM PECAN PIE
Prep: 10 minutes   Bake: 53 to 60 minutes   Serves: 8

This version of pecan pie features a creamy custard filling.

1½ cups pecan halves
3 large eggs
¾ cup packed brown sugar
¾ cup dark corn syrup
½ cup heavy cream
3 tablespoons dark rum

2 tablespoons butter, melted
1 teaspoon vanilla extract
1 (9-inch) Partially Baked Pie
   Shell (page 158)

1. Preheat oven to 350°F. Spread out pecans on a small baking sheet. Bake 8 to 10 minutes, or until nuts are lightly browned and fragrant. Let cool.

2. In a medium bowl, beat eggs lightly. Beat in brown sugar, corn syrup, heavy cream, rum, melted butter, and vanilla until smooth. Stir in toasted pecans. Turn into partially baked crust.

3. Bake 45 to 50 minutes, or until just set. Let cool completely on a wire rack.

324   FROZEN MAPLE SUGAR PUMPKIN MOUSSE PIE
Prep: 15 minutes   Bake: 8 to 10 minutes   Freeze: 8 hours
Stand: 1 hour   Serves: 8 to 10

When maple sugar in granulated form appears on the market, it's a special event. Here's a pie that celebrates its full flavor.

1 cup vanilla wafer cookie
   crumbs
1 cup maple sugar
½ cup finely chopped pecans
5⅓ tablespoons (⅓ cup) butter,
   melted
1 (16-ounce) can solid-pack
   pumpkin
½ teaspoon maple extract

½ teaspoon cinnamon
¼ teaspoon ground ginger
¼ teaspoon grated nutmeg
Pinch of salt
1 cup heavy cream
Maple Whipped Cream
   (page 251)

1. Preheat oven to 375°F. In a medium bowl, combine cookie crumbs, ¼ cup maple sugar, and pecans. Stir in melted butter, tossing until mixture is evenly moistened. Press into a 9-inch pie plate. Bake crust 8 to 10 minutes, or until golden brown. Let cool on a wire rack.

2. In a medium bowl, combine pumpkin, remaining ¾ cup maple sugar, maple extract, cinnamon, ginger, nutmeg, and salt until blended.

3. In a large bowl, beat cream with an electric mixer until stiff. Fold into pumpkin mixture with a rubber spatula. Turn filling into baked crust. Loosely cover and freeze until firm, about 8 hours.

4. One hour before serving, remove pie from freezer and let stand at room temperature. Just before serving, decorate top with Maple Whipped Cream.

325 MAPLE WHIPPED CREAM
Prep: 5 minutes   Cook: none   Makes: 2½ cups

1 cup heavy cream
2 tablespoons powdered
   sugar

⅓ cup pure maple syrup
½ teaspoon ground ginger

In a large bowl, beat cream with an electric mixer until soft peaks form. Add powdered sugar, maple syrup, and ginger and continue to beat to stiff peaks.

326 PRALINE CRUNCH CRANBERRY-APPLE PIE
Prep: 30 minutes   Bake: 72 to 80 minutes   Serves: 8

1 cup pecans
1 cup packed dark brown
   sugar
3 tablespoons flour
1½ teaspoons cinnamon
   Pinch of salt
½ cup plus 1 tablespoon heavy
   cream
2 pounds tart apples, peeled
   and cut into ¾-inch-thick
   wedges (4 cups)

2 cups coarsely chopped fresh
   or frozen cranberries
2 tablespoons butter, cut up
   Mostly Butter Pastry for a
   9-inch double crust pie
   (page 159)
2 tablespoons granulated
   sugar

1. Preheat oven to 350°F. Spread out pecans on a small baking sheet. Bake 7 to 10 minutes, or until nuts are lightly browned and fragrant. Let cool, then coarsely chop. Increase oven temperature to 425°F.

2. In a large bowl, combine brown sugar, flour, cinnamon, and salt. Whisk in ½ cup heavy cream until smooth. Stir in pecans, apples, and cranberries, tossing to coat.

3. On a lightly floured surface, roll out larger pastry disk into a ⅛-inch-thick round. Fold in half and ease gently into a 9-inch pie pan. Unfold dough, letting pastry overhang edge. Trim pastry 1 inch from rim of pan. Turn filling into pie shell and dot with butter.

4. Roll remaining pastry disk into a ⅛-inch-thick round; place over filling. Fold edge of top pastry over lower pastry; flute rim. Cut vents for steam. Brush top of pie with remaining 1 tablespoon cream, then sprinkle with granulated sugar.

5. Place pie on cookie sheet and bake 15 minutes. Reduce oven temperature to 350°F. Bake 50 to 55 minutes longer, or until filling is bubbly and crust is golden. Transfer to a wire rack. Serve warm or let cool completely.

327   ESPRESSO PECAN FUDGE PIE
Prep: 20 minutes   Bake: 53 to 60 minutes   Serves: 12

This ultra-rich nut pie should be served in small slivers.

1½ cups pecans
3 (1-ounce) squares
   unsweetened chocolate,
   cut up
3 tablespoons butter
1 teaspoon instant espresso
   powder
3 large eggs, lightly beaten
1 cup sugar

1 cup light corn syrup
2 tablespoons coffee-flavored
   liqueur
1 teaspoon vanilla extract
1 (9-inch) Partially Baked Pie
   Shell (page 158)
   Sweetened Whipped Cream
   (page 265)

1. Preheat oven to 350°F. Spread out pecans on a small baking sheet. Bake 8 to 10 minutes, until nuts are lightly browned and fragrant. Let cool.

2. In a medium glass bowl, combine chocolate and butter. Microwave on Medium 2 to 2½ minutes, or until butter is melted. Stir until chocolate is smooth, then stir in espresso powder until completely dissolved. Blend in eggs, sugar, corn syrup, coffee liqueur, and vanilla until smooth. Stir in toasted pecans. Turn into partially baked crust.

3. Bake 45 to 50 minutes, or until filling is just set in center. Let cool completely on a wire rack. Serve with Sweetened Whipped Cream.

328   SWEET MAPLE MARLBOROUGH PIE
Prep: 10 minutes   Bake: 40 to 45 minutes   Serves: 8

This is a Thanksgiving classic from New England. Bake the crust ahead, then fill the pie shortly before dinner. It's wonderful served warm, with whipped cream on the side.

2 cups applesauce
⅓ cup pure maple syrup
⅓ cup sugar
3 large eggs
2 tablespoons fresh lemon
   juice
2 tablespoons butter, melted

¼ teaspoon grated nutmeg
¼ teaspoon salt
½ cup heavy cream
1 (9-inch) Partially Baked Pie
   Shell (page 158)

1. Preheat oven to 425°F. In a large bowl, whisk applesauce, maple syrup, and sugar together until smooth. Whisk in eggs, 1 at a time, until blended. Whisk in lemon juice, melted butter, nutmeg, and salt. Mix in cream. Pour filling into pastry crust.

2. Bake 15 minutes. Reduce oven temperature to 350°F. Bake 25 to 30 minutes longer, or until filling is just set in center. Transfer to a wire rack. Serve warm or let cool completely.

329   PEANUT BUTTER PECAN PIE
Prep: 20 minutes   Bake: 58 to 65 minutes   Serves: 8

1½ cups pecans
⅔ cup smooth peanut butter
2 tablespoons butter, melted
1 teaspoon vanilla extract
¾ cup light corn syrup

¾ cup packed brown sugar
3 large eggs
1 (9-inch) Partially Baked Pie
   Shell (page 158)

1. Preheat oven to 350°F. Spread out pecans on a small baking sheet. Bake 8 to 10 minutes, until nuts are lightly browned and fragrant. Let cool.

2. In a medium bowl, whisk peanut butter, melted butter, and vanilla until smooth. Beat in corn syrup, brown sugar, and eggs until well blended. Stir in toasted pecans. Turn into partially baked crust.

3. Bake 50 to 55 minutes, or until filling is just set in center. Let cool completely on a wire rack.

330   SWEET POTATO CUSTARD PIE
Prep: 30 minutes   Cook: 15 to 20 minutes
Bake: 45 to 50 minutes   Serves: 8

Fresh sweet potatoes are definitely worth cooking up for this delicate custard pie, and they only take minutes in the microwave.

2 pounds fresh sweet potatoes
   (4 medium)
3 large eggs
¼ cup packed brown sugar
1 cup heavy cream
½ cup pure maple syrup
1 teaspoon maple extract
1 teaspoon grated lemon zest

1 teaspoon cinnamon
¼ teaspoon grated nutmeg
¼ teaspoon ground allspice
¼ teaspoon salt
1 (9-inch) Partially Baked Pie
   Shell (page 158)

1. Peel sweet potatoes and cut into 1-inch cubes. Place in a steamer rack over boiling water. Cover and steam 15 to 20 minutes, or until tender when pierced with a fork. (To microwave: Scrub potatoes and prick each several times with a fork. Arrange at least 1 inch apart on a paper towel in microwave oven. Microwave on High 9 to 13 minutes, turning and rearranging halfway through, or until fork-tender. Let stand 5 minutes. Carefully peel off skins with a small sharp knife.) Immediately transfer hot potatoes to a large bowl and beat with electric mixer until smooth. Let cool slightly.

2. Preheat oven to 350°F. With mixer on medium-low speed, beat eggs and brown sugar with sweet potatoes until smooth. Beat in cream, maple syrup, maple extract, lemon zest, cinnamon, nutmeg, allspice, and salt until well blended. Turn into partially baked crust.

3. Bake 45 to 50 minutes, or until filling is just set in center. Let cool completely on a wire rack.

331   NEW ENGLAND CRANBERRY-PECAN PIE
Prep: 20 minutes   Bake: 58 to 70 minutes   Serves: 8

Cranberries lend a beautiful color and just the right amount of tartness to this nut-filled pie flavored with pure maple syrup.

1 cup pecans
3 large eggs
1 cup pure maple syrup
¾ cup sugar
6 tablespoons butter, melted
1 teaspoon vanilla extract
1 teaspoon grated lemon zest

¼ teaspoon grated nutmeg
  Pinch of salt
1 cup coarsely chopped fresh
  or frozen cranberries
1 (9-inch) Partially Baked Pie
  Shell (page 158)

1. Preheat oven to 350°F. Spread out pecans on a small baking sheet. Bake 8 to 10 minutes, until nuts are lightly browned and fragrant. Let cool.

2. In a medium bowl, beat eggs lightly. Beat in maple syrup, sugar, melted butter, vanilla, lemon zest, nutmeg, and salt until smooth. Stir in pecans and cranberries. Turn into partially baked crust.

3. Bake 50 to 60 minutes, or until center is just set. Let cool completely on a wire rack.

332   HOLIDAY MINCEFRUIT PIE
Prep: 40 minutes   Cook: 35 minutes
Bake: 61 to 66 minutes   Serves: 10

Here is the best of mincemeat—without any meat! It's best to prepare this filling a day ahead to allow all the flavors to develop.

3 tart apples, peeled and diced
3 pears, peeled and diced
1 cup chopped dried figs
½ cup dried cherries or raisins
½ cup chopped dried apricots
½ cup chopped dried prunes
2 tablespoons chopped
  candied citron
½ cup packed brown sugar
2 tablespoons cider vinegar
½ teaspoon grated lemon zest
½ teaspoon cinnamon

¼ teaspoon grated nutmeg
¼ teaspoon freshly ground
  pepper
  Pinch of ground allspice
3 tablespoons dark rum
1 cup walnuts
  Mostly Butter Pastry for a
  9-inch double crust pie
  (page 159)
2 tablespoons butter, cut up
1 large egg yolk
  Vanilla ice cream

1. In a large nonreactive saucepan, combine apples, pears, figs, dried cherries, apricots, prunes, citron, brown sugar, vinegar, lemon zest, cinnamon, nutmeg, pepper, allspice, and 1¼ cups water. Bring to boil; reduce heat and simmer, stirring occasionally, until fruits are tender and mixture is thickened, about 35 minutes. Remove from heat; stir in rum and let cool.

2. Preheat oven to 425°F. Spread out walnuts on a small baking sheet. Bake 6 minutes, or until nuts are lightly browned and fragrant. Let cool, then coarsely chop and stir into fruit filling.

3. On a lightly floured surface, roll out larger pastry disk into a ⅛-inch-thick round. Fold in half and ease gently into a 9-inch pie pan. Unfold dough, letting pastry overhang edge. Trim pastry 1 inch from rim of pan. Spoon filling into pie shell and dot with butter.

4. Roll out remaining pastry disk into a ⅛-inch-thick round. Cut into ¾-inch-wide strips and arrange in a lattice pattern on top of filling. Fold edge of bottom pastry up over ends of strips, building a high edge. Seal and flute. In a cup, beat egg yolk with 1 tablespoon water. Brush lattice top with egg glaze.

5. Place pie on a cookie sheet and bake 10 minutes. Reduce oven temperature to 375°F. Bake 45 to 50 minutes longer, or until filling is bubbly and crust is golden. Transfer to a wire rack. Serve warm or at room temperature with vanilla ice cream.

333 UPSIDE-DOWN APPLE PECAN PIE
Prep: 25 minutes   Bake: 55 to 60 minutes   Serves: 10

This pie is an all-time favorite from my mother. It's best served warm, but it can be prepared ahead and reheated gently in a warm oven.

6 tablespoons butter
⅓ cup packed brown sugar
1 cup pecans
½ cup granulated sugar
4 teaspoons flour
1 teaspoon cinnamon
¼ teaspoon grated nutmeg

Pinch of salt
2½ pounds tart apples, peeled and thinly sliced
Mostly Butter Pastry for a 10-inch double crust pie (page 159)
Vanilla ice cream

1. In a small saucepan, melt butter over medium heat. Stir in brown sugar and cook until melted and smooth, about 1 minute. Stir in pecans. Spread over bottom of a 10-inch pie plate. Let cool.

2. Preheat oven to 425°F. In a large bowl, combine granulated sugar, flour, cinnamon, nutmeg, and salt. Stir in apples, tossing to coat.

3. On a lightly floured surface, roll out larger pastry disk into a ⅛-inch-thick round. Fold in half and ease gently over nuts in pie pan. Unfold dough, letting pastry overhang edge. Trim pastry 1 inch from rim of pan. Spoon apple filling into pie shell.

4. Roll remaining pastry disk into a ⅛-inch-thick round; place on top of pie. Fold edge of top pastry over lower pastry; flute. Cut vents for steam.

5. Place pie on a cookie sheet and bake 15 minutes. Reduce oven temperature to 375°F. Bake 40 to 45 minutes longer, or until filling is bubbly and crust is golden brown. Transfer to a wire rack and let stand 5 minutes. Immediately invert onto a large serving plate. Serve warm with vanilla ice cream.

334 BUTTERNUT SQUASH SATIN PIE
Prep: 35 minutes   Cook: 23 to 30 minutes
Bake: 50 to 55 minutes   Serves: 8

Fresh butternut squash is always a fall favorite, and in this pie it stars with a delicate molasses-cream custard.

1¾ pounds fresh butternut squash	1 teaspoon cinnamon
¾ cup heavy cream	½ teaspoon ground ginger
¾ cup milk	½ teaspoon grated nutmeg
¾ cup sugar	½ teaspoon salt
¼ cup unsulphured molasses	1 (10-inch) Partially Baked Pie
3 large eggs	Shell (page 158)

1. Cut squash in half, scoop out seeds, and cut squash into large chunks. Place in a steamer rack over boiling water. Cover and steam 20 to 25 minutes, or until tender when pierced with a fork. Let cool, then peel off skin with a small sharp knife. Transfer to a food processor and puree until smooth.

2. Preheat oven to 375°F. In a small saucepan, combine cream, milk, and sugar. Cook over medium heat, stirring to dissolve sugar, until hot, 3 to 5 minutes. (Do not boil.)

3. In a medium bowl, whisk together squash puree, molasses, eggs, cinnamon, ginger, nutmeg, and salt until smooth. Slowly whisk in hot cream mixture. Immediately turn into partially baked pastry crust.

4. Bake 10 minutes. Reduce oven temperature to 350°F. Bake 40 to 45 minutes longer, or until filling is just set in center. Let cool completely on a wire rack.

335 CRANBERRY-PEAR LATTICE PIE
Prep: 35 minutes   Cook: 12 minutes
Bake: 50 to 55 minutes   Serves: 8

⅔ cup packed brown sugar	¼ teaspoon salt
3 pounds pears, peeled and cut into 1-inch chunks	3 tablespoons cornstarch
1½ cups fresh or frozen cranberries	2 tablespoons butter, cut up
½ teaspoon grated lemon zest	Flaky Pastry for a 9-inch double crust pie (page 157)
¼ teaspoon grated nutmeg	

1. In a large saucepan, combine brown sugar and ½ cup water. Bring to boil, reduce heat, and simmer 5 minutes. Add pears, cranberries, lemon zest, nutmeg, and salt. Simmer until cranberries pop, about 5 minutes.

2. In a small bowl, dissolve cornstarch in 2 tablespoons water. Stir into cranberry mixture. Bring to a boil, reduce heat, and simmer 2 minutes. Remove from heat and stir in butter until melted. Let cool.

3. Preheat oven to 425°F. On a lightly floured surface, roll out larger pastry disk into a ⅛-inch-thick round. Fold in half and ease gently into a 9-inch pie pan. Unfold dough, letting pastry overhang edge. Trim pastry to 1 inch from rim of pan. Spoon filling into pie shell.

4. Roll remaining pastry disk into a ⅛-inch-thick round. Cut into ¾-inch-wide strips and arrange in a lattice pattern on top of filling. Fold edge of bottom pastry up over ends of strips, building a high edge. Seal and flute.

5. Place pie on a cookie sheet and bake 15 minutes. Reduce oven temperature to 375°F. Bake 35 to 40 minutes longer, or until filling is bubbly in center. Let cool completely on a wire rack before serving.

336 BUTTERMILK SWEET POTATO PRALINE PIE

Prep: 30 minutes   Cook: 15 to 20 minutes
Bake: 47 to 52 minutes   Broil: 1½ to 2 minutes   Serves: 8

2 **pounds fresh sweet potatoes**	½ **teaspoon cinnamon**
(4 medium)	½ **teaspoon grated nutmeg**
3 **large eggs**	**Pinch of salt**
1 **cup sugar**	1 **(9-inch) Partially Baked Pie**
1½ **cups buttermilk**	**Shell (page 158)**
2 **tablespoons butter, melted**	**Pecan Crunch Topping**
1 **teaspoon vanilla extract**	**(page 246)**

1. Peel the fresh sweet potatoes and cut into 1-inch cubes. Place in a steamer rack over boiling water. Cover and steam 15 to 20 minutes, or until tender when pierced with a fork. (To microwave: Scrub potatoes and prick each several times with a fork. Arrange at least 1 inch apart on a paper towel in a microwave oven. Microwave on High 9 to 13 minutes, turning and rearranging halfway through. Let stand 5 minutes. Carefully peel off skins with a small sharp knife.) Immediately transfer hot potatoes to a large bowl and beat with an electric mixer until smooth. Let cool.

2. Preheat oven to 375°F. With mixer on medium-low speed, beat eggs and sugar into sweet potatoes until smooth. Beat in buttermilk, melted butter, vanilla, cinnamon, nutmeg, and salt until well blended. Turn into partially baked crust.

3. Bake 45 to 50 minutes, or until filling is just set in center. Let cool on a wire rack 15 minutes.

4. Preheat broiler. Sprinkle Pecan Crunch Topping evenly over top of pie. Cover edge of pastry crust with foil. Broil 7 inches from heat, 1½ to 2 minutes, or until topping is golden and sugar is melted. Serve warm or at room temperature.

337 SWEET POTATO WALNUT PIE
Prep: 30 minutes   Cook: 15 to 20 minutes
Bake: 58 to 65 minutes   Serves: 8

1 pound fresh sweet potatoes
   (2 medium)
1 cup walnuts
3 large eggs
¾ cup packed brown sugar
¼ cup heavy cream
1 tablespoon dark rum
½ teaspoon cinnamon

¼ teaspoon ground ginger
   Pinch of ground cloves
   Pinch of salt
1 (9-inch) Partially Baked Pie
   Shell (page 158)
⅔ cup dark corn syrup
2 tablespoons butter, melted
½ teaspoon vanilla extract

1. Peel sweet potatoes and cut into 1-inch cubes. Place in a steamer rack over boiling water. Cover and steam 15 to 20 minutes, or until tender when pierced with a fork. (To microwave: Scrub potatoes and prick each several times with a fork. Arrange in microwave oven 1 inch apart on a paper towel. Microwave on High 6 to 7 minutes, turning and rearranging halfway through. Let stand 5 minutes and peel carefully.) Immediately transfer hot potatoes to a large bowl and beat with electric mixer until smooth. Let cool.

2. Preheat oven to 350°F. Spread out walnuts on a small baking sheet. Bake 8 to 10 minutes, until nuts are lightly browned and fragrant. Let cool, then coarsely chop.

3. Add 1 egg, ¼ cup brown sugar, cream, rum, cinnamon, ginger, cloves, and salt to sweet potatoes and whisk until well blended. Spread evenly in bottom of partially baked crust.

4. In another bowl, whisk together remaining 2 eggs and ½ cup brown sugar with corn syrup, melted butter, and vanilla until smooth. Stir in walnuts. Spoon over sweet potato layer. Bake 50 to 55 minutes, or until filling is just set in center. Let cool completely on a wire rack.

Chapter 14

Classic Custard and Cream Pies

When the time is ripe to indulge and you crave a smooth, decadently rich, creamy dessert, there's nothing like the sweet satisfaction of a custard or cream pie. One slice will take you back to the corner drugstore or Mom's kitchen. Each bite is a cloud of subtle comfort, impossible to resist. This chapter offers a variety of filling flavors, from the simplest vanilla and chocolate to coconut, banana, lemon, buttermilk, butterscotch, and caramel. They feel right at home nestled in your favorite flaky pastry crust or equally comfortable served in a simple crust of crushed cookie crumbs. Custard and cream pies can be transformed into mile-high beauties with a cloak of golden meringue or a generous dollop of whipped cream.

Custard pies have a filling made with milk, sugar, and spices, thickened with eggs. When properly baked, this simple combination of ingredients becomes very delicate, silky, and smooth. Baking a custard pie for too long or at too high a temperature can cause the filling to separate and become watery. A custard filling is ready when the edges are set and the center jiggles slightly. As the pie cools, the filling will firm up to just the right texture. A good way to ensure a crisp bottom pastry and avoid overcooking the filling is to partially bake your empty pastry crust first, which you can do in advance. Custard pies are best served the day they are made, and if there are any leftovers, be sure to refrigerate them.

Cream pies have the same milk, sugar, and egg base filling as custard pies, but the fillings, thickened with cornstarch or flour, are cooked on the stovetop, and the assembled pie needs no baking. Since the filling is spooned into a fully baked pie or crumb crust and chilled until set, many are wonderful do-ahead pies. Cream pie fillings prepared with cornstarch have a smooth, velvety texture. Flour-based fillings are similar but a bit denser. When using cornstarch, combine it thoroughly with sugar and other dry ingredients before adding the cold liquid. Gradually stir in the liquid until the mixture is completely smooth. It's important to stir the filling constantly but gently over moderate heat. Stirring too vigorously can cause the custard to break down. Cooking at too high a temperature can cause lumping and curdling if the filling contains eggs. Once the cornstarch mixture has reached a full boil, continue to boil for 1 minute longer, then immediately remove from the heat. At this point, the filling will have thickened sufficiently, and any additional cooking may cause it to become too thin.

There's little doubt that many of our favorite custard and cream pies have a meringue topping. To prevent your meringue from shrinking or weeping, always apply the beaten whites to the pie filling while it is still hot and then bake the meringue immediately. I prepare my filling first, then cover and keep it warm while beating the egg whites and sugar. Make sure the meringue is spread all over the surface of the filling so that it touches the edges of the pie crust to form a tight seal. Bake just until the decorative peaks turn a golden brown, rotating the pie if necessary to brown the topping evenly. Let the pie cool to room temperature on a wire rack, then refrigerate, if desired.

Counted among my favorite custard pies are Lemon-Lime Meringue, Old-Fashioned Chocolate Custard with a toasted hazelnut crust, Brandy Pear Custard, Buttermilk-Cherry Chess, and Piña Colada Chess Pie. Banana Cream Pie is perfection served in a Pecan Praline Crust; Black Bottom Coconut Cream Pie is scrumptious with bittersweet chocolate.

338 BANANA CREAM PIE WITH PECAN PRALINE CRUST

Prep: 20 minutes   Cook: 6 to 7 minutes   Chill: 3 hours   Serves: 8

⅔ cup sugar
¼ cup cornstarch
¼ teaspoon salt
2⅓ cups milk
⅔ cup heavy cream
3 large egg yolks
1 tablespoon butter

2 teaspoons vanilla extract
¼ cup apricot preserves
  Pecan Praline Crust (page 248)
3 medium ripe bananas
  Whipped cream

1. In a large saucepan, combine sugar, cornstarch, and salt. Gradually whisk in milk and cream until smooth. Cook over medium heat, stirring gently, until mixture reaches a boil, 4 to 5 minutes. Boil 1 minute; remove from heat.

2. In a small bowl, beat egg yolks lightly. Gradually whisk in 1 cup hot milk mixture. Return to saucepan, whisking constantly. Return to a boil and boil 1 minute longer. Remove from heat; whisk in butter and vanilla to blend well. Cover surface of custard with wax paper or plastic wrap. Let cool slightly, about 20 minutes.

3. In a small saucepan, heat apricot preserves over medium heat until melted and bubbly, 1 to 2 minutes. Spread over bottom and sides of Pecan Praline Crust. Slice 2 bananas and arrange on top. Spread custard evenly over bananas. Cover and refrigerate until cold, 3 hours or overnight.

4. Just before serving, uncover pie; slice remaining banana and arrange on top of pie. Decorate with dollops of whipped cream.

339 BUTTERSCOTCH PIE WITH PRALINE PECAN BRITTLE

Prep: 20 minutes   Cook: 9 minutes   Chill: 3 hours   Serves: 8

6 tablespoons butter
1 cup packed dark brown sugar
½ cup boiling water
3 tablespoons cornstarch
2 tablespoons flour
¼ teaspoon salt
2¼ cups milk

3 large egg yolks
1 teaspoon vanilla extract
1 (9-inch) Fully Baked Pie Shell (page 158)
Whipped cream
Praline Pecan Brittle (recipe follows)

1. In a large heavy skillet, melt butter over medium heat until golden brown, about 5 minutes. Add brown sugar and cook, stirring, until melted and bubbling, 1 to 2 minutes. Boil 1 minute. Carefully stir in boiling water and boil 1 minute longer, stirring constantly, until smooth. Remove from heat.

2. In a large saucepan, combine cornstarch, flour, and salt. Gradually whisk in milk, then stir in brown sugar mixture. Bring to a boil over medium heat, stirring gently; boil 1 minute. Remove from heat.

3. In a small bowl, beat egg yolks lightly. Gradually whisk in 1 cup hot filling mixture. Return to saucepan, whisking constantly. Bring to a boil and boil 1 minute. Remove from heat. Stir in vanilla. Cover surface of custard with wax paper or plastic wrap. Let cool slightly, about 20 minutes.

4. Spread custard evenly in baked crust. Cover filling and refrigerate until cold, 3 hours or overnight. Just before serving, uncover and decorate top with dollops of whipped cream, then sprinkle with Praline Pecan Brittle.

340 PRALINE PECAN BRITTLE

Prep: 10 minutes   Bake: 8 to 10 minutes   Cook: 5 minutes
Makes: about ½ cup

The ingredients in this cookie-like topping can easily be doubled. Save any leftovers to sprinkle over your favorite flavor of ice cream.

¼ cup pecans

¼ cup sugar

1. Preheat oven to 350°F. Line a cookie sheet with foil and oil lightly. Spread out pecans on a small baking sheet. Bake 8 to 10 minutes, until nuts are lightly browned and fragrant.

2. In a small heavy skillet, cook sugar over medium heat, swirling pan but not stirring, until sugar melts and forms an amber syrup, about 5 minutes. Stir in nuts and immediately spread on prepared cookie sheet. Let cool completely. Peel off foil. Transfer praline to a plastic storage bag and seal. Crush with a rolling pin into small pieces.

341 CHOCOLATE MALTED CREAM PIE
Prep: 35 minutes   Cook: 10 minutes   Bake: 8 to 10 minutes
Serves: 8

Either regular or chocolate malted milk powder is dandy in this candy bar-like filling. If you prefer a whipped cream topping, try adding a couple of tablespoons of malted milk powder to the cream for a super flavor.

⅔ cup sugar
½ cup instant malted milk
   powder
¼ cup cornstarch
¼ teaspoon salt
2¾ cups milk
3 large egg yolks
1 (1-ounce) square
   unsweetened chocolate,
   cut up

1 tablespoon butter
½ teaspoon vanilla extract
   Fluffy Meringue Topping
   (recipe follows)
1 (9-inch) Fully Baked Pie
   Shell (page 158)

1. Preheat oven to 350°F. In a large saucepan, combine sugar, malted milk powder, cornstarch, and salt. Gradually whisk in milk until smooth. Bring to a boil over medium heat, stirring gently, and boil 1 minute. Remove from heat.

2. In a small bowl, beat egg yolks lightly. Gradually whisk in 1 cup hot malted milk mixture. Return to saucepan, whisking constantly. Return to boil and boil 1 minute longer. Remove from heat. Whisk in chocolate, butter, and vanilla until chocolate is melted and custard is completely smooth. Cover surface with wax paper and keep hot while you prepare Fluffy Meringue Topping.

3. Pour hot filling mixture into baked crust. Immediately spoon half of Fluffy Meringue Topping around edge of prepared pie filling, then spread onto edge of pastry crust to form a tight seal. Pile remainder of meringue in center of pie, then spread to meet meringue around edge. Lift meringue with back of spoon to form decorative peaks.

4. Bake 8 to 10 minutes, or until meringue peaks are golden brown. Let cool completely on a wire rack. Serve at room temperature or chilled.

342 FLUFFY MERINGUE TOPPING
Prep: 10 minutes   Cook: none   Makes: Topping for one 9-inch pie

4 large egg whites, at room
   temperature

¼ teaspoon cream of tartar
½ cup sugar

In a large bowl, beat egg whites and cream of tartar with an electric mixer on medium speed until soft peaks form. Gradually beat in sugar, 1 tablespoon at a time, beating well after each addition. Continue to beat on medium speed until stiff peaks form when beaters are lifted, 4 to 5 minutes longer.

343   SOUR CREAM RAISIN PIE WITH BROWN SUGAR MERINGUE

Prep: 15 minutes   Cook: 4 to 6 minutes   Bake: 6 to 8 minutes
Serves: 8

Any dried fruit—dark or golden raisins, currants, dried cranberries, or dried cherries—would be perfect in this easy sour cream custard pie.

3 large egg yolks	½ teaspoon vanilla extract
2 cups sour cream	Brown Sugar Meringue
⅔ cup sugar	(recipe follows)
2 tablespoons cornstarch	1 (9-inch) Fully Baked Pie
¼ teaspoon salt	Shell (page 158)
½ cup raisins	

1. Preheat oven to 375°F. In a medium bowl, whisk together egg yolks and sour cream until blended.

2. In a large saucepan, combine sugar, cornstarch, and salt. Whisk in sour cream mixture until smooth. Cook over medium heat, stirring gently, until mixture boils, about 3 to 5 minutes. Boil 1 minute; remove from heat. Whisk gently until smooth. Stir in raisins and vanilla. Cover to keep hot while you prepare Brown Sugar Meringue.

3. Pour hot filling into baked crust. Immediately spoon half of Brown Sugar Meringue around edge of prepared pie filling, then spread onto edge of pastry crust to form a tight seal. Pile remainder of meringue in center of pie, then spread to meet meringue around edge. Lift meringue with back of a spoon to form decorative peaks. Bake 6 to 8 minutes, or until meringue peaks are golden brown. Let cool completely on a wire rack. Serve at room temperature or chilled.

344   BROWN SUGAR MERINGUE

Prep: 10 minutes   Cook: none   Makes: Topping for one 9-inch pie

½ cup packed brown sugar	¼ teaspoon cream of tartar
4 large egg whites, at room temperature	½ teaspoon vanilla extract

Press brown sugar through a fine sieve. In a large bowl, beat egg whites and cream of tartar with an electric mixer on medium speed until soft peaks form. Gradually beat in strained brown sugar, 1 tablespoon at a time, beating well after each addition. Continue to beat on medium speed until stiff peaks form when beaters are lifted, 4 to 5 minutes longer. Beat in vanilla.

345 FRESH GINGER CREAM CHEESE PIE
Prep: 15 minutes   Bake: 25 to 30 minutes   Chill: 2 hours   Serves: 8

This pie is fabulous with fresh berries. It can also be frozen, then thawed in the refrigerator overnight for the perfect do-ahead dessert.

4 (3-ounce) packages cream
   cheese, at room
   temperature
¾ cup sugar
1½ teaspoons grated fresh
   ginger
1 teaspoon fresh lemon juice

1 teaspoon vanilla extract
   Pinch of salt
2 large eggs, at room
   temperature
¼ cup heavy cream
   Gingersnap Crumb Crust
   (page 165)

1. Preheat oven to 350°F. In a large bowl, beat cream cheese with an electric mixer on medium speed until light and fluffy. Gradually beat in sugar, scraping down sides of bowl with a rubber spatula, until completely smooth. Beat in ginger, lemon juice, vanilla, and salt. Add eggs, 1 at a time, beating until just blended after each addition. Add cream and beat until smooth.

2. Pour filling into Gingersnap Crumb Crust. Bake 25 to 30 minutes, or until filling is just set. Let cool completely on a wire rack. Refrigerate until cold, 2 hours or overnight.

346 SHAKER SLICE OF LEMON PIE
Prep: 20 minutes   Bake: 35 to 40 minutes   Serves: 8

This old-time double crust pie with a melt-in-your-mouth fresh lemon filling is a winner. Be sure to discard the bitter white pith of the lemons before slicing.

2 small lemons
2 cups plus 1 tablespoon
   sugar
⅓ cup flour
¼ teaspoon salt
2 tablespoons butter, softened
   and cut up

3 large eggs
   Mostly Butter Pastry for a
   9-inch double crust pie
   (page 159)
¼ teaspoon cinnamon

1. Preheat oven to 400°F. Grate 1 teaspoon lemon zest from 1 lemon and set zest aside. With a small sharp knife, cut away remaining peel and white pith from both lemons and discard. Slice lemons ⅛ inch thick and remove seeds.

2. In a large bowl, combine 2 cups sugar with flour and salt. Whisk in ⅔ cup water, butter, eggs, and reserved lemon zest. Stir in lemon slices.

3. Roll out larger pastry disk into a ⅛-inch-thick round. Fold in half and ease gently into a 9-inch pie pan. Unfold dough, letting pastry overhang edge. Trim pastry 1 inch from rim of pan. Spoon filling into pie shell.

4. Roll remaining pastry disk into a ⅛-inch-thick round; place on top of pie. Fold edge of top pastry over lower pastry; flute. Cut vents for steam. In a cup, combine remaining 1 tablespoon sugar and cinnamon; sprinkle over top of pie.

5. Bake 35 to 40 minutes, or until filling is bubbly and crust is golden. Let cool completely on a wire rack.

347 SATIN CARAMEL CUSTARD PIE
Prep: 15 minutes   Cook: 8 to 11 minutes   Bake: 50 to 55 minutes
Serves: 8

Here's an elegant pie for caramel lovers. It's rich and golden but not too sweet, thanks to a burnished sugar syrup.

½ cup plus 2 tablespoons sugar	1½ teaspoons vanilla extract
½ cup boiling water	⅛ teaspoon salt
4 large eggs	1 (9-inch) Partially Baked Pie Shell (page 158)
1 cup milk	Sweetened Whipped Cream
1 cup heavy cream	(recipe follows)

1. Preheat oven to 350°F. In a small saucepan, cook ½ cup sugar over medium-low heat, swirling pan occasionally, until sugar is melted and syrup is a deep amber color, 6 to 8 minutes. Immediately remove from heat and gradually stir in boiling water with a long-handled spoon. (Mixture will bubble vigorously.) Return to heat and continue to cook, stirring, until caramel is melted, 2 to 3 minutes. Remove from heat and let cool.

2. In a large bowl, whisk eggs and remaining 2 tablespoons sugar until well blended. Mix in caramel syrup, milk, cream, vanilla, and salt.

3. Pour filling into partially baked crust. Bake 50 to 55 minutes, until a cake tester inserted into custard 1 inch from edge comes out clean. (Center may look a bit wobbly, but do not overbake.) Let cool completely on a wire rack. Serve with Sweetened Whipped Cream.

348 SWEETENED WHIPPED CREAM
Prep: 2 minutes   Cook: none   Makes: 2 cups

1 cup heavy cream	1 teaspoon vanilla extract
2 tablespoons powdered sugar	

In a large bowl, beat cream with an electric mixer on medium speed until soft peaks form. Add powdered sugar and vanilla and continue to beat to stiff peaks.

349 BUTTERMILK-CHERRY CHESS PIE
Prep: 30 minutes   Freeze: 20 minutes
Bake: 1 hour 5 to 12 minutes   Serves: 8

Dried cherries add just the right amount of tartness and make this buttery custard pie truly memorable.

1 **(9-inch) Unbaked Pie Shell** (page 158)	3 **large eggs**
1 **cup sugar**	1½ **cups buttermilk**
2 **tablespoons flour**	⅓ **cup butter, melted and cooled slightly**
¼ **teaspoon grated nutmeg**	1 **teaspoon vanilla extract**
Pinch of salt	½ **cup dried cherries or raisins**

1. Preheat oven to 425°F. Freeze pie shell until firm, about 20 minutes.

2. Line pie shell with foil; fill halfway with pie weights, dried beans, or rice. Bake 12 minutes, or until edge of pastry is set and lightly colored. Remove foil and weights. Bake 13 to 15 minutes longer, or until bottom and sides of crust are golden brown. Transfer to a wire rack and let cool completely.

3. Reduce oven temperature to 350°F. In a large bowl, combine sugar, flour, nutmeg, and salt. Whisk in eggs until smooth, then beat in buttermilk, melted butter, and vanilla until blended.

4. Pour filling into baked pastry crust. Sprinkle cherries evenly over top. Bake 40 to 45 minutes, or until filling is just set and golden. Transfer to a wire rack. Serve warm or at room temperature.

350 BRANDY PEAR CUSTARD PIE
Prep: 25 minutes   Bake: 40 to 45 minutes   Serves: 8

Canned pears, packed in syrup or juice and drained well, also work nicely in this pie filling.

3 **cups thinly sliced peeled pears**	1 **large egg**
2 **tablespoons brandy**	1 **cup half-and-half**
½ **cup sugar**	1 **tablespoon melted butter**
3 **tablespoons flour**	½ **teaspoon vanilla extract**
⅛ **teaspoon salt**	1 **(9-inch) Partially Baked Pie Shell (page 158)**

1. Preheat oven to 350°F. In a medium bowl, toss pears with brandy.

2. In a large bowl, combine sugar, flour, and salt; mix well. Whisk in egg, half-and-half, melted butter, and vanilla until smooth. Stir in pears with brandy. Turn into partially baked crust.

3. Bake 40 to 45 minutes, or until custard is just set in center. Let cool completely on a wire rack.

351 LEMON-LIME MERINGUE PIE

Prep: 35 minutes   Cook: 7 minutes   Bake: 8 to 10 minutes
Chill: 4 hours   Serves: 8

1¼ cups sugar
⅓ cup cornstarch
Pinch of salt
4 large egg yolks
¼ cup fresh lemon juice
¼ cup fresh lime juice
1½ teaspoons grated lemon zest

1½ teaspoons grated lime zest
1 tablespoon butter
Fluffy Meringue Topping
(page 262)
1 (9-inch) Fully Baked Pie
Shell (page 158)

1. Preheat oven to 350°F. In a large saucepan, combine sugar, cornstarch, and salt. Gradually whisk in 1½ cups water until smooth. Bring to boil over medium heat, stirring gently; boil 1 minute. Remove from heat.

2. In a small bowl, whisk egg yolks until lightly beaten. Gradually whisk in 1 cup hot filling mixture. Return to saucepan, whisking constantly. Whisk in lemon and lime juices and zest. Return to boil and boil 1 minute more. Remove from heat; whisk in butter until smooth. Cover and keep hot while you prepare Fluffy Meringue Topping.

3. Pour hot filling mixture into baked crust. Immediately spoon half of Fluffy Meringue Topping around edge of prepared pie filling, then spread onto edge of pastry crust to form a tight seal. Pile remainder of meringue in center of pie, then spread to meet meringue around edge. Lift meringue with back of spoon to form decorative peaks.

4. Bake 8 to 10 minutes, or until meringue peaks are golden brown. Let cool completely on wire rack. Refrigerate 4 hours, or just until filling is chilled and firm.

Variation:

CLASSIC LEMON MERINGUE PIE

Prepare Lemon-Lime Meringue Pie as directed, except substitute ½ cup lemon juice and 2 teaspoons grated lemon zest for the lemon and lime juice and zest.

352 CAPPUCCINO CREAM PIE

Prep: 20 minutes   Stand: 30 minutes   Cook: 10 minutes
Chill: 3 hours   Serves: 8

2½ cups milk
¼ cup freshly ground coffee
1 (3-inch) cinnamon stick
¾ cup sugar
¼ cup cornstarch
¼ teaspoon salt
½ cup heavy cream
3 large egg yolks

1 tablespoon butter
1 teaspoon vanilla extract
1 (9-inch) Fully Baked Pie
  Shell (page 158)
Whipped cream and
  chocolate-coated coffee
  beans or mocha-flavored
  coffee bean candies

1. In a small saucepan, heat 1 cup milk until small bubbles appear around edge of pan. Remove from heat and stir in coffee and cinnamon stick. Cover and let stand 30 minutes.

2. In a large saucepan, combine sugar, cornstarch, and salt. Gradually whisk in remaining 1½ cups milk and cream until smooth. Strain coffee mixture through a fine sieve lined with a coffee filter into milk mixture in saucepan; discard coffee grounds and cinnamon stick. Bring to a boil over medium heat, stirring gently; boil 1 minute. Remove from heat.

3. In a small bowl, beat egg yolks. Gradually whisk in 1 cup hot coffee mixture. Return to saucepan, whisking constantly. Return to a boil and boil 1 minute longer. Remove from heat and whisk in butter and vanilla until smooth. Cover surface of custard with wax paper or plastic wrap. Let cool slightly, about 20 minutes.

4. Spread custard evenly in baked crust. Cover filling with plastic wrap and refrigerate until cold, 3 hours or overnight. Just before serving, uncover pie and decorate with whipped cream and chocolate-coated coffee bean candies.

353 OLD-FASHIONED CHOCOLATE CUSTARD PIE

Prep: 30 minutes   Bake: 45 to 50 minutes   Serves: 8

1 cup milk
1 cup heavy cream
3 (1-ounce) squares
  unsweetened chocolate,
  cut into small pieces
4 large eggs
¾ cup sugar

1 teaspoon vanilla extract
¼ teaspoon salt
Toasted Hazelnut Pie Crust
  (recipe follows)
Whipped cream and shaved
  chocolate

1. In a medium saucepan, heat milk and cream until small bubbles form around edge of pan. Remove from heat and add chocolate; stir until completely melted and smooth. Let cool.

2. Preheat oven to 350°F. In a large bowl, whisk together eggs and sugar until light and lemon colored. Whisk in chocolate mixture, vanilla, and salt until blended.

3. Pour filling into Toasted Hazelnut Pie Crust. Bake 45 to 50 minutes, or until a small knife inserted into custard 1 inch from edge comes out clean. (Center may look a bit wobbly, but do not overbake.) Let cool completely on a wire rack. Just before serving, decorate top of pie with whipped cream and shaved chocolate.

354 TOASTED HAZELNUT PIE CRUST

Prep: 15 minutes   Chill: 1 hour   Freeze: 20 minutes
Bake: 40 to 42 minutes   Makes: 1 single 9-inch pie crust

This rich nut and butter crust is made for chocolate and coffee cream pies.

½ **cup hazelnuts**	6 **tablespoons cold butter,**
2 **tablespoons sugar**	**cut up**
1¼ **cups flour**	4 **to 6 tablespoons ice water**
¼ **teaspoon salt**	

1. Preheat oven to 350°F. Spread out hazelnuts on a small baking sheet. Bake 15 minutes, or until nuts are lightly browned and dark skins are cracked. Rub warm nuts in a terrycloth towel to remove as much of skins as possible. Let cool. In a food processor, process hazelnuts and sugar until finely ground.

2. Add flour and salt to ground nuts in processor. Process to blend, about 5 seconds. Add butter; turn machine quickly on and off until mixture is in coarse crumbs. Sprinkle on 1 tablespoon ice water. Turn machine on and off 2 or 3 times. Repeat process with remaining ice water as needed, 1 tablespoon at a time, following each addition of water by 2 quick pulses, just until dough begins to hold together. Turn dough out onto work surface and gather gently into a ball. Flatten dough into a disk, then wrap tightly in plastic wrap. Refrigerate 1 hour or overnight.

3. Roll disk into a ⅛-inch-thick round. Fold in half and ease gently into a 9-inch pie pan. Unfold dough, letting pastry overhang edge. Trim overhanging edge of pastry 1 inch from rim of pan. Fold pastry edge under and flute. Freeze 20 minutes, or until firm.

4. Preheat oven to 400°F. Line pie shell with foil; fill halfway with pie weights, dried beans, or rice. Bake 12 minutes, or until edge of pastry is set and lightly colored. Remove foil and weights. Bake 13 to 15 minutes longer, or until bottom and sides of crust are golden brown. Transfer to a wire rack and let cool completely before filling.

355 CLASSIC KEY LIME PIE

Prep: 30 minutes   Bake: 15 minutes   Chill: 2 hours   Serves: 8

Key lime juice from Florida is available in many specialty food shops, but the juice of regular Persian limes works nicely, too.

4 large egg yolks
1 (14-ounce) can sweetened
  condensed milk
⅔ cup key lime juice or fresh
  lime juice
  Graham Cracker Crumb
  Crust (page 160)

1 cup heavy cream
2 tablespoons powdered
  sugar
1 tablespoon dark rum
1 teaspoon grated lime zest

1. Preheat oven to 350°F. In a large bowl, beat egg yolks until light and lemon colored. Gradually beat in condensed milk and lime juice until blended.

2. Pour filling into baked crust. Bake 15 minutes, or until filling is set. Let cool completely on a wire rack. Refrigerate until cold, 2 hours or overnight.

3. Just before serving, in a large bowl, beat cream with an electric mixer until soft peaks form. Add powdered sugar, rum, and lime zest and continue to beat to stiff peaks. Spread cream decoratively over pie.

356 RED, WHITE, AND BLUEBERRY CUSTARD PIE

Prep: 10 minutes   Bake: 55 to 60 minutes   Serves: 8

This star-spangled treat is perfect for a Fourth of July barbecue.

2 large eggs
¾ cup sugar
2 tablespoons flour
1 cup half-and-half

1 cup fresh blueberries
1 cup fresh raspberries
1 (9-inch) Partially Baked Pie
  Shell (page 158)

1. Preheat oven to 400°F. In a medium bowl, beat eggs until blended. Whisk in sugar and flour until blended. Whisk in half-and-half.

2. Arrange blueberries and raspberries in partially baked pastry crust. Pour custard over fruit.

3. Bake 10 minutes. Reduce oven temperature to 350°F. Bake 45 to 50 minutes longer, or until center of filling is just set. Let cool completely on a wire rack.

357   PIÑA COLADA CHESS PIE
Prep: 15 minutes   Cook: 50 to 55 minutes   Serves: 8

This tropical drink-inspired pie is filled with sweet pineapple chunks, cream of coconut, and rum.

1 (20-ounce) can pineapple
  chunks in juice, drained
3 tablespoons flour
4 tablespoons butter, softened
⅔ cup sugar
¼ teaspoon salt

3 large eggs
½ cup cream of coconut
2 tablespoons dark rum
1 (9-inch) Partially Baked Pie
  Shell (page 158)

1. Preheat oven to 325°F. Cut pineapple chunks in half. In a medium bowl, toss pineapple with 1 tablespoon flour until evenly coated.

2. In a large bowl, beat butter, sugar, and salt with an electric mixer until light and fluffy. Add eggs, 1 at a time, beating well after each addition. Beat in cream of coconut and rum. Beat in remaining 2 tablespoons flour just until blended. Stir in pineapple mixture. (Filling will appear curdled, but it will become smooth and creamy when baked.)

3. Turn filling into partially baked crust. Bake 50 to 55 minutes, or until center of filling is just set. Let cool completely on a wire rack.

358   SWEET CARROT MAPLE PIE
*Prep: 20 minutes   Cook: 15 minutes   Bake: 60 to 65 minutes
Serves: 8*

1 pound carrots, peeled and
  sliced
3 large eggs
2 tablespoons sugar
1 cup heavy cream
½ cup milk
½ cup pure maple syrup

½ teaspoon cinnamon
¼ teaspoon salt
1 partially baked 9-inch
  Whole Wheat Pastry crust
  (page 162)
Whipped cream

1. In a medium saucepan, combine carrots with enough water to cover. Bring to a boil, reduce heat, and simmer until carrots are soft and tender, about 15 minutes; drain. Immediately transfer carrots to a food processor and puree until smooth. Let cool.

2. Preheat oven to 350°F. In a large bowl, whisk eggs until blended. Beat in sugar. Add carrot puree, cream, milk, maple syrup, cinnamon, and salt until smooth. Pour filling into partially baked whole wheat crust.

3. Bake 60 to 65 minutes, or until filling is just set in center, puffed, and golden. Let cool completely on a wire rack. Serve with whipped cream.

359 COCOA CREAM PIE WITH MACAROON MERINGUE

Prep: 20 minutes   Cook: 6 to 7 minutes   Bake: 8 to 10 minutes
Serves: 8

This rich cocoa pudding pie is topped off with a billowy cloud of coconut meringue.

1 cup sugar	3 large egg yolks
6 tablespoons unsweetened	1 tablespoon butter
cocoa powder	½ teaspoon vanilla extract
¼ cup cornstarch	Macaroon Meringue (recipe
¼ teaspoon salt	follows)
2¼ cups milk	1 (9-inch) Fully Baked Pie
½ cup heavy cream	Shell (page 158)

1. Preheat oven to 350°F. In a large saucepan, combine sugar, cocoa powder, cornstarch, and salt. Gradually whisk in milk and cream until smooth. Cook over medium heat, stirring gently, until mixture boils, 5 to 6 minutes. Boil 1 minute; remove from heat.

2. In a small bowl, beat egg yolks lightly. Gradually whisk in 1 cup hot cocoa mixture. Return to saucepan, whisking constantly. Return to a boil and boil 1 minute longer. Remove from heat. Whisk in butter and vanilla until completely smooth. Cover to keep hot while you prepare Macaroon Meringue.

3. Pour hot filling mixture into baked crust. Immediately spoon half of meringue around edge of prepared pie filling, then spread onto edge of pastry crust to form a tight seal. Pile remainder of meringue in center of pie, then spread to meet meringue around edge. Lift meringue with back of spoon to form decorative peaks.

4. Bake 8 to 10 minutes, or until meringue peaks are golden brown. Let cool completely on a wire rack. Serve at room temperature or chilled.

---

360 MACAROON MERINGUE

Prep: 10 minutes   Cook: none   Makes: Topping for one 9-inch pie

4 large egg whites, at room	½ cup sugar
temperature	½ cup flaked coconut
¼ teaspoon cream of tartar	

In a large bowl, beat egg whites and cream of tartar with an electric mixer on medium speed until soft peaks form. Gradually beat in sugar, 1 tablespoon at a time, beating well after each addition. Continue to beat on medium speed until stiff peaks form when beaters are lifted, 4 to 5 minutes. With a rubber spatula, gently fold in coconut.

361 BLACK BOTTOM COCONUT CREAM PIE
Prep: 25 minutes   Cook: 10 to 12 minutes   Chill: 3 hours
Bake: 6 to 8 minutes   Serves: 8

3 ounces semisweet
   chocolate, cut up
2 cups heavy cream
1 (9-inch) Fully Baked Pie
   Shell (page 158)
⅔ cup sugar
¼ cup cornstarch

¼ teaspoon salt
2¼ cups milk
3 large egg yolks
1 tablespoon butter
2 teaspoons vanilla extract
1½ cups flaked coconut

1. In a small glass bowl, combine chocolate and ¼ cup cream. Microwave on Medium 1½ to 2 minutes, or until cream is hot. Whisk until chocolate is melted and smooth. Let cool completely, stirring occasionally, about 15 minutes. Spread chocolate mixture along bottom and halfway up sides of baked crust.

2. In a large saucepan, combine sugar, cornstarch, and salt. Gradually whisk in milk and ¾ cup cream until smooth. Cook over medium heat, stirring gently, until mixture comes to a boil, 4 to 5 minutes. Boil 1 minute; remove from heat.

3. In a small bowl, beat egg yolks lightly. Gradually whisk in 1 cup hot filling mixture. Return to saucepan, whisking constantly. Return to a boil and boil 1 minute longer. Remove from heat and whisk in butter and vanilla to blend well. Gently fold in 1 cup coconut.

4. Cover coconut custard and let cool completely, stirring occasionally, about 30 minutes. Spread custard evenly in prepared crust. Cover surface with wax paper or plastic wrap and refrigerate until cold, 3 hours or overnight.

5. Preheat oven to 350°F. Spread remaining ½ cup coconut on a small cookie sheet. Bake 6 to 8 minutes, until lightly toasted. Just before serving, whip remaining 1 cup cream until stiff. Uncover pie, decorate top with whipped cream, and top with toasted coconut.

362   PAVLOVA ANGEL PIE
Prep: 30 minutes   Cook: 2 minutes   Chill: 1 hour   Serves: 8 to 10

Here's a new interpretation of the Australian dessert classic, featuring a passionfruit cream filling and a coconut meringue pie shell.

10 fresh passionfruit or ½ cup
   frozen passionfruit
   puree, thawed
3 tablespoons granulated
   sugar
2 teaspoons cornstarch
2 tablespoons fresh lime juice

1 cup heavy cream
½ cup powdered sugar
   Coconut Angel Pie Crust
   (recipe follows)
3 kiwifruit, peeled and sliced
½ pint raspberries

1. Cut each fresh passionfruit in half and scoop out pulp and seeds with a spoon. Transfer to a fine sieve set over a bowl; strain pulp through sieve, pressing with back of a spoon to remove seeds. Measure ½ cup puree.

2. In a small saucepan, combine granulated sugar and cornstarch. Stir in passionfruit puree until smooth. Bring to a boil over medium heat, stirring constantly; boil 1 minute. Transfer to a bowl and stir in lime juice. Cover and refrigerate until chilled, about 1 hour.

3. In a large bowl, beat cream and powdered sugar with an electric mixer until stiff peaks form. With a rubber spatula, gently fold ⅓ of cream into passionfruit mixture. Repeat twice more with remaining cream until blended.

4. Spread half passionfruit filling into baked crust. Top with half of kiwifruit and raspberries. Repeat with remaining filling and fruit. Serve immediately or refrigerate up to 2 hours.

363   COCONUT ANGEL PIE CRUST
Prep: 10 minutes   Bake: 2 hours   Makes: 1 (10-inch) pie crust

This versatile meringue crust is perfect with a wide assortment of fillings. Try your favorite ice cream or the Classic Lemon Curd (page 217) and an assortment of fresh berries.

4 large egg whites, at room
   temperature
¼ teaspoon cream of tartar
¼ teaspoon salt
1 cup sugar

½ teaspoon vanilla extract
½ teaspoon almond extract
½ cup flaked coconut, finely
   chopped

1. Preheat oven to 250°F. In a large bowl, beat egg whites with cream of tartar and salt with an electric mixer on medium speed until soft peaks form. Gradually beat in sugar. Increase mixer speed to medium-high, add vanilla and almond extract, and continue to beat until stiff peaks form when beaters are lifted. With a rubber spatula, gently fold in coconut.

2. Spread meringue into a well-greased 10-inch pie pan, building up sides. Bake 2 hours, or until meringue is firm and cream colored. Turn oven off. Leave crust in oven with door ajar until completely cooled.

364   OLD-TIME VINEGAR PIE
Prep: 15 minutes   Bake: 40 to 47 minutes   Serves: 8

This pie, tart and homey, was an old-fashioned standby when lemons were scarce and cider vinegar was used as a substitute. Now, with the addition of sweet raisins, pecans, and whipped cream, it's ready for a comeback.

⅓ **cup pecans**
¾ **cup packed brown sugar**
½ **cup granulated sugar**
¼ **cup flour**
 Pinch of salt
½ **cup cider vinegar**
2 **cups boiling water**

3 **large eggs**
2 **tablespoons butter**
⅓ **cup raisins**
1 **(9-inch) Partially Baked Pie Shell (page 158)**
 Sweetened Whipped Cream (page 265)

1. Preheat oven to 350°F. Spread out pecans on a small baking sheet. Bake 5 to 7 minutes, or until nuts are lightly browned. Let cool, then coarsely chop. Increase oven temperature to 425°F.

2. In a heavy medium saucepan, combine brown sugar, granulated sugar, flour, and salt, pressing out any lumps of brown sugar with back of a spoon. Stir in vinegar and boiling water and bring to a boil, stirring to dissolve sugar. Reduce heat to medium and cook 1 minute. Remove from heat.

3. In a medium bowl, beat eggs until light and lemon colored. Gradually whisk 1 cup hot vinegar mixture into eggs; then stir warm egg mixture back into remaining vinegar mixture in saucepan. Stir in butter until melted. Add raisins and pecans.

4. Turn filling into partially baked crust. Bake 10 minutes. Reduce oven temperature to 350°F. Bake 25 to 30 minutes longer, or until edges of filling are just set. (Center of filling will be somewhat wobbly, but it will firm as it cools; do not overbake.) Let cool completely on a wire rack. Serve with Sweetened Whipped Cream.

365   AMARETTO RICOTTA PIE
Prep: 15 minutes   Bake: 40 to 45 minutes   Serves: 8

1 (15-ounce) container ricotta
    cheese
½ cup sugar
3 large eggs
½ cup heavy cream
2 tablespoons amaretto
    liqueur

½ teaspoon vanilla extract
⅛ teaspoon salt
1 tablespoon flour
1 ounce semisweet chocolate,
    grated
1 (9-inch) Partially Baked Pie
    Shell (page 158)

1. Preheat oven to 350°F. In a food processor or blender, mix ricotta and sugar until smooth. Add eggs, 1 at a time, and process to blend. Add cream, amaretto, vanilla, and salt and process until smooth. Add flour, pulsing machine on and off just until blended. Stir in grated chocolate.

2. Pour filling into partially baked crust. Bake 40 to 45 minutes, or until center of filling is just set. Let cool completely on wire rack. Serve at room temperature or chilled.

Index

Acknowledgments

While working on this project I received encouragement from more friends than I can name, but a special thanks must go to all my friends in the food department at *Ladies' Home Journal*, where I truly learned the art of baking; to Barbara Stratton, Miriam Rubin, Cliff Pepper, Carol Guthrie Dovell, Holly Sheppard, Debra Mintcheff, Lisa Brainerd, and Julia Pemberton, for all their time and special inspirations; and also to my mother, Susan and Rip Westmoreland, and Karen and Chris Tack for so generously sharing their kitchens.

To Jean Galton, for her moral support and top-notch expertise in recipe testing.

A special note of gratitude to Susan Wyler, my editor, who gave me the opportunity to spread my baking wings and create the kind of imaginative dessert book I always dreamed of writing.

To order any of the
365 Ways Cookbooks

visit your local bookseller or call 1-800-331-3761

Our bestselling **365 Ways Cookbooks** are wire-bound to lie flat and have colorful, wipe-clean covers.

Each **365 Ways Cookbook** is $17.95 plus $3.50 per copy shipping and handling. Applicable sales tax will be billed to your account. No CODs. Please allow 4–6 weeks for delivery.

> Please have your VISA, MASTERCARD, or AMERICAN EXPRESS card at
> hand when calling.

♦ 365 ♦

Days of Gardening 0-06-017032-8
Easy Italian Recipes 0-06-016310-0
Easy Low-Calorie Recipes 0-06-016309-7
Easy Mexican Recipes 0-06-016963-X
Easy One-Dish Meals 0-06-016311-9
Great Barbecue & Grilling Recipes 0-06-016224-4
Great Cakes & Pies 0-06-016959-1
Great Chocolate Desserts 0-06-016537-5
Great Cookies and Brownies 0-06-016840-4
One-Minute Golf Lessons 0-06-017087-5
Quick & Easy Microwave Recipes 0-06-016026-8
Snacks, Hors D'Oeuvres & Appetizers 0-06-016536-7
Ways to Cook Chicken 0-06-015539-6
Ways to Cook Fish and Shellfish 0-06-016841-2
Ways to Cook Hamburger & Other Ground Meats
0-06-016535-9
Ways to Cook Chinese 0-06-016961-3
Ways to Cook Pasta 0-06-015865-4
Ways to Cook Vegetarian 0-06-016958-3
Ways to Prepare for Christmas 0-06-017048-4
Ways to Wok 0-06-016643-6

FORTHCOMING TITLES
Great 20-Minute Recipes 0-06-016962-1
Soups and Stews 0-06-016960-5
Low-Fat Recipes 0-06-017137-5
Ways to Cook Eggs 0-06-017138-3
More Ways to Cook Chicken 0-06-017139-1
All-American Favorites 0-06-017294-0
Main-Dish Salads 0-06-017293-2
Jewish Recipes 0-06-017295-9
Asian Recipes 0-06-017292-4